A JEWISH PHILOSOPHY OF HISTORY

A Jewish Philosophy of History

Israel's Degradation & Redemption

Paul Eidelberg

iUniverse, Inc.
New York Lincoln Shanghai

A Jewish Philosophy of History
Israel's Degradation & Redemption

All Rights Reserved © 2004 by Paul Eidelberg

No part of this book may be reproduced or transmitted in any form or by any means, graphic, electronic, or mechanical, including photocopying, recording, taping, or by any information storage retrieval system, without the written permission of the publisher.

iUniverse, Inc.

For information address:
iUniverse, Inc.
2021 Pine Lake Road, Suite 100
Lincoln, NE 68512
www.iuniverse.com

ISBN: 0-595-31695-6 (Pbk)
ISBN: 0-595-66376-1 (Cloth)

Printed in the United States of America

To Eleonora
and in memory of
Suzanne Daniel

Acknowledgments

As in my previous books that interface Torah and Science, the present work is indebted to one of the greatest Torah philosopher and Talmudist of the twentieth century, Dr. Chaim Zimmerman. It was also my good fortune to have physicist Gerald L. Schroeder read and offer some helpful comments on Chapter 7, which interfaces the Book of Genesis with Einstein's general theory of relativity. Indeed, I am very much indebted to Dr. Schroeder's scintillating work, *The Science of God: The Convergence of Scientific and Biblical Wisdom.*

I also want to thank Professor Will Morrisey for reading parts of the manuscript and for helpful comments on Chapter 11 dealing with Christianity.

Abbreviated versions of Chapters 2 and 12, which discuss, respectively, Israel's "Arab Problem" and the clash of civilizations between Islam and the West, were previously published by the *Ariel Center for Policy Research*, whose dauntless director, Professor Arieh Stav, has brought many of my controversial essays to public attention in Israel.

Of course, I alone am responsible for the views contained in this book as well as for its shortcomings.

Contents

Part I

Prologue 3

Chapter 1   Degradation and Redemption 7

Chapter 2   The Arab Problem: On Self-Determination 22

Chapter 3   Political Dimensions of The Jewish Problem 41

Chapter 4   Psychological Dimensions of The Jewish Problem:
"Demophrenia" 54

Chapter 5   Psychological Dimensions of The Jewish Problem:
A Critique of Moral Relativism 72

Chapter 6   Psychological Dimensions of The Jewish Problem:
A Critique of Modern Psychology 85

Chapter 7   The Convergence of Science and Torah 96

Part II

Chapter 8   The Torah's World-Historical Program:
The Chosen People 113

Chapter 9   The Historical Function of The Pre-Socratics 133

Chapter 10 Plato and Aristotle:
In Quest of the Good and the Beautiful 144

Chapter 11 Rome and Christianity 166

Chapter 12 Islam: A Clash of Civilizations 181

Chapter 13 Modernity: In Quest of Morality 206

Chapter 14 Hebraic Civilization: Israel's Final Redemption 224

Appendix   Israel's Return and Restoration:
            An Essay Confirming the Existence of Laws of History 235

Notes 263

Bibliography 295

Index 305

Part I

Prologue

Reflecting on *The Magic Mountain*, Thomas Mann writes: "Since it is certainly not customary for an author to discuss his own work, perhaps a word of apology, or at least of explanation, should occupy the first place."

Almost every Friday morning for eighteen years, I was privileged to sit at the table of an extraordinary Torah philosopher and Talmudist, the late Gaon Dr. Chaim Zimmerman. Rav Chaim was widely known for his prodigious memory. The Babylonian and Jerusalem Talmuds and literally thousands of other Hebrew tomes were stored in his memory as if his mind were a giant computer. But unlike a computer, his was a creative mind. He could interface Torah with science and philosophy as well as with politics and thereby illuminate the Torah as the paradigm of reason and of how man should live.

Pondering the magnificence of the Torah and greatness of the sages of Israel illuminated by Dr. Zimmerman, I became all the more appalled by the lack of Jewish national pride among Israel's political and intellectual elites. Something had to be done to correct this degraded state of affairs. Ands so, with Rav Chaim's encouragement, I wrote *Jerusalem versus Athens: Toward a General Theory of Existence* (1983). The title of that book may remind some people of "Jerusalem and Athens," an essay written by the renowned Professor Leo Strauss with whom I studied at the University of Chicago. *Jerusalem versus Athens* differs profoundly from "Jerusalem *and* Athens."

While writing *Jerusalem versus Athens,* I became aware of a Jewish philosophy of history. It seemed to me that developments in philosophy, science, and world politics since the destruction of the First Temple in 586 BCE were carrying out the world-historical goal of the Torah, namely, the elimination of idolatry on the one hand, and the universal recognition of ethical monotheism on the other. Evidence of a Jewish philosophy of history also appeared in two subsequent books of mine: *Beyond the Secular Mind: A Judaic Response to the Problems of Modernity* (1989), and *Judaic Man: Toward a Reconstruction of Western Civilization* (1996).

It so happened, however, that the existential threat confronting Israel prompted me to write two other books, one concerning the flawed mentality of Israel's political and intellectual leaders, the other concerning Israel's political system, whose fragmented character prevents the government from pursuing a coherent and resolute national strategy against Israel's Arab foes. But now the time has come to weave the threads of that Jewish philosophy of history I had seen two decades ago, especially in view of Israel's current degradation and the despair of so many Jews regarding Israel's future. The time had come to show that this degradation is but a necessary stage of Israel's Final Redemption.

Accordingly, Part I of this book provides an analysis of Israel's malaise and what must be done to overcome it. Chapter 1 discusses Israel's degradation resulting from three basic failings: first and foremost, the government's Secular Zionism, which formed the intellectual foundation of Israel's rebirth in May 1948; second, the government's failure to exploit the victory of the Israel Defense Forces in the Six-Day War of June 1967; third, the government's signing the Oslo or Israel-PLO Declaration of Principles of September 1993.

Chapter 2 analyzes the "Arab problem." It sets forth a national strategy addressed to two interrelated dangers: (1) the danger posed by Israel's burgeoning Arab population, which threatens to transform Israel into an Islamic state; and (2) the danger of an Arab Palestinian state, whose inhabitants are openly dedicated to Israel's extermination. The chapter shows how these two dangers can be overcome by a rigorous application of democratic as well as Jewish principles.

Chapter 3 discusses the *political* dimensions of the "Jewish problem." It shows that Israel's basic dilemmas—including the threat to its existence—are largely the result of its flawed legislative, executive, and judicial institutions. The chapter offers a program of institutional and other reforms that will simultaneously make Israel more Jewish, more democratic, and more capable of overcoming its internal and external dangers.[1]

Chapters 4, 5, and 6 discuss the *psychological* dimensions of the "Jewish problem." Chapter 4 shows that Israel's ruling elites suffer from a pathological syndrome which I call "demophrenia."[2] This syndrome glues them to the suicidal policy of "territory for peace," a policy that entails the establishment of a "Palestinian" state in which an entire generation of Arab children have been taught to emulate homicide bombers. Underlying this syndrome is the doctrine of moral relativism, which renders all "lifestyles" equal. Relativism, which permeates all levels of education in the democratic world, has eroded Jewish national pride and makes Israel's political elites incapable of dealing effectively with the country's internal and external enemies. Chapter 5 refutes this doctrine. It thus provides the basis for refuting, in Chapter 6, modern psychology. Virtually every school of modern psychology posits the primacy of the *emotions* in opposition to Judaism, which affirms the primacy of *reason*.

Chapter 7 discusses the Convergence of Science and Torah and reveals Judaism as the *religion of reason*. We read in the Midrash, "God looked at the letters and words of the Torah and created the world." This reminds us of Plato's cosmological dialogue the *Timeaus*, where the "Demiurge" looked at the eternal Ideas and formed the heavens and the earth. But Plato's Demiurge is a craftsman, not a creator. He fashioned the visible universe from a preexisting, formless matter; he did not create that "matter." There is no *creatio ex nihilo* in Greek philosophy. Thanks to Einstein's theory of general relativity, however, *creatio ex nihilo* has become the reigning cosmology of science. This confirms the account of creation in Genesis 1:1 and lends credence to the idea that the Torah is the "DNA" of Nature and History.[3] Obviously this idea also makes a Jewish philosophy of history possible—the subject of Part II of this book.

Chapter 8 sets forth the World-Historical Program of the Torah, the fulfillment of which requires the Chosen People. The concept of the Chosen People is clarified in terms of history, philosophy, and science. The chapter advances the iconoclastic idea that Jerusalem, not Athens, is the source of philosophy, that Judaism is a comprehensive and verifiable system of truth. This is a necessary precondition of fulfilling the goal of the Torah: to eliminate all forms of idolatry on the one hand, and to promote the universal recognition of ethical monotheism on the other. Suffice to say here that idolatry is the worship of *any* created thing, including the products of the human mind. Idolatry therefore includes (1) the postulation of any physical entity, law, or process as *autonomous* or *independent* of God; and (2) the belief that any scientific theory fully comprehends reality or that any political ideology or system of government formulated by man is wholly adequate for the physical and spiritual happiness of mankind. Obviously there are more or less primitive and more or less refined forms of idolatry.

We start in Chapter 9 with the pre-Socratic philosophers, some of whom flourished at the time of the destruction of the First Temple and were apparently influenced by Jews. The pre-Socratics undermined belief in the Homeric gods by depersonalizing the "forces" of nature. As a consequence, they left nature lifeless and human life meaningless. Enter Plato and Aristotle, two of the greatest legislators of the human mind. As will be seen in Chapter 10, Plato and Aristotle deified human reason and developed an organic and teleological conception of nature that provided norms of how man should live. The demise of Zeus and the Greek pantheon followed. But it took Christianity—"a spark from Zion"—to apply the *coup de grace* to Greek and Roman polytheism. This is discussed in Chapter 11, where we show that Christian antinomianism and the separation of church and state planted the seed for the eventual ascendancy of secularism in the modern world.

Chapter 12 reveals the world-historical functions of Islam and how it is unwittingly contributing to Israel's demise *as a secular democratic state, hence to the ultimate ascendancy of Hebraic Civilization.* This chapter also demonstrates that Islam and the West are involved in a clash of civilizations, the former based on a decadent religious absolutism, the latter based on a decadent secularism-cum-relativism.

Needless to say, the archpriest of secularism is Machiavelli, the father of Modernity—the subject of Chapter 13. This chapter shows how Machiavelli's new political science subverted the Greco-Christian tradition and left man without any morality. Two movements emerged from Machiavelli, nurtured, of course, by his philosophical successors: the undisguised egoism of *Individualism* and the covert egoism of *Statism*. Armed by an ethically-neutral science, these two isms clashed in the two World Wars of the twentieth century. Those wars, which revealed the moral bankruptcy of Western civilization, led to the fulfillment of biblical prophecy, the rebirth of Israel.

This fact, together with the decadence of the West and Islam, calls out silently for a renaissance of Hebraic Civilization, the essence of which is discussed in the concluding chapter.

An Appendix contains my edited version of an essay written by Dr. Zimmerman showing that Israel's rebirth is the result of providential laws of history pointing to Israel's Final Redemption.

Chapter 1
Degradation and Redemption

The Jewish People are in the third of four redemptions. The First Redemption, of course, was the Exodus from Egypt, the second from Babylon. The most conspicuous sign of the Third Redemption was the establishment of the State of Israel in 1948.[4] It is widely recognized that the establishment of the State of Israel was made possible by the murder of six million Jews in the Nazi Holocaust. And yet, today, in the midst of the Third Redemption, no place on earth is more dangerous for Jews than Israel. Regardless of which party or prime minister is in power, more and more Jews are being murdered and maimed by Arab terrorists. The sense of Jewish national pride has evaporated. How are the causes of this degradation to be understood, and what must be done to hasten Israel's Final Redemption?

The Failure of Orthodox Jewry

According to Rav Yisachar Shlomo Teichtal, a Torah giant, the Holocaust, to which he himself fell victim, was very much a consequence of the failure of Europe's orthodox Jewish leaders to heed the teachings of the prophets and the sages to redeem Eretz Yisrael, the Land of Israel, when even gentiles—recall the Balfour Declaration and the League of Nations—supported the return of the Jews to their ancient homeland. He blames rabbis who, by denouncing secular Zionism and opposing immigration to Israel—*aliya*—discouraged Jews from fulfilling their sacred obligation to return to and rebuild the Land of Israel and thereby sanctify God's Name.

Fleeing from the Nazis, and writing in 1943 without books and while Jews were perishing around him, Rav Teichtal composed an extraordinary work entitled *Eim Habanim Semeichah (A Joyous Mother of Children)*.[5] There he cites an incredible number of Torah, Talmudic, and post-Talmudic sources showing that "the purpose of our afflictions is to arouse us to return to Eretz Yisrael." These sources all speak of the crucial importance of the Holy Land. They show that the redemption of the Jewish people can only take place in the Land of Israel.

Rav Teichtal goes further. Contrary to what he had learned from contemporary rabbis and had himself believed prior to the Holocaust, he shows that the secular Zionists were deserving of great praise; for even though they denied the Torah, they were fulfilling the commandment to return to and rebuild the Land of Israel.[6] What is more, further research on his part revealed that many of the great *halachic* authorities—experts in Jewish law—predicted that secularists would restore the Holy Land![7] How is it possible, therefore, that learned orthodox rabbis failed to heed the teachings of Torah masters, such as Maimonides and Nachmanides, regarding the mitzvah of settling in and rebuilding Eretz Yisrael?[8]

To begin with, let us be fair and recall that, in the closing years of the nineteenth century and the early years of the twentieth, the venerable beliefs and customs of the Jewish people had come under the ideological assault of the Socialist and Communist movements along with that of secular Zionism. The defections from tradition, especially in urban areas, were massive. On the surface, therefore, orthodox rabbis had good reasons to oppose the shallow secular Zionism initiated by Theodore Herzl's *The Jewish State*. They saw in this Zionism the denial of the Sinai Covenant and the choseness of the Jewish people. Secular Zionists, influenced by the egalitarianism of the Enlightenment, regarded all nations as equal. They rejected the idea that the Jews were "a nation apart." And yet, had not Jews lived and died for their apartness? Did not the deepest instincts of the Jews call for difference and distance? In contrast, the Zionists envisioned a state in which the Jews would become a "normal" people. No longer would they suffer the scourge of anti-Semitism, of pogroms and humiliation. The dignity of the despised Chosen People would be restored—note the paradox—and at last they would live in peace and security.

To become a "normal" people, however, the Torah, which had sustained and inspired the Jews for thousands of years, would have to be relegated to the home and the synagogue. Judaism would be divorced from public law, would cease to be an all-comprehensive way of life. Such a state was anathema to the rabbis. Besides, they believed that a Zionist state based on non-Torah law could not possibly succeed or endure.

Now it so happens that, three decades before Herzl's pioneering work, certain rabbis did in fact encourage *aliya*. In 1864, Rabbi Tzvi Kalischer published a book, *Derishat Tzion*, which was praised by various *halachic* authorities for its proposed "Organization for the Settlement of Eretz Yisrael." Mention should also be made of the Chofetz Chaim, Rabbi Yisrael Meir HaCohen, one of the greatest Torah scholars of modern times. (His unparalleled *halachic* work, the *Mishna Berura*, is the definitive compendium of Jewish law.) Even in the aftermath of the 1929 Hebron massacre, the Chofetz Chaim encouraged *aliya*. He held that "there is no Torah like the Torah of Eretz Yisrael, and there is no wisdom like the wisdom of Eretz Yisrael" (Midrash Rabbah, Genesis 16:7). Nevertheless, when Rav Teichtal wrote *Eim Habanim Semeichah*, so prevalent was anti-Zionism among European rabbis that he was compelled to cite the *halachic* authorities that had endorsed Kalischer's work in the hope of persuading other rabbis to encourage *aliya* and thereby save as many Jews as possible from the Nazi inferno.

Without wishing to malign these rabbis and thereby arm the wicked, Rav Teichtal nonetheless compared them to the Ten Spies, about whom it says in Psalms 106:25, 24: "*They murmured in their tents…They despised the desirable land*" and thus discouraged the Children of Israel from entering the land promised to the patriarchs. Although the spies were princes of Israel, Rav Teichtal cites various sources that explain their behavior as motivated by self-interest: they were afraid that in Eretz Yisrael they would lose the positions of leadership they held in the desert! (See the Zohar [The Book of Splendor] 3:158a.) "The same holds true in our times," says Rav Teichtal "even of rabbis, rebbes, and chassidim. This one has a good rabbinical position; this one is an established Admor [a prominent Torah master]; and this one has a profitable business or factory or a prestigious job which provides great satisfaction. They are afraid that their status will decline if they go to Eretz Yisrael. People of this sort [though otherwise meritorious] are influenced by their deep-rooted, selfish motives to such an extent that they themselves do not realize that their prejudice speaks on their behalf."[9]

Rav Teichtal quotes numerous sources that extol the great merit of Eretz Yisrael. The Talmud: "He who dwells in Eretz Yisrael is like one who has a God, and he who dwells outside the land is like one who does not have a God" (*Ketuvot* 110b). The Midrash: "It is preferable to dwell in the deserts of Eretz Yisrael than in palaces abroad" (Midrash Rabbah, Genesis 39:8). The Zohar: "I will return in peace to my father's home, for there lies the Holy Land, there I will be perfected…" (1:150b).

Does it not state in Genesis 15:7: "*I am the Lord who brought you* [Avraham] *out of Ur-Kasdim to give you this land to inherit it*"? The Talmud expresses this as follows: "Eretz Yisrael is an inheritance from our forefathers" (*Avodah Zara* 53b). Therein is the basis of the Jewish claim to the Land of Israel.

Now, if Rav Teichtal, a man of extraordinary learning, courage, and love of the Jewish people, could question the motives of prominent rabbis who denounced secular Zionism and thereby discouraged Jews from leaving the fleshpots of Europe for Eretz Yisrael, what shall we say of the descendants of those who established the State of Israel and who now wish to abandon Judea and Samaria, the heartland of the Jewish people? Are their motives any purer?

The Degradation of the Jewish State

Rav Teichtal warned that the failure of orthodox rabbis to encourage European Jewry to make *aliya* would minimize the salutary influence of religious Jews on their alienated secular brothers who were rebuilding the Land of Israel. Without a majority of observant Jews in Eretz Yisrael, assimilated Jews would inevitably establish a state whose governing institutions would be based on gentile rather than Jewish principles. Such a state, instead of having as its goal the reconstruction of Hebraic civilization with all its creativity, would be preoccupied with security and comfort, thus steeped in mediocrity and materialism. This would be the inevitable consequence of forming a state that merely imitated the *goyim*. And lo and behold, did not the founders of the State of Israel pursue a policy of "normalizing" the hundreds of thousands of religious Sephardim and Oriental Jews that entered this state after its establishment in 1948—Jews whom they scorned as "primitives"?[10]

The truth is that were it not for the high birthrate of religious Jews in Israel on the one hand, and the exodus from Israel of hundreds of thousands of secular Jews on the other, Judaism would hardly exist in this so-called Jewish state! Proof: despite the large majority of the Jews in this country who identify with the Jewish heritage, the 1992 Labor-Meretz government proceeded to deJudaize the curriculum of Jewish public schools with the intention of transforming the Jewish state into a "state of its citizens."[11]

Here one may recall the warning of Dr. Isaac Breuer, one of the greatest Jewish philosophers in the first half of the twentieth century. Breuer, an orthodox rabbi, a founder of *Agudat Yisrael*,[12] yet an ardent Zionist who made *aliya* in 1936, declared that only observant Jews can be true Zionists. Secular Zionism, he maintained, is not only a distorted form of Jewish nationalism, but that by having "turned the Torah into a mere religion, a matter of private conscience [secular Zionism has become] the most terrible enemy that has ever risen against the Jewish nation."[13] This dire prediction certainly applies to the ascendancy in Israel of ultra-secularists who have abandoned Zionism along with Judaism.

Consider the Israel-PLO Declaration of Principles commonly known as the Oslo Agreement. That agreement was initiated by the government of Israel without the participation of the United States. Yes, it was signed and sanctified in Washington, and two American administrations have been involved in its implementation—thanks to Israeli complaisance. Evident here is a simple fact: Israeli prime ministers, independently of their attitudes toward secularism and Zionism, have advocated the surrender of parts of Eretz Yisrael to Israel's sworn enemies. Even the religious parties have condoned this desecration of the Holy Land, which eminent rabbis have justified on the grounds of *"pikuach nefesh"*—the saving of Jewish life?[14] Jewish life indeed! The Land of Israel is soaking in Jewish blood. How are we to explain this self-demeaning behavior of these religious and secular Jews? This question will be treated at length in Chapter 4. Here I propose to outline the stages of Israel's degradation, which began *immediately* after its greatest military victory, the Six-Day War, and which appears to have reached its depth under the premiership of Israel's greatest general, Ariel Sharon.

UNDOING THE MIRACLE OF THE SIX-DAY WAR

Israel's degradation may be traced to its government's failure to translate the miracle of the Six-Day War of June 1967 into public policy. Before elaborating, ponder a few remarks from Michael B. Oren, *Six Days of War*.[15] On Day One, in little more than half an hour, the Israel Air Force destroyed 204 planes—half of Egypt's air force—all but nine of them on the ground, while destroying six Egyptian air fields, four in Sinai and two in Egypt. "The Israelis were stunned. No one ever imagined that a single squadron could neutralize an entire air base" (175). On Day Two, Col. Avraham Adan, watching the rout of the Egyptian army, was "stupefied." "You ride past burnt-out vehicles and suddenly you see this immense army, too numerous to count, spread out of a vast area as far as your eyes can see…It was not a pleasant feeling, seeing that gigantic enemy and realizing that you're only a single battalion of tanks" (216). Moshe Dayan was no less puzzled: "Though Israel had gained command of the skies, Egypt's cities were not bombed, and the Egyptian armored units at the front could have fought even without air support" (ibid.). Gen. Avraham Yoffe: "There was no planning before the war about what the army would do beyond the al-'Arish-Jabal Libni axis, not even a discussion. Nobody believed that we could have accomplished more or that the [Egyptian] collapse would be so swift" (ibid.). But as we read in Leviticus 26:8: "*Five of you shall chase away a hundred, and a hundred of you shall put ten thousand to flight…*"

Serious recognition of the miracle, of the hand of God in the Six-Day War, required the government—it was a national unity government—to declare Jewish sovereignty over Judea, Samaria, and Gaza, which the Israel Defense Forces conquered along with the Sinai and the Golan Heights. To fully appreciate this miracle, a brief survey of contemporary events will show that Israel's government could indeed have created a "Greater Israel."

In June 1967 the United States was bogged down in Vietnam and was very much concerned about Soviet expansion in the Middle East in general, and

Soviet penetration of the oil-rich Persian Gulf in particular (on which the entire economy of the West, indeed, the world depends).[16] Recall that Egypt and Syria and Libya were then Soviet clients, and that Egypt had sought to gain control of strategically situated Yemen. Recall, too, that Israel employed French planes and weaponry in its stunning victory over Egypt, Syria, and Jordan. That victory awakened Washington to Israel's strategic value, for it resulted in the closing of the Suez Canal to the Soviet Black Sea fleet. This important arm of the Soviet navy was then compelled to sail through the Straits of Gibraltar and around the Cape of Good Hope to project Soviet power along the east African littoral and in the Indian Ocean, the sea-lanes of oil tankers from the Persian Gulf. Israel's superb air force could also help protect NATO's southern flank in the eastern Mediterranean.

America needed a strong and stable ally in the volatile region of the Middle East.[17] A minuscule Israel, confined to its precarious 1949 armistice lines, could hardly serve this function. Accordingly, in a now declassified secret memorandum dated June 27, 1967, the U.S. Joint Chiefs of Staff recommended that Israel retain control of the Judean and Samarian mountain ridges overlooking its vulnerable population centers on the coastal plain, as well as control of Gaza, the Golan Heights, and a portion of the southern Sinai to secure Israel's access to the Red Sea through the Strait of Tiran.

Viewed in this light, only a feckless and faithless government—it consisted of both secular and religious Jews—would trivialize the historical significance of Israel's victory in the Six-Day War by not declaring Jewish sovereignty over the land conquered by the IDF. Instead, ten days after the war, the government transmitted a proposal to Cairo and Damascus offering to return to the prewar borders for a peace agreement! No wonder so many people throughout the world are oblivious of the fact that Israel has valid legal claims to this land, apart from its having been regained in a war of self-defense. Jordan's annexation of Judea and Samaria in 1950 was never recognized by any state except Pakistan and Britain. Egypt had no claim to Gaza (and its claim to the Sinai was dubious). Jordan and Egypt had invested nothing in these desolate territories, which were occupied by diverse Arab clans *with no indigenous culture linked to this land*. The presence of those Arabs would not have deterred statesmen who believed in God and possessed the courage of their convictions. Such statesmen would have incorporated the land of their forefathers into the State of Israel.

Having failed to translate the miracle of the Six-Day War into Israel's national policy and thereby sanctify God's Name, it was inevitable that subsequent Israeli governments would undo that miracle. Indeed, it was not long before they bowed to UN Resolution 242, which requires Israel to withdraw from territories conquered in the June 1967 war.

The timidity of Israel's ruling elites—say rather their lack of faith in God, their ignorance regarding the spiritual significance of Eretz Yisrael, and their lack of confidence in the justice of Israel's cause—could not but encourage Egypt and Syria as well as Jordan to launch the Yom Kippur War. Yom Kippur, the holiest day in the Jewish calendar, was chosen to degrade Jews and Judaism. To defame the Chosen People and to make a mockery of their relationship to God is the conscious aim of Israel's enemies, especially Muslims who murder Jews in the name of Allah.

The ceasefire negotiations of the Yom Kippur War exposed the feebleness of Israel's government. Recall Henry Kissinger's "shuttle diplomacy" between Israel on the one hand, and Egypt and Syria on the other. His diplomacy was anything but "evenhanded": Syria and Egypt received territorial rewards for their aggression. Of course the United States has strategic interests in the Middle East which cannot but bias its role as a mediator in the so-called Arab-Israel conflict, a misnomer for the Arab war against the Jewish people. Even if it were true, as Bernard Lewis contends, that American mediation "has, on occasion, rendered signal service to the warring parties," he admits that,

> on the whole they are likely to do better when they meet face to face, preferably in secret. With a superpower mediator, the parties will tend to negotiate with the mediator rather than with each other. This is especially relevant to the Israel-Palestine [sic] conflict, where the ultimate issue is the survival or destruction of a nation. Any arrangement short of this is seen as temporary and provisional. On the basic issue, clearly, there is no possibility of compromise or even of meaningful negotiation.[18]

Wise as this assessment may appear, it ignores a necessary precondition of meaningful negotiation, namely, that the people with whom you negotiate must respect you and acknowledge your basic human needs or rights. But surely Lewis knows that Arabs have nothing but contempt for Jews, and deny they have any human rights. Negotiations between Israel and the Arab Palestinians thus become a self-demeaning and self-defeating charade. Lewis also ignores the most pernicious consequences of American mediation. It remains a fact that in every conflict with its adversaries, Israel has been forced by the United States to agree to ceasefire arrangements in which the Jews can only give and their enemies can only take. Washington has thereby created, with the compliance of Israeli governments, the deadly precedent which has no parallel in the world, namely, that *Israel can never win a war*. Unlike any other nation in history, Israel must turn over to its enemies the land they used as a launching pad to attack the Jewish state! How humiliating! But this is not all.

Underlying the anything but "evenhandedness" of American diplomacy is the pernicious doctrine of moral equivalence: the Jewish state (the victim) has been placed on the same level as Arab despotisms (the villains).[19] This degradation of Israel, abetted by its political elites, has been obscured by Israel's intellectual elites, whose mentality has been shaped by the leveling egalitarianism of the democratic world. Even more culpable, however, are the religious parties and their rabbinical leaders, who failed to denounce this amoral—nay, immoral—state of affairs.[20] Elaboration is necessary.

Israel is praised as the "only democracy in the Middle East." If democracy is the criterion of a good regime, then one must pronounce Arab dictatorships as bad regimes. Is it not obvious, therefore, that by negotiating with Arab despots Israeli politicians blur the distinction between the good and the bad, which cannot but demean the Jewish state? Such negotiations also suggest that agreements reached with the rulers of Arab regimes are as reliable as those reached with the leaders of democracies. The bad thus becomes good! (See Isaiah 5:20.) Nihilism was thus injected into the misnamed Arab-Jewish conflict in the aftermath of the Yom Kippur War. Twenty years later this nihilism—this denial of evil—produced a grotesque ceremony in Stockholm where Yitzhak Rabin, Shimon Peres, and Yasser Arafat each received a Nobel Peace Prize for the September 1993 Oslo Agreement. This Covenant of Death, by which Israel's government dignified and legitimized the unspeakable crimes of Yasser Arafat, has damaged and destroyed the lives of more than ten thousand Jews. (See Isaiah 28:15.)

The Yom Kippur War provided the diplomatic and strategic grounds for nullifying the miracle of the Six-Day War. Egypt, which had seemingly lost the Yom Kippur War, deftly won the United States to its cause by shifting its allegiance from Moscow to Washington. The price? The U.S. would pressure Jerusalem to return the Sinai to Egypt. Enter Likud Prime Minister Menachem Begin.

Mr. Begin concluded two related agreements, the Camp David Accords of September 1978 and the Israel-Egyptian peace treaty of March 1979. In the latter, Begin surrendered the Sinai with its Israeli developed oil fields and sophisticated airbases. Also, and with the assistance of his defense minister, Ariel Sharon, he uprooted the Jewish settlement of Yamit. He thereby set a precedent that augurs ill for the 230,000 Jews in Judea and Samaria (as well as for the Jews in Gaza and on the Golan Heights). If this were not enough, the Camp David Agreement became the first international legal document that not only designates Judea and Samaria as the "West Bank," but also describes its Arab inhabitants as the "Palestinian people"! Therein are two of the fictional grounds for a Palestinian state. True, Camp David only prescribed *functional* as opposed to *territorial* autonomy for the Arabs. But such was the broad scope of those functions that the Arabs would inevitably demand statehood—and their demand would win the support of the democratic world as well as Israel's left-wing parties.

And so Menachem Begin, the arch-Zionist, took the first major steps to undo the miracle of the Six-Day War. This undoing has profound psychological and metaphysical consequences. One does not surrender the heartland of the Jewish people without diminishing Jewish pride, disdaining the Prophets and therefore Israel's unique relationship with God. Although secularists may scoff at the idea, this God is a "jealous" God and a God of justice, and Jews will pay—indeed are paying—an awful price for betraying Eretz Yisrael, the land He chose for the Jewish people.[21]

Begin was succeeded by an even more ardent Zionist, Prime Minister Yitzhak Shamir. Although Mr. Shamir abstained in the Knesset vote on the Camp David Agreement, his government brought Israel to a lower level of degradation. Recall the first intifada. In December 1987 Arabs threw stones at Jews as Arabs did centuries ago to humiliate Jewish *dhimmies*. Despite Israel's armed might, the Shamir government refrained from quelling Arab violence. Instead, Shamir went to the U.S.-Soviet sponsored Madrid Peace Conference of October 30, 1991, where he tacitly recognized Yasser Arafat's PLO. Imagine the Jewish state of Israel seeking peace with a gang of murderers, thieves, and drug-traffickers. How degrading! How disgraceful! But how many Jews felt this degradation and disgrace, having already descended from the halcyon heights of the Six-Day War?

How many secular Jews felt ashamed when Labor Prime Minister Yitzhak Rabin shook Arafat's bloodstained hands on the White House lawn on September 13, 1993 to consecrate the Oslo Agreement? How many rabbis protested that shameless handshake and that despicable agreement, which denied the miracle of the Six-Day War and therefore denied the God of Israel? Could Jewish self-abasement sink lower? It could and did. For the government, under the aged warrior of Yitzhak Rabin, not only deJudaized the education of Jewish youth, but deleted the terms "Judaism," "Zionism," and "Eretz Yisrael" from the Soldiers Code of Ethics! Meanwhile, Rabin's (very) foreign minister Shimon Peres applied for Israel's membership in the Arab League, a consortium of corrupt dictatorships dedicated to Israel's destruction. Although any sensible person would deem Peres a fool, such has been the decline of sense and sensibility or honor in Israel that this ridiculous and unprincipled politician is esteemed as an "elder statesman."

Hence Israel descended to a lower level of degradation when Peres became Prime Minister after Rabin's assassination. Here a word from Moshe Sharett, a former Israeli Prime Minister: "I have stated that I totally and utterly reject Peres and consider his rise to prominence a malignant, immoral disgrace. I will rend my clothes in mourning for the State if I see him become a minister in the Israeli government" (*Personal Memoirs*, 1957).

Peres revealed his own contempt for Jews in this excerpt from his interview with *Ha'aretz* following his defeat by Benjamin Netanyahu in the May 1996 prime ministerial election:[22]

Interviewer: *What happened in these elections?*
Peres: We lost.
Interviewer: *Who is we?*
Peres: We, that is the Israelis.
Interviewer: *And who won?*
Peres: All those who do not have an Israeli mentality.
Interviewer: *And who are they?*
Peres: The Jews.

Mr. Peres was mistaken. The Arabs won the 1996 elections, for Prime Minister Benjamin Netanyahu, contrary to what he had led most Jews to believe, proceeded to implement the Oslo Agreement. He not only met with Arafat, but in January 1997 he abandoned 80 percent of Hebron and left its Jewish residents at the mercy of Arab gunfire. Moreover, despite daily Arab violence and violations of the Oslo Agreement, Mr. Netanyahu refrained from abrogating that Covenant of Death. To the contrary, with Ariel Sharon as his foreign minister, he concluded the Wye Memorandum, which prescribes Arab control over most of Judea and Samaria.

Israel descended to a still lower level of degradation with the 1999 election of Prime Minister Ehud Barak (another aged warrior). After his shameless evacuation of Southern Lebanon, Mr. Barak was ready to evacuate almost all of Judea and Samaria, including eastern Jerusalem. As if it were his private property, he offered Arafat shared sovereignty of the Temple Mount, the holiest site of the Jewish people. Could any Israeli government sink even lower? Consider the government under Mr. Sharon.

Sharon received an unprecedented 63 percent of the votes in the February 2001 election. This was a clear mandate to put an end to the wanton murder of Jewish men, women, and children by Arafat's terrorists. But the termination of Arab butchery logically entails the disarming and destruction of the Palestinian Authority (PA), reoccupation of the land turned over to Arafat, hence the abrogation of Oslo. Mr. Sharon, another aged warrior, did nothing of the kind. He appointed Oslo's architect, Simon Peres, foreign minister, continued to negotiate with the PA, and pursued a policy of self-restraint against Arab suicide bombings and rocket attacks. As of this writing, well over 900 Jews have been murdered under Sharon's premiership, a number far exceeding those killed under *all* of his four predecessors. This policy, as one general put it, had the effect of "educating the population to absorb blows."[23] The Jews of this country have been dehumanized.

Sharon knows all about the horrors of war. He hates war and yearns for peace. The trouble is that Israel is confronted by a most cruel and utterly implacable foe. The choice confronting Israel is not between war and peace but between war with victory and war with defeat. This is hardly the time for an aged warrior to be at the helm of the Jewish state.

The Jews, mindful of Sharon's daring and heroism as a general, are all the more confused by his vacillating and feckless behavior as Israel's prime minister. Sharon, who was against a Palestinian state, became one of its strongest supporters. Sharon, who built communities in Judea, Samaria, and Gaza (Yesha), gave orders to uproot them. Sharon, who was firmly opposed to unilateral withdrawal under fire, embraced that very policy. Sharon, who originally mocked the idea of a "security fence," initiated its construction.

That multi-billion dollar fence, which marks the *de facto* borders of a Palestinian state, will obviously not make the 230,000 Jews who live on its eastern side more secure. Even military commanders openly admitted that the only thing that prevents suicide bombers from entering Jewish cities west of the fence is the presence of the IDF in Palestinian cities. Moreover, as one astute commentator pointed out, "While Israel, in building [that fence] is renouncing its claims to everything on the eastern side, the Palestinians, in objecting to [the fence], renounce none of their claims to the western side."[24]

The degradation and folly of the Jewish state under Prime Minister Sharon is mind-boggling.

Thus, in 2003, Sharon, without Knesset or public discussion, accepted the "Road Map" to a Palestinian state, a "two-state" plan inspired by Israel's enemy, Saudi Arabia. The Road Map was drawn up by the so-called Quartet, which includes, in addition to the U.S. and Russia, two other unmitigated enemies of Israel, the UN and the EU (European Union). This would-be peace plan requires Israel to withdraw from Judea, Samaria, and Gaza even without the cessation of Arab terror—as if Israel's withdrawal would transform Hamas and Islamic Jihad into doves! And so it came to pass in February 2004 that Sharon announced his unilateral disengagement plan, with Gaza first on his list. All of Gaza's 8,000 Jews would be uprooted and expelled from their homes. Their synagogues and study centers, their schools and Jewish academies, their vineyards and orchards would be abandoned, and all this treasure would be turned over to Arab terrorists! The plan is not only immoral or unjust; it not only violates Israel's Basic Law: Freedom and Human Dignity; it not only rewards and further encourages terrorism. All this is obvious. But to fully appreciate the heinous character of that plan, ponder this: had a French prime minister said that all Jews must be removed from Paris because their presence arouses violence, he would have been denounced as a racist as well as an anti-Semite!

It has been said that those whom the gods wish to destroy they first drive mad. In January 2004, the Sharon government, in addition to violating Jewish law, which limits the ransom for captives, also violated international law—*nullum crimen sine poena*, "no crime without a punishment"—by releasing some 400 terrorists in exchange for the corpses of three Israeli soldiers, plus a single Israeli citizen who was kidnapped while trying to conclude a drug deal with Hezbollah operatives! This decision was made despite the well-known fact that the release of hundreds of Arab terrorists in 1985 sparked the first *intifada*. The release of those unrepentant terrorists not only augmented their killing power but also their determination to annihilate Israel. Israeli governments have thus been complicit in murder on the one hand, and have conditioned Jews to accept the murder of their loved ones on the other. Indeed, Israel's ruling elites have murdered the sense of justice in the Jewish state. In the process, they have eroded the State's Jewish character, as we shall now see.

In forming his government after the January 2003 elections, Mr. Sharon appointed two leaders of the ultra-secular Shinui Party, chairman Tommy Lapid and Avraham Poraz, to head, respectively, the Justice and Interior Ministries. These two ministries have the power to deJudaize the State of Israel. Sharon placed under Lapid's ministry the Rabbinical Courts. Their subsequent elimination cannot but accelerate the Left's crusade for a "secular revolution" in Israel. Meanwhile, Mr. Poraz, in addition to fostering commercial violation of the Sabbath, eased the entry of gentiles into the country by "flexible" interpretation of the conversion and immigration laws. In fact, he froze the immigration of gentiles who underwent orthodox conversion! Under his anti-religious agenda, citizenship may be granted to the children of foreign workers and to any non-Jew that could make some contribution to the country, whether financial, artistic, scientific, or even athletic. Sharon raised no objection to this blatant attempt to deJudaize Israel, despite the fact that the Jewish majority in Israel has plummeted from 82 percent to 72 percent in twenty years and that almost half the births occurring in Israel are non-Jewish.

If further proof is wanted regarding Sharon's betrayal of the millions of Jews who have come to this country because they wanted to live in a Jewish state, (1) he opposed any amendment of the "grandfather clause" of the Law of Return, which has enabled hundreds of thousands of gentiles to enter Israel;[25] (2) he justified his choice of Avraham Poraz to supervise immigration to Israel by saying, "I see that [a Jew is] whoever comes, sees himself as part of the Jewish people, serves in the army, and fights";[26] (3) he even referred to Judea and Samaria as "occupied territory" and thus made a mockery of Jewish history and Jewish identity. Indeed, Sharon's reference to the heartland of the Jewish People as "occupied territory" reveals, with awesome clarity, that the aged warrior had capitulated to terrorism and American pressure. All that remained was to define the terms of this surrender, while posturing about "peace and security."

The Jews of Israel should tremble when they hear Labor's surrogate prime minister insist on an Arab state in Judea and Samaria. This betrayal of the Jewish heritage and of God's covenant with the Jewish people spells doom. An Arab state in Judea and Samaria will develop a formidable army. With international economic support, it will gradually accommodate a million and more Arab "refugees." It will seek to expand, for the Arab appetite for Jewish land and Jewish blood is insatiable. It will subject the 230,000 Jewish residents of Judea and Samaria to unrelenting violence. These Jews will be forced to leave, and Arab "refugees" will occupy their homes. Terrorist attacks will continue against the pathetic remainder of the Jewish state. Many Jews will emigrate from Eretz Yisrael. Their exodus will accelerate Arab control of the Knesset, thanks to democracy's egalitarian principle of one adult/one vote. Israel's government will be Arabized. This new Arab state will extend from the Jordan River to the Mediterranean Sea—the explicit and undeviating goal of Arafat's PLO. Arafat or his successor will become the ruler of the erstwhile Jewish state. Instead of a "Greater Israel," behold a "Greater Palestine"!

It thus appears that the rabbis who discouraged *aliya* before the Holocaust were correct when they said a Zionist state based on non-Torah law would not succeed or endure. But they were also wrong. For as Rav Teichtal saw, had a million orthodox Jews from Europe made *aliya* during the decades following the publication of Rabbi Tzvi Kalischer book, *Derishat Tzion* in 1864, Israel would not have had a succession of prime ministers whose policies, far from endowing Jews with security and dignity, have sickened their daily life with fear and humiliation. Indeed, countless Jews, especially children, have suffered or are suffering post-traumatic shock syndrome, in dread of, or having witnessed, Arab terrorist attacks, especially suicide bombings that have reduced Jews to body parts.

"Peace" and "Democracy"

It should be borne in mind that the Oslo policy of withdrawing from Yesha was justified not only in the name of "peace," but also in the name of "democracy."

Ruling Arabs in Judea, Samaria, and Gaza is simply undemocratic—or so it has been said by guilt-ridden, approval-seeking or "politically correct" Jews. Israel's secular and religious leaders taught them that "peace" and "democracy" are more exalted than Jewish retention of their ancient heartland. This degradation of God's covenant with the patriarchs—which cannot but incite Arab contempt and violence—has long been the position of Israel's leftwing leaders. To explain their appeasement of the Arab Palestinians in terms of guilt feelings—which may apply to others—ignores the possibility of sinister motives. Surely their motives for abandoning land resplendent with Jewish history (ostensibly for the sake of "peace" and "democracy") is no less selfish than the motives of Jewish leaders who, according to Rav Teichtal, discouraged Jews from redeeming this land prior to the Holocaust. Oslo was not simply the release of a guilty conscience. Nor was it merely a monumental blunder.

The present writer contends that *Oslo was the price for Arab support in Israel's 1992 Knesset elections!* But to make the sale of Judea, Samaria, and Gaza for Arab votes palatable to the public, this betrayal had to be couched in terms of "peace" and "democracy." Peace and democracy required the end of Israeli rule over the Arabs in the "West Bank"—which means peace and democracy required the end of Zionism and the emasculation of the Jewish psyche. Judea and Samaria were engraved in the Jewish people's collective memory. So long as Jews remained in Judea and Samaria, most Jews in Israel would remain bonded to Judaism. This bond had to be severed: Judaism had to be eviscerated and the Jewish soul deconstructed. This was the hidden purpose of Oslo's architects. As Yoram Hazony points out: "In some crucial way, the Oslo agreement had signaled the end of *the* [anti-Zionist] mission, a turn of events that the celebrated author David Grossman described—mimicking the language of the accords, which called for an Israel military redeployment—as a 'redeployment from [and shrinkage of] entire regions of our soul.'"[27] Consistent therewith, the Rabin-Peres government all but eliminated Jewish content from the public school curriculum. Its goal was to transform the Jewish state into a "state of its citizens"—the only way the Left, with its Arab allies, could preserve its political power and perquisites. That the Left could enlist Ariel Sharon in support of its goal of emasculating Judaism by a Palestinian state is indicative of the degrading and terminal consequences of secular Zionism.

Now recall the forebodings of the prophets and sages of Israel. Isaiah prophesies that in the "end of days" Israel will be ruled by fools, by a government so deranged that it calls evil good and good evil (3:4; 5:20; 44:25). The Babylonian Talmud calls this government "paltry," "debased" (*Sanhedrin* 98a). The Mishnah describes this period as devoid of truth as well as shameless like the face of a dog" (*Sotah* 6:14). Ponder these words of the Torah with the

"Palestinians" in mind: *"They [the Children of Israel] have provoked me with their nullities. Now I will provoke them by a non-people, by a vile nation"* (Deuteronomy 32:21).

But there is a bright aside to these maledictions. The Talmud relates that Rabbi Akiva and his colleagues were coming up to Jerusalem, and that just as they approached Mount Scopus they saw a fox emerging from the ruins of the Temple Mount. Rabbi Akiva's colleagues wept while he seemed merry. When asked why he was merry, Rabbi Akiva explained that just as the prophecy has come to pass that Jerusalem will lay in ruins and the Temple Mount will become heaps of rubble (Micah 3:12; Jeremiah 26:18-20), so a future generation will see fulfilled the prophecy of Jerusalem's redemption; indeed, Jerusalem will eventually be called the City of Truth (Zechariah 8:3-4). We must therefore ask: What must be done to restore Jewish national pride and hasten the Final Redemption of the Jewish People? The first step is to identify Israel's enemies and determine what must be done to thwart their hostile designs. This is the purpose of the next chapter.

CHAPTER 2
THE ARAB PROBLEM:
ON SELF-DETERMINATION

INTRODUCTION

MANY of those who oppose the establishment of an independent Arab Palestinian state on the "West Bank" do so for reasons of security. Without the "West Bank" Israel would be reduced to its indefensible 1949 borders. Others reject an Arab Palestinian state for religious reasons. What is called the "West Bank" is nothing less than the biblical land of Judea and Samaria, the heartland of the Jewish People. This land, they argue, belongs to the Jews by Divine law. Still others oppose an Arab Palestinian state in Judea and Samaria on the basis of international law. They argue that the Jews have the only valid legal claims to this land. This argument has been articulated by Moshe Brody:

> With the end of the First World War and the fall of the Turkish Empire, the Allied Powers in the early 1920s signed an international treaty known as the "Mandate for Palestine," which was accorded the status of international law by the League of Nations. The Mandate for Palestine formalized the Balfour Declaration and, among other provisions, recognized "the historical connection of the Jewish People with Palestine" and the "grounds for reconstituting their national home in that country." In particular, the Mandate designated all of Palestine west of the Jordan River for immediate Jewish settlement, and encouraged such settlement. These areas included all of Gaza, the entire city of Jerusalem, the Golan Heights, and all that is now referred to as the "West Bank"—including places such as Hebron, Jenin, and Nablus. Nothing was excluded from Jewish settlement, nor were there any limitations. Of outstanding note was the fact that, while civil and religious rights in Palestine were guaranteed to non-Jewish inhabitants, *national rights to Palestine were conveyed*

solely to the Jewish People. No Arabs, Muslims, or Christians were recognized as having any national rights to any part of Palestine.

In 1946 the United Nations charter reaffirmed the validity of all existing instruments of international law. Being such an instrument, *the Mandate for Palestine remains valid international law today, exactly as it was originally written—and it remains the only international law pertaining to the settlements of Palestine and national rights in Palestine.* This means that under international law, all of "Palestine" is still designated for the Jewish People and Jewish settlement. Even the United Nations General Assembly Partition Resolution 181 of November, 1947, which led to the establishment of Israel and the 1948 War of Independence, did not change this, because General Assembly resolutions are recommendations only and do not have the status of international law. *There is absolutely no basis for any allegation that Jewish settlement anywhere in "Palestine" is "illegal" under international law. Furthermore, no Arabs or Muslims have any national rights to Palestine under international law today.*[28]

While all these arguments are defensible, no one to my knowledge has ever opposed an Arab Palestinian state on *democratic* grounds. The reason is fairly obvious. Virtually everyone believes that the democratic principle of self-determination justifies an Arab Palestinian state in the first place. I shall refute this prejudice.

Before doing so, certain democratic principles must be clarified. The claim that the Palestinian Arabs are entitled to independent statehood is based on the principles of *contemporary* or *normless* democracy. This claim, we shall see, can be refuted by those very principles. The same claim can be refuted by employing the principles of *classical* or *normative* democracy. What are the differences between these two types of democracy?

Although both classical and contemporary democracy emphasize freedom and equality as basic principles, classical or normative democracy derives these principles from the Genesis account of man's creation in the image of God. As a consequence, freedom and equality in classical democracy have rational and moral constraints. This is not the case of contemporary or normless democracy, where moral relativism flourishes and prevents those tainted by relativism from opposing a Palestinian nation-state on moral grounds.[29]

Also, whereas freedom in classical democracy takes precedence over equality, the reverse is the case in contemporary democracy where an indiscriminate egalitarianism reigns supreme. This egalitarianism disposes its victims to assert the equal rights of the Arab Palestinians to independent statehood even though such a state would be another Arab despotism diametrically opposed to equality and not very solicitous about freedom. Furthermore, unlike classical democracy, which exalts *political* freedom, contemporary democracy worships *personal* freedom—another reason why moral relativism flourishes in contemporary democratic societies. But neither political freedom nor personal freedom would thrive in the Arab Palestinian state so ardently advocated by the partisans of contemporary democracy.

Bearing these distinctions in the mind, it will not be necessary, except in certain contexts, to make specific references to classical and contemporary democracy, since both, as will be shown, logically negate Palestinian statehood. This negation will no doubt expose me to the charge "racism" by contemporary democrats, to say nothing of Arabs who are anything but democrats. Undeterred by this canard, the author will show that the only realistic solution to the Arab issue is one that conforms to both democratic and Jewish principles.

Islam Versus Democracy

As will be presently demonstrated, Arab-Islamic culture is utterly opposed to the basic principles of democracy however understood. This being the case, the Arabs of Judea, Samaria, and Gaza have no right, *in this period of history*, to an independent and sovereign state; indeed, the creation of such a state, at this time, would serve neither the good of these Arabs nor the good of Israel. Any claim to the contrary by Arabs is but a ploy to truncate Israel and thereby facilitate its destruction. If such a claim is made by Jewish democrats, it merely reflects abysmal ignorance if not intellectual dishonesty.

That Arab-Islamic culture rejects the basic principles of democracy is so obvious that I must apologize to the reader for enumerating the following well-known facts:

(1) Whereas freedom, including freedom of speech, is one of the two cardinal principles of democracy, Arab-Islamic culture is strictly authoritarian, which is why its media are state-controlled.

(2) Unlike democracy, whose other cardinal principle is equality, Arab-Islamic culture is strictly hierarchical. Top-down leadership is a fundamental principle of Islamic theology. Authority runs down from Allah to Muhammad and from Muhammad to the *imam*, the ruler of the regime.

(3) Democracy is based on the primacy of consent or persuasion. This adorns democratic societies with a certain easy-goingness and civility. Not only are past grievances readily swept aside, but political opponents can be

friends despite their differences. Differences are resolved by mutual concessions, and agreements are usually lasting. In contrast, Arab-Islamic culture is based on the primacy of coercion. Agreements between rival factions do not really terminate animosities, which is why such agreements are so short-lived.

(4) Because democracy is based on the primacy of consent, the pursuit of peace is the norm of democratic states. In contrast, because Arab-Islamic culture is based on the primacy of coercion, the foreign policy norm of Arab-Islamic states is intimidation and conquest. *Jihad* (holy war) is a basic Islamic principle, which is why Muslim violence will be found throughout the world.

(5) Whereas democracy is based on the primacy of the individual, Arab-Islamic culture is based on the primacy of the group—be it the village or the extended family. The individual Muslim has no identity outside the group; it is to the group that he owes all his loyalty. This is one reason why internecine conflict has been endemic among Arabs throughout history.

(6) Contemporary democracy is regarded as a process by which various individuals pursue their private interests and have diverse values or "lifestyles." This is not the case in Arab-Islamic culture, which binds everyone to the set of substantive values prescribed in the Quran and in Islamic law (the *sharia*).

(7) Whereas contemporary democracy is inclined toward moral relativism, Islam is based on absolutism. The former conduces to tolerance, the latter to intolerance. Admittedly, Islamic regimes tolerate non-Islamic minorities, but only as *dhimmis*—virtual pariahs.

(8) Democratic societies are preoccupied with the present (the Now). Conversely, Arab-Islamic culture exists under the aspect of eternity. What dominate Islamic mentality are the past and the future, which is why revenge for past injuries is a dominant motif of the Arab world. And given their group loyalty, Muslims are religiously bound to wreak vengeance against those who have slighted the honor of any Muslim.

(9) The openness or publicity found in democracy stands in striking contrast to the hiddenness, secrecy, and dissimulation characteristic of Islam. As one liberated Arab sociologist writes: "Lying is a widespread habit among the Arabs, and they have a low idea of truth."[30]

(10) Whereas contemporary democracy is rooted in secularism, Arab-Islamic culture is rooted in religion. Even Arab leaders who are not devout Muslims identify with the basic goals of Islam. The radical separation of religion and politics found in democracy is foreign to Islamic regimes.

The ten preceding considerations demonstrate that the democratic concept of national self-determination has no logical application to the Arab Palestinians. Let us examine this concept.

NATIONAL SELF-DETERMINATION

National self-determination involves the question of whether a people has the right to establish any form of government it pleases, be it a Communist, Fascist, or Islamic dictatorship. To answer this question, let us first recall these words of the American Declaration of Independence:

> We hold these truths to be self-evident, that all men are created equal, that they are endowed by their Creator with certain unalienable Rights, that among these are Life, Liberty and the pursuit of Happiness.—That to secure these Rights, Governments are instituted among Men, deriving their just powers from the consent of the governed.

Underlying these words of the Declaration of Independence is the Torah's conception of man's creation in the image of God.[31] This remarkable document portrays man as a rational being who possesses free will and is capable of distinguishing right from wrong. Without such a conception of human nature, the fifty-six signatories of the Declaration would have had no rational or just grounds for rebelling against Great Britain whose laws and colonial governments violated, in the words of those signatories, the "Laws of Nature and of Nature's God."

This "Higher Law" doctrine of the Declaration provides a set of norms or standards by which to determine whether the granting of national self-determination to this or that people or ethnic group can be justified. It certainly cannot be justified among people steeped in ignorance or habituated to violence and servitude. Such a people, as Thomas Jefferson understood, may justly be governed without their consent. John Stuart Mill held the same view. In his classic, *On Liberty*, Mill writes: "Despotism is a legitimate form of government in dealing with barbarians, provided the end be their improvement, and the means justified by actually effecting that end."[32] Mill elaborates in *Representative Government*, which calls to mind certain Arab characteristics! He explains that a people may lack the moderation which representative government requires of them:

> A rude people, though in some degree alive to the benefits of civilized society, may not be able to practice the forbearance which it demands: their passions may be too violent, or their personal pride too exacting, to forego private conflict, and leave to the laws the avenging of their real or supposed wrongs. In such a case, a civilized government, to be really advantageous to them, will require to be in

a considerable degree despotic: one over which they do not themselves exercise control, and which imposes a great degree of forcible restraint upon their actions. A people must be considered unfit for more than a limited and qualified freedom…who will not co-operate actively with the law and the public authorities in the repression of evil-doers.[33]

Remarkably, and apropos of the destruction of the World Trade Center, the eminent historian Paul Johnson said of Arab-Islamic states that harbor terrorists: "Countries that cannot live in peace with their neighbors and wage covert war against the international community cannot expect total independence." He recommends a "new form of United Nations mandate system"![34]

It follows that a people's right to national self-determination is not an absolute: it is limited by rational and moral considerations. It would be irrational and unjust to permit a people, in the name of self-determination, to establish a form of government that denied its neighbor's right to self-determination. This would be the inevitable consequence of establishing an Arab Palestinian state on Israel's doorstep (*the goal of contemporary democrats for whom justice is mere equality and bears no relation to a person's or a people's character or worthiness*).

In view of the fact that the militant beliefs and authoritarian way of life of these Arabs render them hostile to democracy—and I shall soon document their latent savagery—they may be governed without their consent until a humane alternative is forthcoming. Before elaborating on this alternative, it should be emphasized that, contrary to almost universal opinion, the principle of government by the consent of the governed does not mean that democracy is the only just form of government. In fact, the word "democracy" does not appear in the American Declaration of Independence (*or in its Israeli counterpart*). What the Declaration regards as most important is not the *form* but the *ends* of government, namely life, liberty, and the pursuit of happiness. In its own words: "whenever *any* Form of Government becomes destructive of these ends, it is the Right of the People to alter or abolish it." This clearly implies that there are just forms of government other than democracy, an implication relevant to Israeli rule over the Palestinian Arabs.

Now, given the paramount importance of the ends of government, no people have a right to establish a form of government whose very nature is destructive of these ends. When the American Declaration of Independence states that men's rights to life, liberty, and the pursuit of happiness are "unalienable," this means that these rights may neither be taken away *nor voted away*. If self-determination is to be continuously effective, the people must be offered, in periodic elections, alternative public policies, and not the cynical charades played by various despots.

From these considerations it follows that even if the Palestinian Arabs were to vote *unanimously* in favor of establishing an Islamic dictatorship, such an act would not only be irrational—for men cannot rationally divest themselves of the power to determine who shall be their rulers—but it would also be unjust. It would or could deprive future generations and perhaps other nations of their right to life, liberty, and the pursuit of happiness. As Abraham Lincoln has written, "[One] cannot say any people has a right to do what is wrong."[35] The principle of self-determination is not self-justifying. Its justice depends on consequences, namely, whether its application will result in the establishment of a just form of government.

This understanding was still alive at the end of World War II. Neither the German nor the Japanese people were permitted to establish any form of government they desired. To the contrary, American and British statesmen in those days deemed it both reasonable and just to impose on Nazi Germany and Imperial Japan a parliamentary form of democracy in which the principle of self-determination is obviously meaningful and continually operative. By means of periodic multi-party elections and freedom of speech and press, the people of those two countries can determine who shall exercise the powers of government and thereby influence the policies and goals of their respective countries.

On the other hand, the principle of self-determination can be used to stifle democracy. Hitler called for the self-determination of the Germans in the Sudetenland; England complied at Munich, which doomed democratic Czechoslovakia. One may compare the Sudeten Germans to the "West Bank" Arabs. In the name of self-determination, the United States and Europe favor an Arab Palestinian state in the historic heartland of the Jewish people, a state which, in alliance with Egypt and Syria, could doom democratic Israel.

If the truth were told, the Arabs of the "West Bank" exercised far more self-determination under Israel than they now do under Yasser Arafat's PLO-Palestinian Authority! Under Israel's benevolent rule they elected their own mayors and enjoyed rights and opportunities non-existent in the entire Arab-Islamic world. Israel's government established a system of primary and secondary schools which greatly multiplied the number of girls and boys attending classes (where, they were also taught, unfortunately, to hate Jews). Thanks to Israel, Arab colleges and universities appeared for the first time in the "West Bank" (only to become centers for Arab insurrection). Israel's government also established new hospitals, health centers, and nursing schools. Infant mortality was greatly reduced and the standard of health improved beyond recognition. Also, roads as well as water and electric power facilities were constructed. Modern methods of agriculture were introduced. Eventually, tens of thousands of "West Bank" Arabs were employed in Israel. The Arabs' standard of living doubled and quadrupled. (Tourists were amazed to see so many large and luxurious mansions in Arab towns and villages.)

One Arab commentator acknowledged in 1971 that "The Arabs feel, not only that they live better than before [the Six-Day War of] 1967, but say also that they will not choose to live again under a [Jordanian] dictatorship after having experienced the liberal Israeli regime."[36] In that same year the following remark appeared in a Lebanese newspaper: "We have lived a long period under the 'humiliation' of Arab nationalism, and it pains us to say that we had to wait for the Israel 'conquest' in order to become aware of human relationships…"[37]

If this candid attitude was widespread among Arabs west of the Jordan, it did not run very deep: most Arabs cheered and danced on their roof tops in 1991 when Iraqi Scud missiles fell on Israel. They are paying the price of such perversity. Having cursed the seed of Abraham, they are themselves cursed by Arafat, whom they embraced in 1993. Thanks to the Israel-PLO Agreement of that year, they now live impoverished and intimidated by Arafat's military dictatorship: a pretty consequence of the misplaced principle of self-determination. For this we may thank the proponents of contemporary democracy in the governments of Israel and the United States.

With Arafat's "election," self-determination among the Palestinian Arabs ceased the moment it was exercised. Even their civil rights, which they enjoyed under Israeli law, were violated. Darkness has descended upon them. As we shall see in a moment, Arafat liberated their most savage instincts. Here I am reminded of a passage in Jefferson's Declaration of Independence that mentions "the merciless Indian Savages, whose known rule of warfare is an undistinguished destruction of all ages, sexes, and conditions."

Self-determination is a morally neutral and therefore dangerous concept. It flourishes in parliamentary democracy. Let us see why.

Parliamentary Democracy and Human Nature

Self-determination can flourish in parliamentary democracy because parliaments, by definition, are based on the primacy of speech, the distinctively human attribute. What indeed is a human self if not one that governs itself by speech? Speech lets reason in, as force does not. Reasoned speech opens the door to merit; the cleverest rhetoricians fell to Socrates. A parliamentary regime, though capable of dealing forcefully with other nation-states, prefers to deal with them by speech. But only if those nation-states share its fundamental understanding of human nature can this dialogue mean anything other than a charade.[38]

By contrast, consider a Palestinian nation-state under Yasser Arafat. (Alternatively, one might observe it as exemplified by Arafat's patron, Egypt.) We see no promise of meaningful parliamentarism there. Arafat's PLO-Palestinian Authority is a kleptocratic dictatorship. In addition to absconding public funds, it summarily executes critics of the regime, indoctrinates Arab children to hate Jews, and trains them to become suicide bombers. (Incidentally, can anyone take Hosni Mubarak's parliament seriously? No more so than we can look to Egypt's media for reasoned discussions and truthful reports.) The "self-determination" so touchingly proclaimed by Arab propagandists confines itself to the will of the ruling elites. That will has little to do with reasoned speech. For them, consent is a problem resolved by force alone.

The primacy of force in Arab regimes is symptomatic of a radically different view of human nature. Not reason, not merit, but chance rules such regimes: the chance of who happens to get the power to impose his will—for the moment. Reason serves force and force serves the ruler's will, inverting the moral universe of Jeffersonian democracy. It is no accident that military, not civilian, control characterizes these regimes.

Truly, a country's form of government—its true form, not always the form it shows the world—reflects its understanding of human nature. Whereas a nationalism based on that which is distinctively human, on reasoned speech, need not destroy itself by escalating irrational, absolutist demands both in the world and within its own borders, a nationalism based on will, on force, inevitably attacks the world and convulses itself. For the passions cannot restrain themselves. Their only limit is exhaustion or destruction.

ARAB-ISLAMIC BARBARISM

To cite a recent example of Arab-Islamic barbarism, ponder George Will's account of the suicide bombing that occurred in Jerusalem's Sbaro restaurant on August 9, 2001, when 15 Jews were killed and more than 100 were wounded, many maimed for life. Mr. Will first quotes a report by *USA Today's* Jack Kelly, who was 30 yards away when the terrorist detonated a bomb packed with nails:

> The blast…sent flesh flying onto second-story balconies a block away. Three men were blown 30 feet; their heads, separated from their bodies by the blast, rolled down the glass-strewn street.… One

woman had at least six nails embedded in her neck. Another had a nail in her left eye. Two men, one with a six-inch piece of glass in his right temple...tried to walk away.... A man groaned.... His legs were blown off. Blood poured from his torso.... A 3-year old girl, her face covered with glass, walked among the bodies calling her mother's name.... The mother...was dead.... One rabbi found a small hand against a white Subaru parked outside the restaurant.

Mr. Will, a gentile political scientist and one of America's most respected journalist, comments:

> As with the June bombing that killed 21 at a Tel Aviv disco, children were not collateral victims—they were the targets. Abdallah al-Shami, a senior official of Islamic Jihad, celebrated "this successful operation" against "pigs and monkeys." That is a familiar rhetorical trope among those whom the calamitous Oslo "peace process" cast in the role of Israel's "partners for peace." In yet another of the constant violations of the Oslo requirement to stop anti-Jewish incitements, this was a recent broadcast from the moral cesspool that is the official television station of Yasser Arafat's Palestinian Authority: "All weapons must be aimed at the Jews...whom the Koran describes as monkeys and pigs.... We will enter Jerusalem as conquerors.... Blessings to he who shot a bullet into the head of a Jew."[39]

A physicist describes what happens when a conventional bomb is exploded in a contained space, such as a city bus traveling through downtown Jerusalem: "A person sitting nearby would feel, momentarily, a shock wave slamming into his or her body, with an 'overpressure' of 300,000 pounds. Such a blast would crush the chest, rupture liver, spleen, heart and lungs, melt eyes, pull organs away from surrounding tissue, separate hands from arms and feet from legs." (*Toronto Star*, June 19, 2002.) These are among the little Arab "animosities" apologists of the Palestinians speak of in saying that Israelis, including (presumably) the school children who usually fill these buses, have brought upon themselves in the "intifada"—a euphemism for Jihad.

Lest it be thought that Islamic Jihad is an aberration of the Arab-Islamic world, Muslims throughout that benighted world gleefully celebrated the Sbaro massacre. (In fact, one study indicates that 85 percent of Palestinian Arabs support the suicide bombing of Jewish civilians.) To any "politically incorrect" scholar of Islam, it would be obvious that the Islamic religion failed to eradicate—indeed, it can arouse—the paganism submerged in the Arab soul. (Recall the horrifying butchery of two Jewish reserve soldiers in Ramallah, and, more recently, of American soldiers in Fallujah, Iraq.) Even in Jordan with which Israel has a "peace" treaty, Jews are regarded as subhuman. In August 2001, Israeli businessman Yitzhak Snir was murdered outside his home in Amman. The killing was applauded by various Jordanian newspapers, one of which ran a headline that read, "A DOG THAT DIED."[40]

This reduction of the human to the subhuman reveals the nature of Arab terror and distinguishes it from all conventional acts of war. Acts of terror involve the *wanton* slaughter of innocent lives—the lives even of children who do not directly or even indirectly constitute a military threat to the adversary. Such acts are not to be confused with "collateral damage," almost inevitable when they involve military targets. Arab terrorist attacks simply deny the humanity of their victims and differ not at all from those of Nazis who reduced Jews to the ashes of Auschwitz. Accordingly, one does NOT negotiate with terrorists. To do so is to obliterate the distinction between the human and the subhuman, between the rational and the irrational. It is to dignify unmitigated evil, indeed, to reward evil and thereby condition evil-doers to persist in their evil acts. In other words, the failure to punish terrorists *decisively* is to perpetuate their unspeakable crimes.

Our analysis of Arab-Islamic culture and of self-determination, and the evidence of Arab Palestinian savagery (which can be multiplied a thousand-fold), will convince any candid reader that it would be utterly irrational and inconsistent with democracy to allow these Arabs to form an independent nation-state. Such a nation-state on the "West Bank" would eat at Israel's heart: geographically, militarily and, most of all, in spirit. *By definition* that nation-state would never satisfy itself; by its nature it *could* not. This being the case, is there a realistic and humane solution to the Arab Palestinian problem? Stated another way: is there an alternative to Oslo?

HOW TO SOLVE THE ARAB PALESTINIAN PROBLEM

Before addressing this issue, it should be noted that certain politicians advocate a Palestinian state only as a means of solving Israel's Arab demographic problem. It is widely known, but hardly ever made a subject of public discussion, that such is the prolific birthrate of Israel's Arab inhabitants that, sooner or later they will outnumber Jews. The democratic principle of one adult/one vote will then enable these Arabs to control the Knesset and, by perfectly legal means, transform the Jewish state into an Arab state. Obviously such a state will not be democratic. This self-destructive logic of (contemporary) democracy can be avoided, or so some naively believe, by creating a Palestinian state in the "West Bank" to which Israel's Arab population may immigrate and there become citizens. Alternatively, these Arabs may remain in Israel, but their citizenship, hence their Israeli voting rights, will be transferred, as it were, to the new Palestinian state.

This scenario can only be spawned by those who refuse to take Arabs or Islam seriously, or who simply lack the intellectual integrity or moral courage to acknowledge the obvious: the Arabs of Israel are committed to Israel's destruction, and they are multiplying to hasten that end. Year after year these Arabs have committed hundreds of politically motivated assaults including stabbings, shootings, arson, and sabotage. They have collaborated with the PLO and other terrorist organizations and have even formed terrorist cells of their own. Several have been implicated in suicide bombings. But even as early as 1990, no less than 62 percent of these "Israeli" Arabs *openly* supported Saddam Hussein despite his threat to incinerate half of Israel![41] No wonder they are exempt from military service.

These Arabs have no intention of leaving Israel. Here they enjoy all the rights of Jews as well as educational opportunities unequalled in the Arab-Islamic world. In Israel, moreover, they can refrain from paying taxes, commit crimes without punishment, and receive subsidies for large-families to facilitate their eventual political ascendancy. True, they complain of Israeli discrimination, but then they gain the sympathetic support of Israeli politicians anxious to win their votes, which can only be paid for at the expense of Jews and the Jewish character of the state. Hence it is futile and sheer folly to try and solve Israel's internal demographic problem by creating a Palestinian nation-state on Israel's vulnerable eastern border.

Evident here is the desperation of Jewish democrats who stubbornly refuse to take Islam seriously and unwittingly insult Muslims in the process. Unreconstructed academics are especially dangerous. Their sheltered havens are hotbeds of moral relativism, which, by denying the existence of evil, severs Israel's Illuminati from reality. Only Ph.D.s like Yossi Beilin, Yair Hirschfeld, and Ron Pundak could dream up Oslo—could believe that offering the villainous Arafat a Palestinian state and arming his professional Jew-killers would or could put an end to Arab terrorism and solve not only the Palestinian problem, but defuse Israel's demographic time-bomb.

In any event, Israel's internal demographic problem can be solved by vigorously addressing the more urgent Arab Palestinian problem. It has been proposed that the 3.5 million Arabs in Judea, Samaria, and Gaza be made Jordanian citizens, but that this historic land of the Jewish people should be incorporated into the State of Israel. The trouble is, no Jordanian government will cooperate with this proposal, which would destabilize that regime. Besides, and as already indicated, Arafat's PLO-Palestinian Authority has educated a generation of children to hate Jews and Israel and to emulate suicide bombers. It would take decades to overcome such hatred. Long before that, however, there will be far more Arabs than Jews between the Jordan River and the Mediterranean Sea. Even now the 4.7 million Arabs west of the Jordan almost equals Israel's so-called Jewish population, which includes some 400,000 gentiles who immigrated to Israel under the "grandfather clause" of the Law of Return. A more forthright solution to the Arab Palestinian problem is necessary. Accordingly, a future government will:

(1) Abrogate the Oslo Agreement and, in one swift and devastating attack, disarm and dismantle the entire PLO-Palestinian Authority.[42] This should be done without approval-seeking and without fear of UN condemnations and U.S. sanctions. Israel is quite capable of withstanding foreign pressure if its government will only stand up and uphold the rights of the Jewish People instead of sacrificing them to the idol of "peace and security." Any and every effort to justify crushing the PA will be taken as a sign of weakness.

The government must act on the recognition that Yasser Arafat and his minions have no intention of reaching a peaceful settlement. This was made crystal clear in 2000 when Prime Minister Ehud Barak offered him 95 percent of Judea and Samaria (including the removal of Jewish settlements), eastern Jerusalem (leaving the Temple Mount in Arab hands), and partial return of refugees—all this in a sovereign Palestinian state. Yet Arafat said "No." His goal has ever been the elimination of the Jewish state from the Arab Middle East. Thus, in March 1996 the *Middle East Digest* reported that Arafat had told Arab diplomats at a meeting in Stockholm that the "PLO plans to eliminate Israel" by stages.[43] The strategy requires the orchestration of negotiations and terrorist attacks punctuated by cease fires, keeping alive the hopes of Israelis panting for peace with their genocidal enemies.

Arafat knows what he is doing. His strategy of stages merely replicates Muhammad's *al-Hudaibiya* Treaty of 628 with the pagan Meccans. Two years later the prophet of Islam executed his strategy of stages by decimating his Meccan rivals. The same *al-Hudaibiya* treaty was invoked by Egyptian clerics as a precedent for Anwar Sadat's signing an agreement with Israel; and Arafat, himself an Egyptian, has referred to that treaty to signal his real intentions. He was quite serious when he said "peace means the destruction of Israel." Hence it is absolutely essential *not* to negotiate with the Palestinian Authority; indeed, the PA must be utterly destroyed. Eliminating the entire terrorist leadership will demoralize and divide the so-called Palestinians, which actually consist of diverse clans from various Arab states. No leadership will readily develop and command the loyalty of these rival clans. Thus, once the PA is destroyed, the government should

(2) Declare Jewish sovereignty over Judea, Samaria, and Gaza, while broadcasting (for the sake of Jews in the Diaspora) biblical and historical evidence as well as international law affirming Israel's exclusive right to these areas. (The Arabs in these areas will of course retain the personal, religious, and economic rights they enjoyed under Israeli law, but they will not vote in Israeli elections.)

(3) Establish unequivocal jurisdiction over the Temple Mount.

(4) Relocate certain cabinet ministries in Judea, Samaria, and Gaza. (This will convince Arabs that the Jews intend to remain in these areas *permanently*.)[44]

(5) Sell small plots of land in these areas at very low prices to Jews in Israel and abroad with the proviso that they settle on the land, say for a period of six years. This would diminish the dangerous population density of Israel's large cities and, at the same time, encourage Jewish immigration to Israel. (Enfranchising Israelis living abroad would encourage thousands of these Jews to return to their homeland.)

(6) Develop model cities in Judea, Samaria, and Gaza by attracting foreign capital investment on terms favorable to the investors. Based on past experience, and given Israel's gross domestic product, now $122 billion, another 200,000 Jews can be settled in Judea and Samaria within a few years. Their presence, and the curtailment of their employment in Israel, will prompt many Arabs to leave, as 400,000 did between 1949 and 1967, and as tens of thousands are doing even now.[45]

Had such policies been implemented shortly after the Six-Day War, the idea of a Palestinian state would have died before it was born. Moreover, once Israel seizes the initiative vis-à-vis the Palestinian Arabs, it will be psychologically primed to deal with the internal Arab demographic problem.

How to Solve the Arab Demographic Problem

Few people realize that the influence of the Arab vote on Israeli politicians is a basic cause of the Arab Palestinian problem and will continue to hinder the dissolution of that problem. Stated another way, Arab voting power can decisively influence who will be Israel's prime minister and thereby shape not only the character but the *borders* of the state. Israel's political elites have long been aware of this fact. Thus, on May 6, 1976, the year after the UN General Assembly equated Zionism with racism, then Prime Minister Yitzhak Rabin said this to high school graduates about to enter the army:

> The majority of the people living in a Jewish State must be Jewish. We must prevent a situation of an *insufficient* Jewish majority and we dare not have a Jewish minority....The minority is entitled to equal rights as individuals with respect to their distinct religion and culture, *but not more than that.*

Rabin's last sentence obviously refers to Israel's Arab inhabitants. It clearly implies that their rights as individuals do not include equal *political* rights! In May 1976, however, Rabin's Labor Party was not dependent on the Arab vote as it was to become a year later when Labor's 29-year control of Israel's government came to an end. Thereafter it would not be politically expedient to publicly suggest that the rights of Israel's Arab citizens do not include equal political rights. Labor had not only lost the support of the religious parties, but its electoral base was shrinking. Religious Jews, with a much higher birthrate than secular Jews, were shifting to the less secular Likud Party, a loss magnified by the tens of thousands of secularists leaving the country. To regain power Labor had to win the burgeoning Arab vote whose kinsmen were the Palestinian Arabs and whose champion was Yasser Arafat. Enter Professor Harkabi's "Machiavellian dove" Shimon Peres. To put the Arab vote solidly in Labor's camp in the 1992 Knesset elections, it would be necessary (in violation of the law) to contact and solicit the support of Yasser Arafat in Tunis. The price was Oslo. In other words, *Oslo was the price for Arab support in Israel's 1992 Knesset elections!* But as previously indicated, to make the sale of Judea, Samaria, and Gaza for Arab votes palatable to the public, it had to be couched in terms of "peace" and "democracy." Peace and democracy required the end of Israeli rule over the Arabs in the "West Bank"—indeed, the end of Zionism.

In "Death of Zionism" (1993) Dr. Chaim Zimmerman describes the mentality of Israel's left-wing:

Being empty of tradition, they cannot see the importance of *Eretz Yisrael* more than any other place on earth. Their conscience tells them that the right of a Jew to *Eretz Yisrael* is no different than that of an Arab. The chosen land and the chosen nation are to the atheist a myth, a result of racism and the lack of education. They do not see the importance of Yisrael in this mundane world, and its relational spirit to the mental [and moral] world. Hence, they see nothing wrong in giving pieces of the land of *Eretz Yisrael* to the Arabs.

They are trying to make deals with the most vicious and malicious of people to whom killing women, children, the weak and the old is a *jihad*, to whom human life is considered worth less than an animal. They offer land in order to live in peace with them, lacking the most elementary understanding that these people will use the peace process for the logistics of trying to remove the Jews from *Eretz Yisrael*...

But these people are not trustworthy. The expression in the Talmud that—"no man lives with a snake in one basket"—exemplifies this situation.[46]

And so the Jews had to be deceived. They had to be imbued with democratic guilt about ruling Arabs as well as with the devious truth: "We cannot make these Arabs citizens of Israel without destroying Israel's character as a Jewish state!" But dissolving the Jewish character of State was precisely the goal of the Labor Party once it became dependent on the Arab vote and on Arab parties to regain control of the government. Let us therefore restate Oslo's ultimate purpose and show how Israel's internal demographic problem is intimately related to the Palestinian problem.

The purpose of Oslo was not merely to create a Palestinian state in Judea and Samaria. It was not merely to withdraw Jews to Israel's pre-1967 borders but to withdraw *Jewish national consciousness* to those borders, and then to destroy Judaism within those borders by transforming the Jewish state into a "state of its citizens." This was the Left's hidden agenda in the 1992 national elections, which witnessed, for first time in Israel's history, a government whose formation required an alliance between Jewish and Arab parties or proxies of the PLO. Yasser Arafat thus entered Israel's cabinet disguised as Shimon Peres.

The deJudaizing of Israel commenced with a vengeance, especially in the all-important domain of public education. This is not the place to detail this veritable revolution.[47] We need to focus on the fact that the voting power of Israel's Arab citizens transformed Labor into an active and obviously anti-Zionist party. Prior to its defeat in the 1977 elections, Labor spoke not of statehood but of "autonomy" for the Arabs in Judea, Samaria, and Gaza. Indeed, immediately after the Six-Day War, such prominent Labor leaders as Moshe Dayan and Yigal Allon advocated Israeli retention of Judea, Samaria, and Gaza. Even Abba Eban said in a private interview: "We shall make peace not on the basis of territorial claims but on the necessities of our security." Still more revealing, Prime Minister Levi Eshkol declared: "The threat of destruction, that hung over Israel since its establishment and which was about to be implemented, has been removed. Never again shall we permit this threat to be renewed."[48] Oslo has renewed this threat, but primarily because of the political power of Israel's Arab voters, to which problem I now turn.

Even though some one million Arabs citizens of Israel reject Israel's existence, and even though a majority of the suicide bombings occurring in this country were aided by such Arabs, no Israeli government is going to expel its Arab population. Besides, no Arab state will accept them. So, what should be done to save the Jewish state from its burgeoning, hostile Arab inhabitants?

The *only* way to solve Israel's "Arab problem" is to make the State of Israel *increasingly Jewish and proud* on the one hand, and *classically democratic* on the other! This will result in a steady emigration of Arabs and, at the same time, erode the nationalist ambitions of their party leaders. The question is: how can this be accomplished?

Most commentators will say: "Increase the Jewish content of public education." Of course, but no less important, indeed, more urgently required is the radical reform of Israel's political and judicial institutions:

(1) Democratize Israel's parliamentary electoral system to increase the impact of *Jewish convictions* on those who make the laws and policies of the State. The *only* way to do this is to make legislators *individually* accountable to the voters in *multi-district* elections—the practice of virtually all democracies. The existing system makes the entire country a single electoral district in which parties compete on the basis of proportional representation. This makes every vote count in apportioning Knesset seats. As a consequence, virtually every Jewish party seeks the support of Arab voters, which can only be purchased by compromising Jewish national interests.

(2) Replace the inept, divisive, and irresponsible system of multi-party cabinet government with a presidential system comparable to that of the United States. A presidential system will be far more conducive to national unity, energy, and accountability. (*Jewish Statesmanship* examines and refutes the arguments political scientists have set forth against a presidential system,

showing that most of these arguments are not relevant to Israel's unique situation in the Arab Middle East.)

(3) Democratize the method of appointing the Supreme Court, the most powerful branch of Israel's government. Presently, the Court, whose decisions so often violate the abiding beliefs and values of the Jewish people, is widely recognized as a self-perpetuating oligarchy since it has *de facto* control over judicial appointments. (I enlarge on this subject in the next chapter.)

(4) Enforce ***Basic Law: The Knesset***, which prohibits any party that negates the Jewish character of the State.

(5) Enforce the 1952 ***Citizenship Law***, which empowers the Minister of Interior to nullify the citizenship of any Israel national that commits "an act of disloyalty to the State." (The law should be amended to clarify the term "act" to protect freedom of speech and press.)

(6) Rescind large-family allowances, with the understanding that the Jewish Agency will assume the function of providing such allowances to Jewish families, while Arab philanthropic agencies may do the same for Arab families.

(7) Put an end to the notorious tax evasion of Arab citizens and their countless violations of building and zoning laws.

(8) Terminate subsidies to, or expel, Arab university students who call for Israel's destruction, and require Arab schools to include Jewish studies in their curriculum.

(9) Rescind the "grandfather clause" of the Law of Return, which, as previously indicated, has enabled hundreds of thousands of gentiles to enter Israel.

(10) As proposed earlier, enfranchise Israelis living abroad. This will increase the power of the Jewish vote.

(11) Phase out U.S. military aid to Israel (now less than 2 percent of the country's GDP), as well as American participation in Israel-Arab affairs. Both undermine Israel's material interests as well as Jewish national pride.

(12) As Kemal Ataturk did in Turkey, terminate Arabic as an official language of the State and its (required) use in all official documents. This will

negate the anti-Zionist idea that Israel is a bi-national state or that it should be a "state of its citizens."

The above solution to the Arab demographic problem, which I have abbreviated, avoids two simplistic and unrealistic alternatives. The expulsion of Israel's Arab population is politically impossible. On the other hand, no sensible policy can be based on the remote possibility that Arabs will soon forsake their 1,400-year autocratic tradition and become liberal democrats. The problem is not to change the Arabs but to change Israel, whose laws and institutions should be made more Jewish, hence more conducive to Jewish national pride.

Epilogue

Nothing less than a clash of civilizations is enfolding in the Middle East. Such a clash will not be resolved by negotiations. Negotiations with the Arabs have only brought a loss of Jewish lives and Jewish land. Israelis can win on the battlefield, but not at the conference table, where they lack the Arab's long cultivated guile— exactly why the Arabs have learned to prefer negotiations. Israel should shun negotiations like the plague, and should treat Arab despots with coldness if not disdain. Israel's government should adopt the Chinese attitude toward Muslims, which was expressed in the *North China Herald* in 1867: "If politeness and ceremony be observed toward the Mohammedans, they imagine they are feared and become arrogant; but in showing severity and rudeness, they are impressed with fear and respect, and they are supple and manageable."[49]

The Middle East is the place where the Occident and the Orient reveal their nature, their limitations, and their destiny. It is here that the genuinely human confronts absolutist irrationalism. Nevertheless, if Israel were true to its heritage, its example would be the best chance for enlightenment in the Middle East, an enlightenment enriched by Jewish values. This chance will be lost, and Israel's own existence will be jeopardized, if a Palestinian nation-state is established in the "West Bank."

Chapter 3
Political Dimensions of the Jewish Problem

Introduction: Israel's Dysfunctional System of Governance

Solving the Arab problem will ultimately depend on solving a basic aspect of the Jewish problem, namely, Israel's erratic system of governance. With this object in mind, the present author wrote *Jewish Statesmanship: Lest Israel Fall* (2000). Available in English, Hebrew, and Russian, *Jewish Statesmanship* exposes the inherent flaws of Israel's governing institutions and shows how these flaws may be remedied by the application of Jewish as well as democratic principles. Accordingly, *Jewish Statesmanship* interfaces political science and the Torah and thus constitutes perhaps the first systematic handbook for Jewish statesmen.

Certain fundamental facts concerning Israel and its governing institutions need to be borne in mind. First, what makes politics and politicians so erratic in this country is that Israel lacks a written constitution, one that prescribes the powers of the legislative, executive, and judicial branches of government.[50] Instead, Israel has a welter of Basic Laws enacted haphazardly over the course of decades, which laws, far from being "basic," are easily changed and so vague as to allow politicians and judges enormous latitude.[51] Accordingly, what is called the rule of law in Israel is very much the rule of a few men.[52] Arbitrary acts on the part of the government are commonplace. Even the Supreme Court, precisely because it controls the appointment of its own members, feels free to ignore and overturn laws enacted by Israel's Knesset.[53] This anarchic state of affairs allows a prime minister to pursue his own political agenda despite the law and, in the case of Ariel Sharon, regardless of his party label.

Second, ever since the establishment of the State of Israel in 1948, no Labor- or Likud-led government has ever been toppled by a Knesset vote of no confidence. The Knesset, sovereign in theory, is in practice subservient to the government. Lacking, therefore, are institutional checks and balances. This fact allows prime ministers to ignore the Knesset even on matters affecting the borders of the State.

Third, although a large majority of Israel's Jewish population is either orthodox or traditional, the parliamentary representation of Israel's two major parties, Labor and Likud, has never remotely reflected the proportion of religious, traditional, and secular Jews in this country.[54] This is a direct consequence of a very low parliamentary electoral threshold, which has enabled citizens of various religious and secular persuasions to form their own parties. The resulting multiplicity of parties in the Knesset produces a farrago of parties in the cabinet whose rivalry renders it virtually impossible for the government to pursue, let alone for the public to discern, clear and coherent national policies.

Fourth, the existing parliamentary electoral system maximizes the power of the parties—of course those that form the government. Contrary to the practice of 74 out of 75 countries having democratic elections for the lower (or only branch) of the legislature—the entire country constitutes a single electoral district. In this nationwide district a profusion of parties with fixed lists of candidates compete for Knesset seats on the basis of proportional representation. Since no party has ever won a majority of the popular vote—the electoral threshold is a mere 2 percent—several parties must unite after the election to form the government. Until the government is formed, the public is never quite certain of its composition, which gives a prime minister extraordinary leeway.

Fifth, under this system, diverse party leaders—those who top the party lists—become cabinet ministers and dominate the Knesset. Having different agendas, the parties forming the cabinet do so, as David Ben-Gurion said, "not on the basis of a common program but merely to divide up the positions of influence and the national budget."[55] Moreover, since Knesset Members are not *individually* elected by or accountable to the voters, those who become cabinet ministers can ignore public opinion with impunity—and readily do so *between* elections.

To clarify the issue, suppose Israel had single member, multi-district elections. This would shift power from the parties to the voters and to their *personal* representatives in the Knesset. The Knesset would then cease to be subservient to the government. It would also be in a better position to curb the despotic power of the Supreme Court.[56] By making Knesset members *individually* accountable to the people in constituency elections, Israel would have, for the first time, the institutional checks and balances essential to democracy and the rule of law.

To avoid misunderstanding, the present writer is not contending that institutional reform alone will solve Israel's major problems. I do contend, however, that such reform is a *necessary* precondition of changing the disastrous cou[rse] of this country.

Political and judicial institutions must be designed with a clear understanding of how they may affect the vices and virtues of human nature, especially the former. There are no institutional substitutes for virtue, but as we shall see in a moment, and as is the case in Israel, institutions can readily magnify men's vices.

In my treatise, *A Discourse on Statesmanship: The Design and Transformation of the American Polity*, I develop a "psychology of political forms." There I show that the various attributes of institutions influence the character of those who wield their powers: (1) who is eligible to vote in elections; (2) who is eligible to hold office; (3) the mode of election (or electoral laws); (4) the tenure of those elected; (5) the size of the institution; and (6) the powers of the institution will more or less influence the behavior of a country's lawmakers, administrators, and judges. The most important of these attributes is *who* is eligible to vote, followed by *who* is eligible to hold office, for these will ultimately determine who will rule and shape the character of the regime.

To all but doctrinaire democrats, it will be obvious that Jews should rule in a Jewish state, just as Muslims should rule in a Muslim state, if Jews and Muslims are to preserve their respective cultural heritage. In Japan, a parliamentary democracy, not only is citizenship restricted to ethnic Japanese, but the offspring of Japanese parents must be born in Japan to be a Japanese citizen! Such is the concern of the Japanese to preserve, undiluted, their country's cultural integrity. The reforms proposed in this chapter should be viewed in this light.

Turning to the mode of election, this will affect the relationship between the persons elected and their electors, and therefore whether the voters can exercise any constraints on their representatives. If the mode of election facilitates such constraints, this will have a more or less salutary influence on the behavior and character of public officials. Without such constraints, self-aggrandizement will be the rule. This is but to affirm the natural tendency of mankind toward egoism. Men are not by nature animated by the "common good"—else there would be no need for the Ten Commandments! Indeed, as will be seen later, that term will not be found in Machiavelli's *Prince* and *Discourses*.

Now, the longer the tenure of an institution the greater will be the honor and independence (as well as potential power) of its members. Much the same may be said of an institution's size: the smaller its size the greater the honor of being elected to that institution. And so it is with the institution's powers. In a well-designed system of institutional checks and balances, the members of each branch will be jealous of their prerogatives; hence they will guard against the encroachments of other branches. Self-interest will thus serve as a sentinel over the public good. But this means that well-designed institutions can elevate

...ilosophy of History

...ile ill-designed institutions can lower their character. As the ... has written: "At the birth of societies, the rulers of republics ... ns; and afterwards the institutions mould the rulers."[57]

...onal way of reconstructing Israel's governing institutions ... ns of a constitution. However, pursuance of a constitution should not postpone incremental reforms beginning with multi-district elections and elimination of fixed party lists. (*Jewish Statesmanship* nonetheless outlines a constitution that will simultaneously render Israel's governing institutions more democratic and more Jewish.)

MULTI-DISTRICT ELECTIONS

Israel's governing institutions should be designed in such as way as to strengthen the representational bond between citizens and those who are supposed to represent their current opinions and interests as well as their abiding beliefs and values.

Representation is often defined as having one's views reflected in the legislative decision-making process. Representation may also be defined as having one's views reflected in actually enacted policies of government. The first raises the question: How well does the mode of election enable the national electorate to impress its opinions on the legislature? The second raises the question: How well does the actually executed policies of the government represent the opinions of the national electorate?

As indicated above, Israel's single countrywide elections with fixed party lists cannot but insulate Knesset Members from the voters between elections. Hence the "representational bond" between MKs and voters is weak. This is especially true of cabinet ministers, since they occupy safe seats on their party's list. It follows that Israel's method of electing members of the Knesset does not enable the electorate to impress its opinions effectively on the legislative process nor on the actually executed policies of the government. This is hardly consistent with representative democracy, and it conduces to the self-aggrandizement of elected officials.

If Israel had some form of multi-district or regional elections, whereby the people could vote for individual candidates rather than for a party slate, the representational bond between MKs and constituents would be relatively strong. The electorate would thus be more capable of impressing its opinions on the Knesset and on actually enacted government policies. The resulting constraints on elected officials would counter political egoism and diminish abuses of public trust.

Moreover, since more than 50 percent of Israel's Jewish population are traditional Jews while another 25 percent are orthodox, it follows that making the country more democratic by means of district elections—a reform consistent with Deuteronomy 1:13—would also make it more Jewish! Furthermore, district elections would diminish the power of party leaders over their colleagues in the Knesset, so that the latter would be able to exercise more independent judgment vis-à-vis government polices. The Knesset would cease to be a cipher. A stronger Knesset would also restrain the Supreme Court, which has become a super-legislature because of the Knesset's impotence. Multi-district elections would therefore promote a system of checks and balances yet to be seen in Israel.

Unfortunately, many Israelis, including academics, believe that such is the smallness of this country, both in population and geographical area, that multi-district elections are inappropriate. They are wedded to a single countrywide election in which parties compete on the basis of proportional representation (PR). This, they believe, enables distinct groups, be they ideological, ethnic, religious, or otherwise to be represented in the Knesset by correspondingly distinct parties regardless of whether the individuals composing these groups are dispersed throughout the country. They contend, moreover, that representation of geographical districts leads to disproportionate representation of diverse groups as well as gerrymandering. Let us distinguish facts from fictions.

First, of the 74 countries having multi-district or constituency elections for the lower (or only) branch of their legislature, many, as we shall see in a moment, are smaller than Israel. What needs to be stressed, however, is that apart from the Netherlands, a homogeneous constitutional monarchy, Israel is the only reputed democracy in which legislators are not individually accountable to the voters in constituency elections. In other words, in Israel alone, an incumbent politician does not have to defend his voting record against a rival candidate. If the incumbent violated his previous campaign pledges, he need not worry about being publicly exposed by a rival for his seat in the Knesset.

Second, contrary to its advocates, proportional representation of distinct groups in a single national district election does not ensure a party's fidelity to its campaign pledges. In the 1992 election campaign, the Labor Party's platform rejected recognition of, or negotiation with, the PLO, as well as withdrawal from the Golan Heights. Once ensconced in office, however, Labor betrayed the voters. So did the Shas Party, which declared, in that 1992 campaign, that it would not join a Labor-Meretz coalition. Much the same may be said of the Likud in 1996. When Prime Minister Netanyahu declared on CNN that no one ever expected him to accept the Oslo Accords as a basis for the "peace process," or meet with Yasser Arafat, or withdraw from Hebron, he unwittingly admitted that he had betrayed the expectations of those who voted for him. So much for the blessings of proportional representation in the absence of multi-district elections.

The fact that 74 democracies somehow manage to conduct the public's business by means of multi-district elections should dispel the fiction that Israel cannot function well or justly without its existing parliamentary electoral system. More than half a century of fixed party lists competing in a single country-wide election has engendered in Israel the shoddiest politics, culminating in the 1999 elections when 29 Knesset Members hopped over to rival parties, virtually all to obtain safe seats! This unheard phenomenon clearly revealed how much a poorly designed political system can arouse and magnify the all-too-human vice of egoism. Only the ignorant along with self-serving politicians want to preserve such a system. Strange that Israeli political scientists have not united to denounce this pernicious system. Perhaps because contemporary political science, like the social sciences in general, is morally neutral?

Another important fact: Israel's permissive electoral threshold, by far the lowest in the democratic world except for the Netherlands, produces an excessive multiplicity of single-interest parties. This not only incapacitates the Knesset where, to be sure, reasonable diversity is desirable, but it also fragments the government where unity is necessary. The low threshold, coupled to the absence of district or constituency elections, has made the Knesset, as the public recognizes, a haven for mere job-seekers. These two aspects of Israel's parliamentary system doom this country to political ineptitude, paralysis, and anarchy. The government formed as a consequence of this system is inherently incapable of pursuing coherent, rational, and resolute national policies.[58] Is it any wonder that Israeli politicians lack national vision? Is it any wonder that Israel is despised?

Let us suppose, therefore, that Israel were to have multi-district or regional elections. The country would then be divided into several geographical electoral districts. Let us assume that most of these districts are heterogeneous. Those elected in such districts will then have to represent a variety of opinions and interests rather than a single-issue group. This will put an end to most single-issue parties. It would then remain to design a parliamentary electoral system appropriate to Israel.

A profusion of electoral systems exist. The simplest (though it would arouse much opposition in Israel) is the single-member district with plurality rule (SMDP). The candidate receiving the most votes in the district wins. Opponents say SMDP disenfranchises minorities. This is misleading. First of all, the individuals composing "minorities" not only vote, but they also have the opportunity to lobby their district's representative. Second, experience in the United States indicates that minorities are not ignored by congressmen, especially in closely contested districts.

Because SMDP requires elected officials to represent diverse opinions and interests, it can enlarge their intellectual horizons. Even if it is true that plurality rule disproportionately represents diverse groups, it is also true that proportional representation with a low electoral threshold multiplies small parties, paralyzes governments, such that minorities themselves suffer as a consequence. And it bears repeating that Israel's parliamentary system enables politicians to ignore the voters with impunity.

In any event, single member districts with plurality rule is employed in no less than 22 countries, including Canada, the United States, and Great Britain. Of these 22 countries, the following have smaller populations than Israel: *Bahamas, Barbados, Belize,* Botswana, *Dominica, Gambia, Grenada, Jamaica, Micronesia,* New Zealand, *St. Kitts & Nevis, St. Lucia, St. Vincent, Samoa, Trinidad & Tobago, and Zambia.* I have italicized those countries whose geographical area is smaller than Israel. Incidentally, the 50 American states employ SMDP, and their populations range from 500,000 (Wyoming) to 34,500,000 (California).

Of course, single-member districts with plurality rule is not the last word. Some 54 countries employ other methods of representing constituents. Districts may have more than one representative, as in Australia; they may have run-off elections to obtain a majority candidate, as in France; and they may even combine SMDP for part of the legislature and proportional representation for the remainder, as in Germany.

Of the 54 countries just alluded to, the following have smaller populations than Israel: *Cape Verdi,* Costa Rica, Denmark, Finland, Honduras, Ireland, *Liechtenstein,* Lithuania, *Luxembourg, Malta,* Norway, and Uruguay. Again, the geographical area of the countries here italicized is smaller than Israel.

We see, therefore, that 28 countries have smaller populations than Israel, and of these, 18 are smaller in area. This should dispose of objections to multi-district elections on the basis of a country's population or size. By the way, many of these countries are as heterogeneous as Israel.

Of the many regional electoral systems which Israel might adopt for its betterment, two may be mentioned here: the Preferential Vote system used in Australia and Ireland, and Personalized PR used in Germany and Denmark, which systems avoid gerrymandering. (Further details will be found in *Jewish Statesmanship.*) It should be borne in mind, however, that political institutions, however well-designed, do not guarantee wisdom and virtue. Nevertheless, *how* they are designed will either minimize or maximize the *probability* of obtaining wisdom and virtue in the councils of government.

Restructuring the State of Israel

In Plato's *Republic*, the best regime in theory unites, in the philosopher-king, wisdom and power. Knowing, however, that the union of wisdom and power is hardly ever attained, and if attained does not endure, the philosophic statesman may design a constitutional system whose goal is to unite wisdom with *consent*. This would be the goal of *normative* democracy assimilated to the Torah.

The Torah is the repository of wisdom, and the moral and intellectual qualities required of those who make as well as those who execute the laws of a Torah government are exemplary. (See Exodus 18:19 and Deuteronomy 1:13.) Nevertheless, Jewish law embodies the principle of government *with* the consent of the governed. Thus, the Babylonian Talmud states, "No legislation should be imposed on the public unless the majority can conform to it" (*Avoda Zara* 36a). This principle is expressed differently in the Jerusalem Talmud: "…any legislation enacted by a court [meaning the Sanhedrin] but not accepted by the majority of the public is no law" (*Avoda Zara* 2:8). It follows that before enacting legislation, a wise government will investigate whether any proposed law will be acceptable to a majority of the people. Law or the rule of law must therefore unite wisdom and consent. This is a basic Torah principle.

We see, however, that Israel's government is based neither on wisdom nor consent (since it can ignore public opinion with impunity). We are therefore forced to conclude that Israel's government is based on mere power, hence on the arbitrary rule of men. The result is naked self-aggrandizement or egoism.

A Jewish government must be based on the rule of law. The laws enacted by that government must be acceptable to a majority of the Jewish people. As indicated above, a large majority of Israel's Jewish population identifies with the Jewish heritage. In fact, studies indicate that 50 percent believe in the divine origin of the Torah! The rule of law must therefore be consistent with the Torah. It follows that Israel's legislative, executive, and judicial institutions should be designed in such a way as to maximize the *probability* that these institutions will not violate the cherished beliefs and values of the Jewish people. *Jewish Statesmanship* proposes the following governmental institutions:

(1) The Parliament. The parliament will be bicameral. Its two functions, law-making and administrative overview, will be divided between two assemblies, a Senate whose membership is limited to Jews, and a House of Representatives based on universal suffrage. To anticipate objections to a second branch of parliament without law-making power, let us briefly compare it with the existing Knesset.

Israeli cabinets sometimes include more than thirty members of Israel's 120-member Knesset, either as ministers or deputy ministers. This alone makes the Knesset incapable of exercising the important function of administrative overview—*which is why corruption in government is so widespread in Israel*. In contrast, members of the proposed House of Representatives will be excluded from the cabinet, in consequence of which they will be free to determine whether the laws are being faithfully and efficiently administered.

(2) THE GOVERNMENT. As indiucated in the previous chapter, a presidential system will replace Israel's inept and divisive system of multi-party cabinet government. The president and his cabinet will be limited to Jews. The cabinet will no longer consist of competing party leaders. Hence members of the Senate will also be excluded from the cabinet.

(3) THE SUPREME COURT. The judges of the Supreme Court will also be limited to Jews. They will be nominated by the president (advised by a council of men learned in Jewish and secular law) and confirmed by the Senate. Moreover, consistent with the existing Foundations of Law Act 1980, Jewish law will be *primus inter pares* vis-à-vis the foreign legal systems currently used by the court. Jewish civil and criminal law will gradually replace their foreign counterparts, except where the latter fill gaps in the law and conform to reason and justice.

This restructuring of Israel's political and judicial institutions will render government more ethical and efficient, more Jewish and democratic, and more consonant with the rule of law, something sorely lacking in this country.

BEYOND INSTITUTIONAL REFORM

The absence of the rule of law means that anarchy reigns in Israel. That this is the case may be demonstrated as follows:

(1) The single most significant cause of anarchy has been the government's release of Arab terrorists, including many convicted of murder—this, in the specious name of "peace."

(2) Each year the state comptroller reports to the Knesset hundreds of violations of the law and of administrative procedures by various government ministries. However, because the majority of the members of the Knesset are subservient to their party leaders who control the government, these reports seldom lead to legal or remedial action.

(3) Cabinet ministers range abroad and pursue objectives that contradict government policy, the most notorious offender being Shimon Peres. Thus, when Peres served as foreign minister under the national unity government led by Prime Minister Yitzhak Shamir (1984-1988), he campaigned in foreign capitals for an international peace conference on the Middle East, which Mr. Shamir described as "madness" and "suicidal."

(4) The Supreme Court, quite apart from rendering decisions that violate Jewish law, issues rulings that have no basis in Knesset law, or that encroach on domains properly belonging to the government. For example, the Court declared parental spanking a criminal offense, contrary to a consensus of the Knesset. The same Court substituted its judgment for that of the IDF by ruling against the leveling of the very houses Arab terrorists subsequently used to murder a pregnant woman and her four daughters.

(5) Arab students, subsidized by the government, display the PLO flag on Israeli campuses, openly advocate Israel's destruction, and do so with impunity.

(6) The Citizenship Law, which empowers the minister of interior to nullify the citizenship of any Israel national that commits an act of disloyalty to the State, has never been enforced, even though hundreds of Arab citizens are members of terrorist cells, have aided terrorists, and have even committed terrorists acts themselves, including suicide bombings.

(7) Arab Knesset members routinely commit sedition (for example, by organizing illegal trips to hostile Arab states and supporting terrorist organizations). With the exception of MK Azmi Bashara, Arab MKs have never been indicted by the attorney general. (Bishara's indictment was quashed by the Supreme Court.)

(8) Prior to January 19, 1993, while the Prevention of Terrorism Ordinance banning contacts and meetings with terrorist organizations was in force, the law was defied with impunity by prominent left-wing Knesset Members such as Yossi Beilin, Haim Ramon, Yossi Sarid, and Dedi Zucker.[59] (Incidentally, the link for these contacts was an Israeli Arab citizen, Dr. Ahmed Tibi, who became a close adviser to PLO Chairman Yasser Arafat. That an Israeli citizen could serve a declared enemy of the State of Israel, unhampered by the attorney general's

office, exemplifies the criminal negligence of Israel's highest law-enforcement agency.)

(9) The Supreme Court repeatedly refused to adjudicate the merits of petitions showing, *prima facie*, that in signing and implementing the Israel-PLO Declaration of Principles of September 13, 1993, various prime ministers and cabinet ministers violated several Israeli statutes including the law of treason.[60]

(10) Israel's Arab parties brazenly violate Basic Law: The Knesset, which prohibits any party that negates the Jewish character of the state, yet none has been barred from participating in elections, thanks to permissive decisions of the Supreme Court.

(11) Israeli political parties in the Knesset receive funds from foreign sources in brazen violation of the law.

(12) Each year Israeli police make thousands of false arrests, enter homes without a search warrant, and employ excessive force against peaceful (Jewish) demonstrators. Seldom is there any redress of grievances.

Many more instances of anarchy or lawlessness may be cited, but virtually all may be attributed to, or at least are facilitated by, the absence of multi-district elections on the one hand, and the resulting lack of institutional checks and balances on the other. Without personal representatives, citizens have no political means of redressing their grievances. This compels those who can afford the legal fees to take their grievances to the Supreme Court, which has made the court far more powerful than any of its counterparts in the democratic world. Lacking institutional checks and balances—and none can exist with an impotent legislature—the judicial branch will make the laws while the executive branch will be above the laws!

Although anarchy would be significantly mitigated by the reform of Israel's political and judicial institutions, a far more serious dysfunction needs to be remedied. As will be seen more clearly in the next chapter, a hitherto unrecognized mental disorder permeates Israel's ruling elites, a disorder that filters down and taints the general public.

We saw in Chapter 1 that the sense of justice has been murdered in Israel—the consequence of tolerating Arab terrorism via the irrational policy of self-restraint, a policy that arouses the contempt of Arabs and incites them to kill more Jews.

To murder the sense of justice is to destroy the instincts of civilized human beings, in particular the instinct of self-preservation. That instinct is also undermined when Israeli prime ministers hobnob with Arab terrorists—yesterday Arafat, today, some Palestinian Authority "prime minister." By so doing they destroy Jewish pride or honor, which cannot but emasculate Jews and render them incapable of persevering in a protracted conflict. When the sense of honor and of justice no longer animate human beings, they sink toward the subhuman level, where moral distinctions vanish. Venerable beliefs and values dissolve. Family values disintegrate. Gender differences collapse. Authority declines. Children no longer respect their parents. The foundations of civilization crumble.

The sense of justice and of honor are constantly under the attack of Israel's political and judicial elites. Civic virtue has been eroded. The revolting example, mentioned earlier, of 29 MKs abandoning their parties in the 1999 Knesset elections—almost all when their seats became vulnerable—and joining a rival party, produced no moral outrage, no movement for reform. And what of the parties that rewarded this betrayal? This unconscionable behavior reveals not only the flawed character of many members of Israel's parliament but of the flawed nature of Israel's parliamentary electoral system.

To cite a more pernicious example: when a nation is at war, a sober government will be all the more concerned to foster public spiritedness and a due respect for law, as opposed to self-indulgence and leniency. Hence, when judges of the Supreme Court, in war-plagued Israel, issue decisions that encourage perversion and permissiveness and even subversion, one has to wonder not only about their unwisdom but about their connection with reality, i.e., their sanity. Evident here is more than abysmal ignorance of the prerequisites of civilized society. Evident here is *degeneracy*, a leveling of moral distinctions, a will to Jewish self-negation. Thousands of years of human experience mean nothing to these judges who, in their arrogance, have no understanding of what primitive instincts and pagan practices had to be overcome before mankind, thanks very much to the Bible of Israel, emerged from barbarism to civilization. Of course the arrogance of the Supreme Court may be attributed to the conceits and superficiality of contemporary education; but one should not minimize the significance of the Court's mode of appointment. Do not expect intellectual modesty from a Court whose judges are accountable to no one, a Court that is virtually self-appointed and pursues its own anti-Zionist—nay, anti-Jewish—agenda under the façade of the rule of law.

The Knesset, which enacted Basic Law: The Judiciary, and which thereby established the Supreme Court, has the authority to reform this so-called High Court of Justice. Instead, it allows the Court to become a super-legislature, to legalize immorality, undermine authority, and even encourage murder! To infer that the Knesset is dominated by irresponsible fools is surely an understatement. The same may be said of Israel's Chelm-like government, which has inanely or insanely proclaimed self-restraint against Arab barbarism as a form of strength, thus manifesting the Supreme Court's virtual indifference to the murder of Jews. But again, this is not simply a matter of flawed human beings but of the flawed system of multi-party cabinet government, whose ministers, rather than risk the loss of their power and perquisites, risk the lives of Jewish men, women, and children.

Conclusion

In discussing the flaws of Israel's governing institutions and how these flaws may be overcome, this chapter has questioned the sanity of Israel's political and judicial elites. The next chapter will reveal the precise nature of their appalling mentality.

Chapter 4
Psychological Dimensions of the Jewish Problem: "Demophrenia"

Pathological Fear

ALTHOUGH Israel is not a democracy from an *institutional* point of view, the *mentality* of this country, especially of its political, judicial, and intellectual leaders, is thoroughly democratic. This fact prompted the author to write *Demophrenia: Israel and the Malaise of Democracy*. *Demophrenia* is a mental disorder peculiar to contemporary or normless democracy as opposed to classical or normative democracy. This disorder is most pronounced among Israel's ruling elites whose democratic mentality clashes with Zionism. Before defining demophrenia, we must first inquire into the fear that dwells in the Jewish psyche of these elites and how it is compounded by their democratic mentality.

I am alluding to more than the Jewish fear of anti-Semitism, which is nothing but the well-known consequence of two thousand years of statelessness and dispersion, persecution and humiliation, pogroms and holocausts. That fear is simply the inevitable result of perennial and deadly hatred of Jews and Judaism. There is nothing paranoid about this fear. It reflects a sober assessment of a typically hostile world. But this fear has been magnified and rendered pathological by a related fear, one resulting from democracy's ascendancy over Zionism in the mentality of Israel's ruling elites. And now I shall speak only of contemporary democracy whose basic principles, freedom and equality, have no rational and ethical constraints. This normless democracy has become a secular faith—call it "democratism"—which, like various religious faiths, is immune to questioning.

Democracy has replaced Zionism as the one and only justification for the State of Israel. This has had a profound but hitherto unexplored psychological impact on the psyche of Israel's political, judicial, and intellectual elites.

Since 1975, when the United Nations declared Zionism a form of racism, the mentality of Israel's ruling elites has undergone a gradual metamorphosis such that they now derive their legitimacy and respectability from Israel's being the "only democracy in the Middle East." Once America became Israel's patron, emulating America became all the more "natural." Unlike America, however, Israel is burdened by a hostile Arab population in Judea, Samaria, and Gaza, the so-called Palestinians, whose kinsmen in the Middle East inhabit territories and control resources of strategic interest to the United States. How Israel's government treats these Arabs is therefore of concern to Washington and has become a test of Israel's democratic credentials, especially of Israel's policy-makers and opinion-makers. Israel's ruling elites are very fearful and fervent about their democratic reputation, as may be seen in their benevolent treatment of Arabs in Judea, Samaria, and Gaza.

The decade following the Six-Day War of June 1967 witnessed a tremendous rise in the standard of living of these Arabs. As previously noted, Israel's government introduced modern methods of agriculture; built new roads and water and electric power facilities; established new hospitals, health centers, and nursing schools; and constructed primary and secondary schools as well as universities. The government also initiated democratic elections for local self-rule, which elections, however, brought Arabs identified with the PLO to power in 1975. An upsurge in Arab terrorism followed, to which Israel's government reacted with extraordinary self-restraint. A more vigorous policy might have jeopardized the democratic credentials of Israeli prime ministers. Today, crushing the Palestinian Authority means depriving the Arab Palestinians of their vaunted (but never examined) right to self-determination. This could make Israel appear as an oppressive and even fascist state, a prospect that fills Israel's ruling elites with dreadful fear. This fear compounds their fear of anti-Semitism. And so Israel fights with suicidal self-restraint.

To be sure, fear is not the only motive. Kindness, mercy, and magnanimity are characteristic of the Jewish people, inherited from the patriarch Abraham. (See Genesis 14:14-24; 18:3-7, 23-32.) This benevolence of Jews on the one hand, and their having themselves been so often oppressed on the other, tends to inhibit Israeli governments from using overwhelming force against Arab barbarians. To this add the ardent desire of Jews for peace. Some commentators believe that this yearning for peace leads otherwise hard-boiled Jewish politicians to succumb to "wishful thinking" regarding their Arab adversaries. This attitude is prominent among their academic advisers, especially those tainted by cultural relativism. Arabs know how to foster such wishful thinking; indeed, it is part of their Grand Strategy. Arabs use professions of peace and negotiations to obtain "confidence-building" measures, i.e., unilateral concessions from Israel. The release of Arab terrorists is one concession; another is the evacuation of the Israel Defense Forces from Arab cities, which harbor terrorists and weapons factories. But let us go to the heart of the matter.

When Israel's ruling elites repeatedly enter into agreements with Arabs who invariably violate such agreements, when they turn a blind eye to Arab leaders who openly proclaim their intention to destroy the Jewish state, and further, when these Jews continue to negotiate with such Arabs—who exalt suicide bombers—in view of all this, it is hardly sufficient to attribute such Jewish behavior to "wishful thinking." To engage *habitually* in negotiations with such murderers is not merely an exercise in puerility or fatuity; it is to enter into the domain of pathological behavior. Moreover, and as I shall demonstrate in due course, what has induced Israel's ruling elites to enter that domain is the "ethos" of democracy.

Admittedly, *tolerance* of violent behavior and *leniency* in the punishment of such behavior are qualities peculiar to democracy. In beleaguered and battered Israel, however, tolerance and leniency toward Arab terrorism are the result of a mental disorder rooted in, or compounded by, democracy. Let me put this in another way. Christians preach love your enemy. This has never prevented the governments of Christian nations from employing overwhelming force against those who have attacked them. Justice demands retribution. But to prevent further attacks on your people, it may be necessary to inflict upon the enemy devastating punishment. Not only is such reaction to aggression perfectly normal, but, in the long run, it may save many lives, including those of your enemies. In contrast, to suffer thousands of casualties, as Israel has, and to respond by merely brief incursions into terrorist strongholds and "targeted killings" of selected terrorists while calling for "peaceful coexistence"—the policy of the Sharon government—is not normal. Such self-abasement, however, did not begin with that government.

Let us go back to December 1987, when Arab violence broke out in Gaza and quickly spread to Judea and Samaria and even to Israel's pre-1967 borders, especially Jerusalem. Arabs threw stones, fire-bombs, and other deadly objects at Jewish civilians, police, and soldiers. Thus began the *intifada*—meaning *expulsion* in Arabic. (Many of Israel's own Arab citizens participated in this insurrection.) Yitzhak Shamir (Likud) was then Israel's prime minister, while Yitzhak Rabin (Labor) was defense minister—*a national unity government.*

The Shamir government's policy toward Arab violence? Self-restraint. A complex maze of rules and regulations governed the use of different types of firearms against the Arabs. By the time a soldier or police officer could decide whether he was legally entitled to use rubber bullets, plastic bullets, live bullets, or just run away, he might well be dead. Was the government fearful of alienating the media and world opinion (which nonetheless followed)? Was it fearful of UN condemnation? Were the Labor members of this so-called national unity government fearful that killing many Palestinian Arabs would alienate Israeli Arab voters, on whom Labor's political power depends? Was Mr. Shamir fearful that crushing the *intifada* would split this multi-party cabinet government? And what about the politicians' fear of losing their democratic respectability when they visit America and Europe? Israel's ruling elites have many fears, and these surely inhibit the use of force in quelling Arab violence.

Encouraged, however, by the government's self-restraint or timidity, the Arabs escalated the violence. From throwing rocks at individuals they advanced to throwing rocks at moving vehicles and firebombs at buses traveling with passengers. Trucks driven by Arabs forced Jewish cars off the highways, into ravines. Sniper attacks using live ammunition and grenade attacks raised the level of Arab violence. Meanwhile, Arab knifings and kidnappings ending in the sexual mutilations of Jews became more frequent.

The first three years of this *intifada* witnessed 122,218 incidents of rock-throwing, road blocks, and rioting in Judea, Samaria, and Gaza; some 2,495 firebomb attacks; 157 sniper attacks; 58 grenade attacks; 1,004 reported cases of arson; close to 4,000 Jews injured and 57 killed.[61] The government tolerated and thereby encouraged this violence, which was further encouraged by the leniency of the courts. For example, the courts imposed a fine of only 2,500 shekels (then $1,250) on Arabs who threw rocks at moving vehicles—an act classified as attempted murder in American and Israeli law![62] (The fines were easily covered by the coffers of the PLO.)

Given this democratic leniency, it is unsurprising that by April 1993 the number of Jewish men, women, and children killed by Arabs jumped to 170. When a Haifa court acquits an Israeli Arab of incitement to violence who, in his poem, repeatedly urges Muslims to smash the heads of Jews; or when an Israeli Arab newspaper (*al-Sirat*) can with impunity call upon the "heroes of the *intifada*...to uproot the venomous fangs of the crusader snakes," and "to silence the barks of the Jewish dogs with a knife," referring to them as "murderers and drug dealers from the darkened alleyways of New York," we see here something more than examples of democratic permissiveness. We see here a unique mental disorder, where otherwise normal people—judges and politicians—virtually encourage Israel's own Arab citizens to incite other Arabs to murder Jews and uproot the Jewish state.[63] This *permissive subversion* is a pathological tendency of contemporary democracy, whose basic principles, freedom and equality, have no rational or ethical constraints. Israel's political and judicial elites imbibed this tendency when they jettisoned Zionism (to say nothing of Judaism) for democracy.

Fear of anti-Semitism magnified by the fear of losing their democratic respectability drives these elites to outdo the permissiveness of their American counterparts. Thus, whereas the American government imposed a media blackout during its invasion of Grenada and severely restricted and even manipulated the media during the 1991 Persian Gulf War, Israel's government placed few constraints on the movement of foreign television crews and journalists that covered the *intifada*. The media's ensuing defamation of the Jewish state was therefore facilitated by Israel's own government.[64]

No less astonishing, Israel television joined the chorus of foreign abuse and disinformation. It repeatedly portrayed the Arabs and the *intifada* in a sympathetic light, the effect of which was to delegitimize Jewish retention of Judea, Samaria, and Gaza. Similarly, various local newspapers, in English as well as in Hebrew, published statements and articles by prominent Jewish citizens of Israel who likened their country to Nazi Germany and the West Bank to a concentration camp.[65] Thus, day after day, while Israel's own media actually justified, and thereby incited, Arab violence, the Shamir government behaved as if it were suffering from aphasia. It was rendered speechless by the principle of freedom of speech and press. This dogma of democracy—more immune to questioning than any dogma of religion—produced the most ludicrous anomaly: the only place in the Middle East where the PLO was permitted to have its own press was in Jerusalem. And what is more, the Arab press was free to publish pro-Iraqi and anti-American propaganda during the Persian Gulf War while Israel was being bombed by Scud missiles![66] So concerned were Israel's ruling elites to appear as champions of liberal democracy that they exposed their country to risks no gentile government would dare expose its people.

Now consider the second "*intifada*," which broke out on September 29, 2000 and issued in a crescendo of Arab suicide bombings. During the first thirty-six months of this war against the Jewish people, Arabs killed more than 1,150 Jews—proportionately equal to 55,000 Americans! Most of these killings occurred under the premiership of Ariel Sharon, whose policy of self-restraint emboldened the Arabs to kill more Jews and gave the terrorists more time to obtain and manufacture more and deadlier weapons. Suicide bombings in Jerusalem made the nation's capital appear, at night, like a ghost town. Drive-by shootings made it unsafe to drive on Israeli roads. Tourism, on which the Israeli economy so much depends, dropped by more than 50 percent. The economy plummeted. Unemployment soared. People were demoralized. More and more Jews felt betrayed and abandoned by the prime minister they had elected to put an end to Arab violence.

The government nonetheless persisted in its supine policy of self-restraint. The self-abasement underlying this policy may be seen in the activism of the

Supreme Court, which quashed the indictment of Arab Knesset Member Talib a-Sana, who, in an interview on Abu-Dubai TV, not only praised a suicide bombing attack in Israel but also called for more of the same. It follows from the logic of the Court's decision that it would be permissible for Arab MKs to praise the Arab terrorists who murdered cabinet minister Rehavam Ze'evi! This is judicial madness. I call it "*demophrenia.*"

The policy of self-restraint has conditioned Jews to accept the murder of other Jews. It has emasculated them, dehumanized them, and made them the passive victims of Arab terrorism. What must be borne in mind, however, is that this dehumanization is the consequence of democracy having replaced Zionism as the one thing that endows Israel's political and judicial elites with political legitimacy and personal respectability. To safeguard their democratic reputation, they must be more democratic than their American counterparts. Meanwhile, they themselves have become dehumanized. Their pathological policy of self-restraint toward Arab barbarism betrays an absence of moral outrage.

Having absorbed the ethos of democracy into their psyche, Israel's ruling elites have also imbibed the moral relativism that dominates the democratic mind. No longer can they wholeheartedly believe in the absolute justice of Israel's cause. This is why Ariel Sharon could say in an interview in *Ha'aretz* that he no longer thinks in "black and white" terms in dealing with the PLO-Palestinian Authority—another motive for not crushing that terrorist regime.

Employing overwhelming force to eliminate Arab terrorists would signify Jewish national pride—something fearful Jewish leaders can ill-afford. Jews must be meek: better to be victims than victors. Jews must always yield to the demands of their enemies, must take risks for peace with their enemies, must sacrifice their holy of holies to pacify their enemies. Heaven forbid that Jews should stand upright and maintain their God-given right to Eretz Yisrael! No! No! That would smack of racism. That would nullify the democratic respectability of Israeli politicians, judges, academics, journalists, and not a few rabbis! Democracy is their life raft. But it is precisely democracy, with its permissiveness and moral egalitarianism that has sickened the minds of Israel's ruling elites. These elites are suffering from *demophrenia!*

DEMOPHRENIA

Demophrenia is a mental disorder in which conscious thought replicates the alogical and amoral nature of the unconscious. Because this pathology is peculiar to contemporary democracy, it may be defined as a compulsive and indiscriminate application of the democratic principles of equality and freedom to political problems and ideological conflicts which are impervious to, and even exacerbated by, those principles. Demophrenia is most advanced in Israel because the democratic mentality of its fear-ridden government not only clashes with Zionism but with the anti-democratic mentality of Israel's Arab inhabitants and neighbors.

Demophrenia originates in institutions of higher education, more specifically, in the doctrine of moral relativism propagated by the social sciences and humanities. This doctrine denies the existence of objective standards by which to determine whether the way of life of one individual, group, or nation is intrinsically superior to that of another or more conducive to human excellence. Those influenced by moral relativism tend to regard all lifestyles as morally equal, which negates even the concept of human excellence. In other words, moral relativism leads to indiscriminate egalitarianism also known as "moral equivalence."

As the educational institutions of a democracy become permeated by moral equivalence, opinion-makers and policy-makers become less capable of making intellectual and moral distinctions. For example, in January 2002, Israel's semi-governmental Council on Higher Education, animated by egalitarianism, decided to remove virtually all entrance requirements and standards for admission to Israeli universities.[67] The Council ignored the fact that whereas Jewish students support the State of Israel, Arab students prance around Israeli campuses with PLO flags and call for Israel's destruction!

The inability to make moral distinctions is characteristic of the *unconscious*. When this inability habitually shapes conscious or public life—and this is the tendency of those influenced by moral relativism—it becomes a mental disorder. Those tainted by relativism habitually blur moral distinctions or trivialize acts that would outrage ordinary or normal people. Mention has already been made of Ariel Sharon's renouncing black and white distinctions and the Supreme Court's quashing the indictment of an Arab MK who praised a suicide bomber and called for more of the same.

I shall now proceed to a more theoretical discussion of demophrenia. However, to show that demophrenia is indeed a widespread but hitherto unrecognized mental disorder, it will first be necessary to review some of the literature on schizophrenia to which demophrenia is intimately related.

Schizophrenia is regarded as the core concept of modern psychiatry. Yet, after one hundred years of research, there is no commonly recognized *causal* explanation of this mental malady. In fact, the editor of a collection of essays written by clinical psychologists suggests that schizophrenia is not a meaningful scientific concept, that it does not refer to any empirically verifiable and naturally occurring entity, hence, that it should be abandoned.[68]

Nevertheless, various researchers distinguish between positive- and negative-symptom schizophrenia. The former includes hallucinations, delusions, and thought disorder; the latter includes escapism, apathy, depersonalization, autism, stereotypic behaviors, flattened emotional or affective reactions, impairment of volition, lack of self-esteem, paranoia, etc. Obviously these negative symptoms exist on a continuum with normal behavior. Indeed, some psychologists contend that mental illnesses merely form the end-points of continuously variable behavior (91, 161, 169). In any event, it should be borne in mind that schizophrenia is not necessarily an all-encompassing illness that sets the patient apart from his fellow man (61). A World Health Organization (WHO) study concludes that schizophrenics, for all their vulnerabilities, are in the full sense responsive social beings like the rest of us (63).

Still, those vulnerabilities can and do result in bizarre behavior. The renowned clinical psychologist Dr. David Shakow distinguishes four types of schizophrenic responses to diverse stimuli which, to my initial surprise, accurately describe the reactions of Israel's ruling elites to the typically *bellicose* behavior of Arab-Islamic rulers on the one hand, and to their occasionally *pacific* utterances on the other:

> (1) The central, directly meaningful stimulus is avoided, apparently because it is disturbing; instead the peripheral is endowed with meaning. (2) A casual attitude appears in which [only] part of the field is accepted as the stimulus. (3) The subject has a fixed idea and resorts to it without regard for the [central and contradictory] stimulus. (4) The peripheral is…selectively attended to, captures attention, and is adhered to.[69]

Moreover, to his false perception a schizophrenic's response may be appropriate or inappropriate to that perception. Alternatively, his perception may be veridical but his response will be inappropriate. The consequence, of course, is maladapted responses to reality.

Although WHO studies have shown that the prognosis of schizophrenia is worse in the urbanized and industrialized West than in the Third World (66), no systematic attempt has been made to determine whether the moral relativism and chaotic pluralism engendered by contemporary democracy contributes to schizophrenia. This lacuna may be attributed to the relativism that modulates the disciplines of psychology and psychiatry, as well as to the tendency of the medical profession to trace schizophrenia to biophysical causes (83, 93, 286).

The absence of research on the possible adverse effects of moral relativism on mental health is all the more curious when one considers that psychologists include alienation, anxiety, and loss of identity among the symptoms of schizophrenia. These symptoms are conspicuous in secular, egalitarian societies where moral relativism thrives. Surely a loss of belief in objective moral standards has emotional and behavioral consequences, some of which may be deleterious. Indeed, many psychotherapists maintain that belief-modification can mitigate various schizophrenic symptoms (244, 274). But if moral relativism or indiscriminate egalitarianism has adverse effects on the mental health of individuals, it may also impair, imperceptibly, the rationality of their political and judicial leaders in matters of vital public concern. (To the extent that such individuals have received a university education, they are more prone than ordinary people to moral relativism, since the latter is a university-bred doctrine.)

A unique analysis of schizophrenia, with far-reaching significance for contemporary democracy, will be found in Ignacio Matte-Blanco's essay, "Basic Logico-Mathematical Structures in Schizophrenia."[70] A profound student of Freud, Matte-Blanco takes his bearing (as does Shakow above) from the Freudian insight that the unconscious, as manifested in dreams, obliterates differences as if it were governed by an egalitarian logic which is anything but logical. Freud writes: "…the most insignificant point in common between two elements is enough to enable the dream-work to replace one by the other for any other purpose. Indeed, even contraries are not kept apart but are treated as though they were identical, so that in the manifest dream [and, according to Matte-Blanco, in the productions of more important psychical structures] any element may also stand for its contrary." Which means that, "The governing laws of logic have no sway in the unconscious; it might be called the Kingdom of the Illogical."[71] Using Blanconian principles, I shall relate this Kingdom of the Illogical to the mentality and behavior of Israel's ruling elites.

As a practicing psychoanalyst, Matte-Blanco examines schizophrenic as well as normal mentality in *logical*, and not simply in *dynamic*, terms. Ordinary thinking deals with things (objects, persons, or concepts) which are in some way distinguishable from one another and with the *relations* existing between them. To be more precise, the mind recognizes, or makes propositions about one thing, another thing, and their relation. The relation between things, using Matte-Blanco's terminology, can be either "symmetrical" or "asymmetrical." For example, in the proposition A is different from B, the relation is symmetrical, whereas in the proposition A is part of B, the relation is asymmetrical. Underlying such propositions are certain logical assumptions or principles, such as: (1) the principle of identity: A is identical to A; (2) the concept of two-valued or Aristotelian logic: either A or not A (either proposition A is true or not true); (3) the principle of formal contradiction: two contradictory assertions cannot be both true at the same time; (4) the principle of incompatibility: A cannot be different from and totally equal to B.[72] This said, let us examine Matte-Blanco's examples of symmetrical and asymmetrical relations:

> If John is the brother of Peter, the converse is: Peter is the brother of John. The relation which exists between them is symmetrical, because the converse is identical with the direct relation. But if John is the father of Peter, the converse is: Peter is the son of John. In this case the relation and the converse are not identical. This type of relation which is always different from its converse is called asymmetrical (213).

Now, according to Matte-Blanco, the principle of symmetry is not only a defining characteristic of the unconscious, but the unconscious treats asymmetrical relations as if they were symmetrical. This means that the unconscious uses a symmetrical logic that homogenizes the differences between things. Thus:

> If John is the father of Peter, then Peter is the father of John. In Aristotelian logic this is absurd; in the logic of the unconscious it is normal....[In other words], the principle of symmetry represents the most formidable departure from the logic upon which all the scientific and philosophical thinking of mankind has been based. We see it constantly in operation in schizophrenic and unconscious thinking (ibid.).

To appreciate the political significance of the principle of symmetry, we must first note that in classifying diverse things (objects, persons, or concepts), the logical mind selects some characteristic which they have in common without negating their differences. To illustrate: Jacob (a Jew) is a member of a set or class of Israelis, and so is Ahmed (a Muslim). This means that both satisfy some characteristic—say "born in Israel"—which defines or determines the class (which characteristic does not logically negate Jacob and Ahmed's religious or other differences). But in view of Matte-Blanco's understanding of schizophrenia,

> When the principle of symmetry is applied, all members of a set or class are treated as identical to one another and to the whole set or class, and are therefore interchangeable with respect to the characteristic which defines the class and also with respect to all the characteristics which differentiate them.

In Aristotelian logic each member of a class fully expresses the characteristic of the class, but it also expresses other characteristics as well, and it is in these other characteristics that the members of a class are different from one another. But if the principle of symmetry is applied this is no longer so (213-214).[73]

For example—and here I shall only substitute my own individuals and classes for those used by Matte-Blanco: Jacob is a member of the class "Israelis" and so is Ahmed; this means that both satisfy the attribute which defines that class. But Jacob may also be a member of a number of other classes, such as "Zionists," "secularists," "humanists," etc. Ahmed, on the other hand, is not an element of these other classes to which Jacob belongs. The difference between Jacob and Ahmed can be described precisely in terms of those characteristics which they do not have in common. If Ahmed were an element of all the classes to which Jacob belongs, then there would be no difference whatsoever between them. But if the principle of symmetry is applied, it is sufficient that both are elements of *one* class ("Israelis") for Jacob and Ahmed to be *identical*. In scientific logic this is absurd (214).

It follows that when the principle of symmetry is applied to the members of the class "Israelis," there occurs a negation of Jacob and Ahmed's ideological differences, which differences may well involve diametrically opposed goals or loyalties. Clearly, the principle of symmetry is a logical extension of the democratic principle of equality, one corollary of which is moral egalitarianism. We are now prepared to examine the relationship between the principle of symmetry and the negative symptoms of schizophrenia, which, to repeat include escapism, apathy, depersonalization, flattened emotional or affective reactions, impairment of volition, lack of self-esteem, and paranoia.

When, as a consequence of the principle of symmetry, all members of a set or class are treated as identical to one another regardless of their ideological antagonisms, a leveling of affects or emotional reactions occurs. To paraphrase Matte-Blanco:

> The subtlety of responses to diverse stimuli presupposes the subtlety of differentiation. Confronted by an ensemble or set which contains everything, the individual's affective reactions should be diverse and contain contradictory affects. But under the influence of the principle of symmetry, the affects are homogenized. Any sudden changes of affect can be understood as flashes of asymmetrization in the midst of a world immersed in symmetrical unity (219).

For example, individuals influenced by the principle of symmetry tend to dissolve the ideological difference between A, who uses force as a means of destroying a democracy, and B who uses force as a means of preserving that democracy. They focus on the *means* and disregard or homogenize the *ends*. A case in point is the use of the term "cycle of violence" to describe Arab terrorist attacks and Israel's response. This mode of thinking conforms to what Harry Stack Sullivan termed "selective inattention." Here again the members of a set or class (Arabs and Israelis) are treated as identical to one another and to the whole set or class, and are therefore interchangeable with respect to the characteristic which defines the class ("violence") and also with respect to all the characteristics which differentiate them.

Another example: when an interviewer asked Shimon Peres about the Tanzim, reputed as the extremist "right wing" of the PLO, Peres replied: "I asked Arafat, 'What about Marwan Barghuti [the Tanzim leader]?' Instead of answering my question, Arafat asked me about one of the right wing ministers in the Israeli government."[74] Mr. Peres succumbed to Arafat's semantic legerdemain. It were as if the anti-logical and amoral nature of the unconscious had invaded Peres' consciousness, such that the profound differences between a notorious Arab terrorist and an Israeli cabinet minister were homogenized by the term "right wing"! This anti-logical leveling of moral distinctions conforms to schizophrenia. As Dr. Blanco puts it:

> If we study the essential structural aspects of schizophrenic manifestations and the characteristics of the unconscious processes we find that all of them constitute examples of different degrees of this process of unification and homogenization....[Hence] there is not only in schizophrenia but in all normal human beings, an aspect which tends to treat reality as though it were homogeneous and indivisible. This contrasts with the thinking-logical aspect of man, which tends to distinguish things from one another (224-225).

It follows from Dr. Blanco's ideas that schizophrenia is a misnomer, that the "classical term 'splitting' [of the personality] is hardly appropriate to what is observed in this respect," that it actually corresponds to an "invasion" or an increase of symmetrical relations in areas of life where such symmetries do not exist or appear in a lesser degree. What happens in schizophrenia is not "splitting" but the exact opposite, "namely the formation of more inclusive classes or sets, to which the principle of symmetry is applied: as a result, everything becomes a transparent, unstructured, colossal unity" (223). Might not the term *demophrenia*, in the horizontal and classless societies of the democratic world, be a more accurate designation for negative-symptom schizophrenia?

Like many schizophrenics, those afflicted by demophrenia are capable of dealing effectively with various areas of social reality. In other areas, however, they, too, suffer from a lack of congruity between the three elements that form the personality: intellect, will, and the affective reactions. This classical understanding of schizophrenia, modified by the Blanconian principle of symmetry, may best be studied in the Jewish and democratic State of Israel, a state ensconced in a hostile Arab-Islamic sea. There demophrenics exhibit selective inattention to, as well as symmetrization of, contradictory aspects of cultural reality. While they ordinarily treat all the members of a set or population as identical to one another with respect to the general characteristic which defines the set or population, they typically ignore those characteristics which radically differentiate the members of that population. The result, as indicated above, is cognitive, volitional, and emotional impairment.

The subject may be further clarified by examining the phenomenon of semantic subversion to which democracies are especially susceptible. Suppose A and Q constitute a set or class of governments whose defining characteristic is the "profession of peace" (p). But A is also a member of other classes and subclasses of which Q is not a member. Thus, whereas A is a democracy, Q is a dictatorship. Accordingly, while the principle of civilian supremacy prevails in A, the principle of military supremacy ($q1$) prevails in Q. Moreover, whereas a free press, publicity, and political candor are subclasses of A, a controlled press ($q2$), secrecy ($q3$), and political deviousness ($q4$) are subclasses of Q. Nevertheless, the demophrenic type of personality, a type common to A, will ignore these differentiating (and disturbing) characteristics of Q and fixate on Q's (comforting) "professions of peace" (p), the one characteristic that renders Q ostensibly identical to A. Q's ruler, cognizant of this tendency of A, repeatedly professes a desire for "peace" as a means of disarming A via A's opinion-makers. This is semantic subversion.

This anti-logical process may be formulated in terms of the symmetrical logic of demophrenia. Consider the relation "p is part of Q." If the converse of this relation is identical with it, that is, if the relation is symmetrical, we may say "p is a part of Q = Q is a part of p." In other words, the part is identical with the whole, from which it follows logically that it is also identical with any other part. To express this again in symbolic logic: p, $q1$, $q2$, and $q3$ are subclasses of Q. If Q is identical to p, then p is identical to $q1$, $q2$, and $q3$ (even though these other subclasses of Q may be inconsistent with p). Of course, that a subclass may be identical with any other subclass of the same class is absurd. But this conforms to the "logic" of symmetrical thinking involved in semantic subversion. Stated still another way: by fixating on Q's professions of peace (p), the contradictory significance of Q's "negative characteristics" (q1, q2, and q3) becomes lost in symmetrical unity. In fact, the law of contradiction is negated by symmetrical logic.

Although demophrenia encompasses these and other negative symptoms associated with schizophrenia, the malady is far more complex and difficult to recognize if only because it involves the dominant, democratic mentality of our age, one that has produced many blessings. Nevertheless, our discussion of the behavior of two national unity governments during the *intifadas* indicates that we are dealing here with a national pathology and not merely with some random instances of obtuseness on the part of Israel's political and judicial leaders. What now needs to be explored is the demophrenic character of Israel's intellectual elites, for these are the educators of Israeli politicians and judges. For this purpose it will suffice to study the late Professor Yehoshafat Harkabi.

A Case Study

I single out Professor Harkabi because he was not only an internationally prominent academic and reputed expert on Islam and on the (misnamed) Arab-Israeli conflict. Harkabi, who held the rank of Maj. General, was also head of Israeli Military Intelligence as well as the mentor of Shimon Peres.

Consider his first book *Arab Attitudes to Israel*.[75] The book was written in Hebrew just before the Six-Day War of June 1967. The English edition appeared in 1972, that is, before the Yom Kippur War. The book is replete with hundreds of quotes from diverse Arab sources, all vilifying Jews and Israel in the most lurid terms and promising the eventual annihilation of the Jewish state. In 541 pages one finds not a single exception to this ventilation of Arab hatred—not even from Islamic scholars. Yet Harkabi was convinced before the Six-Day War as well as before the Yom Kippur War that a peaceful and political solution to the Arab-Israeli conflict was possible. Which means that Harkabi draws conclusions that logically contradict the abundant evidence assembled in his book! This paradox, we shall see, can be explained by demophrenia.

Indeed, I know of no one who better exemplifies the demophrenic mentality of Israel's ruling elites than Professor Harkabi, a self-professed moral or cultural relativist.[76] His (unconscious) application of symmetrical logic to the Arab-Israeli conflict is starkly evident in *Arab Attitudes to Israel*. The book, consistent with relativism, is dedicated to Jews and Arabs alike! Its central and directly meaningful stimulus, that of unmitigated Arab hostility, is selectively negated or "wrapped" in symmetrical unity, via the idea of "peace." This idea is the fixation to which Harkabi resorts despite incessant contradictory Arab stimuli.

In his more recent book, *Israel's Fateful Hour* (1989), which is also dedicated to Jews and Arabs, Harkabi urges Israel's government to negotiate with the PLO and permit the establishment of a Palestinian Arab state in Judea, Samaria, and Gaza. "Human history," he writes, "repeatedly demonstrates the ability of peoples to transcend the negative characteristics that were once justifiably ascribed to them."[77]

Unfortunately, Professor Harkabi does not offer any examples of such peoples. Hence he does not permit us to know *how* they transcended their "negative characteristics." It makes all the difference in the world to know whether the peoples he has in mind were conquered in war (like Nazi Germany and Japan), or whether their "negative characteristics" were overcome as a result of evolution or of revolution. Nor does Harkabi enlighten us about these "negative characteristics." We are left to wonder whether they were part of a people's religious mentality or whether they were of a political and therefore of a more pliable and transient nature. But inasmuch as Harkabi advocates the establishment of a PLO-Palestinian state, he is obviously alluding to the "negative characteristics" of Muslims.

He reveals these characteristics in *Arab Attitudes to Israel*. Writing at a time when one did not have to fear the mindless charge of racism, Harkabi refers to Islam as a "combatant," "expansionist," and "authoritarian" creed. He admits that "The idea of the *jihad* is fundamental in Islam," in consequence of which "hatred," "hostility," and "conflict" are endemic to Arab culture (133). Moreover, and of profound significance, he acknowledges that "the use of falsehood," "distortions of the truth," and "misleading slogans" are typical of Arab political life. "Political scientists, sociologists and historians," he musingly writes, "seem to feel reluctant to mention this aspect of their analysis of the Arab world" (337). Harkabi goes so far as to suggest that mendacity is "second nature" to the Arabs, that one may rightly regard "falsehood as an expression of [Arab] national character." For support he quotes our liberated Arab sociologist, Sonia Hamady: "Lying is a widespread habit among the Arabs, and they have a low idea of truth" (348).

Nevertheless, Harkabi is convinced that the Arabs in question have either transcended these "negative characteristics," or will readily shed them once Israel withdraws from Judea, Samaria, and Gaza and permits the PLO to establish thereon a Palestinian state. The fact that Israel's own Arab citizens, along with the Palestinian Arabs, applauded Saddam Hussein's annexation of Kuwait in 1990 did not make Harkabi recant. (The same may be said of Shimon Peres' steadfast refusal to renounce the Oslo Agreement—a disaster obvious to all but those afflicted by demophrenia.) Evident in Harkabi (and Peres) is selective inattention to contradictory aspects of reality. But now recall Dr. Shakow's enumeration of four types of schizophrenic responses to diverse stimuli:

> (1) The central, directly meaningful stimulus is avoided, apparently because it is disturbing; instead the peripheral is endowed with meaning. (2) A casual attitude appears in which [only] part of the field is accepted as the stimulus. (3) The subject has a fixed idea and resorts to it without regard for the [central and contradictory] stimulus. (4) The peripheral is...selectively attended to, captures attention, and is adhered to.

This enumeration of schizophrenic responses to diverse stimuli clearly applies to the mentor of Shimon Peres. But now let us consider how Harkabi's demophrenic mentality impairs his judgment and induced him to advocate a Palestinian state.

Let A represent the class "Israel" and Q represent the class "Arab Palestinians." Q has four subclasses, p, q1, q2, and q3. Subclass p represents Q's positive public pronouncements regarding "peace" and a "two-state solution to the Palestinian-Israeli conflict." Subclass q1 represents the mendacious character of Arabs (according to Harkabi), q2 the Arab Palestinians' religious *beliefs* and *practices*, and q3 their allies, the Arab League. Not only are q1 and q2 *logically* inconsistent with p, but so is q3 since the Arab League is openly committed to Israel's destruction. Harkabi emphasizes subclass p and deemphasizes subclasses q1, q2, and q3 such that the part p appears virtually identical to the whole Q. It were as if the alogical and amoral nature of the unconscious had invaded Harkabi's thought processes. Alternatively, one can say that his moral relativism had induced him to submerge the "negative characteristics" of Q into the oblivion of symmetrical unity.

Now consider Harkabi's assessment of a statement made by a top aide of Yasser Arafat, one Bassam Abu Sharif who, in May 1988, declared: "We believe that all peoples—the Jews and the Palestinians included—have the right to [self-determination, i.e., to] run their own affairs.... The key to a Palestinian-Israeli settlement lies in talks between Palestinians and the Israelis....The Palestinians would accept, indeed insist, on international guarantees for the security of all states in the region, including Palestine and Israel." Harkabi evaluates this statement as indicative of a significant transformation in the PLO's character because Sharif had hitherto been identified with one of its "extremist" groups. He accepts Sharif's statement at face value and describes it as "humane and sensible."[78] One would think that a former head of Israeli Military Intelligence would be more skeptical about such PLO pronouncements, especially the author of *Arab Attitudes to Israel*, from whom we learn that prevarication is "second nature" to the Arabs. But if we view Harkabi's response in terms of Dr. Shakow's four-fold classification of responses to diverse stimuli as well as in terms of the principle of symmetry, it will be evident that Harkabi's fixation on p has relegated q1, q2, and q3 to the oblivion of symmetrical unity.

Suppose, however, that Harkabi had grounds for believing that the Arabs would indeed transcend their "negative characteristics"—quite an insult—if granted Palestinian statehood. Common sense would dictate that Israel should not withdraw to its vulnerable 1949 armistice lines until the leaders of the PLO not only preach peace instead of war, but show tangible evidence that they are not engaging in prevarication. After all, deception is a basic principle of war, *a fortiori* of warlike regimes. From which it logically follows that Israel's withdrawal would only encourage the bellicose qualities Harkabi attributes to Islam. His fixation on peace, however, dissolves the logical significance of contrary stimuli.

It should also be noted that Harkabi's use of the term "negative" to describe certain characteristics of the Arabs is a euphemism. A more forthright and accurate (but less polite and scholarly) term to describe a militaristic people would be "ruthless" or "cruel." However, such judgmental terms about Arabs would not be logically consistent with his moral relativism as well as with his advocacy of a Palestinian state. On the other hand, the fact that he dedicated two books to both Jews and Arabs indicates that he does not take the latter's "negative characteristics" seriously. This remarkable display of moral egalitarianism would explain why Harkabi could so casually contend, without a shred of evidence, that the Arabs can transcend their "negative characteristics."

Alternatively, one may see in a particular area of Harkabi's consciousness—where diverse and contradictory stimuli appear—an "invasion" of symmetrical relations where such symmetries do not normally exist. Instead of diverse and contradictory affects, a more inclusive class or set is formed, to which the principle of symmetry is applied, such that everything becomes an unstructured, colossal unity. Expressed symbolically, instead of two contradictory stimuli, p and q, which would normally produce contradictory affective reactions, a class Q is formed such that p and q become subsets of Q and cease to produce contradictory affects. What makes the formation of Q possible is the amoral and antilogical nature of the unconscious intruding into consciousness. From this one may draw the startling conclusion that *the amoral doctrine of moral relativism or moral equivalence may itself be a manifestation of the unconscious.* This would explain how Professor Harkabi could acknowledge the "negative characteristics" of the Arabs and yet, contrary to logic *and morality*, advocate a Palestinian state.

(Recall the critique of a Palestinian state in Chapter 2.) It would also explain why Shimon Peres and others, including Ariel Sharon, persist in supporting the Israel-PLO Agreement despite overwhelming evidence that it has been an unmitigated disaster—and not only for Jews. We have, in demophrenia, a deadly syndrome of world-historical significance.

Conclusion

If it is true that the doctrine of moral relativism is a product of the amoral and alogical nature of the unconscious, then, given the demonstrable fact that moral relativism permeates the mentality of the democratic world, it would follow that this world carries within itself the seed of insanity. I shall enlarge on this theme in the next chapter. Here let us recall that negative-symptom schizophrenia includes lack of self-esteem, escapism, stereotypic behaviors, flattened emotional or affective reactions, impairment of volition, and paranoia. Recall, too, delusions listed under positive-symptom schizophrenia. All these symptoms, which admittedly exist on a continuum with normal behavior, describe the *public* behavior of Israel's ruling elites throughout the course of the Middle East "peace process"!

Underlying their behavior is fear of anti-Semitism, intensified and rendered pathological by the fear of losing their democratic image in the eyes of the world. To preserve their respectability as genuine democrats, they *must* repeatedly profess and act on the belief that Jews and Arabs, despite their antagonistic ways of life (and unequal birthrates!) can live in peace and equality (and even multiply!) in the minuscule Land of Israel. Their minds have been subtly influenced by the moral relativism that dominates education in the democratic world. This demotic area of their minds exhibits the amoral and anti-logical nature of the unconscious. Residing in that demotic area is the fixed idea of "peace," to which they resort without regard for countless contradictory stimuli: the periodic eruptions of Arab violence against Jews since the Balfour Declaration, indeed, the ravages Jews have suffered throughout history. An acute victim of demophrenia, Shimon Peres, Israel's "elder statesman," has said: "I have become totally tired of history, because I feel history is a long misunderstanding."[79]

Enough has been said in this chapter about the psychological dimensions of the Jewish problem. I now turn to a critique of its underlying cause, moral relativism.

CHAPTER 5
PSYCHOLOGICAL DIMENSIONS OF THE JEWISH PROBLEM: A CRITIQUE OF MORAL RELATIVISM

INTRODUCTION

SO PERVASIVE is moral or cultural relativism in the democratic world that evidence of this doctrine can be found even at the religious Bar-Ian University, whose observant faculty members surely believe that the Torah is the source of Truth and the paradigm of how man should live. Even there, where the present writer taught for twenty years, one could hear the cynical remark: "Who is to say what is good and bad, right and wrong?" This vulgarism was evident even among officers of the Israel Defense Forces studying at the university!

One can only wonder how a Jewish state, surrounded by hostile Arab-Islamic regimes, can survive when the educators of its political and military elites do not believe in the absolute justice of Israel's cause. Professor Harkabi, who once served as head of the Israel Army Staff and Command College, concludes *Arab Attitudes to Israel* with this demoralizing remark: "The study of the [Arab-Israel] conflict reveals the relativity of the attitudes of the parties."[80] Influenced by such relativism, former General Ehud Barak, during his campaign for Israel's premiership, was quoted as saying (in the United States) that had he been born an Arab, he would have been a terrorist! And we have already mentioned the relativism of former General Ariel Sharon.

Raised and educated in this decadent atmosphere, Tel Aviv University professor of philosophy Asa Kasher, under the authority of the late Prime Minister Yitzhak Rabin, and with the acquiescence of then Chief of Staff Ehud Barak, erased the words "Judaism" and "Zionism" as well as "Eretz Israel" from the Soldiers Code of Ethics! Who but minds afflicted by demophrenia would want to transform the Jewish state into a multicultural "state of its citizens"?

Israel is not multicultural America, the most powerful nation on earth. There relativism can permeate every level of education without immediately endangering that democracy's existence—especially with benign Canada and feeble Mexico on its borders. But minuscule Israel, with Arab-Islamic dictatorships as neighbors, can hardly afford a diet of moral relativism. Yet this has been the fare of countless Israeli students.

Thus, in his book *The Middle East*, Israeli political scientist Yair Evron teaches: "Only by avoiding questions of right and wrong and also by limiting oneself to an analysis of patterns of behavior and strategies in conflict, can we approach this complex [Arab-Israel] conflict not in any emotional or apologetic way but scientifically and analytically."[81] We see here a tension between the apparent needs of "science" and the needs of society. To persevere in the Arab-Israel conflict, the people of Israel require steadfast belief in the justice of Israel's cause. But for academics to preserve their "scientific," i.e., academic credentials, they must adopt a morally neutral attitude toward that conflict. But wait! Evron's book was published in 1973. To appreciate the pernicious impact of his relativism, come with me to the year 2003, and let us see what has happened to students attending Israeli universities.

Caroline B. Glick, an editor and gifted writer of *The Jerusalem Post*, addressed some 150 political science students at Tel Aviv University, where she spoke of her experience as an embedded reporter with the U.S. Army's Third Infantry Division during the Iraq war. Any person not corrupted by moral relativism would favor, as she did, the U.S. over the dictatorship of Saddam Hussein. Yet the general attitude of her audience was expressed by a student who asked, "Who are you to make moral judgments?" Now ponder this exchange between Ms. Glick and a student who spoke with a heavy Russian accent:

> Student: "How can you say that democracy is better than dictatorial rule?"
> Glick: "Because it is better to be free than to be a slave."
> Student: "How can you support America when the U.S. is a totalitarian state?"
> Glick: "Did you learn that in Russia?"
> Student: "No, here."
> Glick: "Here at Tel Aviv University?"
> Student: "Yes, that is what my professors say."

Ms. Glick spoke at five liberal Israeli universities. She learned that all are dominated by moral relativists who indoctrinate their students and ban "politically incorrect" publications. The deadly consequences are clear: "A survey carried out by the leftwing Israel Democracy Institute on Israeli attitudes toward the state [indicates that]…a mere 58 percent of Israelis are proud of being Israeli, while 97 percent of Americans and Poles are proud of their national identity." Ms. Glick concludes: "Is it possible that our academic tyrants have something to do with the inability of 42 percent of Israelis to take pride in who they are?"[82]

One might think that moral relativists would adopt a neutral attitude in the conflict between Jews and the Palestinian Arabs—as political scientists like Yair Evron might have done back in 1973. To the contrary, today's relativists have demonized Israel. Never mind the well-known fact that Arabs use their own women and children as human bombs. Because moral relativists—typically liberals—cannot acknowledge the enormity of evil, they not only ignore the genocidal intentions of Israel's enemies, but they identify Jews as the cause of the conflict! Moral relativism has thus produced *moral reversal*!

MORAL RELATIVISM AND RELATIVITY

Before probing more deeply into moral relativism, we must remove an error which relates that doctrine to Einstein's special theory of relativity which deals with the velocity of light. Although that theory is logically unrelated to moral relativism, it has fostered throughout all ranks of liberal democratic society the vulgar notion that "everything is relative." Actually, the postulate that light is a universal constant on which the entire theory of relativity is based indicates that everything is *not* relative. In fact, Einstein called his findings the principle of *invariance*; it was others that referred to them as "relativity," which name stuck.

In any event, the relativism of the physicist differs profoundly from that of the moral relativist or pluralist. The theory of relativity denies the classical notions of absolute space, absolute time, and absolute motion; it does not deny the absolute. Far from excusing an easygoing pluralism, it appeals to scientists by virtue of what Einstein calls its comprehensive simplicity. The theory would explain "all events in nature by structure laws valid always and everywhere."[83] Indeed, "Without the belief that it is possible to grasp reality with our theoretical constructions, without the belief in the inner harmony of our world, there would be no science."[84]

Even the moral relativist Hans Reichenbach (of whom more later) understood that "philosophers who regard it as an ultimate wisdom that everything is relative are mistaken when they believe that Einstein's theory supplies evidence for such sweeping generalizations; and their error is even deeper when they transfer such relativity to the field of ethics…"[85] Bertrand Russell, another moral relativist, perhaps had in mind the half-educated intellectual when he wrote: "A certain type of superior person is fond of asserting that 'everything' is relative. This is, of course, nonsense, because if everything were relative, there would be nothing for it to be relative to."[86] As Max Planck remarks: "Everything that is relative presupposes something that is absolute."[87]

As for Einstein himself, one may find in his philosophical ruminations expressions of moral relativism, but not in his sober and somber moments. In *Out of My Later Years*, first published in 1950, he writes:

> I am firmly convinced that the passionate will for justice and truth has done more to improve man's condition than calculating political shrewdness which in the long run breeds general mistrust. Who can doubt that Moses was a better leader of mankind than Machiavelli?[88]

But two pages later one reads:

> I know that it is a hopeless undertaking to debate about fundamental value judgments. For instance, if someone approves, as a goal, the extirpation of the human race from the earth, one cannot refute such a viewpoint on rational grounds.[89]

Evident here is the influence of logical positivism on Einstein, who wrote those words only five years after Hitler and his followers had murdered six million Jews and almost six million non-Jews. It was as if positivism had erased everything in the vastness of his *rational* mind with which to condemn this evil.[90] And yet he did condemn this evil, moreover, in words the government of Israel should heed in dealing with Hitler's successors! Thus, in a message honoring the heroes of the Warsaw ghetto, Einstein declared:

> The Germans as an entire people are responsible for the mass murders and must be punished as a people if there is justice in the world and if the consciousness of collective responsibility in the nations is not to perish from the earth entirely. Behind the Nazi party stands the German people, who elected Hitler after he had in his book [*Mein Kampf*] and in his speeches made his shameful [genocidal] intentions clear beyond the possibility of misunderstanding.[91]

Two Kinds of Moral Relativism

Israel has imported two kinds of relativism. Many Israeli academics, beginning with the founders of the Hebrew University, were influenced by German historicism. Historicists maintain that *all* human thought is historical, hence unable ever to grasp trans-historical truths. All philosophy, religion, morality, and even science belong to a particular "historical epoch" or "culture," "civilization," or "Weltanschauung."

Historicism was introduced into the Hebrew University by such German-educated intellectuals as Martin Buber. Buber's book, *Two Kinds of Faith*, tacitly denies the possibility that Judaism is true and Christianity false; they are simply different kinds of faith. Not only did Buber reject the notion of the Jews as the Chosen People, but when confronted by the issue of the Jewish versus the Arab claim to Eretz Israel, Buber held, "There is no scale of values for the [world-historical] function of peoples. One cannot be ranked above another."[92] Buber, who married out of his faith, was not simply an anti-Zionist. His opposition to a Jewish state was rooted in historical relativism.

Inasmuch as historicism has been refuted by Professor Leo Strauss,[93] the remainder of this chapter will be devoted to a refutation of positivism and the relativism associated therewith. Lest this be regarded as a merely academic exercise, I shall show how positivism-cum-relativism underlies Israel's policy of "territory for peace," a policy that is dismembering the Jewish state.

Most social scientists have been influenced by logical positivism, which acknowledges the possibility of objective truths in the domain of science, but not in the domain of moral and aesthetic values. It should be noted, however, that the positivist conception of science is based on a narrow, empiricist epistemology discarded by contemporary theoretical physicists. Einstein rejected the positivist principle that any formal statement that cannot be verified by sense experience is meaningless. The great physicist maintained that "*It is the theory which decides what we observe.*"[94] In fact, Einstein developed his special theory of relativity (1905) without knowledge of the Michelson-Morley experiment (1887). Moreover, his general theory of relativity (1915) postulated the curvature of space-time, the mathematics of which was provided by Riemannian geometry formulated in the mid-nineteenth century without reference to empirical reality. It should also be noted that the empiricist bias of positivism makes nonsense of quantum mechanics, which transcends space and time and therefore what is observable. As Nobel physicist Steven Weinberg has written, "The idea that quarks and gluons can in principle never be observed in isolation has become part of the accepted wisdom of modern elementary particle physics, but it does not stop us from describing neutrons and protons and mesons as composed of quarks."[95] By description Weinberg obviously means mathematical description.

The mathematical understanding of nature is precisely that which distinguishes modern from pre-modern science. Mankind has paid a price for this intellectual revolution. The reduction of science to quantitative analysis (beginning with Galileo and Newton) renders it incapable of telling us anything about the rich, qualitative world of sense-perception and human values. Unlike classical and medieval science, modern science discards all considerations based on aesthetic and ethical principles. Distinctions between the beautiful and the obscene, the good and the bad, collapse into mere emotions or subrational forces.[96] In other words, the discovery of mathematical laws of nature automatically implies the subjectivity and relativity of everything not susceptible to exact measurement. This obviously includes religious and moral values or ideologies. Hence, in the conflict between Jews and Muslims, there are no rational grounds for preferring one side to the other. We have entered the mental world of positivism-cum-relativism.

The philosopher of science, Hans Reichenbach, elaborates: "Ethical axioms are not necessary truths because they are not truths of any kind. Truth is a predicate of statements; but the linguistic expressions of ethics are not statements. They are directives [or imperatives]. A directive [e.g., "do not murder"] cannot be classified as true or false…"[97] Accordingly, if one says "murder is bad," he would simply be expressing an emotion not a fact. This leads to the "fact-value" dichotomy of logical positivism and its emotive theory of values.

Thus, to say "X is good" is equivalent to saying "I like X." By translating ethical into non-ethical or psychological language, positivism devaluates all values, especially aristocratic ones. The plebeian philosopher Thomas Hobbes performed this leveling or democratic operation in the seventeenth century. He offers, in his *Leviathan*, the most lucid and succinct definition of relativism:

> Whatever is the object of any man's appetite or desire, that is it which he for his part calleth good; and the object of his hate or aversion, evil…. For these words of good [and] evil…are ever used with relation to the person that useth them: there being nothing simply and absolutely so, where there is no commonwealth.[98]

It follows that what one calls "good" or "evil" is no more valid than what another calls "good" or "evil." All moralities are therefore equal (since none is objectively true).

We have here a democratic conception of man. Man is simply an ensemble of desires—which Freud will call the *id*. The purpose of man's reason is to determine how to obtain the object of his desires. As Hobbes puts it: "The thoughts are to the desires, as scouts and spies, to range abroad, and find the way to the things desired."[99] Freud will call this instrumental reason the *ego*. And of course man will call the object of his desires "good"—which Freud will call the *super-ego*.[100]

Hitherto, when people said "X is good," they meant that X is intrinsically good—good independently of their personal likes and dislikes. Although the emotive theory of values rejects this traditional view of morality, it retains one of its commonsense assumptions, namely, that a person who sincerely states "X is good" does in fact like X. In other words, logical positivism assumes that the likes or desires of a sane or normal person will be in accord with his moral convictions. This assumption is questionable: a person may well like or desire that which he deems bad, or, conversely, dislike that which he deems good.

Suppose a person lives in "Tovland," where a large majority of its inhabitants have a settled conviction that X is good—it may be Zionism or capitalism—which they like profoundly. If this person says "X is good" and likes it, he will be regarded as "sane" or "normal." If he says "X is good" and dislikes it, a Tovland psychiatrist would have reason to regard him as "insane" or "abnormal." On the other hand, suppose our subject is a member of the minority convinced that X is bad. If he dislikes X, the psychiatrist would deem him "normal," whereas if he likes X, the discordance between his moral conviction and emotion would be symptomatic of abnormality. The following model represents the moral or mental climate of Tovland.

TOVLAND: X IS GOOD

	CONVICTION	EMOTION	DIAGNOSIS
Majority	Positive}	Positive	Normal
		Negative	Abnormal
Minority	Negative}	Negative	Normal
		Positive	Abnormal

Now let us go to "Lotovland," where the majority of its inhabitants believe that X is bad, and therefore agree with the minority in Tovland.

LOTOVLAND: X IS BAD			
	CONVICTION	EMOTION	DIAGNOSIS
Majority	Negative}	Negative	Normal
		Positive	Abnormal
Minority	Positive}	Positive	Normal
		Negative	Abnormal

Notice that what is "normal" in Lotovland is "abnormal" in Tovland—a simple manifestation of moral (or cultural) relativism.

Suppose, now, that all the educators or opinion-makers of Tovland are logical positivists, and that, as a consequence, all the people of Tovland no longer say "X is good," having been taught that such an utterance means nothing more than "I like X." In other words, the Tovlanders will no longer have moral convictions.

Let us therefore rename the country of such people "Pluriland," and let us add that if any Plurilanders happen to have retained any moral convictions or still believe that X is intrinsically good, they would be classified as "reactionaries" or stupid. They may be ignored in the next model. Accordingly, Plurilanders will be divided into a majority that likes X and a minority that dislikes X.

PLURILAND: I LIKE X			
	CONVICTION	EMOTION	DIAGNOSIS
Majority	None	Positive	?
Minority	None	Negative	?

Bizarre consequences follow from this model. First, notice that with the absence of moral convictions in Pluriland, the distinction between sanity and insanity has been obliterated or rendered problematic. Lest the reader doubt the possibility of such a state of affairs, let us briefly recall the anti-psychiatry movement fathered by two psychiatrists, Dr. Robert D. Lang in England, and Dr. Thomas Szasz in the United States, who denied the distinction between sanity and insanity. Indeed, such was the impact of their writings on Anglo-American universities, where positivism-cum-relativism is rampant, that a 1986 poll found that 55 percent of the American public did not believe there was such a thing as mental illness"![101] But what needs to be stressed is this: the inability of mainstream psychiatry to combat the anti-psychiatry movement stemmed from the fact that modern psychology is steeped in moral relativism, which readily lends itself to a denial of the distinction between "normal" and "abnormal" behavior.

Returning to Pluriland, where relativism underlies the mentality of its inhabitants, the need for psychiatrists is problematic in theory (though not in practice). It would be pointless for a visiting psychiatrist—say a tourist from Tovland—to ask a Plurilander his reason for liking X: *his likes are self-justifying*. Since nothing is intrinsically good or bad, Plurilanders do not have to explain or defend their likes and dislikes. It follows that one should not expect rational public debate in Pluriland on issues involving religious or moral values. The mentality of Plurilanders has been conditioned by the "fact-value" dichotomy of social science positivism, that is, by educators who regard religious or moral values as "emotional imperatives" and not as "facts" susceptible to empirical verification.

Here I am reminded of Moshe Dayan's speech to the Israel Army Staff and Command College in 1968, where he spoke of Dr. Arthur Ruppin who, in 1926, founded the Brit-Shalom movement to foster the idea of a bi-national or Arab-Jewish state in Palestine. According to Dayan, the German-educated Ruppin had hoped that "facts" on the ground, especially economic strength and an increasing Jewish population, would induce Arabs to accept Israel's political existence. Such facts, says Dayan, have indeed come to pass, but have not altered Arab rejection of a Jewish state. Dayan then adds this revealing remark: "Perhaps Ruppin's error on this point stemmed from the fact that he thought in rational categories, whereas Arab opposition stems from emotions."[102]

Surely the exact opposite is closer to the truth. Surely it is rational for Arabs to oppose Jewish settlement on land they deem (rightly or wrongly) their own. Conversely, having conquered this land, it is irrational—a surrender to emotion—for Jews to expect Arab friendship. But what is to be singled out here is that Dayan (as well as Ruppin) simply failed to take Arab-Islamic culture seriously, precisely because in the self-effacing or egalitarian mentality of relativism, religion has no rational foundation or is rooted in the emotions (as Freud asserts in *The Future of an Illusion*). We are in Pluriland!

Having been taught the emotive theory of values, the rulers of Pluriland will not be motivated by any moral or religious ideology. Their all-consuming goal will be "peace," meaning comfortable self-preservation (which Hobbes prescribed as the purpose of the Leviathan). They will not take the moral values or religious convictions of any adversarial nation like Lotovland seriously. They will regard the Lotovlanders' ideology as devoid of cognitive validity, a myth that serves their material interests. They will think that the rulers of Lotovland can be pacified by the promise of land or of economic prosperity.

(This is precisely the attitude of Israel's ruling elites, certainly of those who advocate a Palestinian state. They are unwitting Hobbesians!)

Suppose, however, that the Plurilanders have miscalculated. Suppose the moral or religious convictions of Lotovland, even if false, are not reducible to the Lotovlanders' emotions, but rather strengthen and sustain them. In that case, other things being equal, any protracted conflict between the two countries would end in the victory of Lotovland over Pluriland. This would certainly be the outcome if the X of Pluriland were intrinsically bad, as the Lotovlanders may believe. Indeed, even if it had no enemies, how could Pluriland survive when its people or rulers like what may in truth be bad, and dislike what may in truth be good? This leads to a fourth model.

Imagine a society, "Zedland," where the dominant majority believes that X is bad but *like* it! (Longfellow's epithet, "The world loves a spice of wickedness," would raise no eyebrows in Zedland.) If a Zedlander disapproves of X but likes it, he would be regarded as "normal"; for consistent with the majority, his moral conviction and emotion would be *discordant* with each other. But if he disapproves of X and dislikes it, a Zedland psychiatrist would deem him "abnormal." On the other hand, suppose our Zedlander is a member of the minority that believes X is good. If he likes X he would be declared "abnormal," even though, or rather, precisely because, his moral conviction and emotion are in *agreement* with each other. Here is a model of Zedland.

ZEDLAND: X IS BAD			
	CONVICTION	EMOTION	DIAGNOSIS
Majority	Negative	Positive	Normal
Minority	Positive	Positive	Abnormal

Contrast this model with that of Tovland. Notice that whereas a Tovlandian psychiatrist would have to get the moral convictions and emotions of his patients into phase with each other, sanity would require a Zedland psychiatrist to get the moral convictions and emotions of his patients out of phase with each other! The "normal" in one society would be "abnormal" in the other, and vice versa—a commentary on cultural relativism, but also on the fact that man's *will* can oppose the rule of the emotions (as well as the rule of reason).

MACHIAVELLI

This said, we must now go beyond Hobbes to his master, Machiavelli, whom few penetrate and whom almost no one can imitate. Machiavelli will be discussed at length as the father of Modernity in Chapter 13. There I shall focus on Chapter 15 of *The Prince,* where he lays down the foundation for a new political science, involving a new way of understanding and *using* morality and dealing with the emotions. Machiavelli enumerates various virtues and vices that bring rulers praise or blame, qualities which a ruler, "if he wishes to maintain himself," must be able to "use" and "not use" "according to necessity." A ruler whose mind is so cunning and flexible that he can employ virtues and vices "according to necessity" must be devoid of all emotion, except the desire for power. To harbor emotions is to be susceptible to *habits,* and it is precisely habits that prevent a ruler from being a perfect *opportunist.* A ruler must therefore be capable of changing his "nature" with the times and circumstances, which means he must have no emotional predispositions (other than the desire to maintain and increase his power). This would be possible only if man is nothing more than a creature of habits—habits that can be conquered by men of the caliber of Machiavelli.

We are now prepared to construct a model for a nation ruled by Machiavellians. Let us call this nation "Rashaland." The rulers of Rashaland regard virtue and vice as mere instruments of power; they stand beyond good and evil. For such men the only sin is stupidity. As for the people, they are politically irrelevant. (In dealing with Rashaland, one deals with its rulers, not with its people.)

RASHALAND			
	CONVICTION	EMOTION	DIAGNOSIS
Rulers	None	None	Cunning

Although the rulers of Rashaland would call the Pluriland leaders stupid, the two have this much in common: they lack moral convictions. The lack of moral convictions among Pluriland leaders multiplies their people's desires and renders them incapable of uniting on behalf of a common cause. This is not the case of the rulers of Rashaland. Lacking moral convictions and unhampered by emotions, they are animated solely by the desire for power. In Pluriland we find a democracy of desires and a corresponding democracy of thoughts. In Rashaland the ruler's thoughts are focused on one paramount objective: *dominion.* Let us apply what we have thus far learned to Israel.

To the extent that Israel's ruling elites are comparable to those of Pluriland, they can no more compete with the rulers of Rashaland than those of Lotovland. But what needs to be borne in mind is the invisible cause of Israel's infirmity, namely, the influence of democratic relativism on the mentality of its intellectual and political elites. It follows that Israel's survival will ultimately depend on the ascendancy of new elites whose mentality differs profoundly from that of the present ones, which is basically secular. This will require fundamental changes in the philosophical foundations of higher education in this country. Israel will have to become, in thought and in action, a truly *Jewish* state.

Fortunately, relativism is not pronounced among the vast majority of Israel's Jewish population. Most Jews in Israel identify with the Torah, which is obviously opposed to relativism. This alone explains why the Labor Party, despite its uninterrupted control of all the levers of state power between 1948 and 1977, never won a majority of the Jewish vote in any national election. But this suggests that the most expeditious way of transforming Israel's educational institutions is to increase the people's influence on the legislative, executive, and judicial branches of government. This can only be done by making the elections to these branches more democratic, as indicated in Chapter 3.

We must now return to Hobbes. Consider again his statement, "The thoughts are to the desires, as scouts and spies, to range abroad, and find the way to the things desired." But surely this applies to Hobbes' own thoughts, unless he can show—which he does not—that *his* thoughts are exempt from his own conclusions! Hobbes' thoughts are nothing but the instrument of his own desires. Of man's desires he mentions "the desire of power, of riches, of knowledge, and of honour. All of which may be reduced to the first, that is, desire of power. For riches, knowledge, and honour, are but several sorts of power."[103] It follows that his *Leviathan* is a manifestation of Hobbes' desire for power, or what Nietzsche termed a "species of autobiography." But this means that the doctrine of moral relativism, as set forth in the *Leviathan*, has no objective validity! Yet this doctrine, as presented in that work, dominates the mentality of the modern world. In other words, modernity is largely the manifestation of the will to power of Thomas Hobbes, who more or less elaborated the thoughts, and therefore advanced the world-historical project, of Machiavelli.

Clearly, modernity is based on volition, not on reason. But this means that modernity, to an indeterminate extent, is irrational. This can be demonstrated by a logical analysis of democracy, modernity's standard of what is worthy of praise or blame, of what is "good" or "bad."

The *sine qua non* of democracy is the egalitarian principle of "one adult/one vote." This principle implies the theoretical equality of adults holding contradictory opinions, which suggests that their contradictory opinions are equally valid. This is logically absurd. Moreover, the theoretical equality of all opinions includes opinions regarding good and bad, right and wrong—the position of moral relativism, a doctrine most prevalent in democratic societies. Democracy therefore manifests the *alogical* as well as *amoral* nature of the unconscious. Hence it is difficult to avoid the conclusion that modernity, despite the triumphs of mathematical physics, is indeed based on the irrational. One may even say that modernity fosters insanity. This seemingly outrageous statement is supported by evidence presented in Chapter 4. There it was said:

> The absence of research on the possible adverse effects of moral relativism on mental health is all the more curious when one considers that psychologists include alienation, anxiety, and loss of identity among the symptoms of schizophrenia. These symptoms are conspicuous in secular, egalitarian societies where moral relativism thrives. Surely a loss of belief in objective moral standards has emotional and behavioral consequences, some of which may be deleterious. Indeed, many psychotherapists maintain that belief-modification can mitigate various schizophrenic symptoms.

Apparently, there are more psychiatrists in the United States than in all other countries combined; and it has been reported that a frightful percentage commit suicide. This said, let us examine modern psychology.

Chapter 6
Psychological Dimensions of
The Jewish Problem:
A Critique of Modern Psychology

The Torah's conception of human nature, that man is created in the image of God, implies that man is endowed with reason and free will, hence that he is capable of choosing between good and evil. Modern psychology is diametrically opposed to this understanding of human nature. Quite apart from its agnosticism, if not atheism, modern psychology denies the primacy of reason on the one hand, and tends to be deterministic on the other. Since modern psychology is part of the curriculum of higher education in Israel, it cannot but influence Israel's ruling elites, the more so in view of the fact that modern psychology's conception of man influences all the social sciences, including the one most pertinent to government, political science. Israel's Final Redemption, therefore, requires a refutation of modern psychology and its replacement by a Torah psychology. Here I will reproduce, with hardly any revision, the refutation of modern psychology that appears in my essay, "The Malaise of Modern Psychology," which was published in the *Journal of Psychology* in March 1992. As for a Torah psychology, its rudiments will be found in *Judaic Man*.[104]

From Hobbes to Freud

When Hobbes wrote, "The thoughts are to the desires as scouts, and spies to range abroad, and find the way to the things desired," he was laying the foundation for modern psychology. Hobbes relegates thought or reason to the role of a mere instrument of man's desires. Instead of the primacy of the intellect, we have the primacy of the emotions (which Spinoza regarded as "modifications" of desire). Since the emotions do not grasp universals—the existence of which Hobbes denies—the consequence is the ubiquitous doctrine of moral relativism. No one has stated this doctrine more clearly than Hobbes himself. Allow me to repeat the relevant passage in his *Leviathan*:

But whatever is the object of any man's appetite or desire, that is it which he for his part calleth good; and the object of his hate or aversion, evil; and of his contempt, vile and inconsiderable. For these words of good, evil, and contemptible, are ever used with relation to the person that useth them: there being nothing simply and absolutely so; nor any common rule of good and evil, to be taken from the nature of the objects themselves; but from the person of the man, where there is no commonwealth.

To appreciate Hobbes' influence on contemporary psychology, ponder this recent deliverance of a clinical psychologist: "Whether behavior is referred to as [normal or] abnormal is based upon a social designation rather than qualities which inhere in the behavior itself."[105] Hobbes' moral relativism has spawned a relativistic conception of "normal" and "abnormal" behavior. Thus, what is deemed "normal" in one country may be deemed "abnormal" in another—precisely the position presented in the previous chapter's discussion of Tovland and Lotovland.

By virtue of its subordination of reason to the passions, modern psychology denies not only the possibility of objective knowledge of good and evil, but also the distinction between *mind and nature* (a pantheistic notion found in Einstein). The mind, no longer autonomous, becomes a natural object, such that intellectual activity will henceforth be understood in terms of material causes.

This naturalistic psychology was reinforced by Karl Marx: "The *phantoms* formed in the brain are...*sublimates* of [man's] material life-process, which is empirically verifiable and bound to material premises. Morality, religion, metaphysics, all the rest of ideology and their corresponding forms of consciousness, thus no longer retain the semblance of independence."[106] Marx was curiously delighted by the publication of Darwin's doctrine of evolution, that is, of man's descent from lower forms. This doctrine makes that which supposedly occurs earlier in phylogeny (such as the instincts) determinative of what occurs later (such as thought). Darwinism influenced the psychology of William James, who regarded the doctrine of natural selection as "quite convincing." Even before Freud postulated the primacy of the *id*, James concocted a physiological theory of the emotions that placed in question the objective validity of moral and aesthetic values.[107] As we shall see later, however, James was too refined or too sensible to remain consistently mired in a reductionist and relativistic psychology, one that explains the higher—the distinctively human—in terms of the lower.

Freud accepted "the evolution of animals into men" with alacrity.[108] Indeed, like Hobbes, he regarded the "psychical apparatus" of man and the higher animals as equivalent.[109] Enter the Freudian id. The id is the total ensemble of instincts or passions, the most important of which is the libido. The id, writes Freud, "expresses the true purpose of the individual organism's life," which "is directed exclusively to obtaining pleasure."[110] It is from the id—from the impact of external stimuli on the body—that the ego is formed. The ego is the thinking servant of the id. It functions as the organism's "reality principle"—Hobbes' "scouts" and "spies"—which may warn the id to limit or postpone the gratification of its pleasure-seeking principle. Encouraged by evolution, Freud went so far as to say that "The differentiation between the ego and the id must be attributed not only to primitive man but even to much simpler forms of life."[111]

Such has been the influence of evolution on psychology that even cognitive psychologists contend that "cognitive functions…evolved with phylogeny."[112] They not only claim (with Hobbes and Freud) that "Emotional processes have to be primal in human behavior," but they insist on "the primacy of biological events in the emotion-cognitive nexus."[113] Here they commit the classical logical fallacy of *post hoc propter hoc* ("after this, because of this").

In any event, to say or imply that moral values, or ideas concerning how man should live, are determined by subrational or biological drives or instincts, is to say, in effect, that what we believe to be "right" or "wrong," "good" or "bad," "just" or "unjust," depends on our personal likes and dislikes. Hence there are no qualitative differences between the motivations of the vulgar and of the refined: all men are equally animated by egoism. From this moral egalitarianism it follows that all the emotions, love included, are self-regarding. The only natural good is the private good.

Modern psychology therefore liberates the emotions from the restraints of reason. Moreover, the relativism or subjectivism of modern psychology applies not only to moral values but, as James indicates, to aesthetics values, to ideas of the beautiful. Formerly, beauty was linked to goodness and truth. The True, the Good, and the Beautiful, though distinct, were thought to be inseparable. (Indeed, we still speak colloquially of a "beautiful idea" or of a "beautiful deed.") This is no longer so in modern halls of learning. Beauty has been separated from truth and goodness (hence the flood of soul-destroying pornography and that which follows, the crass vulgarity of speech that infects all ranks of society). The separation of beauty from truth and goodness has emancipated the imagination, further liberating the emotions. The casualty is reason, indeed, sanity.

The derogation of reason will be found in the psychoanalytical, behavioral, and biomedical models of mental disorders. Each model involves a mechanistic or deterministic conception of human behavior. The psychoanalytical model exaggerates the influence of unconscious forces (the id, libido, and Oedipus complex) as well as the permanency of childhood traumatic experiences. The behavioral model exaggerates the influence of external stimuli or conditioning. The biomedical model exaggerates the influence on mentality of neural and genetic mechanisms.

Each model has its critics, more or less polemical and more or less empirical. No less than Carl Jung declared: "What Freud has to say about sexuality, infantile pleasure, and their conflict with the 'reality principle,' as well as what he says about incest and the like, can be taken as the truest expression of his own psychic make-up." "Freud's teaching," he adds, "generalizes from facts that are relevant only to neurotic states of mind…" His "is not a psychology of the healthy mind."[114]

D. G. Garan contends that Freudian psychology is a prescientific "personification" of mysterious psychic forces.[115] (To those mentioned above, one may add Eros, Thanatos, the "censor," penis envy, and the castration complex.) Some of these unseen forces are described as autonomous. They operate in the unconscious where they are (mysteriously) endowed by Freud with the capacity to reason, react, evaluate, plot, and carry out complex mental acts affecting "normal" and "abnormal" behavior.[116]

S. J. Rachman is more specific. His studies of people subjected to life-threatening events such as aerial bombardment, as well as current research on various forms of panic such as agoraphobia, refute not only Freud's contention that phobias originate in libido repression,[117] but also the behavioral view that phobias result from traumatic conditioning. "I can think of no psychological theory…that would have predicted the prompt return of the Hiroshima survivors or their extraordinary psychological resistance." Moreover, in a study of 218 military bomb disposal operators, Rachman reveals that "there was no relationship between psychometric or psychiatric results and the performances of dangerous duties, and the few cases of psychological disturbance were not predicted by psychological tests or by psychiatric interview." He concludes that contemporary psychological theories regarding phobias "are designed for creatures more timorous than human beings."[118]

Consider, finally, the biomedical model of mental disorders, specifically its emphasis on drug therapy. While various drugs can be therapeutic per se and also facilitate psychotherapy, so, to a lesser extent, can placebos. It should be noted, moreover, that neuroleptic drugs can be addictive and produce irreversible side effects. One study "estimates that around half of the world's 150 million recipients of major tranquilizers suffer from some degree of tardive dyskinesia."[119]

Although biochemical drugs produced by the organism itself (endorphins, for example) are thought to be non-addictive and promising, man is far too complicated for such simplistic panaceas. Mention should also be made, therefore, of electroconvulsive therapy. Whatever its curative impact on simple physiological depressions, shock treatment can result in permanent damage to a patient's neurological system and memory.[120]

It will be evident from the preceding discussion that modern psychology is in a state of disarray. One psychologist says of the members of his profession that many are bewildered by the fact that "behavior therapy, psychoanalysis, family therapy, a witch doctor, friends, and sometimes no intervention at all bring about successful therapeutic outcomes."[121] Another psychologist writes: "One cannot help but wonder how much in this field is theory and technique, how much is personal charisma, art, religious conviction, or science." Still another contends that "all psychotherapies are theoretically misguided, that…there are common mechanisms by which all therapies work, but their exact nature still remains unclear."[122]

Dr. S. Kellam of the National Institute of Mental Health (NIMH) offers a more radical assessment: "[The] major effort in psychiatry today is to reduce the degree to which the physician and mental hospitals stand in the way of patient's own capacity to get better."[123] Consistent therewith, it has been reported that "More than half the patients derive no benefit from psychoanalysis and for 60 percent of these patients it is harmful. At the same time…two thirds of all neurotics recover without any treatment whatever…"[124] Garan concludes that "Mental patients…recover better without psychotherapies, by living through their 'disease' as a pressure back to normality."[125] One suspects that psychiatry may even be hazardous to your health.

A recent NIMH study indicates that one out of every five adult Americans suffers from some mental disorder (Garan, 1987, p. 140). (This compares with an estimated rate of one-in-ten in the 1960s and one-in-twenty in the 1940s.) The study also shows that of the thirty million adults now suffering from mental disorders, only one-fifth seek professional help, and mostly from general physicians, not psychiatrists.[126]

No doubt the misery of so many people is to be attributed to a multitude of causes. But surely one of those causes, and no minor one, is the moral relativism generated by modern psychology. What needs to be emphasized, however, is this largely unknown fact: the Hobbesian subordination of thought to the passions has led to the emancipation of imagination—and no psychology is more the product of imagination than that of Sigmund Freud, the most influential psychologist of the twentieth century.

The imagination of men, couched in pseudo-scientific jargon, has spawned a welter of contradictory psychologies. Jung candidly admitted in 1933 that "The very number of present-day 'psychologies' amounts to a confession of perplexity."[127] Some 200 different psychotherapies are now reported in the democratic world, of which more than 60 are said to be flourishing.[128] Such pluralism is neither conducive to sanity nor consistent with science.

The multiplicity of contradictory psychotherapies is symptomatic of the widespread confusion among psychologists and other social scientists regarding the nature of man on the one hand, and what constitutes a healthy form of political society on the other. The first thing that needs to be recognized is that the human mind is not a natural object, that the attempt to establish a naturalistic psychology was not only bound to fail but to have pernicious consequences. A fallacious conception of human nature cannot but have detrimental effects on mental health and public happiness.

Unlike mathematical physics, psychology is not an exact science. The question of free will aside, psychology falls far short of being an exact science because neither thought nor emotion has quantifiable units.[129] Suppose, however, that the emotions, conceived in terms of energy, could be quantified. Given a reductionist and mechanistic psychology, what would be the cognitive significance, say, of an erg of specific emotional energy?

A reductionist and mechanistic psychology is a self-effacing contradiction in terms as well as a purblind denial of human creativity. Such a psychology entails insuperable epistemological problems, as the following will show.

If abnormal behavior is reducible to biochemical causes, then normal behavior must also be reducible to biochemical causes. But to reduce behavior to biochemistry is epistemologically absurd, for it would then follow that this theory of behavior is itself reducible to biochemical causes. Similarly, if behavior is Skinnerian, a mere resultant of social conditioning, or if behavior is Freudian, the consequence of a cauldron of instincts modulated by childhood experiences preserved in the unconscious, what is the scientific status of the intellectual products of these psychologists? By exempting their own psychophysiological processes from their conclusions regarding the determinants of human behavior, they call to mind the sign at the sideshow in Swift: "THE LARGEST ELEPHANT IN THE WORLD EXCEPT HIMSELF TO BE SEEN HERE." Such is the epistemological consequence of denying the primacy and potential autonomy of the intellect vis-à-vis the passions.

The fact that the prevailing schools of modern psychology purvey a deterministic conception of human behavior is paradoxical, for they do so in an era that boasts of freedom. This democratic era, however, is also given to moral laxity and to a spiraling rate of mental disorders. Here another look at Freud may be instructive.

Although Freud attributed all that is most precious in human civilization to repression of the instincts, he nonetheless held that psychopathological symptoms are "an indication of and substitute for an unachieved instinctual gratification."[130] In other words, Freudian (and much of post-Freudian) psychology is based on the assumption that the causes of mental disorders reside in repression of the natural desire for pleasure. Garan argues to the contrary that neuroses and psychoses usually result from over-enjoyment, whether by the use of physical or of psychological stimulation. The distressed person reacts to, and seeks to avoid, the negative aftereffects of excessive pleasure by more intense stimulation, thereby initiating a vicious cycle having devastating consequences. For Garan, the claim that repression of the instincts is the cause of disorders—Freud called it "the pillar on which the edifice of psychoanalysis rests"—is a monumental error and dangerous fallacy.[131]

French psychiatrist and professor of medicine Henri Baruk goes further. He offers clinical evidence that mental illness, nowadays, is caused not by repression of the instincts so much as by the total absence of moral restraint. Baruk, who credits Hebraic biology for his findings, has published papers indicating that diminishing the ability of people to distinguish between good and evil produces subtle changes in the chemistry and circulation of their blood and, remarkably, various neuroses and psychoses.[132]

Although Freud, at the end of his psychological ruminations, is said to have discarded the notion of repression and replaced it with "nongratification," this did nothing to mitigate the hedonistic tendency of his doctrine. Release of the emotions by removing restraints on sensual pleasures has very much become the goal of therapy as well as the norm of democracy. The postulation of the primacy of the passions has thus led to their liberation. This liberation undermines all authority: it ruins the family and therefore society. Man, it seems, is being dispossessed of all moral responsibility. The aggressive emotions are gaining ascendancy. The end result is manifest: escalating crime and violence.[133]

Summing up: without denying its accomplishments in perception and learning theory, modern psychology has rightly been called the "psychology without a soul." The ordered or hierarchical soul has been replaced by the "self," by an ensemble of desires. The gratification of desire—of any desire—is fostered by moral relativism. Relativism cannot say No to any desire or to incessant pleasure-seeking. Excessive enjoyment of any pleasure leads to a spiraling pleasure-pain chain reaction ending in mental as well as physiological disorders. As noted above, the number of people afflicted by such disorders in democratic societies is of epidemic proportions. Because such societies are consumer oriented and preoccupied with effort-eliminating technology, they attempt to maximize pleasure by multiplying and stimulating desires and by discarding internal inhibitions and external restrictions. The results are everywhere evident: stress, alienation, loss of concentration, fatigue, mental impoverishment, disease, drug addiction, and, of course, pain. As Garan has put it: "Never have people enjoyed more of everything they have always wanted.... But never have men suffered more from anxiety, which fifty years ago was not even known as a problem."[134]

Physical and mental health, like existence in general, requires night as well as day, the negative as well as the positive, restraint as well as freedom, privation as well as satisfaction. Evident here is the Torah principle—see *Ecclesiastes*—that everything in creation requires its opposite. To ignore this principle is to court disaster.

Desperately needed is a new psychology, a new understanding of human nature, especially one that reveals the true relationship between the intellect and the emotions. The principles of such a psychology are at hand. Needed only is a more explicit, detailed, and systematic analysis, one rooted in the Torah. Here I offer a thought-experiment that illustrates the primacy of the intellect.

A Thought-Experiment

The thought-experiment I have in mind is embarrassingly simple, embarrassing because anyone can perform this experiment and, in the process, turn much of modern psychology on its head. In fact, after making the experiment, the reader may conclude that I have either grossly over-simplified modern psychology by saying it is based on the primacy of the passions, or that modern psychology, far from revealing what is distinctively human, is little more than an explanation of animal-like behavior. But let us make the experiment after a word from one of the architects of modern psychology, Spinoza.

Following a mode of thought inaugurated by Machiavelli and elaborated by Hobbes, Spinoza held that "desire is the actual essence of man," and that emotions are modifications of that essence. From this it would follow that "an emotion cannot be destroyed or controlled except by a contrary and stronger emotion."[135] Spinoza does not explain how one emotion can be stronger than another. Clearly the emotions have different degrees of intensity. Whereas one person's love of family or of country may overcome his fear of violent death, another's may not. On the other hand, a person may risk his life rescuing a complete stranger. Spinoza sheds no light on these questions.

Obviously no emotion or desire can impede itself. Desires are not self-qualifying. A person's desire for "X" may well be constrained and overcome by fear that gratifying the desire may result in ruinous consequences.[136] Such consequences, however, must be anticipated or cognized to arouse that fear. To conclude, therefore, that an emotion can be controlled only by a contrary and stronger emotion will not stand the test of critical analysis. The following thought-experiment will bear this out.

Probably all of us have regretted a moment of anger, especially when, after having given vent to that emotion, we discover that the offending person, the victim of our wrath, was innocent of any wrongdoing. As soon as we discover the truth of the matter, we cease to be angry with the person in question and even apologize. This common experience clearly demonstrates that our initial anger was activated by a misperception or hasty judgment on our part, and that as soon as we learn of our mistake, our reason or intellect not only turned off the emotion of anger, but turned on the emotion of remorse.[137]

Here it may be objected that love alone can transform anger to remorse. Perhaps, but the process is not simply an emotional one. Often ignored is the fact that every human emotion involves an idea or concept, else one emotion could not be distinguished from another. Moreover, every emotion has gradations of intensity depending, in part, on the object that may arouse it. We love, say, our friends, our children, our parents, our teachers, our country, God. But the order and intensity of these loves varies with the ideas associated with these subjects. Such was Abraham's love of God that he was prepared to sacrifice his beloved son. Such was Isaac's love of God that he was willing to be sacrificed. In each case, however, love was modulated by the patriarch's understanding of his world-historical purpose or relationship to his Creator.

Furthermore, love itself may be turned off by an act of the intellect, by the recognition that someone we love is unworthy of our love. Similarly, hatred, followed by reflection and judgment, may be transformed into disdain or mere indifference. On the other hand, as a result of new knowledge or insight, hatred may give way to love, just as love may give way to hatred. Even the fear of violent death may be overcome by meditation and understanding. All of which suggests that the human soul is too complicated to be adequately explained by a mode of material causality, as if it were merely a stimulus-response mechanism.[138]

But to further reveal the primacy of the intellect vis-à-vis the emotions, let us return to the feeling of remorse resulting from an error in judgment. This remorse signifies a negative judgment against ourself. We feel guilty for having committed an injustice or for having fallen short of self-expectation. Even if we feared retribution, the fear would be rational, meaning, it would have been caused by the cognitive awareness that our anger had no rational justification.

Probing deeper, quite apart from the harm caused to the innocent victim of our anger, the mere realization that we had erred in our judgment may mortify us. This suggests the operation, within us, of intellectual or mortal probity to which no other mortal is privy and which therefore is not concerned about public opinion. James held a similar view despite his theory of the emotions: "We are frequently more ashamed of our blunders afterwards than we were at the moment of making them; and in general our whole higher prudential and moral life is based on the fact that material sensations actually present may have a weaker influence on our action than ideas of remoter facts."[139] To admit, however, that ideas can make us feel ashamed is to admit that the intellect can trigger emotions and even physiological changes. This rather obvious fact, incidentally, underlies the use of lie-detectors or polygraphs.[140]

And so, even though lying is commonplace, the desire or concern for truth is more basic to human nature (else science and society and even modern psychology would be impossible). This is but to suggest that we possess an intellectual-moral faculty that hates any error in our mind concerning reality, a faculty that deplores self-delusion even apart from its practical consequences. "How could I have been so stupid?" we sometimes say to ourselves, even when the stupidity is known to no other person and results in no tangible loss. Thus Plato in the *Republic*: "…to be ignorant in the soul concerning reality, to hold and possess falsehood there, is the last thing any man would desire. Men hate falsehood in such a case above all" (382a). This capacity for self-criticism not only distinguishes the human from the subhuman, as well as the urbane from the vulgar, but it reveals the intrinsic supremacy of the intellect over the emotions.

Finally, if we should believe in a God Who knows our every thought and deed, and Who judges us in the scales of Graciousness and Justice measured by Truth, our capacity for self-criticism cannot but be more refined and elevated. And if we have learned very much about the Torah of this God, Who is slow to anger, we ourselves would become more deliberate in judgment and be far less likely to actuate that hostile emotion. Indeed, the fear of displeasing this God would make us all the wiser, especially if that emotion is associated with love, a love resulting, like Abraham's, from profound knowledge.

Conclusion

Although modern psychology has degraded man, it has nonetheless served a constructive world-historical purpose by facilitating the conquest of nature. We ordinarily thank modern science, beginning with Newtonian physics, for the conquest of nature, but this is superficial. The conquest of nature required the liberation of man's acquisitive instincts, and this was facilitated by modern psychology. The liberation of man's acquisitive instincts, however, required a political vehicle, namely, democracy. Democracy, with its separation of church and state, of morality and public law, terminated the rule of a religious landed aristocracy and opened the door to capitalism: unlimited greed and the preoccupation with material well-being. In other words, by reducing reason to an instrument of physical desires, modern psychology closed the mind to the nonphysical world and thereby hastened the conquest of the material world. This is why Israel's ruling elites believe they can buy peace from Islam, a world oblivious of Hobbes.

How ironic. Hobbes based his political philosophy on the "fear of violent death," which he deemed the *summum malum*, the greatest evil. This fear, he contends, induces mankind to seek "peace." That may well be the underlying and dominant motive of countless seekers of peace in Israel. It stands in stark contrast to Israel's enemies, who exalt suicide terrorist bombers motivated by the desire for the pleasures of paradise!

Chapter 7
The Convergence of Science and Torah

To demonstrate the credibility of a Jewish philosophy of history, it will first be necessary to reveal the convergence of science and the cosmology of the Torah, more precisely the principle of *creatio ex nihilo* set forth in the first verse of Genesis.

Genesis and the Big Bang

Physicist Gerald L. Schroeder writes: "Of all the ancient accounts of creation, only that of Genesis has warranted a second reading by the scientific community. It alone records a sequence of events that approaches the scientific account of our cosmic origin."[141] Dr. Schroeder has especially in mind the Big Bang theory. Based on Einstein's general theory of relativity, the abundance of evidence confirming the Big Bang has made *creatio ex nihilo* the reigning cosmological principle in the community of scientists. The dogma of the eternity of the universe, which held sway for millennia in philosophy and science as well as among eastern religions, has thus been discarded. In fact, more and more astronomers, astrophysicists, physicists, and mathematicians—hitherto atheists or agnostics—now admit that the universe had a Beginning, which suggests even to them a Beginner.

Genesis 1:1, "In the beginning God created (*bara*) the heavens and the earth…" contains a unique and seldom used word in the Torah, namely, *bara*. This word, translated as "created," has as its primary definition "bringing into existence something that did not exist before." In Genesis 1:1, *bara* means creation from nothing. Here "nothing" signifies the absence of matter and energy as well as the dimensions of space and time—hence nothing which any human being can detect and measure. The Big Bang theory therefore accords with the Genesis account of Creation. Actually, cosmologists are currently investigating dozens of variations of the Big Bang. What all these theories have in common are the following: (1) a cosmic beginning that began a finite time ago; (2) a continuous, universal cosmic expansion; and (3) a cosmic cooling from an extremely hot initial state. How did scientists arrive at the Big Bang?

When Einstein proposed his theory of general relativity in 1915, the cosmological doctrine of an eternal universe held in a static state throughout infinite time reigned supreme. Although his field equations predicted an expanding universe, Einstein was trying to construct a static model universe that would not collapse as a result of its own self-gravitation. But since Hubble's discovery in 1929 of the recession of the galaxies, the theory of an expanding universe has dominated cosmology.[142] Knowing the rate at which the universe is expanding, one can extrapolate backwards to determine the size of the universe "in the beginning," that is, at the moment when expansion began. At that moment, about 15 billion (Earth) years ago, the entire universe—all the galaxies, with their millions of stars, the dust and gas, the intergalactic matter, all the energy and even the four dimensions of space and time—was squeezed into an "atomic nucleus" or "singularity" of infinite or near infinite density, temperature, and pressure. That singularity, at which all the known laws of physics come to an end, was itself created (*bara*) from "nothing." From that singularity, whose volume is estimated by some to have been much smaller than the period at the end of this sentence, the universe burst forth and expanded, and it continues to expand. What an incredible and *unintended* confirmation, *by science*—indeed, *by a Jew who was not even a believer*—of the infinite power and majesty of God! Strange indeed are God's ways. Strange too that estimates of the age of the universe from Jewish sources antedating the fifteenth century range from 2.5 to 17.5 billion years.[143]

Ponder, therefore, the words of the great Torah scholar and Kabalist Nahmanides (1194-1270). Commenting on Genesis 1:1 some seven hundred and fifty years ago, Nahmanides writes:

> The Holy One, blessed be He, created all things from absolute non-existence. Now we have no expression in the sacred language for bringing [into existence] something from "nothing" other than the word *bara* (created). Everything that exists under the sun or above was not made from non-existence at the outset. Instead He brought forth from total and absolute nothing a very thin substance devoid of corporeality but having a power of potency, fit to assume form and to proceed from potentiality into reality. This was the primary matter created by God.[144]

This "primary matter" is nothing but energy, which can be converted into matter (and vice versa) according to Einstein's famous formula $E=mc^2$. Commenting further on Genesis 1:1, Nahmanides says, "with this creation, which was like a very small point having no substance, everything in the heavens and on the earth was created." That point is the "singularity" from which the Big Bang originated. Nahmanides derived this knowledge from the Talmud (c. 500 CE). Physics has thus confirmed the first verse of Genesis, whose meaning was known 1,500 years ago by Rabbis who had received this secret knowledge via the oral tradition going back to the time of Moses.

According to Nobel physicist Steven Weinberg, the strongest support for the Big Bang comes from measuring the cosmic background radiation left over from the hot early stages of the universe. This radiation, predicted by George Gamow in 1948 and discovered by Arno Penzias and Robert Wilson in 1965, was measured by the Cosmic Background Explorer (COBE) satellite beginning in 1989. The measurements recorded in 1992 were awesome. In mapping the sky, COBE detected nonuniformities in the temperature of radiation that had separated from the dense matter of the universe about a million years after the Big Bang. It is believed that these nonuniformities or ripples were the effects of the gravitational field produced by clumps of matter when the universe was first becoming transparent to radiation. COBE thus revealed what astrophysicists had been seeking: the mechanism for the (eventual) formation of star clusters and the galaxies! The renowned theoretical physicist Stephen Hawking called the COBE findings "the discovery of the century, if not of all time." Astronomer George Smoot, project leader for the COBE satellite, declared, "What we have found is evidence for the birth of the universe…It's like looking at God."[145]

Since the Big Bang theory entails a finite universe, the question arises: What is there *beyond*? Outside the universe there is no space. The notion of emptiness, as opposed to fullness, applies only inside the universe. It bears repeating that space was created at the moment of the Big Bang. Hence there are no dimensions outside the universe (and of course the human mind reasons and calculates in terms of spatial dimensions). The same applies to time. The question of what went on *before* the Big Bang is meaningless, since time itself was created with that awesome event.[146]

Leaving aside the two religions derived from Judaism, only the Torah unambiguously states that time is finite, that time has a beginning, and that God created time, as should now ring true from the Genesis account of Creation. Indeed, Dr. Schroeder, using Einstein's equation for gravitational time dilation, shows that the duration and events of the billions of years which followed the Big Bang, and the events of the first six days of Genesis, are in fact one and the same! Here are some relevant passages from *The Science of God*. Schroeder suggests that we read

> the opening chapter of Genesis a few times, paying particular attention to the description of the events and the flow of time related to those

events. Then read any other chapter in the entire Bible, again concentrating on the flow of events and the related flow of time. Note how the context changes. The description of time in the Bible is divided into two categories: the first six days and all the time thereafter.

During those six days, blocks of time are described and then we are told that a day passed. This is repeated in a totally objective fashion six times....There is no intimate relation between the events and the passage of time....Rather, we are told that the land and waters separated, plant life appeared, "And there was evening and there was morning a third day" (Gen. 1:9-13). No hint is given for the time each of these major events took.

With the appearance of humankind the accounting changes dramatically. The events now become the cause of the flow of time. Adam and Eve live 130 years and are the parents of Seth (Gen. 4:25; 5:3). Seth lived 105 years and is father to Enoch (Gen. 5:6). The passage of time is totally tied to the earthly events being described. These are indeed years of an earthly calendar.

Now here's a puzzle. If, as th[e] ancient commentators claimed, the six days of Genesis are twenty-four-hour days, then why not include them in the calendar? Why not have the calendar start six days earlier? And why must these commentators tell me the days are twenty-four hours each? The Bible says "day." I know a day takes twenty-four hours to pass. Why did they think I would think otherwise?

[Actually]...our questions were anticipated thousands of years ago. The six days are not included in the calendar because within those (six twenty-four-hour) days are all the secrets and ages of the universe. The confusion mounts. How can six days contain the ages of the universe? And if they are truly ages, then why refer to them as days?

The ancient realization that somehow the days of Genesis contained the generations of the cosmos is based on two biblical verses: "These are the *generations* of the heavens and the earth when they were created in the *day* that the Eternal God made the earth and the heavens" (Gen. 2:4); and "This is the book of the *generations* of Adam in the *day* that God created Adam" (Gen. 5:1). In both verses, generations are juxtaposed to days [that is, to one day] of Genesis.

If the six twenty-four-hour days of Genesis were adequate to include all the days of the universe, the cosmic flow from the creation at the Big Bang to the creation of humankind, we clearly require an understanding of time that is not obvious to our unaided senses. Albert Einstein provided that understanding....

> The law of relativity tells us that the flow of time at a location with high gravity or high velocity is actually slower than at a location with lower gravity or lower velocity. This means that the duration between ticks of a clock...in the high-G (or high-V) environment is actually longer than the duration between ticks on a clock...in the low-G (or low-V) environment. These differences in time's passage are known as time dilation....[147]

After explaining the equality between the six days of Genesis and fifteen billion Earth years during which the entire universe was created, Dr. Schroeder refers to Nahmanides' above quoted commentary on Genesis 1:1, and points out that the great Kabalist learned from his teachers that the first word of the Bible, *beresheet*—*"In the beginning of"*—means in the beginning of time. Biblical time thus begins with the appearance of matter—an extraordinary insight. Of course, it remained for the mathematics of general relativity to show how the six days of Creation recorded in Genesis is equal to fifteen billion (Earth) years.

It follows from the preceding discussion that the modern dichotomy between science and religion, or rather, between science and the Torah, has been placed in question by science itself. Indeed, a recent scientific article in one of the foremost international journals of physics bears the title, "Creation of the Universe from Nothing":

> At the 1990 meeting of the American Astronomical Society, Professor John Mather of Columbia University, an astrophysicist who also served on the staff of NASA's Goddard Center, presented "the most dramatic support ever" for an open universe [i.e., one which supports a cosmological proof of God's existence]. According to a journalist present, Mather's keynote address was greeted with thunderous applause, which led the meeting's chairman, Dr. Geoffrey Burbidge [an atheist astronomer], to comment: "It seems clear that the audience is in favor of the book of Genesis—at least the first verse or so, which seems to have been confirmed."[148]

QUANTUM MECHANICS

We must now discuss quantum mechanics (QM), which competes with general relativity for the laurels of science. Whereas general relativity describes gravity and the macrophysical world of space and time, QM deals with microphysical world where space and time do not seem to exist, thus confirming the Torah's cosmological principle of *creatio ex nihilo*.

It should first be noted that QM holds that microphysical events are governed by statistical law. This alone renders dubious the dogma of a self-sustaining, eternal universe. One need only ask: If the universe is eternal, what is it that sustains the stability of the mean associated with statistical law? For however remote the probability, the structure of the universe should have "collapsed" given its supposed eternity and its merely statistical foundations. Some cosmologists might object by resurrecting the model of an oscillating and self-sustaining universe proposed thousands of years ago by the Hindus and adopted by Buddhism and other eastern religions, as well as by various new age philosophies. But such a universe runs against the Second Law of Thermodynamics, that of Energy Decay or Entropy. As I point out elsewhere:

> This law states that every system left to itself always tends to move from order to disorder, its energy tending to be transformed into lower levels of availability, finally reaching the state of complete randomness and unavailability for further work. When all the energy of the universe has been degraded to random motion of molecules of uniform low-temperature, the universe will have died a "heat-death." The fact that the universe is not yet dead is clear evidence that it is not infinitely old. And so, whereas the Second Law, that of energy decay, requires the universe to have a beginning, the First Law, that of Total Energy Conservation, precludes its having begun itself.[149]

The contradiction between the First and Second Law of Thermodynamics is dissolved by the Torah. The statistical laws of quantum mechanics are not self-sustaining and cannot be in a created universe. The universe continues to exist only by virtue of the ceaseless Will of the Creator, but Whose Will manifests itself to man as "laws of nature." Stated another way, what the physicist postulates as a law of nature is in reality what the Talmud calls a *Shevua*, an "oath" or promise that God will not (as a rule) change some stable form or predictable regularity of existence. This applies to the statistical laws governing the microphysical world of QM.

Although QM is said to provide a comprehensive basis for the description of ordinary atomic, physical, and chemical properties of matter, its conceptual framework involves unsolved paradoxes. These originate in Planck's infinitesimal *quantum of action*. Unlike classical physics, with its indivisible atoms of matter, QM postulates indivisible atoms of action in which a definite quantity of energy is associated with a definite period of time. Accordingly, microphysical effects, which would seem to be essentially capable of continuous increase or diminution, actually increase or diminish in discrete "jumps." In the domain of microphysics, the little quantum raises large epistemological problems.

For example, when quantum physicists say that an orbiting electron can jump from one energy level to another without taking any intermediate values, this suggests that quantum transitions are not comprehensible in terms of space and time. If so, it will be very difficult to describe the behavior of an electron or to say just what it is. This prompted J. Robert Oppenheimer to remark in all seriousness:

> If we ask…whether the position of the electron remains the same, we must say "No"; if we ask whether the electron's position changes in time, we must say "No"; if we ask whether it is in motion, we must say "No."[150]

Even to call an electron an elementary "particle" is misleading in view of the fact that microphysical "objects" exhibit wave as well as particle characteristics. Particle-wave duality is a fundamental principle (and conceptual dilemma) of QM. Werner Heisenberg writes:

> The electrons which form an atom's shells are no longer things in the sense of classical physics, things which could be unambiguously described by concepts of location, velocity, energy, and size. When we get down to the atomic level, the objective world of space and time no longer exists, and the mathematical symbols of theoretical physics refer merely to possibilities, not to facts….The very attempt to conjure up a picture [of elementary particles] is wholly to misrepresent them.[151]

The words "particle" and "wave" are nothing more than abstractions used to describe "unitary phenomena." The dual description of these phenomena arises from the inadequacy of our language. Moreover, according to Heisenberg's "uncertainty principle," we can never measure the position and velocity of a particle at the same time. The more accurately we know the one, the less accurately we can know the other. The observer or the instrument of observation (perhaps using photons) affects the position or velocity of the "object" in question. Hence, as Nobel physicist Richard Feynman says, "Nature permits us to calculate only probabilities."

The "uncertainty principle" indicates that QM involves a fundamental indeterminism in nature. Some see this as confirming free will—a controversial issue. Steven Weinberg, a skeptic, says, "I cannot find any messages for human life in quantum mechanics that are different in any important way from those of Newtonian physics."[152] Contrary to Weinberg, Nobel physicist Eugene Wigner contends that "the laws of quantum mechanics cannot be formulated, with all their implications, without reference to the concept of consciousness."[153] Gerald Schroeder puts it this way:

> Quantum mechanics has proven that the visible [or macrophysical] world is not a direct extension of the subatomic [or microphysical] world from which it is constructed. By this it has laid the basis for the biblical concept that the mind is not a mere extension of neurochemical reactions of the brain. QM does something much more important than destroy determinism—it provides the opening *and the mechanism* for choice.[154]

Hardly convincing, but Schroeder will later provide a more compelling basis for free choice.

That subatomic events cannot be understood in terms of space and time means that QM, unlike general relativity, involves a fundamental discontinuity in nature comparable to the absolute discontinuity involved in the Torah principle of *creatio ex nihilo*. This suggests that *the Torah's cosmology dissolves the contradiction between QM and relativity physics at the moment or point of creation*—at which point, says Stephen Hawking, all known laws of physics "break down."[155]

The contradiction between the space-time continuum postulated by relativity physics and the discontinuity postulated by quantum mechanics suggests the need of a new and more comprehensive theory of the universe—more compelling than Hawking's very tentative *Theory of Everything*. Notice that while quantum mechanics and general relativity are conceptually inconsistent with each other, they are in decisive respects conceptually consistent with the Torah. *This suggests that the Torah stands at a higher conceptual level.* How can this conceptual level be articulated, or rather, what evidence can persuade a rational mind of its existence?

According to the Jewish sages, the universe was created for man. (See Hullin 89a.) Hence it is all the more remarkable that during the past three decades, evidence has accumulated which, while eliminating anthropomorphism in physics, has prompted scientists to propose the ultimate anthropomorphism: the "Anthropic Principle"! The essence of this principle was captured by Professor Freeman J. Dyson of the Institute for Advanced Study at Princeton, one of the world's leading mathematical physicists: "As we look out into the universe and identify the many peculiarities of physics and astronomy that have worked together for our benefit, it almost seems as if the universe must in some sense have known that we were coming."[156]

The Anthropic Principle postulates a linkage between the fine-tuning of various physical parameters of the universe and the prerequisites of human existence. For example, the fine-tuning concerning the energy of the Big Bang has been quantified as one part in 10^{120}. As Dr. Schroeder vividly puts it, "If the energy of the Big Bang were different by one point out of

1000000000000000000000000000000000000000000000000000000000000000000000000000000000000000000000000000000000000000000000000

there would be no life anywhere in our universe."[157] Moreover, astronomer Michael A. Corey points out that if the gravitational constant (G)

> were slightly larger, stars would have burned too hot and much too quickly to support the fragile needs of life; but if it were slightly smaller, the intrastellar process of nuclear fusion would have never initiated, and life would have been incapable of arising here. This same rationale can also be applied to the expansion rate of the nascent universe...If the...expansion rate happened to be slightly greater than the presently observed value, life-supporting galaxies would have been unable to form; but if it were slightly smaller, the early universe would have collapsed back in on itself shortly after the Big Bang. Either way and no life forms would have been possible....
>
> The challenge is to find a plausible explanation for this fine-tuning. According to the British mathematical physicist Roger Penrose, the odds that our biocentric universe could have accidentally evolved into its present fine-tuned configuration are an astounding one in 10 to the 10^{123}, which is a number so vast that it couldn't be written on a piece of paper the size of the entire visible universe. This is why many theorists have posited the existence of a "super-calculating intellect" to account for this fine-tuning.[158]

Although the validity of the Anthropic Principle has been challenged by some scientists, consider the statements of these luminaries in the scientific community.[159] Former skeptic Fred Hoyle concludes that "a superintellect has monkeyed with physics, as well as with chemistry and biology." Paul Davies has moved from promoting atheism to conceding, "It seems as though somebody has fine-tuned nature's numbers to make the universe. The impression of design is overwhelming." No less than Stephen Hawking concedes: "It would be very difficult to explain why the universe should have begun in just this way, except as the act of a God who intended to create beings like us."

Still, what has the Anthropic Principle to do with the contradiction between the determinism and space-time continuum of relativity physics and the indeterminism and discontinuity of quantum mechanics? Since neither one nor the other can be regarded as a final and complete theory of reality, it seems to the present writer that both are somehow subordinate to the Anthropic Principle, hence to what is distinctively human—the *mind*. As dreams clearly indicate, the mind transcends space-time and yet is embedded in space-time (the brain). The same may be said of quantum mechanics and also of light, whose speed is independent of any space-time frame of reference. The universe comprehended by QM and relativity physics is a unity of opposites. The same may be said of the mind, the end point of creation intended to be *creation's narrator*, hence to speak of God's infinite wisdom.

"*With wisdom God created the heavens and the earth*" (Proverbs 3:19). It is given to the mind of man to probe this wisdom, impelled today by the apparent contradiction between quantum mechanics and relativity physics. Both involve energy. The wisdom mentioned in Proverbs 3:19 must be more fundamental than energy. If it could be articulated—of course within the limits of finitude—it would transcend the contradiction between relativity physics and quantum mechanics and thereby vastly increase the power of man's mind over nature. As King David said in his praise of the Creator: "*You have made man a little less than God*" (Psalms 8:6).

Here another word is necessary. For King Solomon to say, "*With wisdom God created the heavens and the earth*" is to say, in effect, that the Torah is the genetic material of all that exists, that the letters and words of the Torah are the *means* by which God created the world and by which He continues to supervise all that occurs in the world, including human history (*Shabbat* 88b). The Torah must therefore contain the secret by which to overcome the contradiction between relativity physics and quantum mechanics.

THE LETTERS AND WORDS OF THE TORAH

In 1842, Rabbi Israel Lipschitz of Danzig delivered a remarkable lecture in which he said, in part:

> As regards the past, Rabbi Abahu [c. 300 CE] says at the beginning of Beresheet Rabbah [Genesis 3:7] that the words "and it was evening and it was morning" (in the apparent absence of the sun) indicate

that "there was a series of epochs *before* then; the Holy One built worlds and destroyed them, approving of some and not others."....

This doctrine, which has been handed down in secret for many generations, enables us to understand clearly many verses in Isaiah and Jeremiah which speak of the destruction of the earth, the "rolling up" of the heavens, the "new heavens and the new earth," and many others of similar import.

We are enabled to appreciate to the full the wonderful accuracy of our holy Torah when we see that this secret doctrine, handed down by the word of mouth for so long, and revealed by the sages of the Kabala many centuries ago, has been borne out in the clearest possible manner by the science of our generation.

The questing spirit of man, probing and delving into the recesses of the earth, in the Pyrenees, the Carpathians, the Rocky Mountains in America, and the Himalayas has found them to be formed of mighty layers of rock, lying upon one another in amazing chaotic formations, explicable only in terms of revolutionary transformations of the earth's surface.

Probing still further, geologists have found four distinct layers of rock, and between the layers fossilized remains of creatures; those in the lower layers being of monstrous size and structure, while those in the higher and more recent layers being progressively smaller in size but incomparably more refined in structure and form.

After describing these fossilized creatures in some detail, Rabbi Lipschitz continues:

> From all this we can see that all the Kabalists have told us for so many centuries about the fourfold destruction and renewal of the earth has found its clearest confirmation in our time....
>
> The very first letter of the Torah, with its traditional four *taggin* [i.e., pointers] hints that our present epoch is the fourth, and the fact that it is a *beth* [whose numerical value or *Gematria* is two], and written large, indicates that the greatest peak of creation, a thinking being, now inhabits the world for the second time.
>
> For, in my opinion, the prehistoric men whose remains have been discovered in our time, and who lived long before Adam, are identical with the 974 pre-Adamite generations referred to in the Talmud (*Shabbat* 88[b] and *Hagiga* 14[a]), and lived in the epoch immediately before our own.[160]

What Rabbi Lipschitz means by the "second time" (and, by implication, the "first time") is not clear. Neanderthal appeared about 150,000 years ago. According to paleontologist Stephen Jay Gould, Neanderthal contributed nothing to our immediate genetic heritage.[161] Apparently, they lived in Europe while we emerged in Africa. Aside from their sloped brow and massive jaw, the Neanderthal were similar to us in many morphological respects, including their cranial capacity. Their fossil remains contain stone tools and indicate that they had started to bury their dead. They knew nothing, however, of representational art. They disappear 40,000 years ago and are replaced by Cro-Magnon, although the two had coexisted for tens of thousands of years. The morphology of the new hominids is essentially the same as that of Modern Man. Finely shaped tools and even stone lamps for wicks (suggesting the use of oil) are found in their burial sites. But we have yet to reach *Homo sapiens*.

Let us therefore return to Adam. Genesis 2:7 says that God "breathed into his nostrils the *neshama* of life and *adam* became a living soul." Nahmanides offers the extraordinary interpretation that this verse "is stating that man *wholly* became a living soul and was transformed into *another* man." Which means that *before* the *neshama* there was something like a man, but a man that was not wholly and distinctively human![162]

We may arrive at the same conclusion another way. The six days of Genesis culminate in the *making* and *creating* of Adam: "And God said let us make *adam* in Our image..." (Gen. 1:26); "And God created the *adam* in His image..." (Gen. 1:27). "The making of mankind," Schroeder points out, "relates to the body of Adam. The Hebrew word *adam* has its root in the Hebrew *adamah*, meaning soil. The *creation* of Adam relates to the human soul, the *neshama*."[163] The difference between the "making" and "creation" of Adam applies to the making and creation of the universe. Genesis 1:1 says: "In the beginning God *created* the heavens and the earth." Exodus 31:17 says: "For six days the Eternal *made* the heavens and the earth." The objects of the two verbs, *creating* and *made*, are identical in both verses: "the heavens and the earth." As we have already learned, however, the Hebrew word for create, *bara*, means to create something from "nothing." This, says Schroeder,

> is an instantaneous act. Genesis 1:1 is teaching that in the beginning, in a flash now known as the big bang, God created from absolute nothing the raw materials of the universe. Then, as Exodus 31:17 relates, this primordial stuff during the following six days was fashioned into the universe we know. Making, we see from the verse in Exodus, requires raw materials, and takes place over a period of time. As the Bible says:

> "For *six days* the Lord made the heavens and the earth [from the primordial matter created 'in the beginning']."
>
> The universe was first created (Gen. 1:1) and then made (Ex. 31:17). That order was essential. Before creation there was nothing with which to make.
>
> For Adam the order was reversed. The fact that Adam was first "made" (Gen. 1:26) and only later "created" (Gen 1:27) informs us unequivocally that some amount of time passed during which Adam was fashioned. The *neshama* was implanted only after that vessel was complete. Whether that time was measured in microseconds or millions of years is not certain from the text. What is certain is that the making of Adam's body was not instantaneous and its making preceded the introduction of the *neshama*. Making takes time. The ultimate change from the final form into a human was instantaneous, the creation of the *neshama*.[164]

It appears, however, that creatures with a human morphology—presumably Cro-Magnon—still existed at the time of Adam. This the Talmud deduces from two verses of Genesis. The first tells us: "*And Adam knew again his wife and she bore him a son and called his name Seth*" (Gen. 4:25). Four verses later we read: "*And Adam lived one hundred and thirty years and was father to a son in his own likeness, after his own image and called his name Seth*" (Gen. 5:3). Again Schroeder:

> The Talmud deduces from these two verses that following the trauma of Cain murdering Abel, Adam and Eve separated. It was not until 130 years after Cain and Abel that "Adam knew again his wife [Eve]" (Gen. 4:25).
>
> The Talmud asked why the Bible states "again" in reference to Adam's relations with Eve. Eve was Adam's wife, so obviously it was with her that he had relations. The "again" is superfluous and it therefore teaches something. The answer the Talmud supplies is that during those 130 years of separation, Adam had sexual relations with other beings (the nature of those beings is not clear). From those unions [we learn from the Talmud] came children that "were not human in the true sense of the word. They had not the spirit of God....It is acknowledged that a being who does not possess this spirit is not human but *a mere animal in human shape and form* [!]. Yet such a creature has the power of causing harm and injury, a power which does not belong to other creatures. For those gifts of

intelligence and judgment with which he has been endowed for the purpose of acquiring perfection...are used for wicked and mischievous ends.[165]

The fossil record suggests that these creatures were Cro-Magnon. Lacking Eve's spiritual contributions, however, the offspring of Adam's relations with them would be less than human.

Dr. Schroeder's brilliant reconstruction of the Genesis account of Adam clarifies Rabbi Lipschitz's reference to the pre-Adamite generations referred to in the Talmud. Unlike these pre-Adamites, *Homo sapiens* have a *neshama*. Of course, and as Schroeder indicates, "Archeologists can never discover the fossil remains of *neshama*. It is totally spiritual. That notwithstanding, archeological evidence has confirmed our *biblical* heritage. As it is written: 'The truth shall spring up from the Earth'" (Psalms 85:12).[166]

Rabbi Lipschitz's remarkable lecture, delivered seventeen years before the publication of Darwin's *Origin of the Species*, was printed in a contemporaneous edition of the Mishnah; and its approach was approved by one of the greatest *halachic* authorities of the nineteenth and twentieth centuries, Rabbi Sholom Mordechai Schwadron of Poland.[167]

This is not to suggest any anticipation of, let alone agreement with, the Darwinian doctrine of evolution, namely, that organisms evolve in small cumulative steps into more complex organisms through vast periods of time. This doctrine assumes the existence, in the fossil record, of transitional forms that link one type of organism and another. The rarity of such transitional forms in the fossil record, quips Gould, "persists as the trade secret of paleontology. The history of life," he writes, "is not a continuum of development, but a record punctuated by brief, sometimes geologically instantaneous, episodes of mass extinctions and subsequent diversification."[168] Recent research indicates that terrestrial cataclysms have occurred in the past resulting in the sudden extinction of millions of species. Gould therefore adds "contingency" to the mechanisms of evolution associated with Darwinism: survival of the fittest, adaptation, and natural selection. However, to maintain with neo-Darwinism that life originated as a result of chance is another matter. Indeed, as Schroeder remarks: "Since 1979, articles based on the premise that life arose through random reactions over billions of years are not accepted in reputable journals."[169]

The Book of Genesis proclaimed development 3,300 years ago: first came aquatic animals, then winged creatures and land animals, then mammals and finally humans. There is no inconsistency here between Torah and science. Torah-oriented Jews like Rabbi Lipschitz know that scientific knowledge can only confirm truths hidden in the book of Truth. The illustrious Gaon of Vilna said in the introduction to his work on Euclid: "To the degree that a man is lacking knowledge of secular science he will [be lacking] in the wisdom of the Torah."[170]

No intrinsic contradiction can exist between the Torah and veridical scientific theories because the two reveal the infinite wisdom and power of the one and only God. However, it needs to be emphasized that unlike the Torah, neither general relativity nor quantum mechanics can teach us how man should live. Indeed, so long as mathematical physics remains the paradigm of knowledge—of knowledge severed from the letters and words of the Torah—this tremendous monument of man's intellectual power can only lead mankind to destruction. A "value free" science, one that can teach us nothing about the Good and the Beautiful, requires the conceptual constraints of a higher order of knowledge. Perhaps a Jewish philosophy of history will help open the door to such knowledge.

Epilogue

Kabala teaches that creation is a divine act of *Tzimtzum*, a spiritual contraction by which the Creator removes part of His infinite power to generate the universe. Hence the idea of *creatio ex nihilo*, creation of something from nothing, is misleading.[171] The act of *Tzimzum* signifies the "creation of nothing from something," for God is the only true existent, while the universe is a derived existence dependent wholly on God's providence. Moses, the humblest of men, understood, "*We are nothing.*" (See *Hullin* 89a.) Nor is this all.

Consider the first word of the Torah, *Be'resheet*—usually translated as "In the beginning." The 2,100-year-old Aramaic translation sees *Be'resheet* as a compound word consisting of *Be'*, "with," and "*resheet*," first wisdom," yielding: "*With wisdom God created the heavens and the earth.*" This is exactly what we read in Proverbs 3:19. Wisdom or "ideas"—think of Plato's—constitutes the DNA of the universe. And of course this wisdom, manifested in nature, is accessible to the human intellect. This brings us back to the Anthropic Principle. By postulating the Anthropic Principle, scientists now agree with the sages of the Talmud that the universe was made for man. This principle actually implies a fundamental subordination of nature to human history, which is charmingly confirmed in the story of Joseph. The fulfillment of Joseph's dreams of ascendancy over his family (Genesis 37:5-10) required a famine in Egypt. It was as if God arranged nature (Genesis 50:20) to enable Joseph to become Egypt's viceroy! And of course it was in Egypt that the Jews became a people. Perhaps the Anthropic Principle should be called the "Divine Principle."

Part II

CHAPTER 8
THE TORAH'S WORLD HISTORICAL PROGRAM: THE CHOSEN PEOPLE

Out of all the people that are on the face of the earth, the Lord your God has chosen you to be a people belonging exclusively to Him (Deuteronomy 14:2).

This people have I created that they may relate My praise (Isaiah 43:21).

JEWISH MONOTHEISM

HAVING SHOWN how the Genesis account of Creation is substantiated by general relativity, quantum mechanics, and paleontology, we can now inquire into the Torah's world-historical program, for which purpose let us review the First and Second Commandments:

And God spoke all these words [to the Children of Israel] saying: I am the Lord your God, who brought you out of the land of Egypt, out of the house of bondage. You shall have no other gods before Me (Exodus 20:1-3).

From the First Commandment we learn that the God of Israel intervenes in human affairs. He is not only the God of Nature, but also the God of History. History must therefore have a purpose, and the Jewish People, whom God liberated from Egyptian bondage, must be the instrument of that purpose. "*This people have I created that they may relate My praise*" (Isaiah 43:21). To relate God's praise is to show how God's infinite wisdom, power, and graciousness are manifested in nature and in human history. The Jews were chosen, therefore, to be the educators of mankind. Liberated from Egypt, a state whose ruler was worshipped as a god, and whose people were steeped in paganism and polytheism, the Jews were to exemplify a way of life guided by ethical monotheism.

Alfred North Whitehead writes: "The Jews are the first example of refusal to worship the state [over the individual]."[172] John Adams, Harvard graduate and second president of the United States, said this of the Jews: "They have done more to civilize men than any other Nation."[173] Mark well this extraordinary statement of Nietzsche: "Wherever the Jews have attained to influence, they have taught to analyze more subtly, to argue more acutely, to write more clearly and purely: it has always been their problem to bring people to '*raison*.'"[174]

Although these gentiles testify to the influence of the Jews on mankind, we are still far from articulating a Jewish philosophy of history. To this end we must clarify the meaning of Jewish monotheism.

Although the subject of monotheism was broached in the previous chapter, we shall have to probe more deeply into this subject to show that there are fundamental differences between Jewish monotheism and its Christian and Islamic counterparts. Our initial task is to understand three names of the Creator. The first is the Ineffable Name consisting of four letters *YHVH*, the Tetragrammaton, translated above as "Lord." The Tetragrammaton is a name exclusively used by Jews, for as Judah Halevi states in *The Kuzari*, "no other people knows its meaning."[175] Jews never pronounce the *YHVH*; they refer to it in prayer as "Adonoy" or, more familiarly, as "*HaShem*"—a Hebrew word meaning "the Name." This name is also referred to as the "Eternal." The second name of the Creator is "*Elohim*," translated above as "God." The third name is *EH'YEH* (Exodus 3:14), which refers to God as the Eternal Now.

Consider first, *HaShem*: "*Hear O Israel: HaShem is our God, HaShem is One*" (Deuteronomy 6:4). Only *HaShem* is One; only *HaShem* has Absolute Unity. Absolute Unity is traditionally understood as that which is absolutely separate and distinguishable from all existing things. It is not subject to creation, destruction, change, or limitation; nor can it be described by any physical or mental category. Consequently, there is nothing we can predicate of *HaShem*. We say He is One, not to establish His Unity as we understand that term, but only to exclude plurality. When we attribute to Him existence, eternity, infinity, will, omnipresence, omniscience, omnipotence, lovingkindness, or any other perfection, it is only to negate their contraries, not to establish them as understood by the human mind. "*For My thoughts are not your thoughts*" (Isaiah 55:8). Thus far, the traditional view.

The traditional view also takes cognizance of the anthropomorphisms in the Torah and usually construes them allegorically. Thus, when Moses asks *HaShem* to see His glory, *HaShem* responds by saying that no man can see His "face," only His "back" (Exodus 33:20, 23). Suffice to say the following. *HaShem*, in His essence, is absolutely unknowable. This may be called the a priori aspect of *HaShem*, of which we can say nothing without succumbing to idolatry (a negative theology). But there is also the a posteriori aspect of *HaShem*, of which we can say something without succumbing to idolatry (a positive theology). This second aspect of *HaShem* is described in various ways in the Torah. These descriptions are necessarily anthropomorphic. They apply only to *HaShem's* manifestations or actions, else they would involve contradiction. For example, when *HaShem* asks Cain, who had just murdered Abel, "*Where is your brother?*" (Genesis 4:9), this obviously contradicts *HaShem's* omniscience. The contradiction is dissolved by bringing into juxtaposition two of the most important concepts of the Torah, both of which underlie human freedom and dignity: Repentance on the part of man, and Graciousness on the part of *HaShem*. (See Exodus 34:6.) Neither of these qualities could come into effect had Cain been summarily confronted by his crime, condemned and punished. In this example we see one of the purposes of anthropomorphisms: they help us understand the ways by which *HaShem* relates to men as well as the general ways He would have men relate to each other.

The fact that anthropomorphisms do not describe *HaShem* in Himself but only His manifestations is analogous to one of the strange and revolutionary principles of quantum mechanics. According to quantum theory, the macrophysical world—the world of sense perception—is a derived world. Though real, it is not, physically speaking, the ultimately real. To discover the latter we must grasp the microphysical world, the world of subatomic processes. What is distinctive here is that we can only know about the microphysical world indirectly, that is, by its macrophysical or observable effects. The spatial and temporal concepts used to describe these effects are really metaphors. They do not apply literally to the microphysical world itself (just as anthropomorphisms do not apply to *HaShem* in Himself). In fact, to attribute spatio-temporal properties to microphysical processes is to succumb to anthropomorphism in science.

Returning to the First Commandment—"*I am the Lord your God, who brought you out of the land of Egypt, out of the house of bondage*" (Exodus 20:2)—this is the basis for Deuteronomy's referring to the Chosen People as "*belonging exclusively to Him.*" The First Commandment involves far more than a belief system affirming the existence of God. According to the philosopher Rabbi Joseph B. Soloveitchik, man must serve and try to commune with God, and this he can do through four media of experience: intellectual, volitional, emotional, and dialogical (i.e., prayer). In the present context we can only elaborate on the intellectual medium:

> The intellectual approach to God is closely bound up either with scientific-metaphysical research and knowledge or with the study of the Torah. Maimonides considered both of these cognitive performances to be an expression of man's clinging to God. Thinking in terms of eternal truth, whether theoretical or ethical, is an act of craving for

God.... At this intellectual level, Judaism considered the study of the Torah as the most sublime kind of worship, a way of meeting God, of breaking through the barrier separating the Absolute from the contingent and the relative....[176]

Israel's first Chief Rabbi, Avraham Yitzhak Kook (1865-1935), who was also well versed in philosophy, writes: "Monotheism seeks to probe the unity of the world, of man, of the entire range of reality..." Rabbi Kook also maintained that Israel alone affirms "undiluted monotheism."[177] He admits, of course, that there are in the gentile world pious men, philosophers, men of God, but there is not a nation—besides Israel—whose soul, whose way of life, whose *raison d'etre*, signifies the Divine Idea in the world.[178]

Also significant for Rabbi Kook is that unlike Judaism, gentile religions remain locked in a persistent struggle with indigenous cultures. These religions, he sees, were imposed on pagan nations which often revert to barbarism. Notice the frequent eruption of fratricidal wars of Arab-Islamic states. Notice, too, that Christian Europe has been periodically drenched in rivers of blood.[179] Notice, moreover, that unlike the Quran and the New Testament, the Torah is not the recorded source of a religion but the history of the divine founding of a nation. In Israel alone one cannot separate religion and nationality without destroying Israel's essence. This fact distinguishes its monotheism from that of Islam and Christianity.

Moreover, the founders of Islam and Christianity form an integral part of the faith. Thus, it is not sufficient to believe in the gospels of these messengers, but in the messengers themselves. This is why "holy" wars and forced conversions punctuate the history of these religions. How unlike Judaism, which claims no monopoly on heaven and prohibits proselytizing. Moreover, the Talmud teaches that "a heathen that studies the Torah is equal to a High Priest" (*Avoda Zara* 3a). We have here a magnanimous and gracious monotheism. Indeed, the Torah repeatedly reminds Jews that because they were slaves in Egypt, they should be all the more disposed to treat strangers in their midst with kindness. This does not mean they are to tolerate those who do not abide by the Seven Noahide Laws, especially the prohibition against idolatry. According to Judaism, idolatry is the initial cause of every evil, for example, the slaughtering of children in Moloch worship.

Clearly, the First Commandment logically entails the Second, the elimination of all forms of idolatry. As previously defined, idolatry is the worship of any created thing, including the products of the human intellect, be it a philosophic or scientific theory, a political or religious ideology, or a particular form of government. Consistent therewith, let us equate idolatry with "reification," which may be defined as the postulation of any physical or mental existent, process, or law as autonomous or self-sustaining. Reification thus applies to any philosophic or scientific monism, dualism, or pluralism which attempts to explain the totality or any part of existence in terms of one or more independent or self-subsisting entities. The Torah therefore rejects the exaltation or fixation of any humanly constructed system of governance. It forbids fetishism or the complete devotion of the self to that which is bounded. Hence the Fourth Commandment: *"Six days shall you work and accomplish all your tasks; but the seventh day is Sabbath to HaShem; you shall not do any work…"* (Exodus 20:8). Autonomy is thus to be attained through devotion to the unbounded God. The prohibition against idolatry thus provides a foundation for rational freedom and progress.

Let us now consider the name *Elohim*, which means "the Master of all forces" spread throughout Creation. The Malbim notes that the verb describing *Elohim's* actions appear always in the singular form, attesting to the Creator's being uniquely one, devoid of all multiplicity.[180] Significantly, the name *Elohim* is used exclusively during the first six days of Creation. Not until the seventh day, the Sabbath, is the name *Elohim* conjoined with the Ineffable Name, *YHVH*. The difference between the two is this. *YHVH* is God in Himself, the ultimate source of all existence. But when referred to as the one who place limits, measures, and stable form on the forces of creation, He is called *Elohim* (see Deut. 4:39). This is why *YHVH* relates to freedom and graciousness, while *Elohim* relates to the rigor of law or justice.

Going further, the Zohar states that the phrase "And Elohim *said*," is a creative utterance, a supernal form of energy, so that the universe may be understood as the concretized thought of *HaShem*.[181] "*By the word of HaShem the heavens were made*" (Psalms 33:6); and recall Proverbs 3:19: "*With wisdom HaShem created the heavens and the earth.*" Perhaps the Tetragrammaton, *YHVH*, contains the secret of how the Creator can transcend and yet be immanent in creation? Since the Hebrew root of *YHVH* means "to be," perhaps it would not be wrong to say that *HaShem*, as the ultimate source of all existence, unites Being and Becoming, hence that His oneness is a unity of opposites?

Turning to the third name of the Creator, *EH'YEH*—this is the name God instructed Moses to relate to the Israelites upon informing them of their forthcoming liberation from Egyptian bondage. Their liberation was but the fulfillment of God's promise to Abraham:

> *Know with certainty that your progeny shall be aliens in a land not their own, they will serve them, and they will oppress them for four hundred years. But also the nation that they shall serve, I shall judge, and afterwards they shall leave…*(Genesis 15:13-14).

In view of that lengthy passage of time, the enslaved Israelites needed to be taught that the God of their fathers should also be understood as *EH'YEH*, whose Hebrew letters spell the verb "to be" in its three tenses: I was, I am, I will be. This name explicitly reveals that the past, present, and future are all contained within the Eternal (which explains, by the way, how His foreknowledge does not logically exclude human free will). The name *EH'YEH* guarantees the fulfillment of God's covenant with Abraham, hence with the Jewish people, the vehicle of the Torah's world-historical program.

Remarkably, the idea of an Eternal Present in theology has its counterpart in relativity physics. Dr. Schroeder explains as follows:

> Einstein theorized and later experiments proved that the faster one travels relative to another object, the slower time flows for the traveler relative to the flow of time measured by the stationary observer. At the speed of light (the highest speed attainable in our universe), time ceases to flow altogether. The time of all events becomes compressed into the present, an unending now. The laws of physics have changed timeless existence from a theological claim to a physical reality.[182]

The above names of the Creator indicate that Jewish monotheism involves a personal God Who is both transcendent and immanent (contrary to Islam whose Allah is impersonal and absolutely transcendent). Moreover, in Jewish monotheism there exists no intermediary between God and man (contrary to Christianity). However, even when men have acknowledged the First Commandment, they have ever exhibited a powerful tendency to violate the Second Commandment (for example, by worshipping the stars as a way of exalting *HaShem*). One may say, therefore, that the primary purpose of the Torah is to destroy idolatry—the worship of false gods. Indeed, mankind has produced an infinite variety of false gods, and none has a greater hold or longevity than the productions of the human mind. Men have exalted a phantasmagoria of political and religious ideologies, and they have blindly adhered to a welter of philosophic and scientific theories, such as those which posit an eternal rather than a created universe. By diverting men from worshipping the one and only true God, idolatry leads to the glorification of what is merely human.

Now, what is distinctively human as well as most godlike is the human intellect. Therein is the most subtle cause of idolatry: intellectual pride. Strange as it may seem, but as shown in Chapter 3 of *Judaic Man*, intellectual pride, as opposed to the *Jewish* concept of humility (*anava*), actually narrows the scope of human knowledge. *The belief that man can solve the dilemma of his existence by the unaided human intellect is the supreme form of idolatry.* This is the teaching of the revelation at Mount Sinai, the Torah.

Because the human mind thinks in terms of space and time, the unaided human intellect readily succumbs to reification. It was very much this human tendency that prevented philosophers and scientists from acknowledging *creatio ex nihilo* until the advent of the Big Bang theory in the twentieth century. To this extent, however, science is unwittingly contributing to the fulfillment of the Torah's world-historical program. It is eliminating refined as well as primitive forms of idolatry. However, not until Israel achieves its Final Redemption will mankind truly recognize the ethical monotheism proclaimed in the Torah. This leads me to the Chosen People.

THE CHOSEN PEOPLE

If the Jews are the Chosen People, it appears that they have been chosen to suffer every conceivable misery. That they have nonetheless survived two thousand years of exile, persecution, torture, pogroms, and holocaust is a phenomenon that defies any known or supposed laws of history, sociology, or anthropology.

Some 3,300 years ago the Children of Israel accepted the laws of the Torah at Mount Sinai. This same system of jurisprudence is alive and vibrant today. All the old religions of the nations have either been abandoned or have been so changed that their founders would not now be able to recognize them. In contrast, despite the vicissitudes of time, the Jews, a stateless and tormented people, retained their portable homeland, the Torah. Indeed, never in Jewish history have so many Jews returned to the Torah, and never before have they established so many academies of Jewish learning. Moreover, during the past three decades, a veritable renaissance has been taking place in Jewish philosophy. Mathematicians, physicists, and biologists, are interfacing science with the Torah. Torah principles and values are being employed to illuminate and hopefully elevate the character of democracy, now in a state of moral decay. Thus, despite the murderous hatred and humiliation of Jews down through history, Judaism continues to flourish.

To begin to appreciate the concept of the Chosen People within the context of a Jewish philosophy of history, I shall present a survey of what gentile philosophers, historians, statesmen, and other writers have said about Jews and Judaism during the past twenty-three centuries—and the reader should bear in mind the degradation and exiles and tortures Jews had to endure during these millennia.

ANCIENT AND MODERN PHILO-SEMITISM

In contrast to the vilification of Jews by the generality of mankind, many of the most learned gentiles have admired the Jewish people. Theophrastus (372-287 BCE), Aristotle's student and successor at the Lyceum, referred to the Jews as "a nation of philosophers."[183] Clearchus, another student of Aristotle, and in the first rank of peripatetic philosophers, records his having heard his master tell of an encounter with a Jew from Judea (the ancient name of "Palestine"). Aristotle relates that the man spoke Greek, and adds: "During my stay in Asia, he visited the same places as I did, and came to converse with me and some other scholars, to test our learning. But as one who has been intimate with many cultivated persons, it was rather he who imparted more to us than we to him."[184]

Numenius (fl. 150-176 CE), a Syrian philosopher who is regarded as a founder of neo-Platonism, greatly admired the Jews, especially Moses. He is recorded as having said, "For what else is Plato than Moses speaking Attic Greek."[185] Porphyry records a direct quotation from Genesis by Numenius, whose frequent use of both the Pentateuch and the prophets, which he interpreted allegorically, is attested by Origen (c. 184-254 CE), the well-known early Christian theologian.

Numenius was probably influenced by the voluminous writings of Philo of Alexandria (c. 20 BCE-50 CE), as was the second century Clement of Alexandria, Origen's teacher. Thoroughly versed in Greek philosophy and culture—he was a precursor of neo-Platonism—Philo regarded the teachings of all Greek philosophers and lawgivers as a natural development of the revelatory teachings of Moses. Nevertheless, the influence of Judaism on Greek philosophy, recorded in the fragments of ancient writers, was ignored or denied by modern historians until recent decades.[186] Most interesting is evidence of Jewish influence on Thales and Pythagoras, to be discussed in the next chapter.

What made the Jews philosophers par excellence is that they regarded every aspect of existence as part of an integrated whole. Where others saw chance, they saw God incognito. Where others saw blind fate they saw Providence. For the God of the Bible is not only the God of Nature but the God of History. Hence history has to be rational and purposeful. Historian Paul Johnson writes: "The Jews, therefore, stand at the center of the perennial attempt to give human life the dignity of a purpose."[187] This Jewish idea of purpose, which underlies

Western philosophies of history cannot but elevate the thoughts of statesmen. Allow me to quote at greater length what John Adams said of the Jews:

> They have done more to civilize men than any other Nation. They are the most glorious Nation that ever inhabited the earth. The Romans and their Empire were but a bauble in comparison to the Jews. They have given religion to three-quarters of the globe and have influenced the affairs of Mankind more, and more happily than any other Nation, ancient or modern.[188]

Winston Churchill, another admirer of Jews, is quoted as saying: "Some people like the Jews, and some do not. But no thoughtful man can deny the fact that they are, beyond any question, the most formidable and the most remarkable race which has appeared in the world."[189]

That marvelous poet (and literary critic) Matthew Arnold has written: "As long as the world lasts, all who want to make progress in righteousness will come to Israel for inspiration…"[190]

Olive Schreiner's praise of the Jewish People reminds us of the prophecy in Genesis 12:1-3 (quoted below): "The study of history of Europe during the past centuries teaches us one uniform lesson: That the nations which received and in any way dealt fairly and mercifully with the Jew have prospered; and that the nations that have tortured and oppressed him have written out their own curse."[191]

Historian and statesman Thomas B. Macaulay poured scorn on his fellow parliamentarians when he declared, in a debate in 1833 in the British House of Commons over whether Jews should have their legal and political disabilities removed by law:

> In the infancy of civilization, when our island was as savage as New Guinea, when letters and arts were still unknown in Athens, when scarcely a thatched hut stood on what was afterwards the site of Rome, this condemned people had their fenced cities and cedar palaces, their splendid temple…their schools of sacred learning, their great statesmen and soldiers, their natural philosophers, their historians and poets.[192]

Macaulay's reference to the Temple of the Jews, as well as to their schools of sacred learning and natural philosophers, suggests that the civilization of ancient Israel harbored no tension or dichotomy between religion and science (i.e., natural philosophy), which is why Judaism has been called the religion of reason.

In fact, the term religion (*dat*) is the greatest obstacle to an understanding of Judaism. The word itself does not even appear in the Hebrew Bible, except in the Book of Esther, and there it means law or decree. Although the Torah has certain aspects of religion, the term cannot capture the vast intellectual breadth of the Torah, which embraces, in addition to ethics, cosmology, astronomy, agronomy, zoology, anatomy, medicine, hygiene, family purity, economics, government, civil and criminal law—subjects in which Jews have been the teachers of mankind.

Ponder in this connection the views of Henri Baruk, a biologist, psychopharmacologist, psychologist, sociologist, and a member of the Medical Academy of Paris. Professor Baruk used Torah laws for both individual and group therapy and with remarkable success. Applied with expertise, these laws, he discovered, overcome toxicities, psychopathologies, and intra-group conflict. Having characterized the Torah as "the most complete science of man," Baruk writes:

> Though this extensive science has been vulgarized by the religions which have spring from it, it still remains little known and even misunderstood. The[se] religions...took mainly from its moral principles with, moreover, various modifications which left out Hebraic Law, Hebraic biology, Hebraic sociology, etc., in a word, the concrete and material parts of the Torah. Complete and scrupulously exact study of the Torah is indispensable if one is to capture its spirit. Then again the Torah forms an indivisible whole, and one cannot study it in borrowed versions or excerpts without completely falsifying its meaning and spirit.[193]

Perhaps no gentile thinker has appreciated the magnificence of the Jewish people more than Nietzsche. I quote from *The Dawn of Day*, where he speaks of "The People of Israel":

> In Europe they have gone through a school of eighteen centuries, such as no other nation can boast of...In consequence whereof the resourcefulness in soul and intellect of our modern Jews is extraordinary. In times of extremity they, least of all the inhabitants of Europe, try to escape any great dilemma by recourse to drink or to suicide which less gifted people are so apt to fly to. Each Jew finds in the history of his fathers and grandfathers a voluminous record of instances of the greatest coolness and perseverance in terrible positions, of the most artful and clever fencing with misfortune and

chance; their bravery under the cloak of wretched submissiveness, their heroism in the *spernere se sperni* [despising their despisers] surpass the virtues of all the saints.

People wanted to make them contemptible by treating them scornfully for twenty centuries, by refusing to them the approach to all dignities and honorable positions, and by pushing them all the deeper down into the mean trades and, indeed, they have not become genteel under this process. But contemptible? They have never ceased believing themselves qualified for the highest functions; neither have the virtues of all suffering people ever failed to adorn them. Their manner of honoring parents and children, the reasonableness of their marriages and marriage customs make them conspicuous among Europeans. Besides, they know how to derive a sense of power and lasting revenge from the very trades which were left to them (or to which they were abandoned).... Yet their vengeance never carries them too far, for they all have that liberality even of the soul in which the frequent change of place, climate, customs, neighbors, and oppressors schools man; they have by far the greatest experience in human relationships....

Now Nietzsche concludes his encomium:

> Where shall this accumulated wealth of great impressions, which forms the Jewish history in every Jewish family, this wealth of passions, virtues, resolutions, resignations, struggles, victories of all sorts, where shall it find an outlet, if not in great intellectual people and work? On the day when the Jews will be able to show as their handiwork such jewels and golden vessels as the European nations of shorter and less thorough experience neither can nor could produce, when Israel will have turned its eternal vengeance into an eternal blessing of Europe: then once more that seventh day will appear, when the God of the Jews may rejoice in Himself, His creation, and His Chosen People and all of us will rejoice with Him![194]

THE ORIGIN OF THE CHOSEN PEOPLE

The concept of the Chosen People has its origin in Abraham, the father of the Jewish people. God said to "Abram":

> *Go for yourself—away from your land, from your birthplace, and from the home of your father, to the land that I will show you. I will make you into a great nation. I will bless you and make you great. You shall become a blessing. I will bless those who bless you, and he that curses you, I will curse. All the families of the earth shall be blessed through you* (Genesis 12:1-3).

That blessing is nothing less than ethical monotheism, which has civilized much of mankind. By itself, monotheism, as the great philosopher-mathematician Alfred North Whitehead discerned, is the basis of modern science. Whitehead saw that monotheism involves the idea of a rationally ordered universe, a presupposition of scientific inquiry. No wonder Jews have excelled in science! When divorced from ethics, however, science has become a curse. Let us therefore try to understand the man who conferred the blessing of ethical monotheism upon mankind.[195]

Without any teacher, and in opposition to the polytheism and vicious practices of his pagan contemporaries, Abraham discovered, through reason and observation, that this vast multifarious universe is an integrated whole created by one supreme and transcendent Being of infinite wisdom and power (Genesis 14:22). Over the course of years thousands of people gathered about him and became part of his household. Such was his greatness as a teacher and leader of men that he was called a Prince of God (Genesis 23:6). He discerned the providential kindliness of God and deduced therefrom His code of conduct for men (Genesis 26:5). Abraham saw that the world was designed for man's use and happiness, hence that Man is the purpose of creation. He reasoned that since the Creator showed nothing of Himself but His deeds, then it is His will that men should know Him by the graciousness of His deeds, an attribute they ought to emulate in their relations with one another.

Abraham also reasoned that it is proper for men to be grateful to their Benefactor by thanking Him and by speaking of His graciousness, as well as of His wisdom and power, and to demonstrate their gratitude by consecrating their lives to His service (Genesis 12-14). Accordingly, Abraham devoted all his thoughts and efforts to serving God (Genesis 18:27). He disciplined himself until he learned absolute self-control (*Nedarim* 32b). Through the commandment of circumcision he gained mastery over his body. No difficulty was too great for him, and the greatest sacrifices did not hinder him. Despite his greatness, he was ever humble, regarding himself as mere dust and ashes (Genesis 16:17). In his dealings with men—even enemies—he manifested unequalled hospitality and magnanimity, for which reason he is the exemplar of graciousness (*Hesed*), that purely voluntary and overflowing kindness that seeks neither reward nor recognition (Genesis 14:22-23, 18:1-8, 23). He taught these principles and this manner of service to his household and to all that would listen to him. In short, Abraham developed in himself superior intellectual and moral qualities which became part of his being and were transmitted to his seed forever (*Megilla* 13b). It was because of his superlative character that God changed his name to Abraham, which means father of multitude of nations (Genesis 17:5), and sent him forth to found a new nation in a new land. This nation, Israel, was to be an Abraham writ large.

The ethical monotheism discovered by Abraham and transmitted to his descendants is the only solid and rational basis for the moral unity of the human race or the idea of the human community. Isaac Breuer, who studied philosophy, history, and German philology at the universities of Marburg and Berlin, and who received a doctorate in law at the University of Salzberg, writes:

> The idea of the human community is one of the most beautiful pearls in the treasure of Jewish doctrine; it is a basic truth of Judaism; it is that Jewish idea which first set out on its triumphal procession from the Jewish camp into the whole world; it is the first message of salvation which Israel brought to a society of states which knew only force and the misuse of power. "*God created man in His image. In the likeness of God He created him*" [Genesis 1:27]. Here we have the lapidary sentence from Holy Writ which proclaims through all ages the inalienable, godlike nobility of man as such.[196]

Breuer emphasizes that although the idea of the human community is a Jewish concept, it is obviously not the sole concept or even the basis of Judaism. (As that penetrating literary critic Edward Alexander once wrote, "universalism is the parochialism of the Jews"!) The basis of Judaism is not the *universalism* it bestowed on mankind, but *particularism*. If Jewish nationhood means anything it means a distinctive way of life, namely that illuminated by the laws and teachings of the Torah. For example, of the many laws that distinguish Jews from non-Jews, suffice to mention those pertaining to the Sabbath, the dietary laws, and those governing marriage and family purity. These laws preserved the identity of the Jewish people down through the ages. They not only distinguished the Jewish nation from all other nations, but spared them from the fate of nations whose existence depended on having a land of their own. Some nations have been conquered and eradicated. Others have been amalgamated with their conquerors. Still other nations have undergone evolutions and revolutions that fundamentally altered their character. Only the Jews have preserved their 3,300-year-old national identity. This they could do because, in whichever country they lived, regardless of its beliefs and customs, they adhered to the laws of their Torah, such as those just mentioned.

It should be borne in mind that God created a world not only for diverse individuals but for nations with distinct ways of life. However, for these ways of life to be mutually reinforcing and not mutually obstructive, they require the rational constraints of the Seven Noahide Laws of Universal Morality.[197] Rooted in ethical monotheism, these laws prohibit blasphemy, murder, stealing, immorality, and cruelty to animals, while also requiring the establishment of courts of justice to try violations of these prohibitions.

As previously stated, idolatry involves the worship of *any* created thing, including the products of the human intellect, be it a philosophic or scientific theory, a political or religious ideology, or a particular form of government. Such is the loftiness of the human intellect, that only its Creator is worthy of worship. It follows that to desecrate the Name of the Creator is to degrade humanity as well. Those who deny the Creator not only deny the source of human perfection; they also undermine the highest possible development of man's intellectual faculties. Also, when men reject their Creator, they end by worshipping themselves or their own creations, be it an ideology or anything that gratifies their passions. The typical result is either tyranny or bestiality or vulgarity. Moreover, given man's creation in God's image, each individual is a center of purposes known to God alone. We must therefore be duly concerned about the life, property, and the honor of other human beings. (In Judaism, damaging a person's reputation is tantamount to murder.) Finally, given the fallibility of man's intellect, the Torah requires the establishment of courts of justice. (In Jewish law a person is presumed innocent until proven guilty, and not by circumstantial evidence, but only on the oral testimony of righteous eye-witnesses meticulously examined in open court by judges of impeccable character.)

The seven universal laws of morality may rightly be called a "genial orthodoxy." This genial orthodoxy transcends the social and economic distinctions among men. It holds all men equal before the law. It places constraints on governors and governed alike and habituates men to the rule of law. It subordinates to the rule of law any ethnic differences that may exist among the groups composing a society. It moderates their demands and facilitates coordination of their diverse interests and talents. In short, this Hebraic orthodoxy conduces to social harmony and prosperity.

As just implied, the Noahide Laws can be elaborated in various ways and are therefore applicable to the variety of nations comprising mankind. Israel's world-historical function, therefore, is to provide mankind the example of a nation that synthesizes particularism and universalism, which it can only do as a nation consecrated to God. By affirming a plurality of nations, and by qualifying this particularism with laws of universal morality, Israel avoids the political, cultural, and religious imperialism of Islam and which once animated Christianity. At the same time, Israel avoids the moral decay evident among democracies that have separated morality from public law. Despite its moral decay, contemporary democracy is commonly regarded as the touchstone of what is good and bad. Democracy thus constitutes the idolatry of the modern era. Mankind desperately needs Israel—of course, an Israel dedicated to God.

Only a nation dedicated to God can inspire and elevate mankind. Leo Jung eloquently writes:

> Had Judaism been entrusted to all nations, it would have lost color and intensity. As everybody's concern it would have remained nobody's concern.... Ideals are better entrusted to minorities as their differentiating asset, because of which they live.... Judaism, given at once to the shapeless multitudes of the world, would have become a meaningless phrase...Hence it was bestowed upon one nation as its heirloom, as the single reason for its existence, as the single argument of its national life, as the aim and end of its struggles and labors.
>
> The Jewish people thus received a charge that was to inspire its life, but the benefit of which was to accrue to all the world. At the beginning of Jewish history, Abraham, the first Jew, received the universal call, "And thou shalt be a blessing to all the nations of the world." For the consummation of this ideal, Israel is to walk apart. It will not be counted among the nations.... Guided exclusively by the will of God, living by His commandments and dying if need be for the sanctification of His Name, Israel is to present the example of a whole nation elevated, ennobled, illumined by the life in God and encouraging thereby a universal *imitatio Dei*.[198]

Although this is not proof that the Jews are the Chosen People, it provides evidence for the necessity of such a people. Gerald Schroeder puts it this way:

> In his closing address, Moses adjures the people to "Remember the days of old, consider the years of each generation" (Deut. 32:7). Kabala tells us these "days of old" are the six days of Genesis, and "the years of each generation" are the historical records of civilization. Understanding the events of our cosmic and social past is a key to discovering the immanence of God. The Bible insists the evidence is

> there for us to discover God in this world: "You shall know that I am the Eternal" (Ex. 6:7; Ex. 29:46; Deut. 4:39).
>
> If studying history is indeed the path for all humanity to discover God, then the reason for one of the more contentious and misunderstood issues of the Bible becomes clear. Having a people chosen to be "holy" becomes a necessity, both biblically and scientifically. The Hebrew word for holy is *kodesh*, which means separate, set apart....In the language of experimental science, this "holy" people is an identifiable control group set apart against which the flow of history can be compared..."
>
> The best control is one that is present in the actual environment. The problem becomes how to maintain the separate identity of that people even while they are part of society in general. The Torah accomplishes this by presenting them with a list of constraints (foods, clothing, holidays). For three thousand years it has succeeded. To compensate for the burden of being set aside, those chosen to be separate needed a reward to offset the difficulty of the task. According to the Bible, that reward included a method, not necessarily unique or exclusive, to help in discovering and understanding the transcendental unity that forms the base of our universe.[199]

Schroeder points out that being "holy" does not mean being intrinsically better. "God tells the Israelites that their being chosen is not because they have inherently superior virtues as a people" (Deut. 9:4-6). Being chosen "means being made visible as a symbol." It is in this light that we are to understand why the Jews alone have a universal history and were destined, after horrific dispersion (Deut. 30:1-5), to return to the Land of Israel where they are now the focus of mankind's ("incomprehensible") attention. But now we can better understand why the Jews have always been in the forefront of science!

WHY JUDAISM IS NOT A RELIGION

The time has come to clarify the term religion by way of its competitors, philosophy and science. Conventionally understood, whereas religion is based on revelation, philosophy is based on reason; and whereas religion is rooted in the particularity and subjectivity of faith, science is based on the universality and objectivity of verifiable knowledge. Reason as opposed to revelation, knowledge as opposed to faith, are basic dichotomies or tensions of Western civilization.

It so happens, however, that various modern philosophers have come to the conclusion that philosophy, once defined as purely objective knowledge of the moral and metaphysical universe, is inherently impossible. Having forsaken the classical quest for the True, the Good, and the Beautiful, major schools of philosophy today limit their subject matter to logic and linguistic analysis. Meanwhile, although general relativity and quantum mechanics as theories of ultimate reality contradict each and prompt some scientists to say that modern physics is in a state of conceptual disarray,[200] we have nonetheless seen the convergence of both of these sciences with the Genesis account of Creation.[201] Nor is this all.

The advent of computer research into the Torah reveals a profusion of codified information concerning persons and events that post-date the Bible, indeed, of persons and events familiar in our own day! Based on the hypothesis that the Torah is a giant cipher, the Five Books of Moses were stored, not word by word, but letter by letter into a computer. This entire continuum was scanned by skipping letters at equal intervals, and in a wide range of numbers. The object was to search for the existence of any systematic structures, key words, or names encoded in the text in equidistant letter sequences. The findings then underwent statistical analysis to determine whether or not any positive results were merely fortuitous. The results were astonishing.[202] In fact, and as will be seen in Chapter 10, the eminent philosopher-mathematician Gian Carlo Duranti, a gentile, has related various hidden codes of the Torah to certain esoteric aspects of Euclid's *Elements!*

In this connection I must emphasize the following proposition: *The mathematical discovery of hidden codes in the Torah overcomes the dichotomy of reason versus revelation that has plagued philosophy for some 2,400 years.* Here I can offer only the briefest explanation.

What is decisive in revelation (or prophecy) and in scientific insight alike is not the *subjective process* by which the mind gains knowledge of some reality, but the *linguistic product* of that process, which alone can be communicated and tested by logical and empirical means. The Torah is, of course, a linguistic product. Computer analysis of that linguistic product suggests that the Torah contains, in code form, the genetic blueprint of the universe—long ago the conclusion of Torah scholars, many of whom were quite knowledgeable in mathematics, science, and philosophy.[203]

Moreover, the present writer regards the history and progress of science, along with developments in philosophy, religion, and world politics, as having been programmed for the rebirth of Israel on whose Final Redemption ultimately depends the universal acceptance of the ethical monotheism that issued from Mount Sinai. Obviously the Jewish people must hearken to the Torah if they are to fulfill their world-historical mission, which began with Abraham:

All the nations of the world shall be blessed through your descendants because you [Abraham] have hearkened to My voice (Genesis 22:18).

If you [Israel] hearken to Me and observe My Covenant, you shall be My special treasure among all the nations. Even though all the world is Mine, you shall be a kingdom of Kohanim [of preceptors] *and a holy nation* (Exodus 19:5-6).

If Israel, as a nation, observes the Torah and sanctifies God's Name by making His infinite wisdom, power, and graciousness known to the world, it will have fulfilled the universal mission for which it was chosen. Israel will thus have to reveal the Torah as the paradigm of how man should live. One step in this direction is to reveal the inadequacies of the Torah's major competitors. Having shown the shortcomings of democracy in previous works (if not in earlier chapters), I shall limit myself to the two offspring of Judaism, Christianity, and Islam.[204] However, lest I be accused of Jewish bias, let us examine the views of two gentiles, the historian Arnold Toynbee and the philosopher Friedrich Nietzsche.

Professor Toynbee once described the Jewish people as a fossilized relic of an obsolete culture. Consider, however, his more recent assessment:

> I dare say that Judaism will bring a new message to the world. Looking from the outside, it seems extraordinary that twice in the course of history the Jews have allowed outsiders to run away with their religion to spread it over the world in garbled form. I am talking, of course, of early Christianity and Islam. It is something almost comic that outsiders should seize some of the essential truths of Judaism and put them in, what must seem to the Jews, a garbled form of Judaism, and make a worldwide religion of them while the Jews themselves kept their religion to themselves.
>
> Is not the real future of the Jews and Judaism to spread Judaism in its authentic form rather than its Christian and Moslem forms over the whole world and human race! After all, the Jews must have a more authentic form of Jewish monotheism than the Christians or Moslems have. And is that not going to be the ultimate solution of the relations between Jews and the rest of the world?[205]

Of course, only Jews who devote their lives to the study of the Torah can plumb its wisdom and therapeutic power. Unfortunately, countless Jews are oblivious of the Torah's grandeur, of which Nietzsche says:

> In the Jewish "Old Testament," the book of divine justice, there are human beings, things, and speeches in so grand a style that Greek and Indian literature have nothing to compare with it. With terror and reverence one stands before these tremendous remnants of what man once was, and will have sad thoughts about ancient Asia and its protruding little peninsula Europe, which wants by all means to signify as against Asia the "progress of man." To be sure, whoever is himself merely a meager, tame domestic animal (like our educated people of today, including the Christians of "educated" Christianity) has no cause for amazement or sorrow among these ruins—the taste of the Old Testament is a touchstone for "great" and "small"—perhaps he will find the *New* Testament…rather more after his heart…"[206]

The ruins of which Nietzsche speaks will also be found in present-day Israel, whose political, judicial, and cultural elites are abysmally ignorant of the "Old Testament" and therefore hinder Israel's Final Redemption. Nevertheless, that redemption will necessarily come.

> *God is not a man that he should lie, nor a human being that he should change His mind. Would He promise and not do it, or speak and not confirm it?* (Numbers 23:19).

As will be seen with startling clarity in the Appendix, the Final Redemption is "programmed," the "script" is not. A glimpse of this program is given in Deuteronomy 4:25-31:

> *When you beget children and grandchildren and will have been long in the land, you will grow decadent and…*[commit idolatry], *an evil act in the eyes of HaShem your God…I call heaven and earth to bear witness against you that you will surely perish quickly from the land to which you are crossing the Jordan to possess. You will not remain there very long, lest you be completely destroyed* [or succumb to complete apostasy].
>
> *HaShem shall* [therefore] *scatter you among the peoples and you will remain few in number among the nations where HaShem will lead*

you…Then you will begin to seek HaShem your God, and you will find Him, if you search for Him with all your heart and all your soul.

In the end of days, when you are in distress…you will return unto HaShem your God, and hearken to His voice. For HaShem your God is merciful. He will not abandon you. He will not forget the Covenant which He swore to your forefathers.

The Covenant points to Israel's restoration and Final Redemption: "*I see it, but not now, I gaze at it but it is not near: A star has started its path from Jacob and a scepter has arisen from Israel…*" (Numbers 24:17). HaShem, the God of History, will therefore bring about the Final Redemption of His Chosen People. Illuminated by the Torah, Israel will shine forth "*as a light unto the nations*" (Isaiah 42:6). Let us see how a spark from the Torah was brought to ancient Greece.

Chapter 9
The Historical Function of the Pre-Socratics

Introduction

This and the remaining chapters attempt to outline the Jewish philosophy of history mentioned in the Prologue. Better minds will have to flesh out this philosophy. They will first have to show, with greater precision and comprehensiveness than I am capable, how diverse philosophers, scientists, and empires since the destruction of the First Temple twenty-six centuries ago have been carrying out, unwittingly, the Torah's world-historical program succinctly stated in the First and Second Commandments. We begin with the pre-Socratic philosophers.

Our knowledge of the pre-Socratics is very limited. We have no more than fragments of their writings, and sometimes not even that. Any reconstruction of the statements of these philosophers or attributed to them must remain conjectural. *Verbatim* reconstruction is of course impossible. Nevertheless, the data allow us to catch glimpses of their worldview. Indeed, a Jewish philosophy of history will not only correct the efforts of historians who ignore or deny the influence of Judaism on Greek philosophy, but it will also shed new light on the efforts of Greek philosophers to understand the totality of existence.

It should first be noted that the historic function of Greek philosophy, taken as a whole, was to destroy the Homeric gods, or paganism-cum-polytheism, and thereby prepare the grounds for a more ethical and rational understanding of the universe. A word about paganism is necessary.

Paganism is nothing less than the idolatry of human power and glory, the pursuit of which required the subjugation of other human beings. Military conquest inflated the self-confidence of pagan nations and military success amounted to a demonstration that their deities, on which they depended, and which they identified with various forces of nature, were on their side. (We shall see that this remains characteristic of the Arabs.) Moreover, people steeped in paganism believed that they could propitiate or manipulate their deities by human sacrifice.

Turning to Greek mythology, it was not believed that the gods created the universe but rather that the universe created the gods. (See Plato, *Timaeus* 41.) By eliminating the gods, Greek philosophers were left with an uncreated universe, a premise they never transcended—or so it seems. If the gods, often portrayed as arbitrary, were forces of nature, then their elimination would leave nature open to human cognition and more subject to human will.

Here are three examples of the Homeric gods and the forces of nature they represented: Zeus—the storm wind; Poseidon—the earth-shaker; Hephaestus—fire. I have selected these gods or forces of nature because they correspond to the following verses of I Kings 19:11-12:

> *Go forth, and stand upon the mount before HaShem. And behold, HaShem passed by and a great strong wind rent the mountains, and broke in pieces the rocks before HaShem; but HaShem was not in the wind; and after the wind an earthquake; but HaShem was not in the earthquake; and after the earthquake a fire; but HaShem was not in the fire.*

This depersonalization of nature was a necessary precondition for the development of natural philosophy, as science was called even after the time of Newton. But more fundamental than natural philosophy is theology. According to Josephus (37-101 CE), the Jewish idea of an uncreated, immutable, and eternal God, "known to us by His powers, yet unknown to us as to His essence" fructified Greek philosophy.[207] How is not clear.

THALES

As if Moses as well as King David and King Solomon never lived, historians of antiquity inform us that Thales (634-546 BCE) was the first philosopher. Also ignored is the fact that Thales flourished at the time of the destruction of the First Temple (586 BCE), i.e., during the first dispersion of the Jews from Judea (the Land of Israel).

The major source for Thales is Aristotle, who identified Thales as the first *Greek* philosopher and as the founder of the school of natural philosophy. (The Greeks called these natural philosophers "*physikoi*.") Thales himself was not a Greek, as reputed, but a Phoenician. Phoenicia was the Greek name for Canaan, much of which became Judea. It was from the Canaanites, a Semitic people, that the Greeks derived their alphabet.[208]

That Thales was expelled from Canaan or Judea and became a citizen of Miletus, a Greek city, suggests the possibility that his expulsion was the result of the Babylonian invasion of Judea when King Nebuchadnezzar sacked Jerusalem. In any event, it is reasonable to assume that Thales knew Hebrew. Indeed, as historian Elliot A. Green suggests, his name may be a Greek rendering of the Hebrew word *tal*, which means "dew."

Although no writings of Thales are extant, he apparently investigated almost all areas of knowledge—philosophy, history, science, mathematics, geography, and politics. He is credited by ancient historians as having regarded the earth as spherical. According to Herodotus, Thales predicted the year of the May 28, 585 BCE solar eclipse, which indicates that he figured out that the heavens move in regular ways that accord with mathematical reasoning. Thales therefore provided naturalistic explanations of cosmological events. His questioning approach to the understanding of heavenly phenomena was the beginning of Greek astronomy. He paved the way toward scientific endeavor and initiated the first western enlightenment. He was highly esteemed in ancient times as the first and most eminent of the Seven Sages. But Thales was not merely a natural philosopher.

Asked, what is the divine? Thales replied, "That which has neither beginning nor end"—clearly a Jewish teaching. (See Plato, *Phaedrus* 245d1-6.) So too, it seems, is the following: Asked which was older, night or day? Thales replied, "Night is the older by one day." The question is puzzling, unless the word "day" means morning; and the response is also puzzling, for night is not older than "day" by one [whole] day. Let us therefore rephrase the question and Thales' answer as follows. Asked which was older (or earlier) night (meaning *evening*) or day (meaning *morning*), Thales replied, "Evening is older (or earlier) than morning." This is what we read at the close of each of the six days of Creation in Genesis: "*And there was evening and there was morning.*" Coming from Canaan or Judea, Thales probably knew that "evening" in Hebrew is *erev* and that morning in Hebrew is *boker*. If so, he would surely have known that whereas the root of *erev* means disorder, the root of *boker* means being orderly or able to be discerned.

Here I am applying to Thales Gerald Schroeder's knowledge of Hebrew, who writes in *The Science of God*: "In the subtle language of evening and morning, centuries before the Greek words chaos and cosmos were ever written…the Bible described a step-by-step flow from disorder (*erev*) to order (*boker*)…"[209] It is therefore quite possible that Thales held the view that the order discernible in the universe was preceded by disorder (*erev*). Such a philosopher—indeed, *any* philosopher—would wonder *who* or *what* produced this order. But if that philosopher were influenced by Judaism, as was likely the case of the sage from Canaan or Judea, he would surely have contemplated the idea of monotheism.

Of course I am speculating, and this will be regarded as tendentious speculation until we consider the following. Thales is reported to have said there were three blessings for which he was grateful: "First, that I was born a human being and not one of the brutes; next, that I was born a man and not a woman; thirdly a Greek [as he may have preferred, or was, preferred by others, to be known] and not a barbarian."[210] These blessings parallel the morning prayers of Jews! Since these blessings were not common among Greeks, one should not even dismiss the possibility that Thales was Jewish. Consistent with this possibility, Diogenes Laertius also ascribes to Thales the following sayings, all of which are consistent with the cosmology of Genesis and Jewish philosophy:

- Of all things that are, the most ancient is God, for he is uncreated.
- The most beautiful is the universe, for it is God's workmanship.
- The greatest is space, for it holds all things.

From these three sayings it is hard to avoid the conclusion that Thales, if he was not Jewish, was influenced by Jewish monotheism, hence that he rejected the polytheism of antiquity.

Judging from what is said of Thales, his influence on Greek philosophy must have been profound. Not only is he frequently referred to by Aristotle, but a letter cited by Laertius, and purporting to be from Anaximenes to Pythagoras, advised that all their discourses should begin with a reference to Thales.

Just as scientists today are in quest of a unified theory, indeed, a "theory of everything," Thales is said to have postulated "water" as the elementary cosmic substance underlying the diverse aspects and transformations of nature. Some speculate that Thales based this concept on the observation that water, which manifests the three states of liquid, vapor, and ice, exhibits sensible changes more obviously than any other substance. If so, he would not have literally regarded water as eternal after having said that, "Of all things that are, the most ancient is God, for he is uncreated"—a view that leaves open the possibility of *creatio ex nihilo*. According to Cicero (of whom more later), Thales held there was a divine mind which formed all things out of "water." This would be understandable to any Jew knowing that "water" is a symbol for the Torah! This remark may be deemed outrageous to historians of Greek philosophy. Let me then offer an alternative interpretation.

No man of common sense, let alone a natural philosopher, seeing any metal such as silver or gold or the making of an alloy such as brass or bronze, would regard "water" *literally* as the elementary cosmic substance. Surely it is more reasonable to assume that Thales used the term "water" as a metaphor, perhaps to convey the idea that the elementary substance of all things is formless or "indefinite." The latter is exactly the teaching of Anaximander, his younger associate (possibly his student). And when we consider that Anaximander was followed by Anaximines who postulated "air" as the elementary cosmic substance, it is probable that these philosophers believed that something invisible was the root of all things, but used metaphors to convey an esoteric teaching.

Summing up: although the ideas and sayings attributed to Thales clearly suggest Jewish influence and therefore the influence of monotheism, the latter remained apparently foreign to Greek philosophy, or so we are given to believe by conventional historians. In any event, it is reasonable to conclude that Thales' impact on the *physikoi* undermined the polytheism of the Aegean world.

ANAXIMANDER

It may be of significance that Anaximander (c. 610-546 BCE) is regarded as the first *Greek* philosopher. According to Aristotle and Theophrastus, the first Greek philosophers raised the fundamental question, "What is the *origin* or *principle* [the Greek word "*archê*" has both meanings] of all things?" Anaximander called it "*apeiron*," i.e., "that which has no boundaries." Some scholars translate *apeiron* as the "Indefinite," others as the "Infinite." This agrees with Anaximander's view that "a being which possesses definite qualities and consists of them can never be the origin and principle of things."[211] Since the "Indefinite" or "Infinite" is the origin of all things, it can itself have no origin, in which case it would be uncreated or eternal.

Two interpretations are possible. If Anaximander held, with Thales, that that which is uncreated is divine, then the "Indefinite" may be an *esoteric* substitute for God—a teaching intended for the philosophic few rather than for the unphilosophic and polytheistic many. Alternatively, the "Indefinite" may be an incorporeal substance coeternal with God and from which substance God formed the universe. This would contradict the Jewish principle of creation from nothing. But we have no evidence or extant report of a creator-God in Anaximander, and this poses an insuperable problem. How did the "Indefinite" or *apeiron* become all things? Stated another way, if the *apeiron* is Anaximander's answer to the question, "What is the ultimate stuff?"—the second question would be, "How does this stuff change and become a multiplicity of things?" Apparently, and perhaps to the annoyance of his contemporaries, Anaximander had no answer to this second question, or perhaps he did not deem it prudent to publicize it. (As we shall see in the next chapter, however,

Plato refines Anaximander's "Indefinite," and in a way that is conceptually linked to modern science.)

In any event, by saying that "a being which possesses definite qualities and consists of them can never be the origin and principle of things," Anaximander conveys a radical skepticism regarding the visible and tangible world: he is rejecting the evidence of the senses as providing true knowledge of ultimate reality. This was a milestone in the progress of science, for however one interprets his *apeiron*, one conclusion is unavoidable: the visible world must be understood in terms of an invisible and perhaps incorporeal substance. Another important step has been taken to eliminate the Homeric gods.

Pythagoras

Far more famous and influential than Anaximander is Thales' younger student Pythagoras (c. 569-475 BCE). Various ancient sources say that Pythagoras was also from Canaan, and that he lived for a considerable time on Mount Carmel. The prophet Elijah lived on Mount Carmel, as did his disciple Elisha and other prophets. Josephus states that Pythagoras not only "knew our doctrines, but was in very great measure a follower and admirer of them."[212] More specific reports indicate that Pythagoras' teachings and practices parallel those of the Nazirites, such as Samson, Samuel, and Daniel. For example, Pythagoras did not drink wine or eat animal food, and he did not cut his hair.

Pythagoras is often described as the first pure mathematician. Although he is an extremely important figure in the development of mathematics and philosophy—he is often cited by Plato and Aristotle—we have nothing of Pythagoras's writings. As a pure mathematician, Pythagoras was interested in the principles of mathematics, the concept of number, the concept of a triangle and of other mathematical figures. He is popularly known for his Pythagorean Theorem, which is defined in Book I, Proposition 47, of Euclid's *Elements*: "In right-angled triangles the square of the side opposite the right angle equals the sum of the squares on the sides containing the right angle."

The importance of mathematics can hardly be exaggerated. Mathematics trains the mind to think logically, to apply logic not only to the investigation of nature but also to the laws governing human societies. In addition to establishing a philosophical and religious school, Pythagoras was the founder and legislator of a society in southern Italy. He had many followers who were known as *mathematikoi* and who, like their master, were vegetarians. Among their beliefs mention may be made of the following:

- At its deepest level, all existing objects and their relations are expressible in numbers.
- Certain numbers have a symbolic [hence qualitative] significance.

Pythagoras is reported to have said, "Number rules the universe," and, "Number is within all things." (This is consistent with the "letter-numbers"—*Gematria*—of the Torah, understood as the genetic material of the universe.) The numerical or mathematical conception of the universe posited by Pythagoras has influenced science to this day.

Inasmuch as Pythagoras traveled around the eastern Mediterranean world, including Babylonia, which had a large community of exiled Jews, it would be remarkable indeed if he did not come into contact with some members of this "nation of philosophers"—to recall Theophrastus' description of these students of the Torah. Pythagoras is reported to have said, "*Every* man has been made by God in order to acquire knowledge and contemplate." This is a Jewish, not a Greek, idea.

Now let us return for a moment to Anaximander. His *apeiron*, though devoid of sensible qualities, may nonetheless be a physical and formless substance. Therefore, his attempt to explain the visible world in terms of something invisible—the "Indefinite"—does not preclude materialism, since the invisible may consist not of Pythagorean numbers but of Democritean atoms (discussed below). This is why the philosophy of Anaximander has been classified by modern scholars as materialistic monism. That they have also endowed Thales with this label renders their assessment questionable—and for two reasons.

First of all, what we have learned about Thales as well as about his student Pythagoras stands in striking contrast with the materialistic monism modern scholars attribute to Anaximander. Second, they seem to ignore the fact that living in a polytheistic society, it would have been suicidal for Anaximander to openly question the Greek gods. This may well be the reason why he did not explain what he meant by *apeiron*, a concept that makes nonsense of Zeus and the Greek pantheon. Anaxagoras, discussed below, had to flee Athens when he publicized his teachings about "*Nous*," and Socrates was given the hemlock for substituting human reason for the Olympian gods. Pythagoras knew what he was doing when he established a society in remote southern Italy, and required his students to maintain an oath of secrecy regarding his teachings and the beliefs of that society. (As Josephus points out, "Protagoras also, who was thought to have written something that was owned for truth by the Athenians about the gods, would have been seized upon, and put to death, had he not fled away immediately.")[213] Admittedly, even if Anaximander's *apeiron* was a corporeal substance, such a teaching would

...n subversive. Let us therefore leave the question of his materialistic ...onism open. We may now continue.

PARMENIDES VERSUS HERACLITUS

No such question applies to Parmenides (b. 510 BCE), the philosopher of Being, who held that the world is an uncreated and eternal corporeal plenum—homogeneous, motionless, and immutable. Plurality and variability within the world are mere appearances. Moreover, Parmenides is reported as saying, "The thing that can be thought and that for the sake of which the thought exists is the same"—which brings materialistic monism to its ultimate logical conclusion.[214] The distinction between body and mind evaporates. We are reminded of pantheism and Spinoza who, like Parmenides, deifies the mind.[215] Actually, pantheism comes close to the biblical conception of the universe as an integrated whole. Absent from pantheism, however, is the cosmological principle of *creatio ex nihilo,* which Parmenides (like Spinoza) clearly denies. *Creatio ex nihilo* has ever been a standing offence to the philosopher's pride, thwarting his quest to comprehend the organizing principles of the universe in purely logical terms. But materialistic monism, however logical, renders science impossible by denying motion and change. Being is barren without Becoming.

Turn, therefore, to Heraclites (536-470 BCE), the philosopher of Becoming, who famously said, "You cannot step twice into the same river." Heraclites held that what *is,* far from being homogeneous, indivisible, and motionless, is a unity of opposites, that the tension between opposites generates change, that only change is real. All things are in ceaseless motion; nothing is; all is Becoming. Recall Ecclesiastes (3:1-8): *"To every thing there is a season…A time to be born, and a time to die;…A time to love, and a time to hate; A time for war, and a time for peace."*

The controversy over the essence of Being left its imprint on all Greek philosophy down to the Stoics and Epicureans. But it was Heraclitus' Becoming, with its potential for joy that prevailed over the joyless Being of Parmenides. After all, change is an ineluctable principle of human life. Man rebels against uniformity and monotony. He strives for novelty and creativity. And as we shall see later, the exemplar of human creativity is none other than Abraham, the first Jew, who knew how to render change rational and meaningful by synthesizing it with that which is permanent. This is but another way of saying that Abraham discerned the unity of opposites—of Being and Becoming—implicit in *YHVH,* the Creator Who transcends yet is immanent in His creation.

Contrary to Abraham, of course, Heraclites agreed with Parmenides that the universe is uncreated, finite, corporeal, and eternal.[216] (This prevented them from grasping the unity of Being and Becoming implicit in the Tetragrammaton.) Moreover, given the principle of Becoming, a finite and eternal universe must necessarily undergo periodic destruction or eternal cyclicality—Nietzsche's "Eternal Recurrence of the Same." Eternal cyclicality is a recurring theme in the non-Torah world. It harks back to the oscillating universe of the Hindus and persists among some contemporary cosmologists.[217]

As for the status of mind in Heraclites' philosophy, the following fragment suggests that the human intellect transcends the flux of Becoming: "The wise is one only. It is unwilling and willing to be called by the name Zeus."[218] Heraclites seems to deify the mind, which anticipates another *physikoi*, Empedocles, who flourished two decades later. Empedocles, expounder of the once famous four "elements"—fire, air, earth, and water—claimed to be a god, which may only signify his belief in the godlike ability of the human intellect to comprehend the universe. [219]

Deification of the intellect—the greatest *hubris*—is the distinctive trait of the philosopher, and Heraclites, as both Diogenes Laertius[220] and Nietzsche recognized, is the epitome of intellectual pride. In stark contrast to the Jewish view of wisdom, Nietzsche's Heraclites "was not interested in…what other sages before him had been endeavoring to ascertain…. "I sought and investigated myself," he said…as if he and no one else were the true fulfiller and achiever of the Delphic precept: "Know thyself."[221]

No wonder philosophies—Nietzsche deemed philosophy a "species of autobiography"—become tombstones bearing the names of their creators. Unlike the scientist and the scientific student of Torah, the philosopher does not build on the past. Nor does he put his doctrines to the test of experiment. This is why the history of philosophy is a phantasmagoria of contradictions and abandoned edifices. This is not to deny the utility of these failed attempts of the finite mind to comprehend the totality of existence. Even though Heraclites' nature-philosophy, with its strife between opposites, is tinged with anthropomorphism, he nonetheless helped to destroy the anthropomorphism of the Greek pantheon.

ANAXAGORAS

From Heraclites we turn to Anaxagoras (500-428 BCE) of Klazomene, in Asia Minor. Anaxagoras was the teacher of that great Athenian, Pericles. Shortly before the outbreak of the Peloponnesian War, Anaxagoras was charged by the political opponents of Pericles with impiety, that is, with denying the gods recognized by

Athens. Though acquitted through his friend's influence, he felt compelled to emigrate to Lampsacus, where he died soon after. He not only had the honor of giving philosophy a home at Athens, but he was the first Greek philosopher who explicitly introduced a spiritual principle that gives matter *life* and *form*.

Contrary to Empedocles, who had reduced the multiplicity of things to fire, air, earth, and water, Anaxagoras maintained that

> All things were [originally] together, infinite both in number and in smallness...Nor is there a least of what is small, but there is always a smaller...And since these things are so, we must suppose that there are...all sorts of things that are uniting, seeds of all things, with all sorts of shapes and colors...and that men have been formed of them, and the other animals that have life...But before they were separated off, when all things were together not even was any color distinguishable: for the mixture of all things prevented it.... And these things being so we must hold that all things are in the whole.[222]

The whole was originally in a state of utter disorder (recall our interpretation of Thales and the term *erev*). Instead of the homogeneous primal matter of Parmenides, we have in Anaxagoras a "primal mixture" or chaos consisting of an infinite number of "seeds" which, contrary to Heraclitus, are not in motion but at rest. What imparts motion to these seeds and, in the process, segregates them out, is "*Nous*":

> *Nous* [i.e., Mind] is infinite and self-ruled, and is mixed with nothing, but is alone...For it is the thinnest of all things and the purest, and it has all knowledge about everything and the greatest strength; and *Nous* has power over all things both greater and smaller, that have life. And *Nous* had power over the whole revolution, so that it began to revolve in the beginning.[223]

Anaxagoras's description of *Nous* suggests a Divine Mind that created the "seeds" comprising the original chaos, which in turn suggests *creatio ex nihilo*. It may be significant that Aristotle, in a passage dealing with Anaxagoras, refers to "some [who] make existing things out of the non-existent" (*Metaph.* 1075b15). Since *Nous* seems to be omniscient and omnipotent, Anaxagoras's account of "creation" bears analogy with the account in Genesis and therefore suggests that he was a monotheist. Perhaps this is why he had to flee polytheistic Athens.

Be this as it may, *Nous* communicates motion to this primal chaos. The motion begins at some point in this chaos in the form of a little gyration and extends out to ever larger, concentric circles, segregating homogeneous things from homogeneous things.[224] We see here an astonishing cosmology, devoid of anthropomorphism and bearing some analogy to the expanding universe that originated in the Big Bang. What needs to be emphasized, however, is that *Nous* is an *intelligent* being that transforms chaos into a cosmos—a complex but ordered whole. This conforms to Genesis 2:4, where we are told that "God *made* the earth and the heavens" (in contradistinction to Genesis 1:1, where we are told that "God *created* the heavens and the earth"—and notice the reversal of the order.)

DEMOCRITUS

Finally, a word about Plato's older contemporary, Democritus (460-370 BCE). Democritus maintained that all matter consists of atoms, that is, of individual and imperceptibly small particles.[225] These particles are infinite in number and differ not only in substance but also in size or shape. Diversity in nature and change result from different combinations of atoms and their dissolution. (Recall Murray Gell-Mann's attempt in the 1960s to reduce the tremendous complexity of the zoo of particles then known into more simple and elementary particles, which he named "quarks.") Democritus also posited an *infinite* void or space through which the atoms move. Although the motion of the atoms is strictly deterministic, the things which they form seem to be the result of chance, a view later made explicit by Epicurus, who postulated indeterminate atomic "swerves"—one might almost say quantum jumps.

To conclude, in this world of atoms in motion, man's place is uncertain, for Democritus divests nature of objective values—esthetic and moral. Democritean physics, transmitted by way of Lucretius' *De Rerum Natura,* was to have considerable impact on Galileo and Hobbes, on early modern science as well as on modern political science. Twenty-four centuries ago it required intellectual giants like Plato and Aristotle to overcome the subversive impact of Democritus and his "value-free" physics. It is this kind of physics, however, that now rules the mental horizon of the modern world. Unlike Plato and Aristotle, this physics has no pretension of teaching us anything about the Good and the Beautiful, let alone of the meaning of history. And so the closing lines of Matthew Arnold's *Dover Beach* still haunt the soul of modern man:

> And we are here as on a darkling plane
> Swept with confused alarms of struggle and flight,
> Where ignorant armies clash by night.

Chapter 10
Plato and Aristotle:
In Quest of the Good and the Beautiful

Introduction

With Plato and Aristotle a new type of man appeared in the forefront of world history, Cognitive Man. Cognitive Man is a secularist who regards the unaided human intellect as capable of comprehending the organizing principles of the universe. This is Deification of the Mind. Cognitive Man is therefore to be distinguished from his secular rivals, Volitional Man and Sensual Man. Whereas Cognitive Man seeks to understand the world, Volitional Man wishes to change or conquer it, while Sensual Man wants to enjoy it. Only with the ascendancy of Volitional Man—exemplified by Machiavelli—does secularism come into its own as the regnant force of history.

We are not used to thinking of Platonic-Aristotelian philosophy as secular. Not only do Plato and Aristotle refer to the divine and regard the intellect as divine-like, but the refinement of their writings conveys great piety. What gives the lie to this impression is that neither philosopher regarded piety as a virtue. We must also bear in mind their caution and civic-mindedness. Socrates, the master of irony, was given the hemlock for atheism. And what with the widespread corruption in Athens resulting from affluence, the disastrous Peloponnesian War, and the unabashed atheism of so many sophists or intellectuals, it would have been reckless of these aristocrats of the mind to have joined the scoffers of a religion which, whatever its shortcomings, did provide some salutary restraints on the passions of men.

There are refined and vulgar forms of secularism. Plato and Aristotle's secularism is couched in pious language not only for political and pedagogical reasons, but because, in their species of humanism, the philosopher is virtually divine.[226] For these intellectual and aristocratic giants, Cognitive Man is the passionate lover of wisdom, where wisdom is nothing less than knowledge of the Whole. "The science of the whole," says Aristotle, "enables the wise man to have full intellection of everything" (*Metaph.* 982a21-22). Accordingly, Cognitive Man, whether philosopher or scientist, seeks to reduce the fleeting phenomena of existence to lawfulness. This is as true of Platonic-Aristotelian philosophy as it is of Galilean-Newtonian physics, despite their very different conceptions of lawfulness.[227] Both schools seek to discover the riddle of existence in some scientific order or pattern of the world. This is the aim of Cognitive Man.

However refined the quest of Cognitive Man, what unites him with his secular counterparts, Volitional and Sensual Man, is that, like them, he does not pursue the object of his desire at the behest of God or to glorify God. The reason is rather simple: for Cognitive Man such a God does not exist. Aristotle, like Spinoza, is a pantheist. His Prime Mover is an extrapolation from the principle of motion (*Physics* 251b17-25, 266a5). As for Plato, his "Demiurge" (as previously noted) is not a creator but an artificer that imposes order on a pre-existing chaos (*Timaeus* 30a, 52d-55, 69b). All this aside, however, one thing is clear: both philosophers rejected the idea of a *personal* and *providential* God. Otherwise piety would be a virtue.

Nevertheless, it was left to Plato and Aristotle to apply, philosophically speaking, the *coup de grace* to the Greek pantheon and thereby advance the negative goal of the Torah's world-historical program, the elimination of polytheism. Their explicit teachings—Plato's less than Aristotle's—also support the conclusion that no deity is needed to explain the origin of the universe, which of course contradicts ethical monotheism, the positive goal of the Torah's program.

PLATO

At the outset of Plato's most celebrated dialogue, the *Republic*, we see that Socrates is walking to the Piraeus with Glaucon to attend a religious festival. On the way they are accosted by Polemarchus who invites them to the home of his elderly father, Cephalus. Socrates engages Cephalus in a discussion about justice. Before the discussion gets very far, Cephalus prompts Polemarchus to carry on the dialogue, so that he, Cephalus, can leave to worship the gods. Cephalus never returns, and no more is heard of the religious festival. Philosophy thus replaces religion, the philosopher supplants Zeus. No longer are the gods of the masses to rule mankind; henceforth human reason is to determine how man should live.

For Socrates to question his fellow-Athenians regarding how man should live is to deny that this question can be answered by *tradition*. Socrates thereby undermined the gods of Athens. He was not the first to do so, as we saw in the case of Anaxagoras. Athens, a commercial democracy, was then the center of "culture," of learning. Philosophers and sophists from around the Mediterranean converged on this city which Thucydides has Pericles call the "school of Hellas." The Athenians were thus distracted by a babel of doctrines inhospitable to their religious beliefs. While Democritus severed man from nature and nature from the realm of the Good and the Beautiful, his student, Protagoras, propagated the subversive doctrine of moral relativism: not Zeus but "Man is the measure of all things"—and men differ from one *polis* to another. Zeus had thus become a virtual nonentity, or as Protagoras casually (or cautiously) put it: "Concerning the gods, I am not able to know to a certainty whether they exist or whether they do not."[228]

The relativism and atheism of the sophists—comparable to today's "value-free" social scientists—had engendered a radical egoism that fragmented and corrupted the Athenian *polis*. A "new" morality had taken the place of the old decencies. Socrates' task was to provide a teaching that would reinforce these old decencies on different foundations. Without openly questioning the old gods—for belief in the gods made men better than they would otherwise be—he tried to counter the unrestrained disbelief of the sophists, who catered to the *demos*, the Many, with the restrained disbelief of Socratic philosophy, which appealed to the *aristoi*, the Few.

Still, what was to take the place of the gods in the non-philosophic minds of the Many? Something *impersonal, immutable,* and *eternal* was needed to command the obedience and respect of men. What else could this be but Nature (encompassing *human* nature) as conceived by the philosopher and offered to mankind as a new dispensation (if not as a "noble lie")? By divesting nature of the Homeric gods, whose behavior was arbitrary and mysterious, nature could then become fully accessible to the human mind. Henceforth neither the gods nor man but nature would be the measure of all things and provide the norm of how man should live—a position rejected by the Torah and, for other reasons, by modern physics. No philosopher has made nature the norm with greater clarity and precision than Aristotle. But first we must find man's place and purpose in Plato's physics and cosmology.

When Leonardo de Vinci (1452-1519) warned his readers that "He who is not a mathematician…must not read me," he was paraphrasing the sign above the entrance of Plato's Academy: "Let no one who has not grasped the mathematical enter here!"

Like Pythagoras, Plato made the physical universe fundamentally mathematical. He rejected the materialistic atomism of Democritus and substituted mathematical or geometric "atoms" which combine to form the four "elements" of Empedocles—fire, water, air, and earth. The importance of this step in philosophical thinking, writes Heisenberg, can hardly be overemphasized: "It is not only the origin of natural science in its modern mathematical form, but has by its technical applications changed the whole picture of the world... Among all the different forms of understanding the one form practiced in mathematics is singled out as the 'real' understanding."[229] Moreover, unlike Empedocles' model of the four elements, Plato's mathematical approach will eventually become a means for predicting physical events. But to see how Plato anticipated modern science, and, at the same time, came close to the cosmology of the Torah, we must examine his *Timaeus,* which is not a dialogue so much as the narration of an astronomer-mathematician having that name.

The cosmology in the *Timaeus* is offered as a "plausible," one may say "hypothetical," account of the origin of all things. Timaeus begins by distinguishing between two kinds of entities comprising the universe. One is incorporeal, eternal, immutable, and has no becoming. It is apprehended by reason. The other consists of visible and tangible things apprehended by conjecture or opinion aided by sense-perception. Timaeus then asks whether the universe is eternal and without a beginning, or whether it was created and thus had a beginning. The universe must have been created, he says, because it is a visible and tangible body which, like all sensible things, is either in process of creation or has already been created. Moreover, that which is created must of necessity be created by a cause. But here we are told that "the father and maker of all this universe is past finding out; and even if we found him, to tell of him to all men would be impossible" (28c). Enter Plato's famous "Demiurge," the mysterious "craftsman" of this universe, which will supplant the Olympian gods.

For Plato, all that is visible and tangible in the universe is an imitation of Ideas or Forms (41c-d, 52a). The Ideas constitute the Model or pattern according to which the Demiurge fashions the physical world, including man. The Ideas are not to be construed simply as mental constructs, for they are ungenerated, eternal, and immutable. Harmonizing this noetic pluralism is the "Idea of the Good" (46d). The Idea of the Good (recall Anaxagoras' *Nous*) is the fundamental cause of all knowledge and existence. It is the supreme reality on which all logical, ethical, and aesthetic values of the sensible world depend.

To say that the Idea of the Good is the fundamental cause of all knowledge and existence accords with what was said of the God of the Bible: "*With wisdom God created the heavens and the earth.*"[230] Further, if the Idea of the Good is the cause of *all* existence, then Plato's cosmology or cosmogony would be consistent with the Torah principle of *creatio ex nihilo*. This is not quite the case, however.

We saw that the universe initially required only two kinds of entities: the eternal Ideas which have no becoming, and second, the imitations of these Ideas in all that is visible and tangible and is always becoming or perishing. These two entities cannot wholly account for the origin of all things. The universe requires a third kind of entity, one that is eternal and yet *becomes all things*. Plato admits that this entity is most difficult to describe in words.[231] Still, why does Plato need this third entity—which he also calls the "mother of all Becoming"—and how can it be eternal and still become all things? The reader will soon be surprised.

As previously indicated, Plato does not and cannot regard any visible or tangible entity as a fundamental element of the physical world. The macrophysical world is the derivative of something more fundamental:

> We must gain a view of the real nature of [visible or tangible things such as] fire and water, air and earth *before* the birth of heaven, and the properties they had *before* that time; for at present no one has as yet declared their generation, but we assume that men know what fire is, and each of these [other] things, and we call them principles and that they are elements of the universe.... We shall not now expound the principle of all things...and solely for the reason that it is difficult for us to explain our views while keeping to our present method of exposition [which aims only at "probability"] (48b-e, italics added).

Plato then proceeds to refine his "plausible" and initial account of the origin of all things, but without departing from its hypothetical character (or engaging in a dialectical inquiry, which involves critical analysis of diverse beliefs). He now postulates a primordial, invisible, and formless entity existing *prior* to the construction of the universe.[232] He does this because *that which is to receive all forms must itself have no form*, and this precludes fire, water, air, earth and the like as primary elements. He illustrates this most crucial point as follows: in making figures from clay, the artist will not allow any previous figure to remain visible therein, but will begin by making the clay as smooth as possible before executing his work. Accordingly, if the things that compose the visible and tangible world are to be imitations of the Ideas, they must be derived from an invisible and intangible hence formless substance (49d, 50d-51b). (Recall Anaximander's *apeiron*, the "Indefinite.") In other words, Plato posits an eternal and incorporeal substance which is *pure potentiality* and which can thus become a diversity of physical things corresponding to the diversity of Ideas beheld by the world's artificer, the Demiurge. Moreover, the Ideas are not only patterns, but powers (*Sophist* 247e). Strange as it may seem, Plato is *conceptually* close to quantum physics!

The skeptical reader need only think of sub-atomic particles such as electrons, protons, and neutrons forming the well-known different gaseous, liquid, and solid elements, bearing in mind that "particles," according to QM, are also "waves," and that their behavior defies description, as does Plato's incorporeal substance (and Anaximander's "Indefinite"). One may rightly say that the micro-physical world of QM also consists of "pure potentiality." And this is not all. Since the materialization of Plato's incorporeal substance in the many diverse things comprising the perceptual world requires correspondingly diverse Ideas, but which Ideas Plato associates with mathematical or geometric atoms, we can well appreciate Heisenberg's admiration for this incredible philosopher.

But here we must pause and reflect, lest we make a serious error. Inasmuch as Plato's incorporeal substance is eternal, then, contrary to what was said earlier, the Idea of the Good is not the cause of *all* existence and cannot be identified with the God of Moses. Contrast Philo, who construed Plato's cosmology in the *Timaeus* from the perspective of Scripture:

> When God willed to create this visible world He first fully formed the intelligible world, in order that He might have the use of a pattern wholly God-like and incorporeal in producing the material world, as a later creation, the very image of an earlier, to embrace in itself objects of perception of as many kinds as the other contained objects of intelligence.[233]

Notice that whereas in the *Timaeus*, the Ideas are described as eternal and ungenerated, in Philo the Ideas are not spoken of as ungenerated but rather as created by God. Also, and consistent with Scripture, Philo omits Plato's eternal, incorporeal substance. (Nothing exists that was not created by God.) Plato needed that eternal, incorporeal substance to make what is *transcendent*, the Ideas and the Idea of the Good, *immanent*, which he accomplishes by means of the Demiurge—surely a *deus ex machina*. How Philo deals with the problem of making an absolutely transcendent God (*HaShem*) immanent will be considered later. What needs to be emphasized here is that unlike Philo's God, the Idea of the Good is neither omnipotent nor omniscient. Absent from Plato's cosmology, therefore, is *creatio ex nihilo*, and therein is the most fundamental conflict between Jerusalem and Athens.

It seems that Plato could not offer a "probabilistic" account of creation from nothing—which really means the creation of non-Being from Being—although the Ideas came remarkably close. *Creatio ex nihilo* simply defied the logical mind, and no dialectical method of inquiry would have overcome the lacunae without general relativity and quantum mechanics. Given *creatio ex nihilo*, the human mind, which thinks in terms of space and time, cannot have knowledge of that which "preceded" creation—meaning knowledge of God. Man can only know God through His works, i.e., by studying nature or the created universe, knowledge of which is virtually unlimited.

One other aspect of Plato's cosmology must be mentioned: whether history has any purpose. Reflecting eastern doctrines, the *Timaeus* portrays a finite cosmos involved in eternal cyclicality (37a, 40b)."[234] Man is caught up in a blind, remorseless, indifferent wheel of fate. (No wonder Socrates alludes to the Myth of Sisyphus at the end of the *Apology*.) Despite appearances to the contrary, eternal repetition signifying nothing seems to be Plato's assessment of human history.[235] His Dialogues, or many of them, should be studied as a synthesis of tragedy and comedy. It is no accident that Agathon the tragedian, Aristophanes the comic poet, and of course the ironic Socrates, are the only banqueters to remain awake and sober after the night-long festivities of the *Symposium*.

ANOTHER VIEW OF PLATO

Plato is perhaps the subtlest of philosophers. The philosopher-mathematician Alfred North Whitehead, who was also a historian of science, has said that the history of philosophy is but a series of footnotes to Plato. Since the history of philosophy is replete with conflicting doctrines concerning man and the universe, one should then be able to find many of those contradictions in Plato's Dialogues. Be this as it may, although a *philosophy of history* appears foreign to Plato, he almost certainly pondered the idea.

From the dialogue the *Laws* we learn that in the "present era"—meaning the era in which Plato lived—the government of the cities, even the best of these, must be modeled, he says, on the dogma of "invisible gods" (713b-e). Those dogmas involve laws and notions of good and justice which have mythological, rather than rational, foundations. Since those "invisible gods" have been subverted by philosophic reason as well as by the *physikoi*, political progress should be possible. In fact, Plato's dialogue, *Epinomis*, states that the construction of the city based on reason will only come true when man devotes himself to "gods of whom we have real manifestations" (985d4-986a6). Perhaps Plato had in mind a rational Deity in contradistinction to the irrational gods of the Greek city-states, a Deity whose rationality is evident in nature or in the structure of the cosmos.

We have returned full-circle to the Demiurge, a divine-like being who fashions this cosmos in accordance with the Idea of the Good. The Demiurge may now be regarded as Plato's esoteric way of planting the seed of a new religion, a religion whose deity is the source of rationality, of the Good and the Beautiful. Belief in such a deity would be conducive to the development of the sciences, especially mathematics, the key to a universal, rational, and natural theology. Such a theology would enable men to transcend the "invisible gods" of the cities, whose provincialism, passions, and ambitions periodically convulse the world. We must again recur to Philo.

Of his voluminous writings, his essay *On the Life of Moses* is most pertinent to what was just said about the need to transcend the "invisible gods" of the cities. Philo's contribution to this objective can hardly be exaggerated, but this highlights the influence of Judaism on the non-Jewish world.

When Philo speaks of that influence, he has in mind the remarkable fact that Ptolemy of Alexandria, Egypt (Philadelphus II, 285—247 BCE) commissioned a translation of the Pentateuch into Greek. This enlightened ruler wrote to the high priest, Eleazar, in Jerusalem, and arranged for translators from each of the twelve tribes of Israel to produce what is now known as the "Septuagint." Judging from Philo's remarks, the influence of the Septuagint was widespread and profound. Alexandria, the birthplace of Philo, was a center of learning and of Hellenism in the ancient world. Philo contrasts the laws of the cities of antiquity with the laws of Moses:

> Throughout the world of Greeks and barbarians there is practically no state which honors the laws of any other. Indeed, they can scarcely be said to preserve their own laws, which vary with the vicissitudes of time and circumstances.... It is not so with ours. They attract and win the attention of all, of barbarians, of Greeks...of nations east and west, of Europe and Asia, of the whole inhabitable world from end to end.
>
> For, who has not shown his high respect for that sacred seventh day, by giving rest and relaxation from labor to himself and his neighbors, freemen and slaves alike, and beyond these to beasts? For the holiday extends to every herd and to all creatures made to minister to man...It extends to every kind of trees and plants; for it is not permitted to eat any shoot or branch, or even a leaf, or to pluck any fruit whatsoever. All such are set at liberty on that day, and live as it were in freedom, under the general edict that proclaims that none should touch them.[236]

The sabbath liberates man from preoccupation with the needs of the body, from acquisitiveness, and thus prompts his mind to distinctively human and philosophical interests. The laws of Moses which regulate the ordinary economic and social relations of Jews actually conduce to, and heighten the physical and spiritual enjoyment of, the sabbath. It is in this light that we are to understand why it is that Theophrastus could describe the Jews as a nation of philosophers. Their laws are not based on mythology. While many of them separate Jews from the pernicious influences of the gentile world, many are of universal validity and applicability.

As Philo observes, unlike nations whose laws are ever-changing and so frequently based on whim and accident, the laws of the Jews are "stamped, as it were, with the seal of nature herself, and remain secure from the day when they were first enacted to now…[even] though the nation has undergone so many changes, both to increased prosperity and the reverse."[237] Nothing in their laws has been disturbed because Jews have paid high honor to their venerable and godlike character. Furthermore, unlike nations whose laws depend on coercion for their enforcement, the laws of Moses are based on moral suasion. "In his commands and prohibitions, he suggests and admonishes rather than [merely] commands, and the very numerous and necessary instructions which he essays to give are accompanied by forewords and after-words, in order to exhort rather than to enforce."[238]

Finally, with the *Republic* and the *Timaeus* in mind (but also influenced by Stoicism) Philo remarks that the laws of Moses are "too good and godlike to be confined, as it were, within any earthly walls," that they are "the most faithful image of the world-polity [or 'Metropolis']."[239]

Of course Philo is writing long after the Greek cities were conquered by Rome, indeed, after the Roman Republic was replaced by the Roman Empire. Rome had conquered Europe, North Africa, and the Middle East. Roman paganism was everywhere triumphant, and as will be seen in the next chapter, Rome was steeped in violence and corruption, which could not be stemmed by the ethical teachings of Stoicism, a derivative of Greek philosophy. Eventually, however, a daughter of Judaism, Christianity, modulated by Philo, would conquer the Roman world. But I am getting ahead of my story.

I have suggested that Plato planted the seed of a rational or natural religion, one conducive to a rational understanding of nature and to the progress of the sciences. But in so doing he was very cautious. His *Republic* warns: To "preach dialectic," which involvers criticism of received beliefs on logical grounds, requires great circumspection. Putting this weapon in the hands of the young (be they single individuals or cities) makes it a source of evil, for it fills them with contempt for the dogmas on which parents and governments established good, justice, and all their laws (537d5-539a6). In the "present era," therefore, the philosopher must conceal his deepest insights in the fairest [i.e., "politically correct"] part of his writings (*Epistles* VII, 344c1-d2). Accordingly, Plato's innermost thoughts are veiled, and to gain access to them the "mind" of the reader must overcome various "difficulties" (*Epistles* VII, 340b7-c1).

An example of Plato's esoteric teachings involves mathematics (the most arcane part of the *Timaeus*). *Republic* 526-527 refers to two types of mathematics, one practical, the other theoretical. The former, which may be called "quantitative" mathematics, and which deals with transient phenomena, has ever prevailed in the West. This mathematics—and all sciences based thereon—can teach us nothing about the Good and the Beautiful. In other words, quantitative mathematics is "value-free." But Plato also speaks of a mathematics that aims at knowledge of what is eternal, of the Good and the Beautiful. This mathematics, which may be termed "qualitative," is unknown to the West and has been the subject of painstaking inquiry by Professor Gian Carlo Duranti, to whom we shall return after discussing Plato's greatest student, Aristotle.

ARISTOTLE'S "PRIME MOVER"

The scope of Aristotle's inquiries has not been surpassed in the history of philosophy. He merely set out to comprehend the totality of existence, to reduce heaven and earth and all between to an organized system of theoretical, practical, and productive sciences. To borrow the terminology of the renowned Torah philosopher, Rabbi Joseph B. Soloveitchik, Aristotle would tolerate no randomness or particularity, no mystery to obscure the fleeting events of existence. Everything had to be fixed, clear, necessary, ordered.[240] Nothing was beyond the grasp of the human mind because the Cosmos was an intelligent and therefore intelligible whole.

Like Plato, Aristotle's logical mind could not see how this cosmos could be created from "nothing." He nonetheless postulates a "prime mover." He arrives at this prime mover solely by means of logic. Thus, every motion results from a previous one, which implies an infinite series backwards into eternity (*Physics* 259a). If Aristotle's world is to be intelligible, there must be a first mover which itself is unmoved and eternal. A prime mover is thus required by Aristotle's conception of motion.

It is erroneous to confuse Aristotle's prime mover with a theistic God, let alone the God of Moses.[241] The God of the Jews—the Supreme Being—is not just a principle but a living and personal God with whom one can relate and feel close, otherwise prayer would be meaningless. Aristotle's prime mover is at most the philosopher's edifying surrogate for God. It can neither create nor destroy matter, for "Neither matter nor form comes to be" (*Metaph.* 1069b35), which implies that the prime mover is neither omniscient nor omnipotent. Although Aristotle's *Metaphysics* (1072a-1073a) embellishes his prime mover with various godlike attributes, its lack of omniscience and omnipotence, like Plato's Demiurge, renders it suspect. According to Aristotle, the prime mover is the only being without extension; it is neither finite nor infinite. Yet Aristotle attributes to the prime mover infinite power (*Metaph.* 1073a5-10), contradicting its inability either to create or destroy matter as well as form (*Metaph.*, 1069b35).[242]

Aristotle's conception of motion confirmed the dogma of an uncreated universe. This dogma could have been reached by way of Aristotle's conception of knowledge. To know a thing one must know its causes: its material, efficient, formal, and final causes. In the case of natural objects, the formal and final causes coincide. Aristotle's cosmos cannot have an efficient cause (that by which it comes into being) because the mind cannot grasp its final cause (the *purpose* for which it exists). We cannot know *why* God created the universe. A Creator-God, hence *creatio ex nihilo*, would be utterly inscrutable, an offense to the philosopher's intellect.

The prime mover, we saw, is not a creator. Aristotle defines the prime mover as thought thinking about itself (*Metaph.* 1074b34). He thereby assimilates the prime mover to mind, identifying Being with being known. "Mind is itself thinkable in exactly the same way as its objects are, for in the case of objects which involve no matter, what thinks and what is thought are identical" (*De Anima* 430a1-4). The "god" of the philosopher is nothing more than the metaphysical thoughts of the philosopher's mind (echoing Parmenides and anticipating Spinoza's pantheism). In theory, therefore, the unaided human intellect can comprehend the organizing principles of the universe (which the mind, presumably, could not comprehend if the universe were created *ex nihilo*).

The denial of *creatio ex nihilo* had and continues to have the profoundest implications for human life and society.[243] As mentioned, to postulate a primal and eternal matter entails the denial of an omnipotent and omniscient God Who is both transcendent and immanent. Human history must then be deemed purposeless. To deny a Creator-God is to say, in effect, that neither individuals nor nations are governed by Providence. In Aristotle's finite and eternal universe we succumb, once again, to Nietzsche's Eternal Recurrence. The Second Law of Thermodynamics or increase of entropy may refute Nietzsche, along with Aristotle, but the supposed heat-death of the universe is not a tale for children.

ARISTOTLE'S POLITICAL PHILOSOPHY

When Aristotle inherited the concept of nature from Plato, it had already been demythologized and transformed into the impersonal and immutable standard of how man should live. Aristotle enriched and systematized the idea by developing an organic and teleological theory of nature.[244] Such was the success of this theory that it had no serious rivals in abodes of learning for almost two thousand years. Vestiges of organicism may be found even in Kepler, and it was not until Galileo and Newton, with the rise of the mechanistic conception of nature, that organicism was laid to rest.

What made the teleological theory of nature so alluring and enduring is that it appealed to common sense. Observe the growth of a tree from its seed and it will seem that the processes of nature are inwardly directed toward an end or *telos*. The end is that toward which a living thing strives in order to reach its completion. So it is with man. Neither force imposed from without, nor chance, so much as an immanent impulse prompts man to form associations that can fulfill his potentialities. The most self-sufficient and comprehensive association is the political community, the *polis*, which alone can complete or perfect man's nature. Whatever contributes to that end is called good. Nature is therefore the standard for judging what is good (or bad). There is no other.

Could there be a more impersonal yet intimate and benign substitute for the Olympian gods? Must we not marvel at Aristotle's genius? By creating a new foundation for morality, Aristotle became one of the greatest legislators of mankind. But there is more to his conception of nature.

Also to be seen in nature, and in nature as a whole, is a ruler-ruled relationship or hierarchy. It is natural for men to rule animals, for reason to rule the body, for parents to rule children, for the wise to rule the unwise. To be just, however, political rule must promote the common good; it must contribute to human perfection. The common good thus provides the criterion for distinguishing between just and unjust laws, hence between good and bad regimes.

At this point a brief review of Aristotle's six-fold classification of regimes will facilitate our analysis of his eventual antagonist Machiavelli, the father of democracy.

The three good regimes, in descending order of excellence, are kingship, aristocracy, and "republic" (or "polity"). Their corresponding perversions, in diminishing degree of badness, are tyranny, oligarchy, and democracy. A republic, the best practical regime, combines elements of democracy and oligarchy. It is stabilized by a large agrarian middle class which holds the balance of power between the rich and the poor and whose way of life exhibits temperance or moderation. The best regime in theory, kingship or aristocracy, requires men of exceptional moral and intellectual virtue, and such men are so few in number that their political ascendancy is very much a matter of chance. Nevertheless, the articulation of such a regime provides the model or standard for evaluating and, if possible, improving the laws, institutions, and policies of all existing regimes, good and bad.

The improbability of the best regime in theory or, conversely, the paucity of wise and virtuous men, clearly indicates that "nature" is the exception rather than the rule. Nature is a term of distinction—still intimated when someone is referred to admiringly as a "natural." Only if we understand what is distinctively human can we determine what is good and desirable in the conduct of life, private and public. Required, therefore, is a model of human excellence. Aristotle's *Nicomachean Ethics*, an inseparable part of his political philosophy, contains the paradigm of Secular, i.e., Cognitive Man. It provides a meticulous treatment of the moral and intellectual virtues, those faculties or powers whose perfection is essential for private and public happiness. The better to appreciate our later discussion of Machiavelli, the four cardinal virtues should be borne in mind, namely, *wisdom, justice, moderation,* and *courage*. Their cultivation is the true purpose of politics. And to the extent that rulers pursue this end, the political order will approximate the natural order.

Notice how elegantly Aristotle translates a teleological (and once deemed scientific) conception of nature into a theory of politics with obvious implications for practice. But what needs to be emphasized here is that his theory of nature utterly eliminates the gods from human concern. Oracles, priests, prophets are rendered obsolete. Cognitive Man—the Philosopher—supplants Zeus. Human reason, unaided and autonomous, replaces divine law. In this paradigm of classical political philosophy, which is one of the two sources of Western civilization, we behold an exquisitely modulated secularism, but one more congenial to the Few than to the Many (the *demos* Machiavelli will eventually use to overturn the Greco-Christian Tradition).

One cautionary note is necessary. Leaving the philosopher aside, although classical political philosophy is aristocratic, it exalts the *polis* over the individual. The ultimate reason is theological. Neither Plato's Demiurge and certainly not Aristotle's prime mover is concerned about the individual. Contrast Judaism. Given man's creation in the image of God, the Jerusalem Talmud declares with perfectly logical consistency: "If gentiles [surrounding Israel] demand, 'Surrender one of yourselves to us and we will kill him; otherwise we shall kill all of you,' they must all suffer death rather than surrender a single Israelite to them" (*Terumot* 8, 9). According to Jewish law, no individual may be sacrificed for the sake of his society, a principle foreign to Greek thought. In this respect Judaism appears egalitarian. To the contrary, Judaism projects, in Israel, a universal aristocracy, a nation of "priests"—really noblemen.

QUANTITATIVE MATHEMATICS AND THE IDEA OF EQUALITY

Despite its aristocratic character, classical Greek philosophy generated an idea that turned its hierarchic cosmos on its head—the Idea of Equality. This idea underlies the *quantitative* mathematics which the West derived from the classics, a mathematics which has proven to be the most powerful instrument for advancing an egalitarian conception of the universe. Consider this passage from Whitehead's *The Principle of Relativity*:

> …a discussion of equality embraces in its scope congruence, quantity, measurement, identity and diversity. The importance of equality was discovered by the Greeks. We all know Euclid's axiom, 'things that are equal to the same things are also equal to one another.' This axiom deserves its fame, in that it is one of the first efforts to clarify thought by an accurate statement of premises habitually assumed. It is the most conspicuous example of the decisive trend of Greek thought towards rigid accuracy in detailed expression, to which we owe our modern philosophy, our modern science, and the creeds of the Christian church. But grateful as we are to the Greeks for this axiom and for the whole state of mind which it indicates, we cannot withdraw it from philosophic scrutiny. The whole import of the axiom depends on the meaning of the word equal. What do we mean when we say one thing is equal to another? Suppose we explain by stating that 'equal' means 'equal in magnitude,' that is to say, the things are quantities of the same magnitude. But what is quantity? If we define it as having the property of being measurable in terms of a unit, we are thrown back upon the equality of different examples of the same unit. It is evident that we are in danger of soothing ourselves with a vicious circle whereby equality is explained by reference to quantity and quantity by reference to equality.

Whitehead goes on to say in the sequel: "Let us first drop the special notion of quantitative equality and consider the most general significance of that notion. *The relation of equality denotes a possible diversity of things related by an identity of character qualifying them.*"[245] This definition clearly applies to any qualitative classification system. When applied to qualitative diversity, however, Western mathematics yields, by means of quantitative units, abstract equality. As Aristotle points out, "The most distinctive mark of quantity is that equality and inequality are predicated of it" (*Categories* 6a26). In other words, equality (recall *demophrenia*) obscures qualitative differences, as in the egalitarian principle of "one adult/one vote." *A quantitative mathematics is the ultimate form of reductionism.*

History had to wait for Galileo Galilei before the Idea of Equality became fully manifest as a cosmological principle, one that would deprive man of all moral bearings. Strange as it may seem we must discuss Galileo in this chapter on Plato and Aristotle. But then Galileo deemed himself a Platonist, and in his *Dialogues Concerning Two New Sciences*, he has a tamed Aristotelian, Simplicio, say: "Believe me, if I were again beginning my studies, I should follow the advice of Plato and start with mathematics, a science which proceeds very cautiously and admits nothing until it has been rigidly demonstrated." Natural philosophy, according to Galileo, "is written in that great book that ever lies before our eyes—I mean the universe—but we cannot understand it if we do not first learn the language and grasp the symbols, in which it is written. This book is written in mathematical language, and the symbols are triangles, circles, and other geometrical figures…"[246]

When Galileo writes of mathematics he means Euclidean geometry. Euclid's space is infinite, "flat," and homogeneous. Thus, if "the book of nature is written in geometrical characters," it follows that the universe is infinite (contrary Einstein's general relativity, which employs a non-Euclidean geometry).[247] The idea of an infinite universe revolutionized realms of thought far beyond astronomy. Indeed, for the classics an infinite universe is irrational. In such a universe the "center" would coincide with the "circumference," "straight" with "curvilinear," "motion" with "rest." The world-image of any observer would depend on his place, and no place could claim privilege. Everything would be relative to everything else. Not only would the earth no longer be the center of the universe, but the terrestrial world, regarded somewhat contemptuously by Aristotle, would have the same status as the heavenly spheres.[248] The Idea of Equality had entered cosmology.

The new cosmology shattered the classical and medieval cosmos. It destroyed the idea of a finite, hierarchically-ordered and ontologically differentiated world and posited, in its place, the idea of an infinite universe wherein all things were placed on the same level. The laws of heaven and the laws of earth—astronomy and physics—were now united. With Galileo's mathematical synthesis of astronomy and physics, laws of nature were for the first time established in science. No such laws will be found in Aristotle's physics. Aristotle, we saw, regards nature as teleological; every natural entity possesses an *internal* principle of motion or change directing it to its natural end.[249] In contrast, Galilean physics relates things mechanistically, that is, by *external* causality, leaving nature without an end.

As Whitehead saw, Galilean physics "presupposes the ultimate fact of an irreducible brute matter, or material, spread throughout space in a flux of configurations. In itself, such material is senseless, valueless, and purposeless. It just does what it does do, following a fixed routine imposed by external relations which do not spring from the nature of its being."[250] For Aristotle, "matter" is inseparable from form; it is alive, so-to-speak, with *potentia*. For Galileo matter is dead. To this day there are those who would explain life in terms of what is dead, that is, in terms of lifeless matter in motion. This is one consequence of Galileo's mathematization of nature.

A closely related consequence is the subjectivism resulting from his acceptance of Democritus' atomic theory of matter. Invisible and imperceptible, the atoms possess mathematical qualities whose varied motions, operating upon the senses, cause such experiences as taste, smell, and sound. The mathematization of nature thus resulted in the doctrine of "primary" and "secondary" qualities (developed further by Descartes and Locke). Modern subjectivism begins with Galilean physics: "I judge that, if the ears, the tongue, and the nostrils were taken away, the figure, the number, and the motions [i.e., the primary qualities] would remain, but not the odors nor the tastes nor the sounds, which, without the living animal, I do not believe are anything else than names." [251] In other words: there are certain attributes of matter which we do perceive, such as extension, mass, and shape; these are the "primary" qualities; there are other things which we perceive, such as colors, odors, and sounds, which are not attributes of matter, but are perceived by us as if they were such attributes; these are the "secondary" qualities of matter.[252]

The fact that Galileo's world of matter in motion is amenable to exact quantitative analysis and prediction renders it incapable of telling us anything about the rich, qualitative world of sense-perception. This has greatly simplified and expedited the task of science which hitherto had been bogged down in the anthropomorphisms of sensation and imagination. Galilean physics, although not entirely free of anthropomorphism, reduces the evidence of the senses to phantasmagoria. Hence Whitehead's famous lament:

> Thus nature gets credit which in truth should be reserved for ourselves: the rose for its scent, the nightingale for its song, and the sun

for its radiance. The poets are entirely mistaken. They should address their lyrics to themselves and should turn them into odes of self-congratulation on the excellence of the human mind. Nature is a dull affair, soundless, scentless, colorless; merely the hurrying of material, endlessly, meaninglessly.[253]

Contrast Whitehead's lament with King David:

HaShem, our Master...
When I behold Your heavens, the work of Your fingers,
The moon and the stars, which You have established,
What is man's worth that You should be mindful of him?...
Yet you have made him a little less than God (Elohim).
You have crowned him with dignity and majesty.
You have made him the ruler of the works of Your hands.
You have put everything under his feet and control...
HaShem, our Master,
How powerful is Your Name and Glory in this world (Psalms 8:4-10).[254]

Let us ponder these verses most carefully. "*When I behold Your heavens, the work of Your fingers, the moon and the stars*"—these words do not glorify nature (as in Greek philosophy) but the Creator of nature. Moreover, King David is not comparing man to the moon and the stars. When he declares to HaShem, "*You have made man a little less than God (Elohim),*" he thereby affirms that man is the most important essence in the universe; for having been created in the image of God, man possesses intellect and free will, the highest qualities in creation. King David could therefore say: "*You have endowed man with dignity and majesty. You have made him the ruler of the works of Your hands.*" But when he adds, "*HaShem, our Master, how powerful is Your Name and glory in this world,*" we are here given to learn that the glory of the Creator is manifested through the intellect of man.

The glorification of nature—a tendency of the esthete—is a form of idolatry. Insofar as nature is worthy of admiration, it is only as the work of the Creator. "*The heavens declare the glory of God, and the firmament shows His handiwork*" (Psalms 19:2). Although Galilean science was not intended to glorify God, its mathematical and mechanistic conception of nature put an end to Aristotle's teleological and organic conception of nature and thereby terminated a form of idolatry which, however refined, substitutes Nature for God as the source of the Good and the Beautiful.

The nonhierarchical science emerging from Galileo discards all considerations based on ethical and esthetic principles. Distinctions between the good and the bad, the beautiful and the obscene, the noble and the base, collapse into mere emotions or subrational forces. The realm of fact divorces the realm of value. To this day, and as we have already indicated, *positivism* reigns supreme in all levels of education in the democratic world.[255] Yet this elimination of Aristotle's anthropomorphic conception of nature as a source of ethical and esthetic values has hastened the conquest of nature. However much we may deplore the cost—the consequent decline of religion and morality, of taste and manners—it needs to be emphasized that the prevailing ideas and ideals were based on a farrago of Greco-Christian elements which, having fulfilled their historical function of destroying paganism or primitive idolatry, were now preventing mankind from recognizing the only true God. The atheism generated by scientific materialism degraded man but was also preparing for his ultimate elevation.

QUALITATIVE MATHEMATICS

We have seen that the quantitative mathematics of modern times can tell us nothing about the Good and the Beautiful; and since mathematical thinking is deemed the paradigm of *rational* thinking, statements regarding ethical and esthetic values are said to have no rational foundation. (Recall Hans Reichenbach's positivism.) Needed, therefore, is a qualitative mathematics that can comprehend the Good and the Beautiful on rational grounds. At stake here is nothing less than the preservation of civilized society. So long as contemporary mathematics is deemed the paradigm of rationality, opinions about good and bad, right and wrong, beauty and ugliness will be dismissed as subrational and as having no objective validity. This cannot but undermine the foundations of civilized society, a fact plainly evident in the decay of the West.

Is it not strange, however, that Plato, who regarded mathematics as the touchstone of philosophy, saw no application of mathematics beyond the physical world—as if that mathematics could not reveal the Good and the Beautiful? To clarify this dilemma, let us consult the Italian philosopher-mathematician Gian Carlo Duranti, whose knowledge of classical Greek philosophy has few equals.[256]

According to Duranti, Western mathematics is based on a colossal misinterpretation of Euclid's *Elements*.[257] He maintains that Book X (of the thirteen books comprising the *Elements*) harbors a *qualitative* mathematics based on the esoteric teachings of Plato's *Epinomis*—a dialogue deemed spurious by historians, presumably because they failed to discern its esotericism. Duranti also maintains that Aristotle's *Metaphysics* provides a bridge between *Epinomis* and Book X of the *Elements*.

Apparently, Plato and Aristotle as well as Euclid (who taught in Alexandria) refrained from publicizing truths which would have undermined the religious foundations of the Greek city-states had such truths been divulged "without veils" or "at the wrong time" (Plato, *Epistle* VII 341d-342a1). Precisely such truths are needed in our time in view of the decadence of the West. This circumstance endows Duranti's attempt to restore the qualitative mathematics hidden in Plato and Euclid with enormous potential significance. He pursues this objective in a massive treatise intended solely for mathematicians, hence beyond the scope of this book.[258] Nevertheless, inasmuch as Duranti, a gentile, has informed the present writer of mathematical links between Plato and the Torah, I cannot in good conscience avoid the task of discussing at least the general character of Duranti's extraordinary research. Since the subject is rather arcane, however, it may be advisable for some readers to proceed to the concluding section of this chapter.

It should first be noted that Euclid's masterpiece, the *Elements*, has influenced all branches of science, and none so much as mathematics and the exact sciences. The *Elements* have been studied throughout twenty-four centuries and in many languages. According to Duranti, mathematics in the modern era is a continuation not so much of the *theoretical* mathematics of antiquity as of its *practical* and *applied* mathematics. This circumstance, he says, explains the present crisis in the theoretical foundations of science, testified to by eminent physicists of our time, whose opinions in respect to this problem are cited in large number in Duranti's treatise.[259] The basic flaw in a purely quantitative mathematics is its inability to comprehend the Good and the Beautiful. In the qualitative mathematics he finds in Plato, Duranti sees a "higher rationalism," one superior to the rationalism attributed to modernity.

At the outset of the English-language preface of his treatise, Duranti writes:

> In view of the size and rigor of the edifice of modern mathematics, it would seem that any work seeking to reconstruct Plato's mathematics could only have a purely philological interest, and be aimed principally at a restricted circle of scholars who see in ancient Greek mathematics as the first stirrings of a creature which today has reached its maturity.
>
> At a closer look, however, the mathematics of the ancient Greek philosophers appears to us as being anything but a creature in its infancy. The *Republic* (524d-527c) tells us how those men set their

minds to developing a science of numbers which would be "entirely different from the usual science," and that "instead of applying to all things the concepts of geometry whose sole purpose is to square, apply an area to a segment, add one segment to another, and perform other such [practical] operations," this mathematical system would be aimed at "taking the mind from the sphere of phenomenality to the sphere of pure being, where it can with greater ease perceive the Idea of the Good." As Aristotle says in *Metaphysics* 1078a31-b6: "Of all sciences, mathematics is the best suited to reveal the essence of Beauty as a Cause."

We are, then, dealing with an essentially "qualitative" discipline, whose purpose is neither technical nor to explore corporeal reality, but rather to pursue ends which, in Plato's own words, are "both philosophical and political." After expounding this mathematics, [Plato's] *Epinomis* concludes that only he who has mastered the Genus of numbers upon which it is based can truly lay the foundations of a "City"—especially a City of the Sciences—and be capable of leading it.[260]

No wonder Plato, Aristotle, and Euclid refrained, *in their time*, from divulging this knowledge "without veils"! Aristotle nonetheless declares, "It is impossible…that Plato, after making the search for the 'Good' the purpose of the *Dialogues*, does not allow us [i.e., philosophers] to 'understand clearly what it is'…[Moreover] *Epinomis* begins (973b2/6) by warning us that 'all discourses made up to now would remain unfinished if we did not say what a mortal must learn in order to become wise.'"[261]

Aristotle goes further: "If [Plato's] Ideas were not Numbers, they could not exist at all…"[262] This clearly implies that certain kinds of numbers enable us to understand non-physical realities such as moral and esthetic values. Accordingly, "He who asserts that mathematics has nothing to say about the good and the beautiful is wrong. Instead, it is the most suitable science for showing what the beautiful consists of…The supreme forms of the beautiful are order, commensurability and limit; these things are revealed to us by mathematics. And since essences like order and limit are the causes of many things, it is clear that mathematics concerns what causes order and limit; the beautiful [must then be understood] as a cause."[263] Aristotle goes on to say, "We shall speak more plainly elsewhere about these matters" (*Metaph.* 1078b5). We look in vain, however, for his clarification of this esoteric subject.

Plato regarded quantitative mathematics, which the West has developed with such success, as "limited to practical ends and servile—a science fit for builders and merchants." Not that he disdains the technical sciences per se, but rather any philosophy that limits the totality and significance of number to merely physical phenomena. This should interest today's mathematicians who lament the precariousness of the theoretical foundation of mathematics and its lack of a satisfactory number theory (contained, according to Duranti, in the *Epinomis* and Book X of the *Elements*). Plato recognized that in a world in which science is supreme, "morality cannot stand firmly on principles that depend on 'invisible gods.'"—the gods of Olympus.[264] The salutary consequences of the Big Bang theory and the Anthropic Principle aside, a quantitative mathematics subverts morality along with the gods.

It so happens, however, that a qualitative mathematics is hidden in the Torah.[265] Indeed, as a consequence of an article[266] the present writer sent to Professor Duranti, this extraordinary philosopher published a paper in *Filosofia Oggi* (April 1994) bearing the incredible title, "Codes of the Pentateuch and Egyptian-Platonic Mathematics"! The article I sent Duranti announced that mathematicians in Israel had discovered the existence of key terms encoded in the Pentateuch in equidistant letter sequences (as previously mentioned). The initial research of these mathematicians was conducted in 1985 at Israel's famed Institute of Technology—the Technion. This research revealed to Duranti the surprising appearance and recurrence of the names *Elohim* and the Tetragrammaton (*YHVH*) in letter-skipping intervals of 50, 5, 7, and 49 invariably linked together in all five Books of the Torah:

> These numbers [he writes] are related to fundamental elements of Judaic worship and civilization (the Sabbath, the Jubilee, *Shavuot*, the menorah, etc.); but this does not suffice to justify their roles in the spacing of the "hidden words" [such as *Elohim* and *YHVH*]; indeed, we can only wonder all the more about what sort of "hidden design" lurks behind these recurrences and symbols.[267]

We are thus given to understand that, according to Duranti, certain numerical intervals in the Torah are linked to numerical concepts in Plato's *Epinomis* and Book X of Euclid's *Elements*, which numerical concepts involve a qualitative mathematics capable of grasping the Good and the Beautiful. By ignoring or failing to comprehend the *esoteric* "geometry of the philosophers" contained in Book X of the *Elements*, the West chose the *exoteric* geometry set forth in the first five books of that classic, a geometry that led to a rationality incommensurate with moral and esthetic values. Duranti quotes J. A. Wojciechowski: "We should meditate on the fact that we were successful or unsuccessful according to the kind of rationality we chose."[268] Evidently, the West "chose" a rationality based on a quantitative mathematics, which yielded tremendous success in the mastery of the physical world, but at an enormous price: the loss of objective knowledge regarding the Good and the Beautiful, which requires a qualitative mathematics.

Duranti contends that the qualitative mathematics he sees in Plato and which he links to the codes in the Torah "implies first of all that the Torah founds the City of *YHVH* upon science and reason, and therefore that the Old Testament refuses to be exhausted in that concept of religion to which the histories of philosophy relegate it today."[269] Hence, it bears repeating nothing is a greater obstacle to understanding the uniqueness of the Torah than to place it under the category of religion.[270]

Conclusion

The Idea of Equality, magnified by the mathematization of nature in Galileo's *Two New Sciences* (1638) and perfected by Newton's *Principia* (1687), shattered the hierarchic universe of the classics. Heaven was brought down to earth and Nature was no longer a term of distinction, the norm as to how man should live. In both respects, Galileo and Newton, the architects of classical mechanics, unwittingly furthered the world-historical program of the Torah. The great edifice of classical Greek philosophy has crumbled, and, with it, one of the two pillars of Western civilization. The other pillar is Christianity, to which we now turn.

Chapter 11
Rome and Christianity

Roman Decline and Christian Ascendancy

ALTHOUGH Rome conquered Greece on the battlefield, Greek philosophy conquered the Roman mind and prepared the ground for Christianity. Before enlarging on the subject of Christianity, we must briefly examine two schools of thought derived from Plato's Academy, Skepticism and Hedonism, which contributed to the demise of the Roman gods and thereby served the Torah's goal of eliminating polytheism.

Simply stated, Academic Skepticism denies the possibility of absolute certainty. James E. Holton elaborates: "Man as man, the Skeptics asserted, is limited to opinions of that which is more or less probable. Although man may seek to attain a higher degree of probability by examining, as Socrates did, the relative merits of all opinions, he will never at any point in his inquiry be assured of absolute certainty..."[271] While skepticism may be philosophically defensible, it cannot but undermine the established beliefs of the community. A doctrine which purports to demonstrate that the commonly accepted standard of what is just and unjust must always lack a fully rational and defensible basis may not unduly disturb the philosopher, but the impact of that skepticism on most citizens can become politically disastrous. It can shatter their belief that the common good should be preferred to their private good.

This was well understood by Cicero (106-43 BCE), the great philosopher-statesman of the Roman Republic. He recognized that Skepticism, by placing in question the existence of the gods, would subvert men's traditional beliefs and lead to social chaos. His two dialogues, the *Republic* and the *Laws*, which are very much based on Plato's corresponding dialogues, convey, by means of different interlocutors, "politically correct" opinions while concealing Cicero's own real beliefs. A further word about Cicero is therefore necessary before we discuss Hedonism.

In the *Republic* and the *Laws*, Cicero addresses the fundamental question that guided classical political philosophy as a whole: What is the best regime or political order? In the *Republic*, the more philosophic of his two dialogues, we learn that the best regime in theory is one whose laws are based on pure reason and justice. Since such a regime would require the rule of philosophers, it is not to be expected among the commonality of men. Cicero therefore offers, in the *Laws*, the model of a good practical regime, one based on the primacy of religion and the natural law teachings of the Stoics. In short, whereas the *Republic* is addressed to the Few, the philosophers, the *Laws* is addressed to thoughtful statesmen and is intended as a guide suitable for the Many.[272] The intention of the *Laws*, therefore, was to counter the corrosive skepticism rampant in Rome.

As for Hedonism (which Cicero despised), its most influential exponent was Epicurus (341-270 BCE), who was born in the Athenian colony of Samos, about five years after the death of Plato. Reduced to its simplest level, the goal of his teaching was to rid men of fear, especially the fear of death and of the gods. How better might one do this than by denying the immortality of the soul and making the gods irrelevant by propagating the belief that they have no concern about mankind—a discreet way of denying their existence and avoiding the fate of Socrates. By explaining the origin and structure of the universe and of the human soul in materialistic and mechanistic terms, Epicurus sought to liberate men from ignorant fears and superstitions.

As generally understood, the imperative of Hedonism is to seek pleasure and avoid pain. But Epicurus is no vulgar hedonist. He recommends refined pleasures, above all those of the contemplative life. He cautions against ambition and emphatically rejects the life of politics. Underlying his apolitical hedonism, however, is a morally subversive cynicism. For Epicurus, no pleasure is bad in itself, but he cautions that the means which produce some pleasures may bring pains many times greater. Virtue is to be honored if it gives pleasure; but if it does not give pleasure, we must bid virtue farewell. As for justice, it is merely a compact not to harm or be harmed. Injustice is not an evil in itself, but only in consequence of the fear of being detected and of being unable to escape those appointed to punish such actions (the position Glaucon asks Socrates to refute in Book II of the *Republic*). Justice will therefore vary as the laws or forms of government in different countries vary—the relativistic conclusion of the sophists that undermined Athens.

The most complete exposition of Epicurus is contained in the work of the Roman philosophic poet Lucretius (c. 99-55 BCE). His epic *De Rerum Natura* (*On the Nature of the Universe*) has influenced modern philosophers, especially Hobbes. Read with discernment, Lucretius purveys a doctrine of atheism, notwithstanding his exoteric (or "politically correct") reference to the gods—a caution Hobbes was to adopt in the *Leviathan*.

The life of Lucretius coincided with the decline and fall of the Roman Republic. The period was one of almost ceaseless violence: political assassinations (including Cicero's), civil wars, massacres, revolts, conspiracies, mass executions, and social and economic chaos. A brief chronology of the times paints a grim picture of devastation:

> • 91 BCE: the so-called Social War between Rome and her Italian allies breaks out. No sooner is this bitter struggle ended (88 BCE) than Lucius Cornelius Sulla, a ruthless politician and renegade army commander, marches on Rome, and an even more convulsive and bloody Civil War begins.
>
> • 82 BCE: Sulla becomes dictator. He orders the arrest and execution of more than 4,000 leading citizens, including 40 senators.
>
> • 71 BCE: Spartacus' massive slave revolt (involving an army of 90,000 former slaves and outlaws) is finally put down by Cassius and Pompey. More than 6,000 of the captured rebels are crucified and their bodies left for display along the Appian Way.
>
> • 62 BCE: Defeat and death of Catiline. By this point in his career this former lieutenant of Sulla had become a living plague upon Roman politics and a virtual byword for scandal, intrigue, conspiracy, demagoguery, and vain ambition.

Such was Rome from the rise of Sulla to the fall of Catiline, a period of bloodshed and moral decay. No wonder the precepts of Epicurus—with their emphasis on contemplative pursuits and quiet pleasures and severe strictures against ambition, fame, and the world of politics—struck a responsive chord in the heart of a young Roman poet like Lucretius.[273] Nevertheless, his Epicurean teachings brought no solace or salvation to the Roman masses, which had lost their moral bearings when they lost their immortal gods. Hedonic cynicism led to disillusionment and despair.

Cicero was quite aware of this. In the place of Epicurean atheism and hedonism he offered Stoicism. Stoicism, as conveyed by Cicero—who understood that philosophy could undermine civic morality—held that the gods existed and loved human beings. Both during and after a person's life, the gods rewarded or punished human beings according to their conduct in life. The gods had also provided man with the gift of reason. Since man has this in common with the gods, but animals share our love of pleasure, the Stoics argued, as Socrates had, that the best and most virtuous life was one lived according to reason, not according to the search for pleasure. This did not mean that humans had to shun pleasure, only that it must be enjoyed in the right way. It was fine to enjoy sex, but not with another man's wife. It was fine to enjoy wine, but not to the point of shameful drunkenness. Finally, the Stoics held that mankind must heed the natural law, which arises from reason. The natural law is also the source of all properly made human laws and communities.[274]

This is essentially the Stoic ethical teachings that Cicero urged the Roman elite to adopt—in vain. "The gentile world," writes Rabbi Samson Raphael Hirsch, "was falling into decay. The gods heard their death-knell, sadness dwelt in the hearts of men. Innocence and human worth were laughed at; bestial indulgence and shameless lust took the prize, folly and weakness ascended the throne.... Humanity had lost its divinity, men sighed for a new God."[275]

EARLY CHRISTIANITY

Although Jews were prominent in Rome and many Romans converted or sought to convert to Judaism, it required antinomian Christianity—Christianity divorced from Jewish law—to save Rome from utter barbarism.

Transcending the divisions of nations and ethnic diversity, Christian universalism ignited a spark from the Torah, the Genesis conception of man's creation in the image of God. From this monumental Jewish teaching there arose the "idea of the human community." Isaac Breuer writes:

> The idea of the human community was unknown to the whole of antiquity. The noblest and most sensitive moral philosophers of Greece only dared hint at it and shied away in awe before its consequences which spelt the destruction of the whole structure of classical society. It appears quietly and shyly in Roman law, too, and the great legal minds provided it with a sparse home in the so-called natural law [of the Stoic philosophy], which it vainly tried to wrest for itself in the Civil Code. It was reserved only for Judaism to bring it to validity with full lucidity at the end of antiquity, and this deed is the highest glory which Judaism acquired in the battle for the religious progress of the human community. It was the idea of the human community whose consoling beam and strengthening balsam at the end of antiquity drove all the miserable and the burdened, the pursued and enslaved among the gentiles, as

well as the great and the distinguished for whom Greek skepticism embittered all joy of being, into the arms of Judaism. It was the idea of the human community whose banner Christianity borrowed from Judaism, and under whose standard the ingenious propaganda of a Paul made the world subservient to itself.[276]

Jewish Christians inverted pagan hedonism, with its Bacchanalian rites and cultic obscenities, and preached a complete asceticism or renunciation of the bodily self. This ascetic dualism of body and soul marked a radical break from holistic Judaism, which held that the body as well as the soul must be dedicated to God. The early Christians therefore needed a new bible for the new religion, one based on yet superceding the old bible—in particular the Five Books of Moses. The Pentateuch contained an ethics rooted in law which could hardly be assimilated by the pagan world. It contained a theology that contrasted sharply with that of Greek philosophy and Greco-Roman polytheism. The leaders of the new religion had to formulate, or so they believed, a morality divorced from Jewish law, as well as a theology distinct from Jewish monotheism. No such theology could be developed or win converts among Roman and Greek intellectuals without taking into account Plato and Aristotle, the Pythagoreans and the Stoics, to say nothing of a welter of eastern religious doctrines that competed for the minds of men. It remained for a Jew, however, to provide a philosophical foundation for the development of Christianity—Philo of Alexandria.

Despite his eclecticism, which early Christianity probably needed, Philo was the greatest Jewish philosopher and theologian of the Greco-Roman period. His life (20 BCE-50 CE) coincided with Jesus (c. 6 BCE-30 CE) and the early years of Paul's apostolic missions (45-57), which is not to suggest any direct contact or conscious borrowing. However, by the end of the first century, Philo, thanks to his vast knowledge of Greek philosophy and the allegorical method of interpreting Scriptures, becomes decisive for the articulation of Christian theology and Christian exegesis.

Influenced by Philo, Clement of Alexandria (150-213), the first church father, attempted a synthesis of Platonic and Christian thought. Clement's protégé, Origen, the first significant Christian theologian, possessed copies of most of Philo's works. The *Ecclesiastical History* of Eusebius, Bishop of Caesarea (260-341), includes a catalogue of Philo's writings. (Sixty-five of Philo's books are listed in early Christian codices.) Philo's writings were translated into Latin and were known in Italy. Indeed, Ambrose, Bishop of Milan from 374 to 397, used Philo's works more than any other church father. Such was Philo's impact on Christianity that he was regarded as an honorary church father until the seventeenth century, which is not to imply that he ever renounced Judaism.[277] But all this suggests that Philo must have influenced the development of Christianity's most significant doctrine, the Trinity (of which, more below). In fact, he has even been called the "father" of Arius, whose dispute with Athanaseus over that doctrine culminated in Arius' excommunication!

That Philo was a Hellenistic Jew was crucial for the syncretization of Christianity and Greek philosophy. It should be borne in mind, however, that when Philo speaks of God and of man's relation to Him—as he so often does—the Hellene in Philo gives way to the Hebrew. (This must be one reason why his influence on Christianity was sometimes resented by the church fathers.)

To see how Philo is a link between Christianity and Hellenism, we must return to his neo-Platonism. Philo recognized that Plato was confronted by the problem of how the Ideas can be manifested in the multiplicity of diverse things composing the physical universe; in other words, how can that which is transcendent also be immanent. Recall that Plato needed not only a third entity, an incorporeal substance, but the Demiurge to transform that incorporeal substance into the physical world. Similarly, Philo addressed the theological problem of how God, Who is absolutely removed from us, can also be infinitely close to us.

Inspired by the Torah, Philo was the first philosopher to develop the doctrine that the Ideas are the thoughts of God. To describe the thoughts or mind of God, Philo uses the term *Logos* instead of *Nous* (which, for Anaxagoras, is uncreated). God is known through the Logos, for the Logos is the means by which God creates the world. As Wolfson puts it, the relation of God to the Logos is that of the Creator to the created, and the relation of the Logos to the intelligible world is that of the thinking mind to its objects of thought.[278] The physical world may thus be called (as previously mentioned) the crystallized thoughts of God. Lo and behold, Philo has substituted the Logos for Plato's Demiurge. But now, by virtue of the Logos, God, who is ultimately unknowable and absolutely transcendent, becomes both knowable and immanent— knowable and immanent in His works or in nature, His creation. This foreshadows neo-Platonism and facilitates the development of Christianity.

In Philo, the Logos naturally becomes the *Word* of God by which God created the universe, as in Psalms 33:6, *"By the word of the Lord were the heavens made."* (Incidentally, the Hebrew term *davar* means both word and thing!) It was also quite natural for Philo to use the term *Wisdom* as the equivalent of Logos. Thus, in Jeremiah 10:12, *"He established the world by His wisdom,"* and recall Proverbs 3:19, *"With wisdom God created the heavens and the earth."* But then Plato himself speaks of wisdom and mind as the supreme cause of the universe (*Philebus* 30c).[279] What we see in Philo's theology is a fusion of Greek and Jewish thought, which profoundly influenced Christianity (but not Judaism) and enabled Christianity to conquer the Roman world. Philo's Logos leads to the doctrine of the Trinity.

THE TRINITY

On its face, the Christian doctrine of the Trinity appears to violate the Second Commandment: "*Do not have any other gods before Me.*" Let us examine this doctrine, beginning with one of the greatest of all Christian theologians, Origen (185-254).

Origen lived during a period when Christianity as a religion had not yet developed a system of theology as a basis of orthodoxy. Many diverse opinions regarding the faith existed, and various sects formed, each claiming to possess the gospel truth. In this environment, Origen was the first thinker to offer a Christian theology that was philosophically more respectable than the mystic speculations of the various Gnostic sects that flourished in his time. I refer to his seminal work of Christian neo-Platonism, *On First Principles*, which is very much indebted to Philo.

Origen assimilated Philo's Logos to the Johannine doctrine, "In the beginning was the Word, and the Word was with God, and the Word was God" (John 1:1). However, in Origen, and infinitely removed from Philo, the Logos becomes incarnate in Christ, the mediator between God and man. In other words, while God is the "Father," the Logos—no longer the Word or Wisdom by which the entire world is made—becomes the "Son." The Holy Spirit completes Origen's divine hierarchical trinity.

Since God the Father, for Origen, is "personal and active," there must always have existed, with Him, an entity upon which to exercise His intellectual activity. This entity is Christ the Son, the Logos. (I ignore the problem of the Son's advent in the world in time.) Although the Son is coeternal with the Father, he is inferior to the Father but superior to all rational creatures, while the Holy Spirit, inferior to the Son, dwells within the "Saints" or those who have achieved salvation. This hierarchy reveals an allotment of power to the second and third members of the trinity: the Father's power is universal, the Son's corresponds only to rational creatures, while the Holy Spirit's power corresponds strictly to the "Saints." But this is not the end of the story. Origen's trinitarian doctrine raises profound problems for Christianity.

In 319, sixty-five years after Origen's death, and almost three hundred years after the death of Jesus, a dispute over the trinitarian doctrine broke out in Egypt between Arius (250-336) of Alexandria and Athanasius (297-373), the Bishop of Alexandria. The dispute is theological: whether Jesus was a created being (Arius) or not created but rather coequal and coeternal with God the Father (Athanasius). We saw in Origen that the Son is coeternal but not coequal with the Father. One can of course find verses in the New Testament that support Arius—"for my Father is greater than I." (John 14:28), as well as Athanasius—"I and the Father are one" (John 10:30).

Underlying the dispute is a basic Christian dilemma. Christians believe that in order for Jesus to be the savior of mankind, he must also be God. If he is not God, then he cannot be the savior. The trinity doctrine was therefore required to explain his divinity. He is man. He is God. He is both. He must be in order to be the savior.

Now it so happens that the theological warfare between the Arius and Athanasius camps arose and became politically divisive during the reign of the Roman emperor Constantine the Great, who called a council at Nicea in 325 to resolve the dispute. Constantine, himself the high priest of a pagan religion, but nonetheless sensitive to ecclesiastical pressures, used his influence to persuade some 300 bishops—a small fraction of all the bishops in his empire—to adopt the Athanasius doctrine. It is referred to as the Nicene Creed.

At this point, it should be emphasized that the Christian doctrine of the Trinity combines two theologies, Jewish monotheism and pagan polytheism, as was admitted by both Gregory of Nyssa (died after 385) and John of Damascus (675-749).[280] The trinity doctrine satisfied the majority of Christians who had come from pagan backgrounds. Throughout the ancient world as far back as Babylon, it was common for pagan polytheists to worship triad gods.[281] Although many would say that paganism was conquered by Christianity, it may be more accurate to say that Christianity assimilated paganism.

Is it not puzzling that despite the otherworldliness of Christianity and its emphasis on love, that Europe, the home of Christianity, has witnessed the fiercest hatred and the bloodiest wars? Is this failure to be attributed merely to Christians and not at all to Christianity, hence, to its theology on the one hand, and its having jettisoned Jewish law on the other? Is it not passing strange that Christianity should deify a Jew who in truth believed in the divine origin of Jewish law and who therefore rejected the deification of any human being? Must we not admit that Jesus was not a Christian?

Christianity posits the doctrine of his virgin birth, a doctrine rejected by many biblical scholars, and not merely because of its antecedents among eastern religions. (Zoroaster, the Persian prophet who lived and preached in ancient Babylon, was also said to have been God-begotten and virgin born.) Tertullian could nonetheless say, *"Credo quia absurdum est"*—*I believe because it is absurd.* Although Tertullian surely did not mean that any absurdity is believable, he also said, *"And He was buried and rose again; it is certain because it is impossible."* Evident here is a religion based on faith untrammeled by reason. This cannot but lead to unmitigated subjectivism from which may follow fanaticism, crusades, and murder on a vast scale.

Many Christians today believe that the Trinity is a major doctrine of Christianity. Many others would say that it is the very foundation of Christianity itself. Let us now consider the issue from a more thorough reading of the Second Commandment:

> *Do not have any other gods before Me. Do not represent [such gods] by any carved statue or picture of anything in the heaven above, on the earth below, or in the water below the earth. Do not bow down to [such gods] or worship them, for I am God your Lord, a God who demands exclusive worship"* (Exodus 20:3-5).

Rabbi Hirsch comments:

> If God is God, then everything except him is 'no-god'…there can be no other god, not the remotest idea of the possibility of any such god shall be given space in our minds. This denies the conception of [a divine association], that error which, without denying God, thinks that it can place another at His side, sharing His Deity, and forgets that the placing of another god at the side of God means doing away altogether with the real idea of God…. The error becomes greater when the idea of the existence of another god is given more concrete expression by making some pictorial representation or image of it.

Maimonides rejected the trinity doctrine as inconsistent with monotheism. On the other hand, Rabbi Jacob Emden (1697-1776), a great scholar, seems to have held a more lenient view, which is not to suggest that he did not regard trinitarianism as a departure from Jewish monotheism. In a letter appealing to the German authorities not to countenance schismatic Jewish sects and anti-Semitism, Rabbi Emden declared:

> [T]he Nazarene and his Apostles did not wish to destroy the Torah from Israel, God forbid; for it is written so in Matthew (5:18-19), the

Nazarene having said, "Do not suppose that I have come to abolish the Torah. I did not come to abolish, but to fulfill. I tell you this: So long as heaven and earth endure, not a letter, not a dot, will disappear from the Torah until it is achieved. If any man therefore sets aside even the least of the Torah's demands, and teaches others to do the same, he will have the lowest place in the Kingdom of Heaven, whereas anyone who keeps the Torah, and teaches others so, will stand high in the Kingdom of Heaven."....

Christian scholars have assumed from certain passages in the Gospels that he [the Nazarene] wished to give a new Torah to take the place of the Torah of Moses. How could he then have said explicitly that he comes only to fulfill it?...[T]he writers of the Gospels never meant to say that the Nazarene came to abolish Judaism, but only *that he came to establish a religion for the gentiles from that time onward.* Nor was it new, but actually ancient; they being the Seven Commandments of the Sons of Noah, which were forgotten. The Apostles of the Nazarene then established them anew....

It is for that reason that they were to abstain from meats offered to idols, and from blood, and from things strangled, and from fornication (Acts 15:29). They also forbade them circumcision and the Sabbath. All of this was in accord with the law and custom of our Torah, as expounded by our sages.... It was they (the sages) who said it was forbidden to circumcise a gentile who does not accept the yoke of (all) the commandments. The sages likewise said that the gentile is enjoined not (fully) to observe the Sabbath.

The Apostles of the Nazarene [foremost Paul, "an attendant of Rabban Gamliel the Elder, well-versed in the laws of the Torah"] therefore chose for those gentiles who do not enter the Jewish faith that instead of circumcision they should practice immersion (for truly immersion is also a condition of full conversion), and a commemoration of the Sabbath was made for them on Sunday.... But the Nazarene and his Apostles observed the Sabbath and circumcision...for they were born as Jews. They observed the Torah fully, until after a period of time a few of them decided to give up the Torah among themselves completely. They said that its [complete] observance was too difficult for them...(Acts 15:10).

They knew that it would be too difficult for the gentiles to [fully] observe the Torah of Moses. They therefore forbade them to circumcise, and it would be sufficient that they observe the Seven Noahide Commandments, as commanded upon them through the *Halacha* from Moses at Sinai.... [Hence] the Nazarene brought about a double kindness in the world. On the one hand, he strengthened the Torah of Moses majestically...And on the other hand, he did much good for the gentiles.[282]

Rabbi Emden seems to regard Pauline Christianity as a religion designed by Jews for the gentile world, that is, to eliminate primitive idolatry. If so, it is doubtful that the trinitarian doctrine would have had the blessings of Jesus. Moreover, in departing from Jewish monotheism Pauline Christianity abandoned, as mentioned, Jewish law. For the ethical and rational discipline of Jewish law Paul substituted *faith*. To be sure, this concept may signify that certain aspects of revelation cannot be proven by unassisted human reason. Nevertheless, the subjectivity of faith and its centrality in Christianity has not only led to Christianity's fragmentation, but to its eventual secularization. Let us see why.

CHRISTIAN ANTINOMIANISM

Christian antinomianism introduced into pagan Rome the idea of separation of religion and state: "Render unto Caesar the things that are Caesar's and to God the things that are God's." To separate religion and state is to confine spiritual concerns to the church and to leave a welter of political, social, and economic matters to the state, that is, to the more or less arbitrary will and contrivances of men. This is the price Christianity had to pay for discarding Jewish law, which the church did to facilitate the acceptance of Christianity in the pagan world. Having no all-embracing revealed law of its own, the church had to adopt and, at the same time, desacralize the partially religious but pagan laws of a then decadent Rome. (To be sure, the ecclesiastical authorities perforce developed an extensive body of canon law for the government of the church and its members.)

Strange as it may seem, Christian antinomianism is a basic cause of secularism in the West. By limiting itself primarily to "spiritual" matters, Christianity leaves its adherents subject to the shifting laws of the nation-state, and of course the laws of the nation-state, in addition to contradicting the laws of other nation-states, may foster irreligion and permissiveness and thus clash with Christianity. (For example, consider various Western nations whose laws now sanctify blasphemy and pornography, sodomy and prostitution, homosexuality and gay marriages.) Moreover, the separation of Christian morality and public law in the West deprived the law of any sanctity and authority while depriving morality of the support of law. The consequence is evident throughout Europe and America—rampant hedonism, immorality, and crime.

Meanwhile, the separation of Christian morality and public law has made Christianity less and less relevant to the daily social and economic activities of men. This split between morality and law cannot but divide the soul of the individual and corrupt the nation of which he is a citizen. Rabbi Abraham Isaac Kook sees the Christian world as "divided, without the unity of body and soul, without an inner joining and synthesis of the spirituality of the world and its corporeality, without an inner connection between deed and thought...."[283] While individual Christians may be pious, the nations are typically unscrupulous. Ponder these words of Isaac Breuer:

> Christianity addresses itself directly and solely to the individual in complete disregard of nations and of their role as basic elements of history. To the suffering individual, the victim of injustice and oppression, Christianity promised reward or salvation in the life hereafter, or in the beyond of history when nations would (supposedly) cease to exist. It urged the pious Christian to turn the other cheek, to resist not evil, instead of seeking to steer his nation on the path of justice. Hence the Christian individual and his nation drifted farther apart. Christian Europe has presented this interesting phenomenon: while individual citizenries of the nations abandoned paganism to become Christian, the nations comprising these very citizens remained pagan [as witness how those nations participated in the Nazi Holocaust]. The dogma, "Render unto Caesar the things that are Caesar's..." armed the wicked, for the State was Caesar. It arrogated to itself absolute sovereignty and recognized no moral law but self-interest.[284]

In Judaism there is no Caesar and there is no Church. Nor is there any split between law and morality. In Jewish morality the Divine Will appears not in an abstract manner, as in Christianity, but in the concrete and rational precepts of the law—the *Halacha*. In fact, what is distinctive about Judaism is not "morality" but *laws* of morality which are concrete and which clearly relate thought and deed.

In contrast, the behavior of Christians is to be governed not by moral laws but "moral precepts" and "love." Both are problematic. Moral precepts are vague generalities. Belief in such precepts leaves mankind with the problem of applying them to diverse circumstances, which requires judicial reasoning linked to a coherent body of laws. As for love, nothing is more dangerous than this emotion when charged by religiosity without the restraints of law. How often has the "religion of love" tortured and slaughtered men to save their souls?

Appalled by the horrific slaughter that took place in Christian Europe in World War I, Rabbi Kook candidly reveals some of the basic flaws and failings of Christianity. "By emptying law of its divine content," Christianity has often succumbed to "the grossest wickedness." "The poison invades the private law of the individual and spreads through the souls of nations, becoming the foundation of national hatred and the evil of bloodshed..."[285] Bearing in mind that Rabbi Kook died in 1935, hence before the Nazi Holocaust (in which even France participated), he writes: "Europe [in contradistinction to America] rightly gave up on God, whom she never knew." He then elaborates:

> Individual humanists adapted to the sublime good, but not an entire nation. No nation or tongue could understand how to aspire to the Good, the All, let alone how to stamp with this the foundation of its existence. Therefore, when in our day nationalism grew strong and penetrated the system of philosophy, the latter was forced to place a big question mark over all the content of absolute ethics, which truly came to Europe only on loan from Judaism, and as any foreign implant, could not be absorbed in its spirit.[286]

Today it is quite evident that Christian Europe has succumbed to moral relativism or the moral decay of "post-modernism." With uncanny insight, Rabbi Kook foresaw this development. He saw that although Christianity had softened "the hard shell of human depravity," he predicted that beneath the veneer of Christianity, paganism "will win out…will resent the sparks of the spirit of Israel…and hatred of Israel will increase."[287] And so it has come to pass. Recall the temporary resurgence of Christianity in Germany immediately after its defeat in World War II. Devastated by the war, Christians flocked to the churches as the only pillar left to lean upon. But soon after Germany's economy was restored, hedonism returned and the neo-Nazi party, steeped in paganism, increased its power. Again hatred of Jews and now of Israel is rampant throughout Europe, as may be seen in its pro-Palestinian posture, Arab barbarism notwithstanding.

To be fair, however, mention should be made of the Vatican's recent recognition of Israel and the countless Christians who are supportive of the Jewish state, indeed, have become Zionists more ardent than many Jews. The present writer has met many American Christians who, distressed by the moral decay of the West, turn to Israel as the fondest hope of mankind. Alas, Israel, the home of Jews from a hundred nations, has yet to achieve the national unity and sense of Jewish national purpose essential to its becoming, once again, the light of mankind.

Conclusion

Christianity departs from Judaism in basic ways, among which are the following. First, of course, is the Christian doctrine of the trinity which, insofar as it strains the credulity of countless academics, diminishes its own salutary influence and that of ethical monotheism in a world steeped in nihilism and barbarism.

Second, the Christian dualism of the secular and the sacred was abhorred by the prophets of Israel as hypocrisy. This dualism leaves mankind split between body and soul, unable to sanctify the physical world, thus leaving the spiritual world incapable of coping with the passions of men. In other words, Christianity, as an otherworldly religion, impairs the ability to unite thought and deed. Its repression of material striving in the name of God succeeds only so long as people are suffering material privation—as the above-mentioned experience of postwar Germany indicates.

Third, Christian antinomianism renders it a faith-based religion all the more conducive to subjectivism and irrationalism. Many believers have held that if God is to be known at all, it is not through reason but directly through emotion and ecstasy. But as Rabbi Joseph B. Soloveitchik has warned: "The reduction of religion into some recondite, subjective current is absolutely perilous. It frees every dark passion and every animal impulse in man. Indeed, it is of greater urgency for religion to cultivate objectivity than perhaps for any other branch of human culture. If God is not the source of the most objectified norm, faith in Him is nothing but an empty phrase."[288]

Unlike Christianity, Judaism is a law-based religion. By "law," however, I do not mean merely rules of human conduct. The Torah unites Jewish law with the laws of the universe, in and through which the Eternal is to be known. This is why Maimonides, the codifier of Jewish law, could say that science is the only path to the knowledge of God.[289] This is why Judaism is rightly called a "religion of reason."

Still, we must credit Christianity for having spread the Noahide Laws of the Torah throughout much of the heathen world. By so doing, Christianity destroyed primitive idolatry and, to this extent, facilitated the universal recognition of ethical monotheism. Let us therefore conclude this chapter with these words from Alfred, Lord Tennyson's most famous poem, *In Memoriam*:

> One God, one law, one element.
> And one far-off divine event,
> To which the whole creation moves.

Thus, England's nineteenth-century poet laureate, a Christian, rendered in a few simple words of profound significance the message of Judaism.

CHAPTER 12
ISLAM: A CLASH OF CIVILIZATIONS

IN *The Dream Palace of the Arabs*, the renowned Lebanese-born scholar, Fouad Ajami of Johns Hopkins University, portrays the thoughts of the most prominent literati of the Arab world who sorrowfully behold the "death of Arab civilization." He himself writes that "Arab society had run through most of its myths, and what remained in the wake of the word, of the many proud statements people had made about themselves and their history, was a new world of cruelty, waste, and confusion."[290] Arab civilization is theologically coterminous with Islam. The death of Arab civilization suggests that the creativity ascribed to Islam in the past has been exhausted. There are theological reasons for this decay.

ALLAH, MUHAMMAD, AND THE QURAN

In this section let us bear in mind the words of Gerald Schroeder: "*The god an atheist does not believe in is usually not the* God of the Bible. Unfortunately, the god of the "believer" is also often not the God of the Bible."[291]

Despite Islam's recognition of prophets, Islam's deity, Allah, appears to be absolutely transcendent. He is absolute will without personality, which precludes human free will or choice. Indeed, Islam postulates absolute predestination of all that we think, say and do. Sinners are as predestined as virtuous believers (a doctrine that clashes with the Jewish concept of *teshuva*, repentance, and the Jewish holy day of Yom Kippur). Islamic fatalism contradicts the free will implied in the Genesis account of man's creation in the image of God.[292]

The clash between Judaism and Islam can even be seen in the architecture of their places of worship. Commenting on Exodus 27:8 involving the rectangular lines of the Altar in the Temple, Rabbi Hirsch writes:

> …in all forms made by organic forces unconsciously or at least unreasoningly, the curved or circular form predominates, or perhaps is even exclusive. It is only the free, self-directed force, of free, reasoning Man, that makes its buildings and creations in straight lines and angles. The circle, the curve, appertains to subjection, to lack of

freewill [hence the spherical mosque such as the Dome of the Rock (P.E.)]...The rectangle is the sign of the freedom of the human will, and of its mastery over the material world....[293]

The Jewish God—the God of Abraham—endows all men with freedom. Abraham can argue and plead with God, as did Moses, because the God of the Jews is a personal God, immanent as well as transcendent. This attestation of human dignity in Judaism is absent in Islam. Hence it is the profoundest error to identify Allah with the God of the Bible, i.e., *YHVH*. The Zohar states that, "*this Name YHVH belongs only to Israel*" (Exodus 96a).

Although the Quran refers to Allah as the "compassionate" and the "merciful," his most conspicuous function in that highly polemical work is to consign unbelievers to hell. Of course, there are in the Quran many verses of peace and tolerance, and also many verses sanctioning and mandating violence against non-believers. Addressing these contradictions, some of the most respected theologians in Islamic history say that when one sees peace in one place of the Quran and violence in another, one must follow what was revealed last. Unfortunately for Muslim moderates—*and they do not represent mainstream Islam*—the violent verses were revealed later and therefore nullify the peaceful verses. Moderates quote the peaceful verses as if the violent ones were non-existent. They obscure the fact that Islam is a religion of war in theory as well as in practice. But now let us demonstrate that the God of Islam should not be identified with the God of Israel.

According to Muhammad's own admission, Islam stands or falls with the person of its prophet. Hence it is appropriate to examine Muhammad's character, for which purpose let us begin with the views of St. Thomas Aquinas. Describing Muhammad as a man of violence, Aquinas writes:

> He seduced the people by promises of carnal pleasures...His teachings also contained precepts that were in conformity with [such] promises...the truths that he taught were mingled with many fables and with doctrines of the greatest falsity...he perverts almost all the testimonies of the Old and New Testaments by making them fabrications of his own, as can be seen by anyone who examines his law. It was, therefore, a shrewd decision on his part to forbid his followers to read the Old and New Testaments, lest these books convict him of falsity.[294]

That Islam is a militant religion follows from the character of Muhammad as a man of war. In her monumental work, *Islam and Dhimmitude: Where Civilizations Collide* (2002), Bat Ye'or avoids discussing the relationship between Muhammad's character and Islamic theology.[295] Instead, she documents Islam's fourteen-century record of plunder, rape, and genocide. One would hardly know of such barbarism reading the doyen of Islamic scholars, Bernard Lewis. Judging from his book *What Went Wrong?* (2002), nothing is *intrinsically* wrong with the religion that enthralls 1.2 billion people.[296] And Lewis, a Jewish scholar, is not known as an apologist of Islam.[297]

Enter Serge Trifkovic, a Christian scholar. His *The Sword of the Prophet* (2002) departs from the moral "neutrality" of academia and provides a "*Politically Incorrect Guide to Islam.*"[298] Trifkovic portrays Muhammad as a simple preacher who became a fanatical warlord in the process of conquering Mecca and Medina. Citing the Quran[299] and the voluminous *Hadiths*—the Traditions or Reports of what Muhammad said and did—he exposes Islam's prophet as cruel, ignorant, and lascivious. Thus, after slaughtering Arab tribesmen and looting their camels, the prophet and his followers kidnapped their women and staged an orgy of rape. One *Hadith* explains:

> We desired them, for we were suffering from the absence of our wives, but at the same time we also desired ransom for them. So we decided to have sexual intercourse with them but by observing 'azl [coitus interruptus]. But we said: We are doing an act whereas Allah's Messenger is amongst us; why not ask him? So we asked Allah's Messenger…and he said: It does not matter if you do not do it, for every soul that is to be born up to the Day of Resurrection will be born [a view consistent with the doctrine of predestination (P.E.)].[300]

To the men of one Jewish tribe, Muhammad offered the choice of conversion to Islam or death. Upon their refusal, up to 900 were decapitated in front of their women and children. "Truly the judgment of Allah was pronounced on high," was Muhammad's comment. The women were subsequently raped. Trifkovic comments: "That Muhammad's actions and words, as immortalized in the Quran and recorded in the Traditions, are frankly shocking by the standards of our time—and punishable by its laws, that range from war crimes and murder to rape and child molestation—almost goes without saying."[301]

Trifkovic is aware of the cultural and historical relativism that would prompt Western intellectuals to say, "we must not extend the judgmental yardstick of our own culture to the members of other cultures who have lived in other eras." He counters this relativism by pointing out that "even in the context of seventh-century Arabia, Muhammad had to resort to divine revelations as a means of suppressing the prevalent moral code of his own milieu."[302] Muhammad is thus revealed as a deeply flawed man by the standards of his own society, as well as those of the Jewish and Christian Scriptures, and even by the law of which he claimed to be the divinely appointed medium and custodian. Trifkovic sums up his assessment of Muhammad by quoting the eminent orientalist Sir William Muir (1819-1905): "the sword of Muhammad and the Quran are the most fatal enemies of civilization, liberty, and truth which the world has yet known."[303]

What about the Quran? Consider its bizarre references to the Hebrew and Christian Scriptures. Abraham Geiger (1810-1874) writes: "The order in which he gives the prophets is interesting, for immediately after the patriarchs he places first Jesus, then Job, Jonah, Aaron, Solomon, and last of all David [Sura 4:161]. In another passage [Sura 6:84-86] the order is still more ridiculous, for here we have David, Solomon, Job, Joseph, Moses, Aaron, Zachariah, John, Jesus, Elijah, Ishmael, Elisha, Jonah, and Lot! The incorrect spellings of the names of these prophets, as well as the parts which [Muhammad] assigns to them in history, proves that he had never even looked into the Hebrew Scriptures."[304]

The disillusioned Ibn Warraq (*Why I am Not a Muslim*) cites a welter of historians and orientalists, according to whom the Quran is punctuated by "Arabian paganism"—for example, the rites and rituals of the Pilgrimage to Mecca (see Suras 2:153; 22:28-30; 5:1-4; 22:23).[305] Islam even owes the term "Allah" to heathen Arabs. Perhaps Warraq's most damaging statement about Islam appears in the very headnote of his book, where he quotes the renowned historian and philologist Ernest Renan (1823-1892):

> Muslims are the first victims of Islam. Many times I have observed in my travels in the Orient, that fanaticism comes from a small number of dangerous men who maintain others in the practice of religion by terror. To liberate the Muslim from his religion is the best service that one can render him.

Now let us turn to the all-important Islamic concept of *jihad*. Trifkovic points out that the notion of "inner" *jihad*—of one's personal fight against his ego and sinful desires—came into being only after the Islamic Empire had been established. Of its countless *jihads* against unbelievers, Trifkovic emphasizes Islam's massacres in India, which "are unparalleled in history, bigger in sheer numbers than the [Nazi] Holocaust, or the massacre of the Armenians by the Turks."[306]

Like Bat Ye'or and Bernard Lewis, he explodes the myth of Islam's "Golden Age."[307] He notes that the medieval philosophers alFarabi and Avicenna, both Persian, "belong to 'Islam' just as much as Voltaire belongs to 'Christianity.'"[308] (Muhsin Mahdi has shown that alFarabi crafted his work on Plato and

Aristotle in an esoteric style. On the surface he appears as a devout Muslim; but a close reading reveals him as a disciple of Greek philosophy.)[309] Contrary to its apologists, the Muslim Empire inherited the knowledge and skills of Greece, Persia, and India (including what are still mistakenly known as "Arabic" numbers.) "Whatever flourished," writes Trifkovic, "it was not by reason of Islam, *it was in spite of Islam.*"[310] He quotes the incomparable nineteenth-century philosopher Alexis de Tocqueville:

> I studied the Quran a great deal. I came away from that study with the conviction that by and large there have been few religions in the world as deadly to men as that of Muhammad. So far as I can see, it is the principal cause of the decadence so visible today in the Muslim world and, though less absurd than the polytheism of old, its social and political tendencies are in my opinion more to be feared, and I therefore regard it as a form of decadence rather than a form of progress in relation to paganism itself.[311]

If de Tocqueville is correct, one cannot simply conclude that Islam's world-historical function, like Christianity's, was to destroy primitive idolatry—which of course it did wherever Islamic monotheism supplanted polytheism. But if Allah ought not be identified with *HaShem*, and if Islam, as de Tocqueville maintains, is "a form of decadence rather than a form of progress in relation to paganism," we shall have to conclude that Islam is not truly consistent with the First and Second Commandments and therefore cannot be said to have advanced the goal of the Torah, that of *ethical* monotheism! After all, in its triumphal march across the Middle East, southeast Asia, North Africa, and southern Europe, Islam not only conquered countries steeped in polytheism, but also destroyed innumerable Christian and Jewish communities. Viewed in this context, Islam's role in history is ambiguous. Perhaps it is only now that Islam is fulfilling its world-historical function?

To clarify that function, let us make a thought-experiment. Let us "remove" Islam from the Middle East; and let us go back to 1948 and "remove" the Arabs from the population then occupying the Land of Israel. Obviously this would preclude the "Arab-Jewish conflict." Equally obvious, Israel today would be very different, but in what fundamental way? In pursuing this question it should be recalled that the elite that founded the State of Israel—David Ben-Gurion, Levi Eshkol, Golda Meir, etc.—was committed to the establishment of a thoroughly secular, egalitarian society. These secularists dominated not only the political and economic institutions of nascent Israel, but also its educational and cultural institutions as well as its mass media. As secularists, they rejected the Torah as the ultimate source of Jewish authority. Considerations of power, and not only of ideology, governed the anti-Torah attitude of the elite.

What is ironic, however, is that the ambition and ideology of the elite complicated its task of constructing an ostensibly Jewish state in the presence of a then predominantly Arab population. Its own egalitarianism required the elite to confer citizenship on the Arabs living within the armistice lines established after the 1948 War of Independence. This could not but render precarious the elite's electoral power base and voting strength in the Knesset. Desperately needed was a large Jewish majority in the Land of Israel. Needed, therefore, was a great influx of Jews not only from war-torn Europe, but also from Asia and Africa. This posed its own dilemma for the secular elite.

The vast majority of Sephardim and Oriental Jews from Africa and Asia were religious and thus constituted an obvious threat to the elite's political power. The secular elite needed these Jews to counterbalance the Arab population and, at the same time, to endow the State of Israel with "legitimacy" as being overwhelmingly Jewish. But the addition of hundreds of thousands of religious voters would obviously eventuate in the elite's political decline. Thus, if the elite were not to commit political suicide and renounce its goal of creating a thoroughly egalitarian society in the Land of Israel, it had to secularize the Sephardim and Oriental Jews.

This it did to no small extent and, sad to say, in unconscionable ways. Immigrant parents who sent their children to religious schools were denied employment until they transferred their children to secular schools. Thousands of Yemenite children, who were brought to Israel by *Youth Aliya* (their parents came later), were herded into secular kibbutzim and other anti-religious institutions. Meanwhile, immigrant transit camps were the scenes of political and anti-religious propaganda designed to turn youth away from their parents. Thus, by means of coercion, segregation, and indoctrination, the secular elite undermined the structure and intense loyalties of countless impoverished immigrant families on the one hand, and their dedication to Torah values on the other.

Nevertheless, because the secularists as a whole were divided such that no single political party under the system of proportional representation could obtain a majority in the Knesset, the secular elite had to make concessions to the religious parties. For example, public transportation and places of entertainment were put under Sabbath restrictions in Jerusalem (and elsewhere). The powers of the Chief Rabbinate under the British Mandate were left intact as were laws governing marriage and personal status. Exemption from military service was given to *yeshiva* students. Public religious schools were established, and public funds were dispensed to *yeshivas* (Jewish academies).

Without these laws and arrangements (all of which were in force until the ascendancy of the Labor government in July 1992), many religious Jews would have left Israel and none but the most desperate would have made *aliya*. Which means that were it not for the Arabs and the need to establish an overwhelming Jewish majority, Israel would have developed into a thoroughly secular and conventional society, one composed of Hebrew-speaking gentiles.

Moreover, because of the hostility of the Islamic world, Israel has had to spend enormous sums for the country's defense. This forced the government to impose on its citizens the highest taxes, which depressed the economy, lowered productivity and capital investment, and thereby prompted the emigration of hundreds of thousands of Jews, *the bulk of whom were secularists*. Having received no spiritual legacy from the secular elite, and seeing the country drift from crisis to crisis while pursuing the will-o'-the-wisp goal of "peace"—something unreconstructed Islam will never give Israel—these Jews saw no solid reason for remaining in the land of their fathers or for not seeking their fortune elsewhere, especially in the United States.

But while the secular elite (which dominates Israeli governments) grows more inept and decrepit (as we saw in Chapter 1), the "return to Torah" movement has been flourishing, along with more and more *yeshivas*. A renaissance has occurred in the study of Jewish law, revealing its rational, humane, and comprehensive character. Add to this, countless new books have been published which interface the Torah with various scientific disciplines. And so, while the secular elite has declined, the Torah has been gaining ascendancy. *But all this would never have happened had there been no Arabs in the Land of Israel.* It thus appears that the *ultimate* historical function of Islam is two-fold: first, to make the success of a secular democratic state in the Holy Land impossible, and second, to facilitate Israel spiritual rebirth—one might almost say to compel Jews to become Jews!

While a renaissance has been occurring in Judaism, the decadence of Islam, which very few commentators have the wherewithal to admit, is obvious. Of course, to speak of the decadence of a religion whose faithful number more than one billion human beings is hardly pleasant and is bound to offend countless people in the West, especially those tainted by cultural relativism. But if it is true that the West, whether it knows it or not, is involved in a clash of civilizations with Islam, it behooves us to understand not only Islam's decadence, but also how that decadence as well as that clash of civilizations is serving the world-historical program of the Torah.

THE DECADENCE OF ISLAM[312]

Islamic decadence is rooted in its impersonal and empty monotheism. Although Daniel Pipes would deny that Islam is decadent, we read in his *Militant Islam Reaches America* (2002) the following assessment of the Islamic world:

> Whatever index one looks at, Muslims can be found clustering toward the bottom, whether in terms of military prowess, political stability, economic development, corruption, lack of human rights, health, longevity, of literacy…Muslims also lag when one looks at the Nobel Prize winners, Olympic medalists, or any other easily gauged international standard. There is a pervasive sense of debilitation…As a Muslim religious leader in Jerusalem put it, "Before we were masters of the world and now we are not even masters of our own mosques."[313]

This assessment appears to be confirmed by the Syrian army magazine, *Jaysh a-Sha'b* (*The People's Army*), which, on April 25, 1967, published an article referring to Islam as one of the "mummies in the museums of history."[314] And yet, this mummy, if intellectually dead, is otherwise alive. Sectarian strife, violence, insurrection, and terrorism erupt repeatedly throughout the Islamic world. This turbulence is described in a study of some fifty countries in which Muslims reside; and it matters not whether these Muslims constitute an overwhelming majority or only a tiny minority. The study was published in 1983 by Dr. Pipes.[315] It makes no difference whether the Muslims are Sunni or Shi'ite Muslims, Arabs or non-Arabs, or even whether they are "fundamentalists," "traditionalists," "reformists," or "secularists"—the story is the same.

The story was well known to the late Professor Harkabi, discussed in Chapter 4. Recall his saying that mendacity is "second nature" to the Arabs, that one may rightly regard "falsehood as an expression of [Arab] national character." No wonder Western orientalists (apologists aside) are sometimes disconcerted by the apparent lack of objectivity on the part of Muslim scholars concerning the Quran and the collection of *Hadith* Reports of what Muhammad said and did.[316] All of these are included in Islamic law, the *sharia*, which prescribes amputation of the hand for theft and enslaves half of humanity—women—wherever it reigns. No less significant, all four schools of Islamic law—*Hanafi, Hanbali, Shafi'i, Maliki*—agree that *jihad* commands offensive war against infidels. The Armenian genocide, perpetrated in the Anatolian and Arab provinces of the Turkish Empire (1915-1917), was programmed by *shari* laws decreed in the eighth century and still not revoked.[317]

Hence it is all the more astonishing that even Western-educated Muslims (with an exception to be mentioned later) ignore the violent and bloody character of Islamic history thoroughly documented by Bat Ye'or. These educated Muslims (and their numerous apologists among American academics)[318] emphasize the "tolerant" and "peace-loving" nature of Islam and describe the Muslim treatment of non-Muslims in idyllic terms.[319] They write about Islam and Islamic history in utter disregard for factuality; they live, as it were, in a dream world intoxicated by their own illusions.[320] But meanwhile many people in the West and not a few in Israel have also succumbed to illusions—to put it kindly. Pipes writes:

> Westerners, and some Israelis, tend to discount the anti-Israel vitriol of Arab leaders as so much rhetoric. "These are only words," is how Shimon Peres puts it: "Let them talk." Others take refuge in the belief that the populations over which demagogues preside are rather more pacifically disposed. As [former President] Jimmy Carter has remarked, "the Arab people need and want peace." But if anything, the opposite appears to be the case: quite a few Arab dictators show greater flexibility in their thinking than do their subjects.
>
> In the topsy-turvy world of Middle East politics, peace depends largely on Arab despots who keep popular passions in check; but even in this region of autocracy, populations ultimately have their way [as will be shown in a moment].

Pipes asks, "What accounts for this seemingly permanent enmity?" and answers:

> Historical memory is one source, fed by the belief that once a land has been conquered and settled by Muslims, it becomes part of an inalienable Islamic patrimony [the *umma*], its loss a robbery that one day must be made good. Three full centuries after the whole of Spain fell to Christians in 1492, Muslims continued actively to dream of a restoration; in Muslim eyes, writes the distinguished scholar Bernard Lewis, this was Islamic ground, "wrongfully taken...and destined to be returned." Where Israel is concerned, there are two further insults: not only the possession by an alien people of sacred Islamic places in Jerusalem, but their possession by Jews, a historically impotent group now insufferably powerful.
>
> Together, the role of historical memory and the passionate intensity of Arab political feeling may account for the special volatility of the Arab political sphere, in which even the most drastic actions— annihilating a state and scattering or killing its people—*have long*

been accepted as commonplaces. The Latin Kingdom of Jerusalem, established by the medieval Crusaders, was destroyed in the 12th century and its subjects were dispersed, an accomplishment *that still serves as a model for modern Arabs.*[321]

That the author of these revealing passages should now deny, after September 11, a clash of civilizations between Islam and the West, is mystifying, more so because he knows very well that *neither personal nor political freedom appears in the Arabic lexicon.*[322] This obscurantism is also dangerous, for it minimizes the enormous challenge confronting the West—especially Israel, surrounded as it is by Arab-Islamic regimes. Turn, therefore, to a novelist, who, unlike academics and journalists, has a license to write candidly about ugly things.

In his 1985 novel, *The Haj*, Leon Uris has the famous Orde Wingate say:

> …every last Arab is a total prisoner of his society. The Jews will eventually have to face up to what you're dealing with here. The Arabs will never love you for what good you've brought them. They don't know how to really love. But hate! Oh God, can they hate! And they have a deep, deep, deep resentment because you [Jews] have jolted them from their delusion of grandeur and shown them for what they are—a decadent, savage people controlled by a religion that has stripped them of all human ambition…except for the few cruel enough and arrogant enough to command them as one commands a mob of sheep. You [Jews] are dealing with a mad society and you'd better learn how to control it.

The novel's central character Haj Ibrahim confides to a Jewish friend:

> During the summer heat my people become frazzled…. They are pent up. They must explode. Nothing directs their frustration like Islam. Hatred is holy in this part of the world. It is also eternal…. You [Jews] do not know how to deal with us. For years, decades, we may seem to be at peace with you, but always in the back of our minds we keep up the hope of vengeance. No dispute is ever really settled in our world. The Jews give us a special reason to continue warring.

Uris has the cultured Dr. Mudhil elaborate:

> We [Arabs] do not have leave to love one another and we have long ago lost the ability. It was so written twelve hundred years earlier. Hate is our overpowering legacy and we have regenerated ourselves by hatred from decade to decade, generation to generation, century to century. The return of the Jews has unleashed that hatred, exploding it wildly.... In ten, twenty, thirty years the world of Islam will begin to consume itself in madness. We cannot live with ourselves...we never have. We are incapable of change.

Later in the novel (as if he were commenting on what Genesis 16:12 says of the descendents of Ishmael) Mudhil remarks: "Islam is unable to live at peace with anyone.... One day our oil will be gone, along with our ability to blackmail. We have contributed nothing to human betterment in centuries, unless you consider the assassin and the terrorist as human gifts."

Some pundits may call Uris a "racist." They lack the novelist's sensitive but clear-headed understanding of Arab culture. Unlike apologists, Uris appreciates the tragedy of a few insightful Arabs who know they are trapped in the decadence of a savage culture which Bat Ye'or calls "A Culture of Hate."[323] Hate incites murder. Ponder this: in all the lands it conquered, Islam replaced indigenous places of worship—Christian, Jewish, Persian, Zoroastrian, Buddhist, Hindu—with Mosques. This could not be done without enormous bloodshed.

What happens to a culture in which hate is a chronic principle? When that principle gains ascendancy, as it has in Islam, it tends to close the Muslim's mind. It breeds intolerance.[324] It precludes self-criticism and undermines any incentive to understand and learn from non-Muslims.

Contrast Judaism. Kindness (*Hesed*) is a fundamental Jewish principle. Although we shall plumb the depths of this principle latter, suffice to say for the present that kindness prompts the Jew not only to help but to understand and learn from non-Jews. (In the Babylonian Talmud, *Pesachim* 94b, Rabbi Judah the Prince, compiler of the Mishna, unhesitatingly declares in favor of a gentile astronomical theory over that of the wise men of Israel.) The kindliness of the Jew enlarges his mind and makes him tolerant toward others. Accordingly, whereas Jews speak of righteous gentiles whose place in heaven is assured, Muslims designate as evil everything that is not Islam and consign all infidels to hell.

Not that Muslims have not borrowed from the West. From time to time various Muslim states have adopted certain Western laws and institutions; but these borrowings cannot be logically and psychologically integrated into an

Islamic country without profound changes in the *sharia* as well as in the cultural mentality of the Muslim masses. Bernard Lewis puts it this way:

> The Egyptian constitution, for example, was adapted after that of Belgium and provided for a limited parliamentary monarchy. When things went badly wrong, Egyptians very naturally judged parliamentary institutions not by the Belgian or other Western European originals, but by the local imitation administered by King Faruq and the pashas.[325]

Faruq was overthrown by the Free Officers Society in 1952. A military dictatorship was eventually established under Gamal Abdal Nasser, who held that the Egyptian masses were not ready for democratic institutions. Apparently, they remain unprepared to this day. Lewis ruefully remarks that attempts at modernization in the lands of Islam (apart from Turkey) have "left a string of shabby tyrannies, ranging from traditional autocracies to new-style dictatorships, modern only in their apparatus of repression and indoctrination."[326]

ISLAMIC LAW: THE *SHARIA*

The West's parliamentary institutions simply clash with fourteen centuries of political autocracy on the part of Muslim rulers on the one hand, and of religious thralldom on the part of the Muslim masses on the other. In fact, this religious thralldom, the core of which is the *sharia*, is more impervious to change than political autocracy. Hence no Muslim ruler should be expected to institute a "Protestant Reformation" that would make parliamentary institutions viable.[327] Bernard Lewis cites an interesting example that took place in Tunisia in 1960:

> President Habib Bourguiba put forward the interesting idea that the month-long fast of Ramadan, with the resulting loss of work and production, was a luxury that a poor and developing country could not afford. For a Muslim ruler simply to abolish or disallow a major prescription of the holy law is unthinkable. What President Bourguiba did was to try to justify its abolition in terms of the holy law itself. This law allows a Muslim to break the fast if he is on a campaign in a holy war, or *jihad*. Bourguiba argued that a developing country was in a state of *jihad* and that the struggle to obtain economic independence by development was comparable with a

defensive war for national independence. In pursuit of this argument he proposed to abolish the rules whereby restaurants, cafes, and other public places were closed by day and by night during the month of Ramadan and oblige them to keep normal hours. In support of this new interpretation of the law, he tried to obtain a *fatwa*, a ruling, from the mufti of Tunis and other religious authorities. The religious authorities refused to give him what he wanted. The great mass of the people observed the fast despite the president's dispensation, and Bourguiba was finally compelled to beat a more or less graceful retreat. Even an autocratic socialist head of state, in pursuit of so worthy an end as economic development, could not set aside a clear ruling of the holy law.[328]

On the one hand, various orientalists maintain that the *sharia* has become a patchwork of petrified laws and contradictions resulting from the haphazard borrowings of Western legal systems.[329] On the other hand, Muslims devoted to the *sharia* find it exceedingly difficult to adapt this body of antiquated law to the demands of the modern, technological society. "The Quran is inadequate as a basis for legislation," said Nilufer Narli, a professor of sociology at the Boazici University in Istanbul."[330]

Here it should be noted that Islamic law does not recognize corporate legal persons: there are no Islamic equivalents to such Western entities as the business corporation, the trade union, the professional association, the college, the church, the political party. This is why Muslim states lack "civil society"—those sources of initiative and independence that can check the ever-encroaching power of the state, especially a state governed by the *sharia*.[331]

It should also be noted that the *sharia* is by no means uniform in the states comprising the Arab-Islamic world. Whereas the Libyan government lashes all adulterers, Pakistan lashes unmarried offenders and stones married ones. And while the Sudan imprisons some and hangs others, Iran adds other punishments, including banishment.[332]

And so the Islamic world is in disarray. Quite apart from the age-old conflicts between Sunni, Shiite, and Sufi Muslims, the *sharia* has been put into partial practice only in the most conservative states—Saudi Arabia, Pakistan, and Sudan. Because it has been ignored or has less than paramount authority, the *sharia* has engendered civil war in Algeria and has placed Egypt under the constant threat of terror by the Muslim Brotherhood.

While Western students of Islam speak of the archaic nature of Islamic law, hardly any go to the fundamental cause of its obsolescence, namely, this: *the sharia is not rooted in the infinite wisdom of God, for only a body of laws so rooted can enable jurists to reconcile permanence and change.* The decadence of Islam is the inevitable consequence of its not being based on divine revelation—and *this is the ultimate reason for Islam's hatred not only of the West, but of modernity, which places the divinity of the Quran in question.*[333] Contrary to what may be gleaned from legions of orientalists, it may well be that what most infuriates believers and impels them to slaughter or subjugate or degrade or convert unbelievers is the dim and discomfiting awareness that their holy of holies is not all that it pretends to be. Perhaps this, more than anything else, prevents them from appropriating, without turmoil, the blessings modernity has to offer mankind.

Actually, modernization has occurred in much of the Islamic world, but without any conceptual framework. Modernization intrudes through the influence of the cinema, music, clothing, satellite antennas, that is, through the globalization of culture (largely American). The trouble is that while modernity encroaches on the Muslim's daily life, it has also frustrated attempts to make the *sharia* a living and coherent system of law. Olivier Roy writes: "The masses who follow the Islamists...live with the values of the modern city...; they left behind the old forms of conviviality, respect for elders and for consensus, when they left their villages. These followers are fascinated by the values of consumerism, imparted by the shop windows of the large metropolises; they live in a world of movie theaters, cafes, jeans, video, and sports..."[334] The contradictions with the *sharia* arouse two fundamentalist reactions:

> One...is the tendency that is ever setting the reformer, the censor, and the tribunal against the corruption of the times and of sovereigns, against foreign influence, political opportunism, moral laxity, and the forgetting of sacred texts. The other tendency, more recent...is that of anti-colonialism, of anti-imperialism, which today has simply become anti-Westernism—from Cairo to Tehran.... The targets are...foreign banks, night clubs, local governments accused of complacency toward the West.[335]

These contradictions not only arouse hatred between diverse fundamentalists and diverse reformists, but it makes all these factions more conscious of and hostile toward the West—the *bette noir* of intra-Muslim conflict.

Roy distinguishes between "fundamentalists" and "neo-fundamentalists." Fundamentalists, usually called "Islamists," have in many respects been Westernized. They would apply the *sharia* to the political space—the state, the economy, urbanization, etc. They deem the state a necessary condition for believers to achieve complete virtue. Here they are trapped in a vicious cycle, for as Roy observes, the state they envision presupposes the complete virtue of its members.[336] As for the neo-fundamentalists, they would shrink the space of the *sharia* to the family and the mosque.

To avoid a common misunderstanding, it should be noted that Islamic fundamentalists, unlike their Christian namesakes, embrace not only their Scripture, the Quran, but also their post-Quranic traditions, including the *sharia*, which is their primary concern.[337] Nevertheless, the Quran is sacrosanct even among Muslim reformists; in fact, it continues to endow Muslim secularists with cultural pride and identity. Roy offers stunning proof: "The [1991 Persian] Gulf War showed that even among secular, Westernized, and 'democratic' Muslim intellectuals [who reject the *sharia*] there was a conscious choice, whether tortured or enthusiastic, in favor of Saddam Hussein, who all agreed was a dictator…a bad Muslim."[338]

What animated their support of Saddam (despite his having violated one of the strongest taboos of inter-Arab politics by invading Kuwait, a friendly Arab state) is a "profound, pervasive, and passionate hatred of the West and all it represents, as a world power, as an ideology, as a way of life…It is a hatred so deep that it has led those who feel it to rally to any plausible enemy of the West—even a racist like Hitler who despised Arabs, [and] an atheist like Stalin who suppressed Islam…"[339] Again we see that Muslims are trapped in a "culture of hate."

Let us now make explicit the following facts. The *sharia* cannot tolerate the segmentation of society that results from the separation of religion and state, hence it cannot tolerate the private groups and institutions that intervene between the state and the family. Nor can Islam tolerate the fragmentation of the *umma*, the worldwide Islamic community, which is divided into more than fifty sovereign nation-states.

Neither fundamentalists nor reformists have developed any political philosophy to deal with these disturbing facts, for which they are all too ready to blame the West. Animated by hatred, they harbor a murderous desire for revenge against Europe's former colonialism and America's present hegemony in Dar al-Islam. The terrorist bombing of the Twin Towers in New York and of the Bali nightclub in Indonesia—symbols of Western mastery and secularity—was not the first manifestation of this hatred.[340] Of course, the other side of this hatred is a desperate desire to restore Islam's past glory. Honor, like revenge, is deeply engrained in Islamic culture. But "no one," says Eric Hoffer, "can be honorable unless he honors mankind."[341]

Islam is Islamism

Whatever Islam's achievements, its rulers and believers have been slaughtering and oppressing men, women, and children in the name of Allah from its very inception. 'Abdallah Laroui, a professor of history in Rabat, admits that the

> ...the Caliph, even in the brilliant periods of Muslim empire, governed according to his own good pleasure; conquered people were persecuted; the state had no other end than the exploitation of subject populations.... It was a reign of violence, fear, the unlimited power of one, and the slavery of all. The Caliph, shadow of God on earth, respected neither the life nor property of his subjects, and his violence, punctuated by brief and bloody revolts, resembled that of all who ruled over the ancient land of Asia.[342]

It could not be otherwise given Quranic doctrine and Islam's military success in history. The empire Islam established within a hundred years of Muhammad—an empire that crossed three continents—involved the subjugation of an untold number of Christian, Jewish, Persian, and Buddhist communities. This history of military victory—inevitably resulting in enormous bloodshed—is viewed by Muslims as a validation of Muhammad's revelation. This is why Islam, unlike Judaism and Christianity, has always been preoccupied with military power and success.

But today the Muslim's overweening pride, his sense of cultural superiority, his confidence in Allah's reward of the faithful, has been shattered by Western dominance. This dominance casts doubt on the truth of Muhammad's revelation and therefore alarms as well as infuriates the Muslim soul.[343] For the traditional Muslim, religion provides not only universal significance; it also constitutes the ultimate basis and focus of his identity and group loyalty.[344] Islamic hatred of the West must therefore be understood in metaphysical as well as in political and psychological terms.

This hatred may be veiled among many Muslims who appear as "moderates," or it may explode in the rage of Muslim "extremists." One thing is clear: the barbarism perpetrated on September 11 was gleefully celebrated in the Muslim street throughout Islamdom. That gruesome display makes the distinction between "moderates" and "extremists" problematic. Bernard Lewis writes:

> Even when Muslims cease believing in Islam, they may retain Islamic habits and attitudes. Thus, among Muslim Marxists, there have been both ulema [doctors of law] and dervishes [popular

mystics], defending the creed and proclaiming the (revolutionary) holy war against the (imperialist) infidel…Even when the faith dies, loyalty survives; even when loyalty fades, the old identity, and with it a complex of old attitudes and desires, remains, as the only reality under the superficial, artificial covering of new values and ideologies.[345]

Not that there are no genuine Muslim moderates, meaning Muslims who sincerely deplore Islamic extremists. Daniel Pipes mentions some notable Muslim moderates. He succumbs to obscurantism, however, when he admits that "militant Islam, with its Westphobia and goal of world hegemony, dominates Islam *in the West* and appears to many to be the only kind of Islam."[346] Why only "in the West"? What about the East—the heart of the Islamic world and its one billion and more inhabitants?

Like so many others, Mr. Pipes obscures the magnitude of the threat Islam poses to the West by waving the flag of Muslim moderates, a minute number which, in war—and the West is at war—is insignificant. He himself has indicated that many "moderate" Muslims may be or become quiescent "extremists," when he quotes the following (presumably moderate) spokesmen: (1) Algerian secularist Said Sadi: "A moderate Islamist is someone who does not have the means of acting ruthlessly to seize power immediately." (2) Osmane Bencherif, former Algerian ambassador to Washington: "It is misguided policy to distinguish between moderate and extreme Islamists. The goal of all is the same: to construct a pure Islamic state, which is bound to be a theocracy and totalitarian." (3) Mohammad Mohaddessin, director of international relations for the People's Mojahadin in Iran, a leading opposition force: "Moderate fundamentalists do not exist…. It's like talking about a moderate Nazi."[347] Although these statements refer to "Islamists" and "fundamentalists," these labels refer to the Islam of the Quran and *sharia*. As Henri Boulad, an Egyptian Jesuit, and a specialist in Islam, states in an article, "L'Islamisme, c'est l'Islam" ("Islamism is Islam"):

> This statement is perfectly consistent with history and geography, with the Quran and the sunna, with the life of Muhammad and the evolution of Islam, with what Islam says about itself. I reject the position of people—Muslims or Christians—who bury their heads in the sand like ostriches…refuse to see the situation objectively, or take their wishes for realities, on behalf of dialogue and tolerance.[348]

Islamism is a cauldron of seething hatred born in Islam. Dr. Pipes presciently warned in 1983: "Keeping Muslim citizens tranquil in Dar al-Harb requires constant vigilance…Too much tolerance or too much strictness spells trouble…. The 'political indigestibility' of Muslim subjects makes them a permanent source of concern to non-Muslim rulers."[349]

It would be misleading to conclude, however, as do complacent American commentators, that the Muslim attack on the World Trade Center and the Pentagon was motivated merely by envious hatred of America's material wealth and power. Muslims disdain and fear American secularism and commercial imperialism, which they see spreading throughout the world and which they regard as an attempt to undermine the Islamic way of life.[350] They view America as the "Great Satan," the great tempter. And so it is! America's global influence constitutes a basic danger to tradition-based societies.

It should be emphasized, however, that Muslims not only regard America as decadent but they also dream of America's destruction as a means of restoring Islam's former glory. What they cannot accept is their own decadence. The Islamist and neo-fundamentalist attempts to overcome this decadence are doomed to failure. Olivier Roy explains:

> First of all, Islamization will mean the destruction of the social space between the state and the family. The Islamic society to which neo-fundamentalism refers never existed….What the Islamists advocate is not the return to an incomparably rich classical age, but the establishment of an empty stage on which the believer strives to realize with each gesture the ethical model of the Prophet. The only place for conviviality here is the family, which is also, but only for men, the only place of pleasure….
>
> What new urban space [can Islamism offer]? We see it in Saudi Arabia. It is an empty space, with neither cinemas nor cafes, only tea houses and restaurants. The streets are patrolled by religious militia, responsible only for enforcing good behavior and imposing religious practice (prayer and fasting). The only space for retreat is the family. But these are no longer the families of the rural world, in which women participate in the work and there is a popular, living culture. The modern family is mainly a place of consumption: television, videos, and so on. The Islamists will never stop the flow of this consumption, precisely because the *sharia* protects family privacy. And what is circulating in the urban family is the opposite of the Islamic way of life: it is the product of the West.[351]

There is no Islamist "culture," and it is futile to blame the West for this decadence. Islamic civilization declined long, long ago. "It has been a long time," says Roy, "since Christianity was Islam's other.... The culture that threatens Muslim society is neither Jewish nor Christian; it is a world culture of consumption and communication, a culture that is secular, atheist, and ultimately empty..."[352] True, but this "culture" was spawned by the West.

No one learned in the classics and in Nietzsche will deny the decadence of the West, whose relativism permeates legions of half-educated intellectuals.[353] To speak of the decadence of a world religion, however, is a more delicate matter. But inasmuch as Islam has become the seedbed of international terrorism, and bearing in mind that Muslims have dispatched their own women and children as human bombs—not even the Nazis resorted to such inhumanity—it is hard to escape the conclusion that Islam has become a descent into depravity and may well be in its death throes. Born in violence, this militant creed, in its pathological hatred of the West, is now destroying itself, having transformed Allah into Satan or a god of death. This is nothing less than idolatry.

Can it be that the irrationalist absolutism of Islam is precisely what is necessary to bring to an end the irrationalist relativism of the West? Can it be that Islamic hatred is the antidote to the moral insensitivity or torpidity of the West born of that relativism? Can it be that the clash between the East and the West is precisely what is necessary to bring about the rise of a civilization that transcends both? But of this, more in the concluding chapter.

THE CLASH

Despite the evidence presented above, various spokesmen in the democratic world deny the existence of a civilizational clash between Islam and the West. To acknowledge such a clash one would then be confronted by the question of whether Western civilization is preferable to Islamic civilization. One might even have to face the question of whether Islam has become a vehicle of evil. But such questions are precluded if one is tainted, however subtly or unconsciously, by relativism.

The intrepid Daniel Pipes has assembled a wealth of information confirming the clash of civilizations that he denies. To minimize the appearance of such a clash, Dr. Pipes states in the preface to the 2002 reprinting of his 1983 book *In the Path of God: Islam and Political Power*, that "militant Islam [is] best understood not as a religion but as a political ideology." To the contrary, Islam has always been a political ideology. The late and learned Ayatollah Khomeini observed that "the Quran contains a hundred times more verses concerning social problems than on devotional subjects. Out of fifty books of Muslim tradition there are perhaps three or four which deal with prayer or with man's duties towards God, a few on morality, and all the rest have to do with society, economics, law, politics and the state..." Islam, according to the same authority, "is political or it is nothing."[354] Fouad Ajami may deplore "theocratic politics," but it describes authentic Islam.

As the very subtitle of Pipes' book—*Islam and Political Power*—suggests, and as its content makes obvious, "However much institutions, attitudes, and customs have changed, the Muslim approach to politics derives from the invariant premises of the religion and from fundamental themes established more than a millennium ago."[355] Surely the most conspicuous theme of that religion, manifested throughout Islamic history, is none other than *jihad*—as Pipes himself demonstrates in a November 2002 article critical of American professors who deny this doctrinal and existential fact.[356] To contend that Islam and the West are not involved in a clash of civilizations when the former is steeped in absolutism, while the latter is mired in relativism, may be "politically correct," but dangerously so and symptomatic of declining confidence in the justice of one's own cause. Relativism and decadence have many shades and degrees.

Benjamin Netanyahu denied a clash of civilizations in the Middle East when he addressed a joint session of Congress shortly after his becoming Israel's prime minister in 1996. Although both Pipes and Netanyahu may be concerned about the canard of "racism," one may suspect additional motives in the case of Mr. Netanyahu. Like most politicians, Netanyahu has long been engaged in the soporific "rhetoric of peace," which compels him to project the illusion of "peaceful coexistence" between the Jewish state and its autocratic Islamic neighbors. This illusion would be dispelled were he to admit of a clash of civilizations; for then, instead of a politics of anesthesia he would have to face the reality of evil, be committed to its *eventual* destruction, and design a strategy to hasten this objective.

Muslims have never had any doubts about the conflict between Islam and the West. They have always divided the world into the territory of Dar al-Islam, where Islam reigns, and the territory of Dar al-Harb, where infidels reign, but which the *sharia* requires Muslims to conquer in the name of Allah. Hasan al-Banna (1906-1949) of Egypt writes: "The Western way of life—bounded in effect on practical and technical knowledge, discovery, invention, and the flooding of world markets with mechanical products—has remained incapable of offering to man's minds a flicker of light, a ray of hope, a grain of faith, or providing anxious persons the smallest path toward rest and tranquility."[357] A leading Egyptian journalist, Muhammad Sid-Ahmed, said in 1994: "There are unmistakable signs of a growing clash between the Judeo-Christian Western ethic and the Islamic revival movement, which is now stretching from the Atlantic in the west to China in the east."[358] A prominent Indian Muslim predicted in 1992 that the West's "next confrontation is definitely going to come from the Muslim world. It is in the sweep of the Islamic nations...that the struggle for a new world order will begin."[359] Samuel Huntington comments:

> On occasion in the past, Muslim leaders did tell their people: "We must Westernize." If any Muslim leader has said that in the last quarter of the twentieth century, however, he is a lonely figure. Indeed, it is hard to find statements by any Muslims, whether politicians, officials, academics, businesspersons, or journalists, praising Western values and institutions. They instead stress the differences between their civilization and Western civilization. The superiority of their culture, and the need to maintain the integrity of that culture against Western onslaught....They see Western culture as materialistic, corrupt, decadent, and immoral.... Increasingly, Muslims attack the West not for adhering to an imperfect, erroneous religion...but for not adhering to any religion at all. In Muslim eyes, *Western secularism, irreligiosity, and hence immorality are worse than the Western Christianity that produced them* (my emphasis).[360]

Huntington has been criticized for having a monolithic view of Islamic civilization. After all, there are Iranian, African, and Indonesian variations of Islam, each representing an autonomous cultural dimension. Nevertheless, the clash between Islam and the West is obvious, as Bernard Lewis made explicit three years before Huntington's 1993 essay "A Clash of Civilizations?" appeared in *Foreign Affairs*. Where Huntington errs, is in his identifying the "West" with "Western civilization." I shall return to this issue later, as well as to his provocative statement to the effect that *Western Christianity produced Western secularism and irreligiosity*. Here I merely want to emphasize Huntington's candid remark that Muslim hatred of the West will be found not only among fundamentalists but also among those whom many in the West would regard as "moderates."

This said, we can now reveal an unknown reason for the Muslim hatred of the West, one relevant to the decadence of Zionism. Thus, under the date line January 9, 1930, the Cairo newspaper *al-Fatah* makes the following remark about European colonizers:

> The real danger approaches us from the spiritual war that Europe is methodically conducting against the spirit of the Orientals in general and of Muslims in particular, with the aid of its philosophical books, novels, theaters and films, and its language. The aim of this

concerted action is of a psychological nature—*to cut off the Oriental peoples from their past.*[361]

Without a past there is no history; without a history there is no cultural or national identity. The loss of cultural identity is precisely what Muslims so much fear and hate about the West. Notice, however, that what foreign colonialists had allegedly done in Egypt is exactly what ultra-secular Jews have in fact been doing to their own people in Israel: *depriving them of cultural or national identity*. They have sought to deJudaize public education in Israel and to transform the Jewish state into a "state of its citizens." If these ultra-secularists were to succeed, so that Israel did indeed become a "state of its citizens," this irreligious state could become an even greater threat to Islamic civilization—reason for Muslims to strive for Israel's destruction!

Israel's ruling elites have willfully refused to address the clash of civilizations described by Lewis and Huntington. They live in a constant state of denial. No matter how often Jewish women and children are murdered by Muslims, no matter how much Jews and Israel are vilified in the Arab-Islamic media—including Egypt's—they refuse to take Islam seriously as a murderous religion whose adherents are dedicated to Israel's annihilation. They close their eyes to the fact that Israel's rebirth and independence and ascendancy constitute a violation of Islamic doctrine, a trespass on Islamic territory, an assault on Islamic pride, hence an intolerable provocation and outright challenge to every Islamic leader. Thus, in a lecture sponsored by the Arab League in Cairo, 'Abd al-Rahman al-Bazzaz, Professor of Law at the University of Baghdad (once Iraq's Prime Minister) declared:

> The existence of Israel nullifies the unity of our homeland, the unity of our nation and the unity of our civilization, which embraces the whole of this one region [Dar al-Islam]. Moreover, the existence of Israel is a flagrant challenge to our philosophy of life and the ideals for which we live, and a total barrier against the values and aims to which we aspire in the world.[362]

Israel is viewed by Muslims as an outpost of the West, the bearer of all the evils mentioned by Huntington, to which add the West's contempt for the past and its denial of trans-historical truths and values. The clash between the West and Islamic civilization hinges on this point: the historical relativism of the West makes history meaningless and purposeless. Recall Shimon Peres' mindless and egotistical statement: "I have become totally tired of history, because I feel history is a long misunderstanding." For Muslims (as well as for Christians and observant Jews), absolute truth was revealed at a supreme moment in history and endowed human life with meaning and purpose.

But now I must correct Huntington's misleading impression that the West and Western civilization are synonymous. Western civilization is a thing of the past: it has succumbed to post-modernism: to multiculturalism, relativism, and feminism.[363] The Great Books of Western civilization are disappearing from university curriculums, and, with this, the idea of the True, the Good, and the Beautiful. Deconstructionism via Jacques Derrida divests the Great Books of all meaning. The Bible, classical Greek philosophy, Shakespeare, Black studies, gay history, and "rap" music are just texts with equally valid perspectives. Academia has thus become the leveler of society.

While universities treat feminism as a major contribution to knowledge, feminists and feminist organizations attack the basic ideas and values of Western civilization. The so-called philosopher Sandra Harding calls modern science "not only sexist but also racist, classist, and culturally coercive"[364]— clearly a rejection of the rationalism underlying the Great Tradition. More conspicuous are radical feminists that seek to deconstruct the family, exposing it as an instrument of male dominance or a source of oppression. Feminists support homosexual rights, gay rights, hence same-sex marriages. The traditional family, which provided the core values and continuity of society, are thus being undermined. As Aristotle understood, it is in the (traditional) family where children are taught self-control and concern for others. It is in the family where they learn modesty, honesty, and respect for authority. These virtues they later manifest as adults in society at large. The family, the heart of the Great Tradition, is being eviscerated by radical feminism.

The decline of the Great Tradition has brought in its wake a depressing vulgarity and mediocrity. No longer are the thoughts of statesmen influenced by the ideas of Plato and Aristotle, or their speeches by the oratory of Demosthenes and Cicero. (Political oratory has been reduced to spin.) No longer does the Old Testament with its eternal verities and examples of great men inspire the West. The Great Tradition, which inspired Lincoln and Churchill, has receded into the background. In the absence of the True, the Good, and the Beautiful, what else can motivate men but a paltry egoism? Indeed, this all-too-human tendency has been sanctified by the social sciences. These disciplines are preoccupied not with greatness, but with measuring and predicting the behavior of the common man, who, generally speaking, is less tainted than legions of academics who purvey the soul-destroying and nationhood-destroying doctrine of moral relativism. Academia has thus become destructive of civilization.

Roger Scruton sees in academia a "culture of repudiation"—repudiation of the Enlightenment or the Age of Reason. He writes:

> ...the spirit of free inquiry is now disappearing from schools and universities in the West. Books are put on or struck off the curriculum on grounds of political correctness; speech codes and counseling services police the language and conduct of both students and teachers; many courses are designed to impart ideological conformity rather than to inspire rational inquiry, and students are often penalized for having drawn some heretical conclusion about the leading issues of the day. In sensitive areas, such as the study of race and sex, censorship is overtly directed not only at students but also at any teacher, however impartial and scrupulous, who comes up with the wrong conclusions. "Racism awareness courses" on American campuses are often used as "correctives"—i.e., punishments—for those whose deviant behavior calls for re-education....
>
> A single theme runs through the humanities as they are regularly taught in American and European universities: the illegitimacy of Western civilization, and the artificial nature of the distinctions on which it has been based. All distinctions are "cultural," therefore "constructed," therefore "ideological," in the sense defined by Marx—manufactured by the ruling classes in order to serve their interests and bolster their power.[365]

CONCLUSION

Since September 11, an "axis of evil" threatens civilized society. It has been given various names: "Islamic fundamentalism," "Islamism," "militant Islam," "Wahhabism," etc. Each of these appellations is said to be an extreme form of Islam. The name of the enemy is of strategic significance. It is one thing to confront what may be a fringe element of Islam; it is quite another if this element lurks in the hearts of Muslims everywhere and can everywhere explode into fanatical fury. That America possesses the wherewithal to win a war against Islam *per se* and then transform various Islamic regimes into democracies is rather dubious. The American government, it seems, would rather appease oil-rich Saudia Arabia, a totalitarian state, than eliminate Riyadh's ruling families—financiers of a thousand mosques that propagate hatred and encourage *jihad*.

Although the American people still display a religiously based patriotism that astonishes jaded Europeans, their political and intellectual and business elites are mired in internationalism or lack the moral clarity and courage to confront the clash of civilizations discussed in this chapter. America can hardly persevere in what promises to be a protracted war when the multiculturalism of which intellectuals boast hinders national solidarity, especially in the absence of a clearly defined enemy. "International terrorism" is too vague. Obscuring or trivializing the nature of the enemy can only hasten the decline of America's national identity. As Samuel Huntington has brilliantly documented, America's burgeoning Hispanic, Muslim, Black, and Oriental populations herald its deconstruction as a predominantly white, dissident-Protestant country, one whose political creed emphasizes democracy, individuality, and limited government.[366] But nothing is more subversive of America's national identity than the university-bred doctrine of moral relativism or pluralism (of which Huntington is strangely silent). This doctrine, while nurturing multiculturalism, saps the nation's confidence in the justice of its cause. Relativism disarms America in the struggle against Islamic absolutism. But as we have seen, relativism is the offspring of contemporary democracy. All the more reason for a Jewish philosophy of history to probe more deeply into the father of democracy, Niccolo Machiavelli.

Chapter 13
Modernity: In Quest of Morality

There are three alternative sources of morality: God, Nature, and Man. Modernity rejected God as well as Nature and has yet to discover a morality in Man.

—Anonymous

When Constantine the Great was on his death bed in 337, he accepted baptism and thus became the first Christian emperor. For almost twelve centuries thereafter the church was joined in unholy matrimony with the state. This tenuous marriage of religion and politics was shattered by Machiavelli, the father of modernity and of modern political science.[367]

Machiavelli

Although Machiavelli is the exemplar of Volitional Man—for his political science is based on the will to power—the great Florentine will best be understood as the creator of Secular Man. By Secular Man, I mean a logically coherent paradigm, not a vague appellation applied to casual and inconsistent non-believers. The secular tendency is as old as Adam. But it was Machiavelli who made secularism a universal ideology. Of course, the elaboration and dissemination of this ideology required philosophical collaborators or disciples such as Hobbes, Locke, Spinoza, Rousseau, and Marx—to mention only a few of the disguised and undisguised atheists who constitute the legislators of the modern mind. These philosophers diluted Secular Man for the multitude, including a multitude of intellectuals. But to see this Promethean diluted, we must see him undiluted.

Machiavelli's deceptively simple book *The Prince*, so often trivialized, marks the Copernican revolution in politics.[368] In that sibylline work Machiavelli undertook the world-historical task of destroying nothing less than the two pillars of Western civilization, classical Greek philosophy and Christianity, whose ethics, whether derived from nature or nature's God, derogate from the complete autonomy of human will and desire.

As previously indicated, the key to modernity will be found in Chapter 15 of *The Prince*.[369] There Machiavelli lists ten pairs of qualities for which men, especially rulers, are praised or blamed—qualities which a ruler, "if he wishes to maintain himself," must be able to "use" and "not use" "according to necessity." [370] Some rulers, he declares, "are held liberal, some miserly...[and/or] rapacious; some cruel, others full of pity; the one faithless, the other faithful; the one effeminate and pusillanimous, the other fierce and spirited; the one human, the other proud; the one lascivious, the other chaste; the one open, the other cunning; the one hard, the other easy; the one grave, the other light; the one religious, the other skeptical, and the like."

Machiavelli elaborates in Chapter 18 of *The Prince*:

> It is not necessary for a prince to have in fact all of the qualities written above, but it is indeed necessary to appear to have them. I shall rather dare to say this: that having them and observing them always, they are harmful, but in appearing to have them, they are useful—so as to *appear* to be full of pity, faithful, human, open, religious, and *to be so*, but with one's mind constructed in such a mode that when the need *not to be* arises, you can, and know how to, change to the contrary.[371]

It bears repeating that a mind so "constructed" must be virtually devoid of all emotion, save the desire for power. To harbor emotions is to be susceptible to *habits*, and it is precisely habits that prevent a ruler from being a Machiavellian, which is to say, a perfect *opportunist*. To be a perfect opportunist, a ruler must change his "nature" with the times and circumstances, which means he must have no emotional predispositions (other than the desire to maintain and increase his power). This would be possible only if man is nothing more than a creature of habits—habits that can be conquered by men of the caliber of Machiavelli. (Long before Rousseau and twentieth-century behaviorists, Machiavelli let it be known that human nature—if man can be said to have a nature—is plastic or malleable.) *But if human nature is malleable, then it should be theoretically possible to shape the mentality of an age!*

This is precisely what Machiavelli set out to do in *The Prince* and its companion work *The Discourses*. Notice that in his list of qualities that bring rulers praise, Machiavelli excludes the four cardinal virtues of Greek political philosophy: *wisdom, justice, moderation,* and *courage!* Moreover, religion (paired with skepticism) is placed last, inverting the Decalogue. Consistent therewith, the central and most significant pair of qualities is designated as "human" and "pride." One would have expected "pride" (the Christian vice) to be paired with "humility" (the Christian virtue), but Machiavelli deliberately omits humility from the list of qualities for which men and princes are praised. Humility, for the creator of Secular Man, is at once the virtue of the weak and the guise of the "proud"—the priests who denigrate pagan *virtu*, i.e., manliness, while lording it over the people in the name of godliness—a devious and impotent form of homotheism.[372] To complete the process of man's deification, the creator of Secular Man simply eliminated every semblance or pretense of godliness, rendering man entirely "human." The seed of *humanism* was thus planted in Chapter 15 of *The Prince*. In that seminal chapter Machiavelli advanced Christianity's historic function, which was to destroy primitive idolatry on the one hand, while facilitating the secularization of mankind on the other.

With justice omitted from the qualities for which rulers are praised, a radically new political science appeared on the stage of world history, one that sanctifies the commonplace, not to say vulgarity, in the name of "realism."[373] In opposition to classical political philosophy, modern political science takes its bearing not from how man *should* live, but from how men *do* live—from the *is*, not from the *ought*. Again Chapter 15: "…there is such a distance between how one lives and how one should live that he who lets go that which is done for that which ought to be done learns his ruin rather than his preservation…Hence it is necessary for a prince, if he wishes to maintain himself, to learn to be able to be not good, and to use it and not use it according to necessity." This separation of morality from politics is the historical consequence of the Christian separation of church and state. Henceforth there are no moral limits as to what man may do. Man is at last fully autonomous. He stands, as Nietzsche was to say, "beyond good and evil."

Furthermore, in direct opposition to the biblical tradition, which exalts truth and truthfulness, the creator of Secular Man teaches would-be rulers to practice deceit and dissimulation constantly. "A prince ought to take great care…that he appears to be, when one sees and hears him, all pity, all faith, all integrity, all humanity, and all religion…. For men, universally, judge more by the eyes than by the hands…Everyone sees what you seem to be, but few touch what you are."[374] We have here a politics keyed to the sense of touch, the most dynamic and erotic of the senses. For unlike sight and hearing—passive receptors of the written and spoken word—the sense of touch, especially in the hands, connects to the will—the *will to power*.

The greatest manifestation of the will to power is not the state but the founding of an entirely new "state." To establish such a state a founder must create "new modes and orders": he must make the "high" low and the "low" high.[375] To do this he must radically alter people's inherited beliefs as to what is deserving of praise and blame. This will require not only great force but monumental fraud or deception. Hence the founder must possess *virtu*, greatness of mind and body. Extraordinary cunning and fierceness—even terror—are essential in the founding of an entirely new state. In no other way can the founder perpetuate his "new modes and orders." Clearly, the "state"—Nietzsche will later say "philosophy"—is a construct of the mind and will of the "prince."[376]

Since all new states originate in force, hence in revolutionary violence, their founders are, and by definition must be, "criminals." Only after they have established new "orders" do they become "legitimate" and respectable. Accordingly, what is decisive in the study of politics is not laws or legal institutions but the dynamics of power, on which alone all laws are ultimately based. Indeed, laws are obligatory only insofar as they can be enforced; otherwise they are mere words having no "effectual truth"—like the best regimes in theory imagined by the philosophers of antiquity. In Chapter 12 of *The Prince*, Machiavelli writes: "The principal foundations which all states have, whether new, old, or mixed, are good laws and good arms. And because there cannot be good laws where there are not good arms, and where there are good arms there needs must be good laws, I shall omit reasoning on laws and speak of arms." Arms are the counterpart of the "effectual truth" mentioned in Chapter 15. There is no such thing as just or unjust laws or just and unjust regimes.

This is precisely the doctrine of legal realism or positivism that identifies the just with the legal, a doctrine that dominates law schools in the democratic world and makes it easier for democracies to recognize and have truck with Arab and other tyrannies. But to deny the distinction between just and unjust laws is to reject the concept of the "common good," a concept which appears nowhere in *The Prince*.[377] Neither does the word "tyrant" (in a book that commends Hiero, Agathocles, Cesare Borgia and others of their ilk as "princes").[378] The term "justice" appears only in Chapter 19 of *The Prince*. There ten Roman emperors are mentioned, only two of which die a natural death—the just and gentle Marcus Aurelius and the unjust and ferocious Septimius Severus. Which means that justice is irrelevant in the world of politics (as implied by its omission in Chapter 15). We have in Machiavelli the Deification of Egoism, the modern euphemism of which is Individualism.

Although Marcus Aurelius' rule was just, whereas Severus' rule was tyrannical, Machiavelli praises both as "virtuous." Why? Because the ultimate criterion of "virtue," as of praise and blame, is success (of which more in a moment). This silent denial of the classical distinction between kingship and tyranny is one of the cornerstones of contemporary political science (which propagates the moral equivalence one hears so much about nowadays). A political science that rejects the traditional distinction between kingship and tyranny can take no account of, in fact must deny, the distinction between the good man and the good citizen. The good citizen is of course the patriot who fights for his country and obeys its laws. His country, however, and therefore its laws, may be unjust—from the traditional point of view. But this means that the good citizen may be a bad man. From which it follows that contemporary political science denies the distinction between good men and bad men—which is why democratic journalists (and only democratic journalists) can publicly proclaim that "one man's terrorist is another man's freedom fighter." These relativists (and their academic mentors) are examples of tamed or democratized Machiavellians.

This leveling of moral distinctions is rooted in a leveling of the distinction between man and beast. The successful ruler, says Machiavelli in Chapter 18 of *The Prince*, will combine, in varying proportions (depending on circumstances), the cunning of the fox and the fierceness of a lion.[379] And just as it would be absurd to condemn a lion for devouring a lamb, so it would be absurd to condemn a "prince" (by calling him a "tyrant") for ravaging or subjugating a nation. As Machiavelli puts it in Chapter 3 of *The Prince*: "It is a thing truly very natural and ordinary to desire to acquire [note the deliberate redundancy]; and when men are able to do so do it, they are always praised or not blamed..." This precept follows an account of Louis XII of France who "was brought into Italy by the ambition of the Venetians...I do not want to blame the part taken by the King for wanting to begin gaining a foothold in Italy..." Machiavelli, the founder of a "value-free" political science, actually shows in Chapter 3 how to conquer his own country! The ultimate criterion of praise and blame is not right and wrong, but success and failure.

We must now ask, what is the world-historical goal of Secular Man? The answer to this question will be found in Chapter 25 of *The Prince*. There Machiavelli subtly equates God with chance (*fortuna*). He then identifies chance with "woman" and playfully proclaims that man's task is to conquer her. What he means is this. "Woman" signifies nature, and man's ultimate goal is to conquer nature, which will require the overcoming of traditional views of human nature. This is why the word "soul" (*anima*) never appears either in *The Prince* or *The Discourses*. We are given to understand, therefore, that man's nature is plastic, is unbound by any moral laws or by "conscience" (another deliberately omitted word in *The Prince*).[380] And so, just as the "Philosopher" replaced the Olympian pantheon with a new conception of nature, so the "Prince" replaces nature (and nature's God) with a new conception of man. This requires elaboration.

The conquest of chance involves the overcoming of God and of all those who have traditionally diminished man by despising the merely "human." The enemy is the "proud," which includes not only the priests who denigrate the body, but also the philosophers who exalt kingship and aristocracy. To conquer chance, therefore, one must lower the goals of human life. For the higher the goals of man the more he is exposed to chance and accident. Turn now to Secular Man diluted, an inevitable bi-product of the undiluted Promethean.

Lowering the goals of human life corresponds to leveling the distinction between man and beast on the one hand, and denying the existence of the soul on the other. Abolish the soul and human reason will have nothing to serve but the wants of the body or sensuality, and such external goods as wealth, power, and prestige. To deny the soul, therefore, is to deify, in effect, the "human, all-too-human"—what the priests referred to, pejoratively, as "human nature."

Machiavelli's deification of the merely "human" is the unembellished meaning of *humanism*; it is the true source of Individualism and Capitalism, of Socialism and Communism, of Fascism and Nazism.

The prerequisites for the Machiavellian conquest of nature can now be more fully appreciated. The first thing needed is a new science of politics, a politics that liberates man's acquisitive instincts in opposition to classical moderation and Christian asceticism. However, the liberation of acquisitiveness necessitates a rejection of priests, nobles, and kings in favor of the *people*. Commentators tend to minimize if not overlook Machiavelli's democratic "bias" (a key to his world-historical project). Machiavelli's political science *had* to be democratic if he was to create a new dispensation for mankind. In other words, he had to destroy classical political science, which is essentially aristocratic, if he was to create a democratic era. *Machiavelli is in fact the first philosopher to contend that democracy is the best regime.* In *The Discourses* he challenges all previous political philosophy by claiming that, "[A]s regards prudence and stability, I say that the people are more prudent and stable, and have better judgment than a prince" (I, 58). And in *The Prince* he boldly declares: "The end of the people is more honest than that of the great.[381] Moreover, in overturning the Great Tradition, which praises *agrarian* as opposed to *commercial* societies as more conducive to virtue, Machiavelli praises commercial republics because such republics, like Rome, are more powerful, are more capable of *dominion*. Machiavelli's political science therefore liberates acquisitiveness and prepares the ground for capitalism (and for much more, as we shall see later). He is indeed the father of Modernity and Democracy.

The Prince must thus be understood as a conspiratorial as well as a Copernican work. (Incidentally, its longest chapter, like that of *The Discourses*, is on conspiracy.) Far from being a tract for the times (as some have foolishly believed), this masterpiece of cunning may be regarded as philosophically-armed propaganda addressed to thinkers who might be tempted to make common cause with the "people" and create a new dispensation for mankind. Needed were "collaborators" who would come after Machiavelli and bring to completion his world-historical project. And they were forthcoming. Before discussing his collaborators, allow me to amuse the reader by the following digression.

MACHIAVELLI'S USE OF "*GEMATRIA*"

Machiavelli was superficially acquainted with *Gematria*, the system by which the Hebrew alphabet is translated into numbers.[382] For example, and as Leo Strauss discerned, Machiavelli makes systematic use of the number 13 (and its multiples) both in *The Prince* and in *The Discourses*.[383] Now it so happens that 13 is the numerical value of the Hebrew word meaning "one"—*echad*. The "prince" is the one par excellence. The "prince," from the Latin *principi*, denotes the "first thing," the "beginning," something radically "new." "A New Prince Must Make Everything New" is the title of the 26th chapter of *The Discourses*, where Machiavelli subtly indicates that a new prince must imitate God. It can hardly be a coincidence that *The Prince* consists of 26 chapters: 26 is the numerical value of the four Hebrew letters comprising the Tetragrammaton, the Ineffable Name of God (as may be seen in note 265).

Turn, now, to Chapter 13 of *The Prince*, the inconspicuous center of the book, and to the very last sentence. Referring to great conquerors and how they "armed and ordered themselves," Machiavelli confides, "to which *orders*, I, in all things, consign myself" (italics added). Thus, in language borrowed from religion, Machiavelli confesses his faith: he bows to one god only, the god of power. (In the chapter's central episode, that of David and Goliath, the knife replaces God.)

But let us go back to the beginning. In Chapter 1 Machiavelli outlines, with remarkable brevity, 13 different modes by which "principates" are acquired. He completes the treatment of the subject in Chapter 11. The central chapter of this group is of course 6. Accordingly, he there decides to "bring forward the greatest examples of "new principates founded by new princes, men who possessed extraordinary "virtue" (a term used 13 times in this chapter). There he mentions Moses in the same breath, as it were, with three pagan law-givers. One of the pagans is Romulus, the mythical founder of Rome, who murdered his twin-brother Remus in order to be "alone," a "first thing," a "new beginning"—a "prince" in the profoundest sense of the term.[384] The discussion is largely symbolic. To be a creator of "new modes and orders" one must destroy or overcome what is nearest and dearest—one's fraternal loyalties, one's subordination to ancestral beliefs and moral convictions.

Now ponder what Machiavelli says in *The Discourses* (I, 9): "Where the act [Romulus' fratricide] accuses, the effect excuses." The *act* of murdering one's brother accuses only because the denunciation of that act represents the established morality—*ordinary* morality. But the *effect* excuses because it inaugurates a new morality—an *extraordinary* morality. With success, however, the extraordinary eventually becomes the ordinary. And so Machiavelli, a "prince"—a "first thing"—destroys the established religious and aristocratic morality and establishes a secular and democratic morality. Nietzsche's creator of new values, the *ubermensch*, is but the descendant of the "Prince."

Returning to Chapter 6 of *The Prince*, by linking Romulus and Moses, Machiavelli prompts the reader to recall that both Romulus and Moses were abandoned as infants. This blurring of distinctions between Romulus (who murdered his brother) and Moses (who saved his brother)—this moral leveling, is diabolically methodical. The number 6 represents the six directions (north, east, south, west, up and down), hence the physical world. Also, the world was created in six days. It is doubly revealing, therefore, that exactly in Chapter 6 of *The Prince* will be found Machiavelli's first reference to God!

It may now be asked: Why does Machiavelli invert the Decalogue in Chapter 15 and not elsewhere? The number 15 reduces to 6 (1+5). Man was created on the sixth day. Man, in the person of Machiavelli, becomes the creator in Chapter 15. In fact, 15 is the *Gematria* for another name of God: *Yod Hei*. Moreover, this is the only chapter of *The Prince* in which Machiavelli does not use historical examples to convey his radically new political science![385] In this chapter he comes into his own as a new prince, a new first thing, a creator of new values.

To be sure, Chapter 24 also reduces to 6 (2+4). It ends with the statement: "And only those defenses are good, are certain, are durable, which depend *on you yourself and on your virtue*" (italics added). God has no place in the world of men. This is an appropriate transition to Chapter 25 where, as we saw, Machiavelli equates God with chance. The number 25 reduces, of course, to 7 (2+5). To many, the number 7 signifies luck or chance. (Interestingly, Chapter 7 deals with Cesare Borgia who obtained power by chance and lost it by chance.) To others the number 7 symbolizes completion or perfection, for it was on the seventh day that God rested from His creation.

Although Machiavelli can be adequately understood without *Gematria* or numerology, his use of the latter is indicative of the great subtlety and painstaking care with which *The Prince* and *The Discourses* were composed. But what is perhaps most significant about his use of numerology is this. By employing numbers and numerical sequences to modulate the communication of his revolutionary thoughts, less room was left to chance. Numerology added spice to his new science of politics and therefore made it more tempting to his unknown "collaborators."

Machiavelli's "Collaborators"

Machiavelli died in 1527. His fellow Florentine, Galileo was born in 1564. Without the conquest of nature made possible by Galilean science, Machiavelli's world-historical project would probably have died with him. While Machiavelli fathered a democratic political science, Galileo fathered the democratic cosmology needed to fashion a new dispensation for man. Recall that Galileo's mathematization of nature—his synthesis of astronomy and physics—overthrew the hierarchically ordered and finite universe of classical (and medieval) philosophy. Heaven and earth now manifested the Idea of Equality. In the mechanistic world inaugurated by Galileo (and perfected by Newton), man can no longer rely on nature or on God for objective and universally valid standards as to how man should live. All ideas on this crucial subject were made equal. Hobbes, who had admired and visited Galileo, saw the consequences of the new "value-free" science: a war of every man against every man, wherein "nothing can be unjust" because in war "the notions of right and wrong, justice and injustice have no place."

> In such condition [writes Hobbes], there is no place for industry; because the fruit thereof is uncertain: and consequently no culture of the earth; no navigation, nor use of commodities that may be imported by sea; no commodious building…no knowledge of the face of the earth; no account of time; no arts; no letters; no society; and which is worst of all, continual fear, and danger of violent death; and the life of man, solitary, poor, nasty, brutish, and short.[386]

Men would resemble so many bodies in ceaseless motion or collision. Accordingly, Hobbes believed that only the most powerful instinct of the human heart, the fear of violent death—Hobbes' *summum malum*—could provide a solid, *natural* foundation for political life. No wonder Hobbes regarded self-preservation as the fundamental law of nature. Only in this debased respect does nature provide a standard for mankind and even dictate a moral imperative: *seek peace*. Peace requires that men renounce their claims to moral or political superiority; it demands *equality*. It also requires the recognition that

> Good, and *evil*, are names that signify our appetites and aversions; which in different tempers, customs, and doctrines of men, are different; and divers men, differ not only in their judgment, on the sense of what is pleasant, and unpleasant to the *taste, smell, hearing, touch,* and sight; but also of what is conformable, or disagreeable to reason, in the actions of common life.[387]

Notice that good and evil, according to Hobbes, have no more rational or objective basis than those secondary qualities of which Galileo said, "I do not believe [that they] are anything but names."

By dispelling men's illusions that their ideas of good and evil have any divine sanction or are rooted in nature, Hobbes would turn mankind's energies away from devastating religious conflicts—his current disciples say "ideological" disputes—to the peaceful conquest of nature. For this purpose he constructed a utilitarian morality based on political hedonism (in contradistinction to the apolitical hedonism of Epicurus).

Kant, who accepted the Galilean-Newtonian physics, preferred a morality based not on men's inclinations or some pleasure-pain calculus, but on the concept of the free moral will. His categorical imperative—"Act only according to that maxim which you can at the same time will that it should become a universal law"[388]—should be understood as an attempt to substitute categories of reason for the two sources of morality undermined by the new physics: Nature and God. Fundamentally egalitarian, Kantian morality is a form of secularized Christianity. Like Christianity, it is intended for men of ordinary reason:

> But the most remarkable thing about ordinary reason in its practical concern is that it may have as much hope as any philosopher of hitting the mark. In fact, it is almost more certain to do so than the philosopher, because he has no principle which the common understanding lacks, while his judgment is easily confused by a mass of irrelevant considerations, so that it can easily turn aside from the

correct way. Would it not, therefore, be wiser in moral matters to acquiesce in the common rational judgment, or at most to call in philosophy in order to make the system of morals more complete and comprehensible and its rules more convenient for use...?[389]

Did not Machiavelli say (quoted above): "[A]s regards prudence and stability, I say that the people are more prudent and stable, and have better judgment than a prince"?

With God and nature having been eliminated as sources of morality, man must find the source of morality in himself. He has tried to do so; every effort has resulted in dismal failure. Bringing heaven down to earth by way of Galileo's cosmic uniformity has leveled mankind.

It need not, according to Judaism. Without degrading man, the notion of cosmic uniformity had been postulated by Rabbi Hasdai Crescas some two hundred years before Galileo. Crescas was of course familiar with the Midrash where the uniformity of nature was explicitly stated eleven centuries earlier! Thus, in Midrash Rabbah (Genesis 12:11) we read:

> Rabbi Huna said in the name of Rabbi Joseph: all that exists, including that which is in heaven and earth, consists of earth. [Which is to say that the heavenly bodies are created of the same fundamental elements as the earth.] As it is written: For as *"the rain and snow come from heaven"* (Isaiah 55:10): just as rain, though it comes from above possesses the same elements as the earth, so everything that exists in the universe, its fundamental elements, are identical to those of earth.[390]

The fact that Adam is made of earth does not negate man's superior rank in the universe. Allow me to repeat the teaching of Psalm 8, where King David asks: *"When I behold Your heavens, the work of Your fingers, the moon and the stars, which You have established, what is man's worth that You should be mindful of him?"* Again, King David is not comparing man to the moon and the stars—which he knew to be made of the same elements as the earth—but to the Creator of the universe. This is why he could say: *"HaShem, our Master...You have made man a little less than God."* Man is the most important essence in the universe; for having been created in the image of God, man possesses intellect and free will, the highest qualities in creation.

We have seen that in the finite, eternal, and hierarchically constructed cosmos of Plato and Aristotle, the cyclic drama of human life did not exclude the Good and the Beautiful while obscuring an ultimate meaninglessness. In the infinite universe of Galileo, in which all things are placed on the same level of being, human life is not only meaningless, but now *publicly* revealed as such, so that we are not even permitted to call anything (objectively) good and beautiful! Nevertheless, by bringing heaven down to earth, and by eliminating, in the process, the prevailing theological and naturalistic sources of ethics, Galilean physics contributed tremendously to man's conquest of nature and to the destruction of idolatry.

Now for a rapid survey of some of Machiavelli's "collaborators" (discussed at greater length in *Jerusalem vs. Athens*). Francis Bacon was a sympathetic reader of Machiavelli. His work, *Of the Interpretation of Nature*, linked science to technology.[391] The purpose of the new science? To alleviate the human condition. For the first time in history, science, divorced from philosophy (the preserve of the Few, i.e., the "proud"), was to serve the Many.

Bearing in mind that the philosophers of modernity regarded religion in general, and Christianity in particular, as their sole competitor as well as the greatest barrier to the conquest of nature and to human progress, Hobbes and Locke engaged in a subtle attack on the Bible. To convey their atheism with some subtlety, Hobbes interspersed references to God by saying everything is matter in motion, while Locke paid homage to the deity by proclaiming that human labor is the source of all value. (By the way, the "state of nature" of these two philosophers is nothing more than a hypothetical construction—really a fiction—on which to propagate a secular, political society.) Influenced by Locke's exaltation of commerce, Adam Smith produced the *Wealth of Nations*, the bible of capitalism, in which he also propagated the novel idea that war could be replaced by economic competition (a prejudice that even two World Wars have yet to dispel).[392]

In Benedict Spinoza, Machiavelli had another collaborator. As may be seen in his *Theological-political Treatise*, Spinoza was the first philosopher who was both a democrat and a liberal; he is also the father of "biblical criticism."[393] His *Treatise* exalts democracy as "the most natural form of government," for there "every man may think what he likes, and say what he thinks."[394]

Jean-Jacque Rousseau, a philosopher of democracy who nonetheless opposed the commercial society, advanced the Machiavellian idea that man's nature is infinitely malleable, a product of historical accident. But whereas Machiavelli said that man is by nature "bad," meaning egoistic, Rousseau held that man is by nature benevolent, that human conflict can be overcome by a "social contract" based on the "general will." Karl Marx went further. As I have written in *Demophrenia*:

Marx not only rejected all hitherto existing morality, but also the belief in the naturalistic foundation of egoism. According to Marx, egoism, no less than morality, is a historical product. And only with the simultaneous disappearance of egoism and morality will man achieve true freedom and equality, meaning genuine as opposed to a factitious democracy. How is this to be understood?

Marx believed that man's exploitation of man is rooted not in any defect of human nature but in the poverty of physical nature. Nature simply does not provide sufficiently for human needs. In other words, not egoism but economic scarcity is the original cause of human conflict and servitude, of human misery and inequality. But with the abolition of private property and the scientific conquest of nature, human exploitation will come to an end. Egoism, which is but a consequence of history, will dissolve, as will morality, which has ever been the morality of the ruling and exploiting class. Henceforth man will be animated by his "generic consciousness," which alone distinguishes human nature from that of mere animals.[395]

What will replace egoism and the restraints of morality will be a spontaneous fraternal disinterestedness. This, for Marx, is the only true humanism, the only true democracy.

DEMOCRACY AND THE DEGRADATION OF MAN

Thanks to Machiavelli and his philosophical successors, Democracy has become the religion or the idolatry of modernity, more immune to questioning than any revealed religion. Democracy, which until Machiavelli, and even well into the eighteenth century, was deemed a bad form of government, is today firmly established as the only good form of government—even though it is the seedbed of moral relativism. Still, it may be argued that the freedom and equality, which thrive in democracy, have facilitated the conquest of nature enjoined in the Torah: "...*replenish the earth and subdue it*" (Genesis 1:28). This was not to be expected of Greek political philosophy, given its aristocratic and agrarian orientation, or of Christianity, given its otherworldliness and asceticism. But this means that the Greco-Christian tradition had to be overcome to facilitate man's conquest of nature. Consider the positive consequences.

The conquest of nature liberated countless men, women, and children from stultifying toil and suffering. Of course, much stultifying toil and suffering were exacted in the process, especially in the early stages of capitalism. But even Marx, in his fusillades against the bourgeoisie, had to admit that capitalism, despite its "naked, shameless, direct, brutal exploitation,"

> has been the first to show what man's activity can bring about. It has accomplished wonders far surpassing Egyptian pyramids, Roman aqueducts, and Gothic cathedrals. It has created enormous cities and has thus rescued a considerable part of the population from the idiocy of rural life.[396]

Meanwhile, liberal democracy has liberated countless people from political bondage. By virtue of equality of opportunity, it opened the door to hitherto suppressed talents. Also, it introduced humane penal codes, approaching, to some extent, the infinitely more humane and rational system of law embodied in the *Halacha*. The Idea of Equality destroyed much good but also contributed to human progress—or so it may be argued. It may also be argued, however, that democracy represents not the progress so much as the degradation of man! Let us explore this hypothesis.

No less a friend of democracy than Alfred North Whitehead has written—and this was before the soul-shattering and stupefying effects of television: "So far as sheer individual freedom is concerned, there was more diffused freedom in the City of London in the year 1663, when Charles the First was King, than there is today in any industrial city in the world."[397] Industrial democracy breeds its own kind of bondage.

True, Democracy put an end to human slavery; but human slavery in the past was not, in all instances, the unmitigated evil it is made out to be, even though its abolition in modern times was certainly justified. Paradoxical as it may seem, the demise of slavery was not the result of moral progress so much as the result of moral decline, as I shall now explain.[398]

Needless to say, there have always been masters unworthy of having slaves. Nevertheless, when individuals were historically important, were of the caliber of a King David or of a Plato, it was fit and proper that they should be served by lesser men. Indeed, it was an honor to serve such great personages, to behold their virtues, to imbibe their words of wisdom.

But when the importance of leading individuals declined and they were no longer worthy of human servitude, Divine Providence brought about the rise of Democracy and Science on the one hand, and the eradication of slavery on the other. The process was gradual. The less men merited slave labor, the more they had to rely on animal and hired labor. Eventually, mankind sunk to so low a level as to be unworthy even of animal labor. (Only consider how biologists began to exult in tracing their genealogy to apes and to be offended by the idea of a higher origin!) Providence therefore accelerated the development of science and technology so that animals could be replaced by machines, progressively automated (and now very much geared to the gratification of paltry desires). In other words, given the increasing selfishness and hedonism of modernity, man no longer merits being served by any living thing.[399]

However, concomitant with the moral decline of the individual, there has been an outward improvement in the character of society. This dichotomy is not paradoxical. The progress of science and technology, the hallmark of Western civilization, was actually the result of egoism or moral decline (facilitated by Machiavelli's corrosive attack on Greco-Christian morality). Rousseau writes in his *First Discourse*, "our souls have been corrupted in proportion to the advancement of our sciences and arts toward perfection."[400] Rousseau was not merely referring to the moral depravity of his own times, the peak of the Enlightenment. He regarded the relationship between corruption and the progress of the arts and sciences as if it were a law of history, a phenomenon, he says, that "has been observed in all times and in all places."[401] By corruption Rousseau had in mind the decline of civic virtue, of dedication to the common good, in other words, the ascendancy of egoism. But as we have seen, egoism is the basis of Machiavelli's godless political science to whose advancement Rousseau contributed.

This political science, whose skepticism or agnosticism underlies all the social sciences and humanities, has thoroughly secularized man, stripped him of sapiential wisdom, while atomizing society. The intellectual functions of Secular Man are limited to the operations of pragmatic reason placed at the service of a welter of desires. The once ordered soul is now the disordered "self." All the emotions of the self, love included, are self-regarding—as the sexual revolution has made clear.[402] The only "natural" good is the private good.[403] Thus Machiavelli.

But now consider the negative aspects of his offspring. Democracy, which enlarged freedom of expression, is witnessing an appalling decline of intellectual standards. Democracy, which elevated the principle of equality, has engendered a leveling of all moral distinctions. Democracy, which championed human dignity, is now yielding to abject vulgarity.

In the process of this degradation, however, Democracy, with its all-pervasive moral relativism, is destroying all ideological competitors to the Torah—including democracy itself![404] The truth is: *Democracy is nothing more than Machiavelli's own creation; it has no intrinsic validity. Democratic freedom and equality have no rational foundation and can have no rational foundation when severed from the Torah and man's creation in the image of God.*

The same may be said of the Sovereign State, another offspring of Machiavelli. If Louis XIV said *L'état c'est moi*, he was only echoing Machiavelli's reference to Louis XII as "France" in Chapter 3 of *The Prince*. The State is simply a human creation, in which respect there is no difference between *L'état c'est moi* and *Vox populi vox Dei*. In both cases law is dependent solely on the will of the sovereign, be it the One, the Few, or the Many. The jurisprudent Isaac Breuer draws the only sensible conclusion: As long as states insist on their sovereignty and recognize no higher authority than their own laws, there can be no social or international peace. "The anarchy of mankind shows itself in continuously recurring historical catastrophes, foretold with tremendous insistence by all the prophets, to which only the law of God can put an end."[405] The experience of more than five decades of the misnamed United Nations—a frequent instigator of conflict—lends weight to this conclusion. But then, is not the UN General Assembly, which renders all nations equal regardless of their moral and intellectual character, the pinnacle of relativism?

DECADENCE AND DISILLUSIONMENT

Relativism will be the epitaph on the gravestone of the West. Ironically, the prevalence of relativism is largely a consequence of the West's greatest intellectual achievement: mathematical physics. The West is trapped in a fundamental dilemma. On the one hand, it regards mathematical physics as the paradigm of knowledge. On the other hand, mathematical physics can tell us nothing about how man should live. The reduction of science to quantitative analysis renders it incapable of telling us anything about moral values.

Although Nietzsche was a relativist, he recognized that relativism is symptomatic of decadence. His paradoxical position may be summarized as follows: Relativism is true but deadly, therefore relativism is false! Why? Because relativism stifles any incentive to pursue a world-historical goal, a psychological precondition of which is belief in the absolute worth of that goal. In other words, relativism undermines the will to creativity on a monumental scale. Hence relativism is deadly, contrary to Life—logically true but existentially false, for Life transcends logic.

Relativism permeates democracy because democracy's two organizing principles, freedom and equality, lack ethical and rational constraints. The West boasts of democracy, ignorant of how it constitutes a basic cause of Western decadence. I define decadence as a retreat from life to death resulting from an inability to confront evil, since evil itself is linked to death. "*I have placed before you today life and good, and death and evil...*" (Deuteronomy

30:15). Unless the ethical is derived from the transcendental, there is no escape from Hume's skepticism and relativistic epistemology.

And so, disgusted with the moral decay of modernity, many people in the West are returning to traditional values, either to Christianity or to the "natural right" doctrine of classical Greek philosophy. But as we have seen, modernity is itself the outgrowth of the secular ingredients of the Greco-Christian tradition. The contemporary phenomenon of Christian fundamentalism, to be applauded as a moral force, lacks the fecundity required for a renaissance of Western civilization. As may be seen in contemporary art, music, architecture, economics, literature, the professions, entertainment, Christianity is conspicuous by its absence. Christian fundamentalism seems to be a historically limited reaction to the neo-paganism now spreading throughout the West. Meanwhile, "liberation theology" contributes to the further secularization of Christianity, which was bound to become an increasingly private affair.

As for the classics, although Jonathan Swift was correct when he likened the ancients to the Brobdingnagians and the moderns to the Lilliputians, the philosophic foundations of the classics are hopelessly obsolete. Newtonian mechanics (fully adequate for macro-objects moving below the speed of light) has relegated to the dust heap of history Aristotle's organic, teleological, and hierarchic conception of nature—exactly Machiavelli's own objective. But to refute Aristotle's conception of nature is to eliminate from serious consideration any return to his source of morality.

If this were not enough, the classics, as indicated, are also burdened by the cosmology of an eternal and cyclical (as opposed to a created and "linear") cosmology. In this most crucial respect there is no difference between Aristotle and Machiavelli who also posited an eternal universe.[406] Classical cosmology, we saw, harbors a fundamental dichotomy: whereas Nature is purposive, History is purposeless. Existentialists also regard history as devoid of purpose. Following the mode of thought inaugurated by Machiavelli and advanced by Nietzsche, existentialism holds that man has no nature, no fixed or permanent nature. Hence there are no immutable standards by which to determine how man should live. Man, i.e., the individual, must choose his own ends or values to endow life with meaning. But this leads to the nihilism deplored by traditionalists who find their (noble but inadequate) standards of criticism in classical political philosophy.

If history is purposeless or meaningless, if humanity is bound to eternal cyclicality, then Plato's and Aristotle's political philosophy is nothing more than a "noble lie," a myth—as it may well have been so understood by one or both of these intellectual giants. In that case, in the quarrel between ancients and moderns, the moderns have at least the advantage of candor, however deadly the consequences. But whatever the intentions of men, the road from Machiavelli's *Prince* to the leveling humanism of the present era may be traced back to the deicide committed in Plato's *Republic*. Looking at this road as traveled today, it is strewn with innumerable casualties seeking meaning in drugs, sex, violence, cults—anything that may help the liberated self escape loneliness, anomie, angst, madness, and self-destruction. This torturous road is viewed, however, from the vantage of a Jewish philosophy of history which denies that history is purposeless or meaningless. This philosophy affords no grounds for pessimism, weapons of mass destruction notwithstanding. For while man acts in freedom and pays the consequences, every act and consequence, good and bad, moves the system of history forward to an end ordained by a just and gracious God.

Consistent with Nietzsche's dialectical philosophy, Rabbi Kook writes:

> The arising of contradictions broadens the scope of existence. Good accentuates Evil and Evil deepens Good, delineating and strengthening it. Just as wine cannot be without dregs, so the world cannot be without wicked people. And just as the dregs serve to preserve the wine, so the coarse will of the wicked strengthens the existence of the flow of life..."[407]

And so two world wars, the bloodiest in human history, led to the restoration of the State of Israel, the subject of our concluding chapter.

CHAPTER 14
HEBRAIC CIVILIZATION:
ISRAEL'S FINAL REDEMPTION

INTRODUCTION

HAVING reached the concluding chapter, perhaps I should apologize for being so selective in my choice of subjects with which to articulate a Jewish philosophy of history. I leave it to others to fill in the gaps of this inquiry. But now let us retrace our steps and provide a brief overview of some of the philosophic, religious, and scientific developments that have occurred since the destruction of the First Temple.

We saw that the basic historical function of Greek philosophy was to destroy the Greek pantheon, that is, primitive idolatry. The Olympian gods represented "forces" of nature. These forces had to be depersonalized if science were to develop. This was the task of the *physikoi*, the Greek natural philosophers. But in the process of demolishing the Olympian gods, these materialists of old also undermined the prevailing religion which, though far from having a refined morality, did place salutary constraints on the behavior of men. We saw that Aristotle transformed the *physikoi's* materialistic or lifeless conception of nature into an organic and teleological one and thereby invested nature with ethical significance far more elevated than the Greek religion. Later, the decay of that religion threatened the Roman world with unmitigated barbarism. Such barbarism was avoided by the advent of Christianity—a "spark from Zion."

In the process of destroying paganism, Christianity also denigrated the sensuality of Roman "naturalism." Thus, whereas Aristotelian philosophy presents nature humane, Christian spirituality presents nature depraved. In this way an otherworldly religion counteracted Aristotle's teleology of nature and its regressive anthropomorphism. It thereby helped to remove a barrier to the further development of science. Nevertheless, such was its otherworldly and ascetic view of man and nature that Christianity, like classical political philosophy, was not conducive to the rise modern science and the subsequent conquest of nature. Machiavelli's corrosive attack on the Greco-Christian tradition therefore provided a partial, albeit most dangerous, corrective to the classical and Christian conceptions of man and nature. By itself, nature—a word that does not appear in the Torah—provides neither a positive nor a negative standard of how man should live. Nature is something subordinate to human will and ingenuity. Paradoxical as it may seem, Machiavelli's "humanism" moved mankind a step toward a Jewish view of nature and promoted, to that extent, the Torah's world-historical program.

Galilean-Newtonian physics completed Machiavelli's neutralization of nature. Mechanistic physics leveled the hierarchical conception of the universe that dominated the mentality of Greco-Christian civilization, and thus facilitated the democratic dispensation projected by Machiavelli in *The Prince*. There Machiavelli laid the foundation for two conflicting movements: Individualism and Statism. Individualism manifested itself primarily as capitalism. Consistent with the teaching of *The Prince*, capitalism removes all restraints on the acquisitive instincts. The growth of capitalism depended, however, on (1) the rise of modern science and (2) democracy, which provided the free labor required for the industrial revolution. Thanks largely to John Locke and Adam Smith, capitalism made its first major appearance in England, where the industrial revolution transformed an agrarian, religious aristocracy into a commercial, secular democracy. Eventually, such was the extent of England's commercial power that, until World War II, the sun never set on the British Empire.

But it is twentieth-century America that represents the pinnacle of individualism and capitalism. That century also witnessed the ascendancy of statism, which took three distinct forms: Communism, Fascism, and Nazism. Here let us pause.

As we saw in Chapter 13 of *The Prince*, power is the basis of the state. Power must therefore be the propelling force of history. Marx adapted Machiavelli to a philosophy of history and posited class conflict as history's "midwife." We saw in the previous chapter that, contrary to Machiavelli (and to the Greco-Christian tradition), Marx held that human conflict is rooted not in human nature, in egoism, but in the poverty of external nature. With the abolition of private property and the scientific conquest of nature, however, egoism and human conflict will come to an end. How does this lead to statism?

The abolition of private property and the conquest of nature require the organization of all the productive forces of society. This necessitates the dictatorship of the proletariat—really its vanguard, the Communist Party. The ascendancy of the state under Communism was inevitable. In this respect there is no difference between Communism and Nazism (National Socialism), and the same may be said of Fascism. These ideologies are based on the primacy of force and their leaders inevitably pursue an imperialistic foreign policy. Hence they were bound to come into conflict with each other and with capitalist democracies, as they did in World War II.

Reflecting on war in general and World War I in particular, Rabbi Kook maintained that great wars, notwithstanding their horrors, are preludes to the rebirth of Israel and its Final Redemption.[408] World War I did in fact produce the Balfour Declaration and the international recognition of the Jewish claim to Palestine. The war also terminated the Ottoman Empire and replaced the Turks in Palestine with the British, thus making possible the establishment of a Jewish state in Eretz Yisrael. The actual establishment of such a state—following the logic of Rabbi Kook—was the result of the more monstrous conflagration of World War II and the Nazi Holocaust. "Out of unspeakable destruction and murder came the salvation of Israel! The death of the righteous granted the Jewish people new life."[409] The most wicked tyranny perished from the world, and Europe, with the help of the United States, entered into an era of peace and prosperity.

However, it needs to be reiterated that *the Nazi Holocaust, for which Christian Europe as a whole was responsible, and in which even democracies were complicit, signaled the end of modernity and the demise of Western civilization.* Despite the Nazi horror, *moral relativism permeates every level of education in the post-modern, democratic world.* Once again the gentile world is without any moral bearings. And so the time had come for the restoration of Israel. Despite the spiritual darkness into which Machiavelli and his philosophical successors had cast mankind, "a spark arose from Zion." The State of Israel was reborn. Its founders, however, were products of a decaying world, as we saw in the first chapter of this book. Nevertheless, from the rotting seed the fruit of a New Israel will emerge. Israel's degradation is approaching its end; its Final Redemption is nearing. Perhaps it will require another war to hasten a renaissance of Hebraic civilization.

Such a war will surely involve weapons of mass destruction, of which nuclear weapons are conceptually the most significant. After all, nuclear weapons are the product of twentieth-century science, of relativity physics and quantum mechanics. No wonder the twentieth century, which marked the triumph of Secular Man, was the bloodiest in human history. The scientific conquest of nature was now at hand, but with it looms the possible devastation of mankind. Like classical physics, relativity physics and QM are morally neutral. Hence Israel's rebirth—the rebirth of Hebraic civilization—was all the more crucial for mankind's salvation.

HEBRAIC CIVILIZATION

For more than 2,500 years of recorded history, the greatest gentile minds in philosophy and science regarded the world as eternal. Not until the end of the twentieth century did the scientific community reject this dogma and arrive at the conclusion that the universe had a beginning, as stated 3,300 years ago in the first verse of the Torah. Moreover, physicists like Nathan Aviezer and Gerald Schroeder have shown that what is said in the Torah regarding the six days of creation is consistent with the findings of astronomy, physics, microbiology, geology, archeology, paleontology, and other sciences. If it took some 2,500 years to overcome the dogma of an eternal universe and to bring the greatest scientific minds to a conclusion regarding the universe that accords with the first verse of the Torah, may it not be that the "Old Testament"—the Book of Truth—will eventually require its religious and non-religious rivals to undergo a fundamental metamorphosis?

In the discussion of Hebraic civilization that follows, we shall want to keep in mind previously mentioned flaws in Islam and the West. Regarding Islam, suffice to mention its Quranic hatred, which stultifies the mind, and its rigid legalism, which frustrates attempts to reconcile permanence and change. Regarding the West, enough to remember the failure of Christian love and moral precepts to compensate for its antinomianism, leaving unrestrained the egoism resulting from the Machiavellian separation of morality from politics.

Now it so happens that the key to understanding Hebraic civilization will be found in *parasha* (weekly Torah portion) *Lech-Lecha*, which portrays the character of the first Jew. God says to Avram:

Lech-Lecha: Go for yourself—away from your land, from your birthplace, and from the home of your father, to the land that I will show you (Genesis 12:1).

Avram is first presented as the archetype of *selfhood*, of *individuality*. But later his name is changed: the letter *Hei*, representing God, is added to his name and Avram becomes Avraham. Whatever else his name means (discussed later), Avraham is the personification of kindness—*Hesed*. At first glance, however, there seems to be a tension between selfhood or self-concern and kindness, concern for others. But this is not so in Avraham, as Rabbi Matis Weinberg, who has plumbed many secular disciplines, will explain. *Hesed-kindness*

> is a profound commitment to Life itself, a commitment that may lead to confrontation, conflict, and even war if such are required to

assure Life's definitive triumph. *Hesed-Kindness*: examine the word. *Kind* means "of one type"; the deepest *kin*ship of all, a shared existence. [What makes *Hesed-kindness* possible, what makes man*kind* possible or gives all men a common source of existence is their creation in] the *Image of God* (Genesis1:27). What clearer statement of monotheism could be made in a word![410]

Now let us consider a unique soliloquy in which God explains why He feels so attached to Avraham:

I love him because he enjoins his children and household after him that they cherish the path of God; that they do charity and justice in order that God bring to Avraham what He promised (Genesis 18:17).

Rabbi Weinberg comments: "But surely 'doing charity'—the *Hesed* which became the hallmark of Avraham for all time—surely *Hesed* must by its very *definition* be driven by selflessness and altruism? Not at all."

The man of Hesed *cares for his own self...*(Proverbs 11:17)

"Self-denial," says Weinberg, "is not associated with *Hesed*. If anything, it is a hallmark of cruelty":

The man of Hesed *cares for his own self, and he who troubles his own flesh is cruel* (Proverbs 11:17).

Rabbi Weinberg admits that what he has thus far said will appear "somewhat subversive" and "outrageous." "Is the Torah seriously suggesting that *Hesed* is meant to be selfish? Is it possible that God would not have loved Avraham had he told his children to keep God's ways 'for the sake of Heaven' instead of 'so that God can bring Avraham his blessings'? After all, the focus on acquiring 'blessings' actually violates a primary element in service of God":

One should not say: I will perform the mitzvot *of the Torah and study its wisdom so that I can obtain the blessings written therein...*

Rambam, Mishne Torah, Hilchot Teshuva. 10:1

"Is it really possible," asks Weinberg, "that Avraham would have failed his test had he insisted on meeting his challenges out of pure love instead of 'for himself'? If so there appears to be an awful contradiction here, for Avraham is held up as the model of service 'for the sake of Heaven,' the paradigm of man motivated by pure love." As the Rambam says:

> The one who serves out of love, will work at Torah and *mitzvot* and walk the paths of wisdom for no ulterior motive whatever—neither from fear of harm nor to secure benefits—he simply does Truth because it is Truth. The benefits will follow in its wake—eventually.... This is the level of Avraham *avinu* [our father], to whom God referred as 'My lover' (Isaiah 41:8) because he did nothing unless out of love.... (ibid.)

Again Rabbi Weinberg:

> I believe that we find all this confusing only because we make many culturally biased—and dangerous—assumptions regarding the nature of *Hesed*. The truth is that these two pictures of Avraham are not contradictory but fully complementary, and each is conceivable only and entirely in light of the other. This is the central teaching of the parasha and of the Avraham model, and only in grappling with its subtleties can we begin to understand what God wanted from Avraham—and what Avraham achieved.

> *Lech-Lecha* describes the job that needs to be done; Rambam describes the motivation for doing it. The *motivation* for Avraham's service to both God and man was pure love. Its *objective* needed to be the consummation of Avraham's own self. But such a motivation can exist only in light of such an objective, and such an objective can only be consummated through such a motivation: if you have not both, you can have neither.

Here is where Judaism departs from both Christianity and Islam. Christianity and Islam praise selflessness and condemn selfishness. Self-sacrifice for the sake of God is the crowning achievement of the Christian saint and the Muslim martyr. Rabbi Weinberg sees, in Avraham's *Hesed*, something far more profound, a love of God and man that affirms selfhood and therefore Life as the essence of Creation.

> "Selflessness," some preach, is a sine qua non of the kind of love expressed in Avraham's *Hesed* and in his service for the sake of

heaven. But in reality, selflessness precludes love. Love, as Rambam defines above, implies being "without ulterior motivation," having no external concern whatsoever. "The one who serves out of love, will work at Torah and *mitzvot* and walk the paths of wisdom for no ulterior motive whatever...."

The motivation must come from *within*. If I want to "*get* something out of it," then clearly I am driven by something that exists outside myself, something *ulterior*. But the only thing that is not ulterior in any way, the only thing "internal," is my own self. And therein lies the problem of selfish selflessness.

A person who does not experience his own self as significant, who finds personal existence meaningless, cannot possibly be moved by anything but "ulterior" motives. He is always trying to "get" something—and all the significance and meaning he manages to wheedle out of life is a lie, because it comes from *outside* his own life. The truly and completely selfish individual is the "selfless" individual—such a one must live on the selves of others in fearful predation. He uses God and other people to find what he cannot himself find within."

Rabbi Weinberg approaches his conclusion:

> History (and for many, personal experience) makes this observation cruelly clear. Those who seek selfless dedication to others, whose objective is to save the world, who make love a religious goal—those have been more successful at mass-murder, terror, and pillage than any Mafia. Only those who are the "servants of God" have succeeded, and continue to succeed, in ruining the lives of countless millions in a sea of blood, tears and, at very least, personal misery....
>
> To taste true love, to participate in *Hesed's* love of pure existence, it is absolutely essential to be "*The man of* Hesed," who "*cares for his own self*." Because the only existence we directly know and experience and love is our own...Either *Hesed* is an expression of love for one's own life or it is based on the worst of ulterior motives—a base and sinful attempt to steal significance.
>
> *Hesed of the nations is a sin* (Proverbs 14:34). "...they do it only to establish their own significance" (Bava Batra, 10b).

Summarizing his illuminating commentary, Rabbi Weinberg writes:

> *Lech-Lecha* inoculated Avraham and his nation against the ravages of selfish religiosity that destroys the service of God. *Lech-Lecha* protected those who embraced it from the hateful destructiveness to which such religion inevitably leads. *Lech-Lecha* created a tradition of *Hesed* based solely on love of life and safeguarded a people from the dangerous lie of selflessness which seeks to destroy all the meaning of Creation.

Here we transcend Christianity, Islam, and the West. Hebraic civilization transcends altruism and egoism. Here we have a civilization based on *Hesed*, on a love of Life, on creativity, which is why the Jewish people are known even by gentiles as the most creative people in history.

Life is creativity (as Nietzsche understood). Thus, when the Torah says "God created man in His own image," this means that just as God is creative in an infinite way, so man is creative in a finite way. This creativity involves a synthesis of reason and free will. By itself, reason is reducible to logic, which is passive. But since it coexists with free will, *reason is also the organ of emphasis on novelty*.[411] As logic, reason sees that novelty must have as its background that which is perennial or unchanging, otherwise novelty will be lost in mere transience and lose all value. Reason in its fullness is therefore dialectical: it prompts man toward conservatism and creativity; it enables him to reconcile permanence and change; its function is to promote the Art of Life.[412]

It is in this light that we are to understand the relationship between the Written Torah, which is fixed, and the Oral Torah, which applies what is fixed to what is changing. The Written Torah alone, based solely on revelation, would produce a static world, without infinite potential for novel response to new situations. A living Torah makes room for change, diversity, growth, creativity—but without vitiating its permanent principles. These principles are vivified by being conceptually linked to change. This linkage is made possible by the judges of the Oral Law, whose interpretations are based not on revelation but on logic, analogy, and intuition. This commitment to permanence linked to change reflects the Jewish people's covenantal relationship with God.[413]

One may even say that permanence and change together constitute a cosmological principle built into the very creation of the universe. The Big Bang represents the most fundamental change—conventionally speaking, from nothing to something. But with the Big Bang the laws of nature were created, laws yielding permanence, reconciling, as it were, Heraclitus and Parmenides.

The reconciliation of permanence and change is the secret of Jewish life and law, of Hebraic civilization. As any Talmud student knows, Jewish law is intended to *educate* the individual, to challenge his mind, such that *creativity, conviction, and voluntary obedience* may follow. The aim of Torah education is to liberate man in such a way that he does freely what nature does blindly, both obeying the laws of God. A great German poet spoke Jewish wisdom when he wrote:

> Dost thou seek the highest perfection?
> Plants can teach thee.
> What they are willy-nilly,
> Thou canst be by thy own free will.[414]

Jewish law is an education in freedom. Because it reconciles permanence and change, its scope is unlimited. Hence, the jurisprudent Rabbi Isaac Breuer could maintain, without chauvinism, that Jewish law "is as comprehensive as any codification of the whole complex of private and public law of a living modern state can possibly be."[415] Far from being obsolete, the *Halacha* has always been a living and creative system of law. As I have elsewhere written:

> Like other legal systems, Jewish law has various branches, for example, civil and criminal law, public and administrative law. Extant Jewish legal knowledge includes 7,000 volumes or 300,000 instances of case law dealing primarily with the social and economic problems of Jewish communities dispersed throughout Europe and North Africa. Prior to the Emancipation in the eighteenth century, these communities possessed juridical autonomy and creatively applied Jewish law to the most diverse social and economic conditions. The enormous body of case law resulting therefrom is being organized at various Israeli universities, and not merely for its historical interest, but for its potential relevance to contemporary problems.[416]

Remarkably, Jewish legal experts in the United States have created a new institute that will educate jurists and others about Jewish law and promote the application of its teachings to contemporary legal disputes and other modern-day problems. Supreme Court Justice Antonin Scalia, in a letter to the institute, acknowledged that Jewish law is one of the "most highly developed systems." One lawyer recently filed a brief to the Supreme Court based on the Talmud's view of capital punishment.[417]

Here is a marvelous example of how Judaism has served the best interests of mankind. But this is implied in the name and deeds of the first Jew, Avraham, of whom the Torah says: *"you shall be the father of a multitude of nations,"* and *"all the nations of the world shall be blessed through your descendants* (Genesis 16:17; 22:18).

Contrary to the God of Islam, who commands Muslims to destroy nationhood by placing all nations under the *sharia*, the God of Israel is infinitely more liberal. He creates unique nations as well as unique individuals; and He wants each to pursue its own perfection in peace. This the nations can do only if they abide by the "genial orthodoxy" of the Seven Noahide Laws of Universal Morality. But God, in His infinite wisdom, saw that mankind would need something more. And so He created an exemplary nation, Israel, and endowed this nation with a unique system of laws which, as previously indicated, has enabled the Jewish people to unite *particularism* and *universalism*. Only when this system of laws is creatively re-established will Israel achieve its Final Redemption and present to mankind the example of a nation in which Freedom dwells with Righteousness, Equality with Excellence, Wealth with Beauty, the here and now with love of the Eternal.

Let us conclude with passages from Holy Writ.

> *And it shall come to pass, when all these things have come upon you—the blessing and the curse which I have presented before you—then you will take it to your heart among all the nations where the Lord your God has scattered you. You will then return to the Lord your God, and listen to His voice, according to everything that I command you today, you and your children, with your whole heart and with all your soul. Then the Lord your God will restore your captives and exiles and have compassion upon you; and He will gather you from all the nations to which He has scattered you. Even if any of yours that are dispersed in the uttermost parts of heaven, from there He will gather you and take you back [as His people]. The Lord your God shall bring you into the land that your forefathers possessed, and you shall possess it again....He will circumcise [remove the barriers from] your hearts and the hearts of your offspring, so that you will love the Lord your God with all your heart and with all your soul* (Deuteronomy 30:1-6).

> *His covenant forever—the Word He commanded to a thousand generations—that He made with Abraham and His vow to Isaac. Then He established it for Jacob as a statute, for Israel as an everlasting covenant, saying, "To you I shall give the land of Canaan, the lot of your inheritance"* (Psalms 105:8-11).

In those days ten men of every nationality, speaking different languages, shall take hold of every Jew by the corner of his garment and say, "Let us go with you, for we have heard that God is with you" (Zechariah 8:23).

The Lord will shine upon you, and His glory shall be seen above you. Nations shall then walk in your light and kings by the radiance of your dawn (Isaiah 60:2-3).

On that day, the Lord will be One, and His Name will be One (Zechariah 14:9).[418]

★   ★   ★

Appendix
Israel's Return and Restoration:
An Essay Confirming the Existence of Laws of History[419]

Introduction

EVERYTHING connected with Israel baffles human understanding. This is because Israel is not governed by the historical and sociological laws that govern the rest of humanity. Obviously the nations do not understand these laws, but neither do most Jews. Indeed, hindering Israel's Final Redemption are not only many secular Jews, but also many of the religious. The latter reject the State of Israel because of its secular founding and character. They repudiate the idea that this secular state has a necessary function in the redemption or restoration of the Jewish people. The present State, they contend, has no basis in Jewish law, the *Halacha*.

Now, this book would be far from complete if it did not discuss the controversy over the *halachic* status of the secular State of Israel. This controversy, however, has to be seen through the eyes of a Torah master. Fortunately, the controversy over Israel's return and restoration has been exhaustively analyzed by one of the Torah giants of our time, the Gaon Dr. Chaim Zimmerman. I refer to his monumental work *Torah and Existence*. The first chapter alone brings to bear on the controversy over Israel's rebirth not only the Written Torah, the prophets, and the Hagiographa, but also the Babylonian and Jerusalem Talmuds, the Midrash, the Zohar, as well as the "*Rishonim*" (including such luminaries as Rashi, the Rambam, and the Ramban), the "*Achronim*" (the successors of the *Rishonim*), and more recent masters (of whom, more later).[420]

In the process of relating this vast amount of material to the controversy in question, Dr. Zimmerman also deals with various concepts of science and philosophy, miracles and free will, prophecy and laws of history. Obviously the discussion of this range of subjects is intended for the scholar rather than the layman. Hence, with Dr. Zimmerman's kind permission, I have condensed and adapted his work on the controversy over Israel's return and restoration for the general public. Rather than discuss such esoteric subjects as miracles and the relationship between laws of history and free will, I shall simply refer the reader to Dr. Zimmerman's reflections on these subjects. We shall now see how a master of the Torah and the Talmud deals with the momentous issue of Israel's return and restoration.

Dr. Zimmerman's central thesis may be stated as follows: The establishment of the State of Israel in 1948 is *halachically* indicative of the Beginning of Israel's Redemption.[421] Israel's complete redemption will necessitate the establishment of a Torah government. Such a government can come into existence by a natural process. Its establishment would require the leadership of a man wholly dedicated to the Torah, a man who, among all the earth's leaders, will stand incomparable in personal rectitude, learning, and wisdom. The Jewish sources refer to such a man as the "*Moshiach*." What follows is an abbreviated version of Dr. Zimmerman's extraordinary erudition on this subject, here adapted for the general reader.

Part I. The Concept of the Moshiach

Dr. Zimmerman's argument employs *halachic* concepts which, though unfamiliar to most readers, are entirely logical and grounded in empirical reality. The argument begins with the concept of the Moshiach. This term, rendered as "Messiah" in English, conjures up in the minds of many people mystical connotations far removed from its logical and empirical origin. The Hebrew term literally means "anointed," and refers to a special oil used in the appointment of kings and high priests of Israel. (See Leviticus 21:10; I Samuel 10:1; II Samuel 2:4.) But let us examine the breadth and depth of this concept.

The first thing to bear in mind is that the concept of Moshiach refers not only to a person but to verifiable stages of history involving the condition and character of the Jewish people. Contrary to the fancies of the superstitious, the Moshiach concept does not allude to any pre-existing being. Nor does it denote a person possessed of supernatural powers. Rather, the Moshiach projected in Jewish law is a thoroughly human personality who, like other Jews, understands the world-historical goal of the Jewish people, but who will be capable of bringing about Israel's complete redemption and, therewith, abiding peace to war-torn humanity. He will not only be a man of flesh and blood, but he will trace his descent to King David through Solomon (something that can readily be done by means of existing genealogical records). Of course, he will emulate his illustrious forebear in his zeal for the Torah. He will implant the love of God and Torah in every heart and home in Israel by virtue of his sterling character and wisdom. (See Isaiah 11:2.) But having said this, it needs to be reiterated that the appearance of the Moshiach depends on the world-historical circumstances as well as on the existential character of the Jewish people. ("Israel," remember, is an ideal construct—really a special creation—whose historical manifestation is governed by "linear" laws to which the concept of the Moshiach, we shall see, is logically related.)

No less than a world-renowned rationalist like Maimonides, who disdained mysticism, held that anyone who denies the concept of the Moshiach denies the Torah as well as the prophets.[422] Such a denial, he held, would be tantamount to a denial of God and of the laws by which He guides history (including the laws of reward and punishment). For this reason, it is of fundamental importance to Judaism to dissociate the concept of the Moshiach from any suggestion of mysticism. This must be done before going deeper into the process of Israel's restoration.

Great reputations have been made by writing on Jewish mysticism, even though there is no such thing.[423] The mystic is someone who abandons his rational faculties and supposedly loses himself in God. No Torah man ever thought it possible for man to overcome the infinite distance that separates him from his Creator. To the contrary, from the Torah perspective the mystic is a fraud, a fabricator of absurd and fantastic myths. The Torah forbids belief in mysticism, as it does any form of idolatry. The Rambam (Maimonides) writes:

> These practices are all false and deceptive, and were the means employed by the ancient idolaters to deceive the people of various countries and induce them to become their followers. It is not proper for Jews, who are highly intelligent, to allow themselves to be deluded by such inanities or imagine that there is anything in them, as it is said, "*For there is no...occult powers in Israel*" (Numbers 23:23); and further, "*The nations that you are driving out listen to astrologers and mystics; but the Lord your God has not suffered you to do so*" (Deuteronomy 18:14).
>
> Whoever believes in these and similar things and, in his heart, holds them to be true and scientific, is nothing but a fool, deficient in understanding, who belongs to the same class with children...whose intellects are immature. Sensible people, however, who possess sound mental faculties, know by clear proofs, that all these practices which the Torah prohibited have no scientific basis but are chimerical and inane. The Torah, therefore, in

forbidding all these follies, exhorts us, "*You shall be wholehearted with the Lord your God*" (ibid., 18:13) (*Mishneh Torah, Book of Knowledge*, "Laws of Idolatry," XI, 16).

Far from having anything to do with mystical fantasies, the concept of the Moshiach is a perfectly rational one. It is part of the logical system of *Halacha*—Jewish law—as the following exposition will make clear.

According to the Torah, the Land of Israel—Eretz Yisrael—belongs to *Klal Yisrael*—the Jewish people. This land is a permanent possession of the Jewish people, whether they occupy it or not. God promised Avraham: "*And I will give unto you and to your seed after you, the land of your sojourning, all the land of Canaan for an everlasting possession*" (Genesis 17:8; and see ibid., 26:3 and 28:13 for a reaffirmation of this promise to Yitzhak and Yaakov). It follows that any loss of Jewish sovereignty over the Land of Israel can only be temporary. "*God is not a man that he should lie, nor a human being that he should change His mind. Would He promise and not do it, or speak and not confirm it?*" (Numbers 23:19).

Now, when the people of Israel transgressed the laws of the Torah, they were expelled from the land. Their exile and dispersion, hence their temporary loss of sovereignty over the land, constitutes a punishment prescribed in the Torah itself. "*You shall therefore keep all My laws and social rules and fulfill them, so that the land to which I bring you to settle in will not spew you out*" (Leviticus 20:22). "*And if you will not hearken unto Me...I, Myself, will bring the land into desolation, and your enemies that settle in it will become desolate on it. But you I will scatter among the nations*" (ibid., 26:27, 32).

And true to the Torah, the Land of Israel, despite its extraordinary fertility, remained desolate and neglected for millennia no matter which foreign nation controlled it: Babylonians, Persians, Greeks, Seleucids, Romans, Byzantines, Arabs, Seljuks, Fatimids, Latins, Mamluks, Turks, or English. (See ibid., 26:43.) What is more, none of these nations ever established a functional state or capital in the Land of Israel; and had any done so, the Jews would not have been able to return to the land, let alone establish therein an independent state as they did in 1948. (Here we have evidence of a law of history modulating, as it were, the local operation of a law of nature.)

We have seen that the expulsion of the Jews from the Land of Israel was a punishment for their having abandoned the Torah, but that the occupation of the land by non-Jews has always and necessarily been temporary. For consistently with His oath to Avraham, Yitzhak, and Yaakov, God promised that, in the proper time of history (1) the subjugation of Jews by the nations will come to an end; (2) the Jews will come back to their land; (3) they will regain their sovereignty; (4) they will do *teshuva*; and (5) they will establish a Torah government comparable to that which existed in the days of King David, who was himself called "Moshiach" (Psalms 84:10, 132:10), because he was anointed with the coronation oil mentioned above. This sequence of stages defines the Torah concept of the Moshiach.

To locate this definition of the Moshiach in the Torah, let us first expand on an earlier reference to the Rambam: "He who does not…look forward to the coming of the Moshiach denies not only the teachings of the prophets but also those of the Torah…for the Torah bears witness to him, as it is said, '*Then the Lord your God will restore your captives and exiles and have compassion upon you; and He will gather you from all the nations to which He has scattered you. Even if any of yours that are dispersed in the uttermost parts of heaven, from there He will gather you and take you back [as His people]. The Lord your God shall bring you back to the land that your forefathers possessed*'" (Deuteronomy 30:3-5) (*Mishneh Torah, Book of Judges*, "Laws on Kings and Wars," XI, I).[424]

Since the word Moshiach is absent from these verses, the concept requires further elaboration. From Deuteronomy 30:3-5 we only learn that the concept of the Moshiach involves these two elements: (1) the end of Jewish subjection to foreign rule, and (2) the return of the Jews to the Land of Israel. But in the sequel to these verses we are told: "*And you shall return and hearken unto the voice of the Lord, and do all these commandments*" (Deuteronomy 30:8). One of these commandments is to appoint a king (ibid., 17:15) whose purpose is to lead the Jewish people in such a way as to fulfill the promise of the Torah. It is sufficient to say, therefore, that the advent of the Moshiach is defined by the expression, "*The Lord your God will return you from your captivity and have compassion upon you; and He will gather you from all the nations to which He has scattered you…and bring you into to the land that your forefathers possessed*," to which must be added the commandment to appoint a king who will imbue Israel with the love of God and Torah. But lest anyone misconceive the character of the future Torah ruler, the Rambam adds (in the sequel to his last mentioned statement): "Do not think that the Moshiach will have to perform signs and wonders, bring anything new into being, revive the dead, or do similar things. It is not so."

We see, therefore, that the Moshiach is nothing more than a superlative human being dedicated to the fulfillment of all the commandments of the Torah. Far from being a mystery, the Moshiach is a concept defined by the *Halacha*. Reading the above words of the Rambam, any student of Jewish law will immediately see the nonsense which outsiders of the Torah have attached to this concept.

Summing up we see that, in accordance with God's oaths to the patriarchs, the Jews will return to the Land of Israel; they will regain their sovereignty over the land; they will return to the Torah; and they will establish a kingdom of Torah in which the Moshiach will be their ruler as in the days of King David, when Israel achieved its highest level of existence.

PART II. SIX NEGATIVE ARGUMENTS[425]

Many people are nonetheless perplexed about the secular State of Israel in relation to various Torah concepts, in particular, the concept of the Redemption—in Hebrew, the *Geula*. This issue cannot be answered by such disciplines as philosophy, political science, or sociology. The issue is a *halachic* one, and like any important problem of *Halacha*, it has practical consequences for Israel's present and future state of affairs. How, indeed, should one consider the secular State of Israel in relation to the Redemption and world-historical function of the Jewish people? This question requires *halachic* investigation and judgment.

Let it first be noted that in the history of many *halachic* problems, different opinions and solutions have arisen and were based on purely logical arguments. Similarly, throughout history, scientists have held different opinions on various scientific problems which they approached by means of different mathematical equations and empirical data. Whatever their solutions, they were based not on personal propensities but on a consistency between logical reasoning and observation. This applies to the *Halacha*. For as with scientific questions, what is decisive in the solution of *halachic* questions is the logical operations of the intellect, not one's emotions or personal predilections.

As already mentioned, many Torah people refuse to accept the establishment of the State of Israel in 1948, or the present State for that matter, as a *halachically* decisive indication of the Beginning of the Redemption. To them Israel is a secular, "Zionist" society, a temporary episode in the history of the Jewish nation, as were other historic movements that appeared in, and disappeared from, the Torah world. In contrast, other Torah people maintain that Israel is really in the initial stage of its restoration, and that any appearances to the contrary notwithstanding, it is progressing toward the fulfillment of its world-historical mission as the light of the nations. Before defending this affirmative position, let us set forth the various arguments of their opponents in the Torah world. Each argument will then be refuted on purely *halachic*, that is to say logical, grounds. Such grounds leave no room for emotionally-charged dogmas or preconceived notions regarding the present State of Israel, even if these dogmas and notions are "religious."

SIX NEGATIVE ARGUMENTS

THE FIRST ARGUMENT

THE PRESENT STATE OF ISRAEL CANNOT BE RELATED TO THE REDEMPTION BECAUSE OF THE ABSENCE OF VISIBLE MIRACLES

One of the most accepted arguments of certain religious people is that the Beginning of Israel's Redemption must coincide with the advent of the Moshiach and be accompanied by miracles.[426] The following *Gemara* ["explanation" in the Talmud] is cited in support of this opinion:

> Ben Zoma said to the sages: Will the Exodus from Egypt be mentioned in the days of Moshiach? Was it not said already: "*Therefore, behold, the days are coming, says the Lord, when they shall no more say, 'As the Lord lives, Who brought up the children of Israel out of the land of Egypt'; but, 'As the Lord lives Who brought up and Who led the seed of the House of Israel out of the north country, and from all the countries into which I have driven them'?*" (Jeremiah 23:7-8). They replied: "This does not mean that the mention of the Exodus from Egypt shall be obliterated, but that [deliverance from] subjection to the other nations shall take the first place and the Exodus from Egypt shall become secondary. Similarly you read: '*Your name shall not be called any more Jacob, but Israel shall be your name*' (Genesis 35:10). This does not mean that the name Jacob shall be obliterated, but that Israel shall be the principal name and Jacob a secondary one. And so it says: '*Remember not the former things, neither consider the things of old.*' '*Remember not the former things*'—this refers to the subjection to the other nations; '*Neither consider the things of old*'—this refers to the Exodus from Egypt" (*Berachot* 12b-13a).

The Gemara clearly implies that the miracles which God will perform at the time of the Moshiach and of Israel's Redemption will be so great as to overshadow the miracles of the Exodus from Egypt. From this and similar Gemaras, the religious people in question regard as axiomatic that the Beginning of the Redemption can only come through unnatural events, events, moreover, that will be accepted by the world as miracles even greater than those of the Exodus. And since no such miracles have occurred in our time, they draw the conclusion that we are not yet in the period of the

Redemption. (Contrary to others, they do not regard the establishment of the State of Israel—three years after the Holocaust—as a supernatural event.)

THE SECOND ARGUMENT

THE REDEMPTION MUST COME THROUGH MOSHIACH

If the Redemption could come through a natural historical process, the Moshiach would be unnecessary. But all the teachings of the Torah, the prophets, and the Talmud bearing on Israel's return and restoration are coined under the emblem of the Moshiach. All the prophecies about the eventual ascendancy and splendor of Israel point to the time of the Moshiach and his ultimate purpose, which is to restore Torah government in the Land of Israel. The Rambam writes:

> If there arise a king from the House of David whose thinking is only in terms of the Torah, and whose aim is the fulfillment of the commandments, as was the aim of his ancestor David, such that he observes all the precepts of the Written and Oral Law, and if, by virtue of his charismatic character and wisdom prevails upon Israel to go in the ways of the Torah and repairs its breaches and fights the battles of God, the probability is that he is the Moshiach. If he does these things and succeeds, rebuilds the Temple on its site, and gathers the dispersed of Israel, then he is certainly the Moshiach. He will influence the whole world to worship God with one accord. As it is written: *"For then I will turn all the nations, that they will communicate in a clear language, that they may all call and understand God's name and worship Him with one mind"* (Zephaniah 3:9) (*Mishneh Torah, Book of Judges,* "Laws of Kings and Wars," XI, 3).

The Rambam here affirms that the laws of the Torah will be re-established in Israel as a result of the outstanding intellect and eminence of the Moshiach. But as many religious people point out, there is not even an infinitesimal sign of the influence of a Moshiach in our time. How, then, can this era be called the Beginning of the Redemption? Such a claim contradicts the tradition and the Talmud as well as the Rambam—or so these people believe.

THE THIRD ARGUMENT

The Redemption Necessitates A Return To The Torah

The Third Argument, that we are not in the period of the Redemption, is based on the statement of the sages that Israel's redemption can come only through *teshuva*, a return to the Torah (*Sanhedrin* 97b). What we see, however, is that the vast majority of the Jews in the world have yet to accept the Torah. Moreover, the laws of the State of Israel are not based fundamentally and entirely on the laws of the Torah, and most Israelis do not completely observe the commandments required by *teshuva*. Hence we cannot call this era the Beginning of the Redemption.

THE FOURTH ARGUMENT

The Redemption Cannot Come Through Those Who Reject The Torah

Many religious people cannot believe that Israel's redemption should come through the efforts of "Zionists" whose doctrines and practices are independent of Torah and entirely differentiated from all the concepts of *Halacha* in their theoretical understanding as well as in their practical functions.

The Gaon Reb Elkhanon Wasserman writes in the name of his Rebbe, the Chofetz Chaim, that the secular "Zionists," whose aim was to destroy the Torah, abandon God, and establish a secular democratic state, will achieve nothing, because a house built against the will of God has neither the power nor the right to exist. As it is written: "*Unless the Lord builds the house, those who build it labor in vain*" (Psalms 127:1).

THE FIFTH ARGUMENT

To Regard The Present State Of Israel As A Factor In The Redemption Is An Appalling And Unacceptable Paradox

It needs to be understood that the man of Torah sees in history the working of God's providence, which has enabled the Jewish people to survive twenty-four hundred years of one decimation after another. The Jews sacrificed themselves to sanctify God's Name in the time of the Greeks and Romans. They survived the Crusades which destroyed one-third of world Jewry. They survived the Spanish Inquisition, the false incriminations of the church, the pogroms and persecutions of Russia. Finally, they survived the Nazi Holocaust, the most monstrous in history. These unparalleled sufferings and slaughters would, without the slightest doubt, have led to the historic death of any other people. Nevertheless, the powerful faith of the Jews—powerful because it is based on the profundity and rationality of Torah learning—preserved them through all these dark tunnels of torture.[427]

Now, in our time, when Klal Yisrael, with the help of God, has reached freedom, the religious man cannot believe that this freedom should result in the abandonment of the Torah. He is appalled by this paradox. In view of all the terrible trials and tragedies the Jewish people had to endure through history for the sake of the Torah, rather than assimilate and become like the nations, the religious man cannot accept the existing State of Israel as a function of the Redemption—not when this State imitates the nations and constantly violates the Torah. Given this emotionally-charged understanding of things, the religious man is not likely to acquiesce in this paradoxical historical situation. Instead of leaving it as a dilemma, he rejects entirely the establishment of the State of Israel as indicative of the Beginning of the Redemption and considers it only as another episode in the Jewish history of survival. In short, if God decided to usher in the Redemption, it makes no sense that He should choose secularists—scorners and enemies of the Torah—instead of Moshiach and lovers of the Torah to rebuild the House of Israel in Eretz Yisrael.

THE SIXTH ARGUMENT

The Establishment Of The State Of Israel Is Contrary To The "Three Oaths"

Finally, we come to the famous argument of the "Three Oaths," specifically, the one in which God abjures the Jews not to come up to and storm the Land of Israel before the proper time (*Ketubot* 111a). This brings us back, full circle, to the First Argument; for the oath in question conclusively indicates—or so many religious people believe—that without miracles (accompanying the Moshiach), no permanent government in the Land of Israel can be established.

All the arguments against the thesis that Israel is in the period of the Beginning of the Redemption have now been stated. These arguments will be refuted in the sequel, and a positive conception of the Beginning of the

Redemption will be articulated by means of a systematic treatment of the Written and Oral Torah.

THE SIX NEGATIVE ARGUMENTS REFUTED

A critical analysis of the six arguments against the Beginning of the Redemption will show that they have no logical and evidential validity.

THE FIRST REFUTATION

Visible Miracles Are Not Required For The Beginning Of The Redemption

The First Argument, that the Beginning of the Redemption must come through miracles, is explicitly refuted by this previously quoted statement of the Rambam: "Do not think that Moshiach will have to perform signs and wonders, bring anything new into being, revive the dead, or do similar things. It is not so." In the immediate sequel the Rambam goes on to say:

> Rabbi Akiba was a great Sage, a teacher of the Mishnah, yet he was also the armor-bearer of ben-Kozeva. He affirmed that the latter was King Moshiach. He and all the sages of his generation thought that ben-Kozeva was King Moshiach until he was slain in his iniquity. Inasmuch as he was killed, it became known that he was not the Moshiach. Yet the sages had not asked him for a sign or token (*Mishneh Torah, Book of Judges*, "Laws of Kings and Wars," XI, 3).

This statement of the Rambam nullifies the First Argument.

THE SECOND REFUTATION

The Beginning Of The Redemption Can Come From The Community To The Individual

The Second Argument, recall, is this: To contend that the Beginning of the Redemption can come through a natural historical process is to contradict the Talmud, which says that all the prophecies in the Torah about Israel's ultimate redemption, ascendancy, and perfection must be related to the time of the

Moshiach and to his basic function, which is to establish Torah government in the Land of Israel. To refute this argument it will first be necessary to clarify certain *halachic* concepts concerning the Beginning of the Redemption.

As stated in Isaiah 60:22 and discussed by the sages in *Sanhedrin* 98a, Israel's redemption can come by two different historical processes, which depending on the existential character of the Jewish people. One is termed *B'Eto*, meaning, "in its time," signifying a natural historical process; the other is termed *Achishena*, meaning "hastened" or "before its time."[428] These two concepts designate two alternative processes of the Divine Redemption of the Jewish people. Accordingly, if Klal Yisrael does *teshuva*—returns to the Torah—they will merit immediate redemption. God will send the Moshiach, a descendant of King David, to take the Jews out of the Exile, just as He did in the time of Moses. With this Moshiach as His servant, God will then perform miracles greater than those He performed in the time of the Exodus from Egypt. This is the *Achishena* or "hastened" process of Israel's redemption.

But even if *Klal Yisrael* does not do *teshuva*, there is a determinate time in history when the Redemption will perforce occur, when no prolongation of the Exile is possible. Just as a determinate period of 400 years had to elapse before the Exodus from Egypt (see Genesis 15:13), so there is a determinate period in which the Exile must be ended, as explicitly mentioned in the *Mishna Eduyot* 2:9.[429] This is the *B'Eto* or "natural" process of Israel's redemption. What needs to be emphasized, however, is that even if Klal Yisrael does not merit the hastening of the Redemption, it will commence by a natural historical process, in stages of development determined by God's infinite supervision [or what may be called the infinite computational system by which God rules history].[430]

Consistent with this *B'Eto* or natural (and unhastened) process of Israel's redemption, consider the incomplete elements of the following stages. First, we see that the Jews (namely those in the free world), are not subjected to gentile rule. Second, we see that the Jews have regained control (of a major part) of the Land of Israel, and that every Jew has a right to settle in Eretz Yisrael (as here qualified). Third, and what is especially significant, more and more Jews (from every walk of life and profession) are returning to the Torah, are doing *teshuva*.[431] Finally, a Jewish government rules over the land (but it is not a Torah government and will not be until Klal Yisrael as a whole returns to the Torah).

The general character of the "unhastened" process of redemption is described by the Jerusalem Talmud—the *Yerushalmi*—as follows:

> Rav Chiya and Rav Shimon ben Chalafta were walking in the valley of Arabel in the early morning, when they saw the morning star, the dawn as it was rising in the sky. Said Rav Chiya to Rav Shimon ben

Chalafta: "Great teacher, thus will be the redemption of Israel: little by little, stage after stage, until the Redemption will be completed. And as the dawn of the morning spreads in the sky, wider and wider, until the entire sky becomes bright by the appearance of the sun, so will be the Redemption, little by little at the Beginning, and gradually becoming wider and wider" (*Berachot* 1.1).

The *Yerushalmi* goes on to illustrate the Redemption by drawing upon the *Book of Esther* and asking:

What is the reason for the statement, "*Even when I sit in darkness, God is my light*" (Micah 7:8)? So also at the Beginning: "*And Mordechai was sitting at the king's gate*" (Esther 2:21). And afterwards: "*Then Haman took the apparel and the horse*" (ibid., 6:11), and afterwards "*and Mordechai returned to the king's gate*" (ibid., 30). And (again) afterwards: "*and Mordechai went forth from the presence of the king in royal apparel*" (ibid., 8:15). And afterwards: "*the Jews had light and gladness, joy, and honor*" (ibid., 16).

The first half of the *Yerushalmi* [referring to Rav Chiya] is quoted by many people who talk about the Beginning of the *Geula*, but the other half—the above quotations from the *Book of Esther*—is not explained by any of the commentaries.

The words of the (always concise) *Yerushalmi* are perplexing. What did Rav Chiya add or disclose when he compared the Redemption to the dawn? In view of the fact that the sages always speak in symbolic language, did a Torah master like Rav Chiya have to explain that the Redemption will come in stages by comparing it to the dawn of morning—as if the statement would not have been clear enough without this analogy?

The intention of the *Yerushalmi* emphatically illustrated by the analogy of the rising sun, is to show that once the *B'Eto* ("unhastened" redemption) process of Klal Yisrael in the Land of Israel begins, it must naturally continue until its completion (in the *Geula Shleima*, the Final Redemption). Just as the spreading of the light in the sky follows an irreversible process governed by natural or physical law, so, when the dawn of the redemption comes, it will continue constantly, little by little, wider and wider. Sometimes the process of redemption may appear in eclipse, as when the dawn is darkened by clouds [like the politics of the present secular State of Israel]. Nevertheless, the general system progresses in accordance with laws which are irreversible. In other words, the *Yerushalmi* used a celestial analogy to emphasize that the system of redemption conforms to a law of history and is no less inexorable than a law of nature. And because the *Geula B'Eto* has to progress in a natural way, the *Yerushalmi* refers to the events recounted in the Book of Esther as an historical instance of this natural process.

And yet the probability of the concatenation of events narrated in the Book of Esther is so minute as to indicate that the saving of Jews, at that time, was a concealed miracle computed by God's infinite wisdom. Similarly, if one carefully considers the sequence of events culminating in the establishment of a Jewish government in the Land of Israel in 1948, it can hardly be doubted that here, too, there occurred, in accordance with the *Halacha* of the laws of probability, another hidden miracle. Again we see God's infinite supervision over Klal Yisrael.

Now let us summarize the basic stages of the "unhastened" (*B'Eto*) process of Israel's redemption (unhastened because the generation, having not returned to the Torah, does not merit immediate redemption). First, the Jews will not be subjected to foreign rule. Second, many of them will return to the Land of Israel and establish their own government. Third, gradually, more and more Jews will return to the Torah. Fourth, their progressive return to the Torah will naturally eventuate in the appointment or leadership of the Moshiach who will establish a Torah government, as the Gemara confirms in *Eruvin* 43b.[432] All the laws of the Torah will be observed. The Sanhedrin will be reinstituted, the wicked will be punished, the righteous will be rewarded, and the Temple will be rebuilt—all under the restored rulership of the House of David. (See Rambam, *Mishneh Torah, Book of Judges*, "Laws of Kings and Wars," XI, 1.)

Had the Redemption occurred in accordance with the laws of *Achishena*, the process would have proceeded from the individual, the Moshiach, to the community, and by way of evident miracles. As we have seen, however, the *Yerushalmi* quoted above illustrates the laws of *B'Eto* which entail a natural process of redemption, one that proceeds from the community to the individual, *beginning with the community's physical development and progressing toward its intellectual and moral perfection.*

The possibility of *Achishena*—of redemption that proceeds from the individual to the community—gives rise to the possibility of false Moshiachs. When such impostors have appeared in history and claimed to possess the ability to perform miracles and bring the Jewish people back to the Land of Israel, their frauds were discovered immediately. It was seen empirically that they could not perform any miracles as Moses did in the period of the Exodus. But when the Redemption proceeds *B'Eto* from the community[433] to the individual, not only is the process a natural one, but as soon as the Jews are no longer subjected as such to foreign rule, one may know for certain that he is in the period of the Beginning of the Redemption (*Atchalta d'Geula*).[434]

It needs to be emphasized that the sages regarded the elimination of subjection to foreign rule as a definitive sign and indication of the Beginning of the Redemption. The Rambam affirms this:

> The period of the Moshiach will be realized in this world, which will continue in its normal course, except that independent sovereignty will be restored to Israel. The ancient sages already said, "The only difference between the present and period of the Moshiach is that political oppression will then cease" (*Mishneh Torah, Book of Knowledge*, "Laws of Repentance," IX, 2.8).

It is also important to stress that throughout the long history of the Jews, there was never a period where redemption proceeded from the community to the individual. What happened was that one or another charlatan tried to deceive the Jews that he was the Moshiach and that he had supernatural powers; but as already noted, his fraudulence was immediately discovered empirically. In contrast, the period in which we now live is a unique state of affairs that logically satisfies the criteria of the Beginning of the Redemption from the community to the individual as described in the Torah, the Prophets, the Babylonian and Jerusalem Talmuds, and, as we shall see later, the Zohar. The Second Argument is therefore refuted.

THE THIRD REFUTATION

Complete Redemption Must Come Through A Return To Torah, But Its Beginning May Come Through A Gradual And Natural Process

The refutation of the Third Argument, that redemption cannot come without *teshuva*, a complete return to Torah, will be found in the Gemara, in tractate *Megilla* 17b. The Gemara explains that the *Shmoneh Esrei*, the Eighteen Benedictions which the observant recite every day, symbolically alludes to the Jews in Exile and to the process of their redemption from its beginning to its end. Each one of the Eighteen Benedictions symbolizes a complete stage.

The Gemara asks: "Why is the Redemption mentioned in the seventh benediction?" The Gemara replies: "Because the Redemption is going to be in the seventh or sabbatical year of rest for the Land [as stated in Exodus 23:10 and Leviticus 25:2-5]. Therefore the Redemption was mentioned in the seventh benediction." The Gemara demurs: "Why is it said that in the sixth year there will be sounds and thunderings, in the seventh year there will be wars, and in the beginning of the eighth year the Moshiach will come?" The Gemara answers: "This is no contradiction because the wars already indicate the Beginning of the Redemption—and that is why redemption is established in the seventh benediction."[435]

The Gemara continues: "What was the reason for mentioning healing in the eighth benediction?" The Gemara replies: "Because circumcision, which requires healing, is appointed for the eighth day, therefore it was established in the eighth benediction." Again the Gemara asks: "What was the reason for placing the prayer for the blessing of the years ninth?" The Gemara answers: "This was directed against those who raise the market price of foodstuffs, as it is written, '*Break the arm of the wicked*' and when David said this he said it in the ninth Psalm."[436]

The Gemara continues: "And why did they see fit to recite the ingathering of the exiles [in the tenth benediction, i.e.] after the blessing of the years?"[437] The Gemara answers: "Because it is written, '*But you, O mountains of Israel, you shall shoot forth your branches and yield your fruit for My people Israel, for they are at hand to come*'" (Ezekiel 36:8).[438] And when the exiles are assembled, judgment will be visited upon the wicked, as it says, "*And I will turn My hand upon you, and purge away your dross as with lye*" (Isaiah 1:25), and as it is written further, "*And I will restore your judges as at the first*" (ibid., 1:26). And when judgment is visited upon the wicked, transgressors cease, and presumptuous sinners are included with them, as it is written, "*But the destruction of the transgressors and of the sinners shall be together, and they that forsake the Lord shall be consumed*" (ibid., 1:28). And when the transgressors have disappeared, the power of the righteous will be exalted, as it is written, "*All the horn of the wicked also will I cut off, but the horn of the righteous shall be lifted up*" (Psalms 75:11).... And where is the horn of the righteous exalted? In Jerusalem, as it says, "*Pray for the peace of Jerusalem, may they prosper that love You*" (ibid., 122:6). And when Jerusalem is built, David will come, as it says, "*Afterwards shall the children of Israel return and seek the Lord their God, and David their king*" (Hosea 3:5)."

Rashi explains that the words "transgressors cease" mean that all will repent, will return to Torah, and that no one in that period will deny that the Torah is God-given. From this it follows that until that period there will not as yet be a complete return to Torah. But the period defined by the cessation of transgressors is several periods after the Beginning of the Redemption mentioned in the seventh benediction (before the appointment of the Moshiach).

We see from this Gemara that, whereas the complete redemption by the Moshiach depends on the Jewish people's return to Torah, the *Beginning* of the Redemption can occur even in a period when the wicked prevail![439] This Gemara clearly refutes the Third Argument.

THE FOURTH REFUTATION

THE ESTABLISHMENT OF THE STATE OF ISRAEL PROVES BY DEFINITION THAT THIS WAS BY THE WILL OF GOD

The Fourth Argument, recall, is the Chofetz Chaim commentary on Psalms127:1: "*Unless the Lord builds the house, those who build it labor in vain.*" The Chofetz Chaim deduced from this axiom the prediction that the secular "Zionists" would not be able to establish a state in the Land of Israel because their aim was to destroy the Torah, abandon God, and build a secular democratic regime. But these secular "Zionists" did in fact establish the present State of Israel. Thus, if one accepts the axiom of the Chofetz Chaim, the proof that we are in the Beginning of the Redemption follows by definition: "*Unless the Lord builds the house, those who build it labor in vain.*" A Jewish state in the Land of Israel cannot be established through human effort alone, but only by the will and supervision of God. Hence, seeing that the Jewish state is a reality, we must conclude that its coming into existence is the Beginning of the Redemption as determined by Divine Laws of History. In short, according to the teaching of the Chofetz Chaim, the proof that we are in the Beginning of the Redemption is the very existence of a Jewish state in the Land of Israel.

THE FIFTH REFUTATION

"THE WICKED WILL PREPARE AND THE RIGHTEOUS SHALL WEAR"

The Fifth Argument considers it unreasonable that the Beginning of the Redemption should come through the efforts of people whose doctrines and practices differ radically from the theoretical understanding and practical functions of the *Halacha*. But the refutation of this argument is clear from the *Halacha* itself. The Rambam writes in his *Introduction to the Mishnah*:

> A man may say: "Behold, we observe the case of a stupid person who lives in tranquility in the world without toiling in it, while others serve him, even a man of wisdom who manages his affairs." But the situation is not as it appears at first glance, because the security of that foolish person and his welfare is a preparation for some other person whom the Creator determined would [eventually] merit it. Although the fool, with his great fortune of money and property, may instruct his servants to construct a beautiful palace, and to plant a vineyard, as

kings do, it is possible that his great palace was unwittingly prepared for a sage who, a thousand years hence, will come and be forced to seek refuge from the sun's heat, and will do so in the shadow of one of the palace's many walls, which, in certain situations, will save his life. As Job says: *"The wicked will prepare and the righteous shall wear"* (27:17). Or, some day, from that vineyard a cup of wine will be taken to make theriac, a medicine that will save a wise and righteous man bitten by a poisonous snake. *This is the wisdom of God, that He can determine in nature causes or means whose effects or consequences will only be seen in the years to come.* (See Isaiah 25:11.)

It seems that the source for this statement of the Rambam is in tractate *Avoda Zara* 2b. There it says that after the Redemption of Klal Yisrael, God is going to judge the whole of humanity. In an allegory intended to convey the meaning and purpose of history, God asks the nations:

> "What was your occupation and goal?" The nations will reply: "Master of the universe, we have established economy and technology and many markets for business. We have advanced hygiene and cleanliness, and have erected many bathhouses and places of entertainment. We have gathered much silver and gold, and all this we did only for the sake of Israel, that they might obtain without great effort their food and pleasures, and have enough time to study Torah."
>
> And God will answer them: "You great fools—all that you have done you have done only for your own interests and for the gratification of your own desires. You have established market places in order to place courtesans therein; baths, to revel in them. As for your accumulation of silver and gold, that is Mine, as it is written: *'Mine is the silver and Mine is the gold, says the Lord of hosts'*" (Haggai 2:8).
>
> And when God asks other nations: "In what were you occupied?" they will reply: "We have built many bridges, we have captured many cities, we have waged many wars, and all this for the sake of Israel, that they might engage in the study of Torah."
>
> Then God will say to them: "You fools—all that you have done you have done for your own interests. You have built bridges in order to extract tolls, you have subdued cities so as to impose forced labor; as to waging wars, *I am the Lord of battles*, as it is said, *'HaShem is a man of war'*" (Exodus 14:13) [which means that the winning of wars is determined by Laws of Divine Guidance].

Here is not the place to explain the profundity of every detail of this allegory and its Gemara. But its general idea must be elucidated in accordance with the logic of the argument.

In the time of the Moshiach, God will judge humanity. He will communicate, so-to-speak, with the nations on the Day of Judgment. Even though they will recognize that God is the Master of the universe, and that past, present, and future are open before Him, the nations will nonetheless think they can deceive God by telling Him that all that they had done was for the sake of Israel, when in fact their political and economic systems, their arts and sciences and technologies, were developed merely to serve their own greed and pleasures, their self-preservation and egoistic aspirations. But how could any nation have the audacity to tell God that it had developed its technology so that Israel should study Torah? How could nations speak falsely to God when they know that God knows the truth? Of course, the words of this Gemara are symbolic. Still, they must be logically related to empirical reality and to truth itself.

The great Gaon, Reb Chaim of Brisk, explains that the reply of the nations is literally true when viewed from the perspective of the Torah system. For according to the Torah itself, and to the prophets and the sages, all of creation—this planet in particular—exists for the sake of Torah, for whose study and fulfillment Israel was created. (Compare Rashi on Genesis 1:1 and Isaiah 43:21: "*This people I have created to relate My praise.*") All the events of human history are correlated and linked to fulfill the purpose of the Torah. The vicissitudes of humanity lead, through an infinite interrelational and transformation system, to the time of the Moshiach, when Israel will be recognized as the goal and peak of human progress. Then everybody will know that "*HaShem is One and His Name is One*" (Zechariah 14:19)—which means that the totality of existence is the result of God's actions. When the Moshiach comes and the nations are judged, everyone will then see that the entire effort of the human race was related and directed to the purpose of the Torah, which is to destroy all forms of idolatry on the one hand, and, on the other, to exalt *HaShem* by revealing his infinite wisdom, power, and graciousness.

Thus, when the nations will say that their arts and sciences and technologies, as well as their political and economic systems and activities, were pursued only for the sake of the Torah, they will be telling the truth; for at that time they will be able to see the logical laws and purpose of history which relate all things to the Torah. But God will answer them: "Of course you now see the true reality of your actions; but in the past, that is, in your historic existence, you did not possess the wisdom to discern the ends to which your actions were being guided. All your labors and mental efforts were motivated by collective egoism and animalistic desires. Lusting for national wealth, power, and glory, you trampled upon the laws of morality. You harnessed your national energies, physical and mental, to destroy the human soul. The knowledge of which you are most proud is merely of matter and body. You closed your eyes and ears to the esthetic beauty of divine creation. You failed to appreciate the higher intellectual levels of existence."

The principle of the Rambam, that "*the wicked will prepare and the righteous shall wear*," is extended here not only from individual to individual in the course of time, but also to the whole history of humanity, that is, to the nations whose actions and technologies were often the result of avarice, vainglory, and a malicious desire to wage war and enslave peoples. However, by virtue of God's providence or infinite interrelational and transformation system, the wickedness of these nations, together with their technologies, contributed to, or helped prepare the grounds for, the period of the Moshiach, Torah government, and the perfection of humanity.

A clear *halachic* principle may be elicited from the above discussion of the sages' understanding of the motives, actions, accomplishments, and ultimate historical purpose of the non-Torah world. The preparation for, or the means to, a Torah end, be it for a righteous individual or an entire generation of Torah, can be effectuated by a wicked person or by an entire generation of wicked people. In this connection, consider the case of a Jew who takes interest from another Jew—both thereby violating the Torah. If the lender dies, his children do not have to return the interest. In support of this *halacha* (i.e., specifict ruling), the Gemara quotes the verse, "*the wicked will prepare and the righteous shall wear*" (*Baba Metzia* 61b).

It is logically incorrect to ask, "How can the wicked be instrumental in bringing about the Beginning of the Redemption?" because that is exactly the explicit rule of the *halacha* just cited; again, "*the wicked will prepare and the righteous shall wear*." We see from the Rambam and the Gemara that this is not only a symbolic expression but a pragmatic function of *Halacha* as well as a fact of history.

It seems that two extremes, the religious and the wicked (for example, atheists who entirely reject the Torah), are committing the same error. The wicked think that they are the cause, and that theirs are the aims, of the State of Israel—of its establishment and development. Meanwhile, their religious antagonists think that that is exactly (and regrettably) the case. They are both mistaken. God's infinite system of supervision determined Israel's redemption. And this redemption is for the sake of the righteous, for those who will return to Torah, for the Moshiach, and for the future of Klal Yisrael, the community of Israel.

This is sufficient for the refutation of the Fifth Argument. Since a clear *halacha* has been established—once again, that "*the wicked will prepare and the righteous shall wear*"—there can be no valid objection to the possibility that the wicked should take part in the Beginning of the Redemption. But they are only helping to prepare the physical foundation for Israel's complete redemption, and for the enjoyment of the righteous, now and in the future.[440]

Because so many religious Jews reject the present State of Israel as a function of the Redemption, some enlargement of the Fifth Refutation may be helpful before turning to the Sixth.

We have seen that various religious Jews cannot believe that the present State of Israel is an instrument of the Beginning of the Redemption because this State is the enemy of, and an obstacle to, the Torah.[441] They deem it paradoxical—as logically absurd and unacceptable—that the Torah, which helped the Jewish people survive 2,000 years of statelessness, dispersion, and repeated slaughter, and which at last brought the Jews back to their own land where they could enjoy freedom under their own government, should nonetheless be abandoned as a result of that regained freedom.

What these religious Jews present here is not a logical paradox but an objection based on offended emotions. The period in which we live is a reality, an existing fact determined by the Divine Laws of History. The existence of this historical fact, like any fact of nature, cannot be explained by sentiment. A fact of nature is not a poetic vision or a mystery. Facts of nature are defined and determined by logical concepts and mathematical relations. They are not influenced by the attitudes of philosophers and poets, or by the feelings of discontented or disillusioned observers. The *halachic* determination of our present period is a matter of reason, not sentiment, whether the sentiment is that of a Torah man or of an outsider of Torah. If this period fits the pattern of the Beginning of the Redemption as defined by the *Halacha*, if its character and historic function do not contradict the teachings of the Written Torah and the logical concepts of the Oral Torah concerning the Divine Plan of Redemption and its relation to empirical reality, then any sentimental, sociological, or philosophical notions to the contrary must be rejected as subjective and irrelevant for understanding the period in which we are now living.

To understand this period *halachically* and to see the logic of its redemption-order, it is enough to recall a few basic principles. First, if the Redemption is by a predetermined time (*B'Eto*), the redemption process unfolds in a natural way. This is the case when the generation—some righteous individuals notwithstanding—lacks the merit to be worthy of miracles. Second, before the complete redemption, the individual has freedom of choice: he can choose to keep the Torah, with all its commandments, or he can reject it entirely.[442] Now, inasmuch as the present generation, as a whole, has not done *teshuva* and, therefore, is not worthy of obvious miracles, the Redemption had to begin by a natural process. It would have been impossible for the Torah people—a small minority—to expel the oppressors from the Land of Israel and establish a Jewish government, if only because no Torah man of that period would have let himself get *halachically* involved in an armed rebellion, where every moment Jewish life is placed at hazard. Any student of Torah would certainly agree that no genuine *Halacha* man of that particular generation would have made decisions involving the slightest doubt of danger to life—*pekuach nefesh*—even for one individual.[443] So, by God's infinite supervision, the idea of overthrowing gentile rule and of establishing a Jewish government in the Land of Israel had to animate the secularists, people who could readily use the weapons of war to establish a Jewish state and to facilitate thereby the ingathering of Jews to Eretz Yisrael. These secularists, inspired by the great ideal of freedom for the Jewish people and of Jewish sovereignty in the Land of Israel, were not aware of, or concerned about, the *Halacha* and its constraints on the risking of Jewish life, to say nothing of other *halachic* rules that would have been impediments to their "Zionist" uprising. And so, inasmuch as the Redemption had to come about by a natural process, it could only have been initiated by non-Torah people.

If the reader will ponder this explanation, he will see that, *halachically*, in our time, the *Atchalta d'Geula*—the Beginning of the Redemption—could not have happened in any other way.

THE SIXTH REFUTATION

The "Three Oaths" Are Not Related To The Jews While They Are In The Land Of Israel

The Sixth Argument, we saw, is based on the famous "Three Oaths" (*Ketubot* 111a).[444] The first of these oaths, which alone is pertinent to this discussion, abjured Israel not to go up and storm Eretz Yisrael—in Hebrew: *shelo yaalu bechoma*. In other words, the Jews are to refrain from attempting to invade the Land of Israel by force in order to liberate the land from foreign rule.

Many commentaries have asked: "What is the source of the oath—not to go up and storm the Land of Israel?" The answer will be found in the Zohar (Exodus 32a).[445] The Zohar states that, even though the Land of Israel is given to the descendants of Avraham through Yitzhak and Yaakov, who have the commandment of circumcision on the eighth day after birth, still, because Ishmael, the offspring of Avraham and Hagar, was circumcised when he was thirteen years old, he merits the privilege to be in Eretz Yisrael while the land is devoid of Jews. And so long as Ishmael's descendants occupy the land, they will prevent the Jews from returning should they attempt to do so by force. But when the Jews settle in Eretz Yisrael, Ishmael's privilege to be in the land will be terminated. Thereafter, if Ishmael's descendants wage war against the Jews, they, the Arabs, will lose. Even if other nations come to the aid of the Arabs, they will not win. The control of the Land of Israel will remain in the hands of the Jews.

This prediction of the Zohar was written many centuries ago and is being realized in our time. But therein is the esoteric as well as the exoteric meaning of the oath abjuring the Jews not to storm the Land of Israel when they are in exile.[446]

The distinction between the status of the Jews when they are in exile and when they are in the Land of Israel helps solve a great difficulty in understanding the Ramban (Nachmanides), a difficulty that has perplexed many generations, but whose solution will completely nullify the Sixth Argument.

Commenting on the Rambam's *Book of Commandments* (*Sefer HaMitzvot*), the Ramban states that "we are commanded to conquer (*lareshet*) the land that God gave to the Children of Israel…and not abandon it to other nations or to desolation, as it says, "*And you shall drive out the inhabitants of the land and dwell therein*" (*viy-horash-tem et ha'aretz viy-shav-tem ba*)" (Numbers 33:53). The two key Hebrew words have been hyphenated. The first, *viy-horash-tem*, corresponds to the word *yerusha* which, according to the Ramban, means "to expel." The Ramban holds, therefore, that the Jews are commanded to conquer the Land of Israel, that this comes under the category of an obligatory war (*milchemet mitzvah*) which applies to every generation, including the present one. As for *viy-shav-tem*, this corresponds to the word *yeshiva* which simply means that the Jews are obliged to settle in the land. Hence, even when the Jews are in exile, the mitzvah of *yerusha* and *yeshiva*, to conquer and dwell in the Land of Israel, is valid.

However, the Rishon Rabbi Yitzchak de Leon raised a substantive question against the Ramban. In his *Megilat Esther*, one of the great commentaries on the *Book of Commandments*, he asks: How can the commandment in question be construed to obligate the Jews to conquer the Land of Israel when the oath *shelo yaalu bechoma* prohibits such conquest? Unable to overcome the contradiction, de Leon remained perplexed about the dictum of the Ramban.

We have here a most interesting fact. The oath which forbids the Jews from storming the Land of Israel, and which today is used as an argument against the thesis that we are witnessing the Beginning of the Redemption or that the State of Israel is an instrument of this redemption process—the same oath was used against the Ramban's understanding of the commandment to conquer the land and dwell therein! We are the heirs of a dilemma that has persisted for centuries. In fact, however [and as Dr. Zimmerman was the first to show], there is no contradiction at all between the oath and the commandment as construed by the Ramban.

The dilemma may be reformulated as follows. According to the Talmud and all the *Rishonim*, whereas the word *yerusha* means to conquer the Land of Israel, the word *yeshiva* means to live in the land. The Ramban holds that Israel is at all times obliged to fulfill this commandment. (Hence the obligatory character of the commandment is not limited to the time of the coming of the Moshiach.) But the question arises: How is it possible that the commandment to conquer and dwell in the land should prevail in our time (or in the Ramban's time, for that matter) in opposition to the oath forbidding the Jews from storming Eretz Yisrael?

To solve this dilemma it will first be necessary to explain certain concepts of Torah and *Halacha*. The Torah was given and written in the language of man, that is, in a language appropriate to the common understanding of man. But the Torah gave the people commandments with which they were unfamiliar. Hence it was necessary for the Torah to state the preliminary procedures required for the fulfillment of these commandments. The preliminary or preparatory stage of a commandment is called, in the Talmud, a *hechsher-mitzvah*—hereafter rendered as "*pre-mitzvah*"—which is distinguished from the actual performance of the commandment as such, which is called *kiyum-ha'mitzvah*—hereafter rendered as "*mitzvah per se*."[447]

For example, the Torah says you shall celebrate the holiday of Succot by dwelling in booths. Building a succah is only a *pre-mitzvah*. To fulfill the *mitzvah per se*, one must dwell in the succah itself. Consistent therewith, no blessing is said over the building of the succah, but only when sitting in the succah. Similarly, the Torah says you shall make *tzitzit* (fringed garments) on the corners of your garments. The *mitzvah per se* is to wear the *tzitzit*; to make them is only a *pre-mitzvah*. Hence we recite the blessing when we put on fringed garments, not when we make them. It is to be noted, however, that whereas the *mitzvah per se* is a constant whose fulfillment cannot be circumvented, the *pre-mitzvah* is only mandatory when it is indispensable for the fulfillment of the *mitzvah per se*. Thus, a man must put on *tefillin* (phylacteries) every day—this is the *mitzvah per se*—but he does not have to manufacture them, which is but a *pre-mitzvah*. And so, in every (positive) commandment, the Torah speaks in the language of a *pre-mitzvah*, the preparatory stage of the *mitzvah per se*. This is a very important rule of Torah scholarship, one that solves many difficulties which have perplexed commentators.

Now, in many instances, there is no determined sequence for the *pre-mitzvah* and the *mitzvah per se*. A *pre-mitzvah* can be done after as well as before a *mitzvah per se*. Thus, a man can fulfill the mitzvah of being in a succah—he could sit in his neighbor's succah—without having first made one himself, and he could then make a succah during the intermediate days of the festival. This said, the supposed contradiction between the "Three Oaths" and the Ramban may now be dissolved.

When the Torah says *viy-horash-tem et ha'aretz viy-shav-tem ba*, and when the Ramban uses the equivalent terms, *yerusha* and *yeshiva*—you shall conquer the land and dwell therein—the conquering of the land is only a *pre-mitzvah*. The *mitzvah per se* is to settle in the land. In other words, the mitzvah proper *is not to conquer the land but to live in it*. (The reader should keep the *halachic* distinction in mind because many people have erred on this subject. They thought that conquering the land—*kibbush ha'aretz*, is a *mitzvah per se*—*kiyum-ha'mitzvah*. This is incorrect. The conquest of the Land, which is expressed by the word *yerusha*, is only a *pre-mitzvah*—*hechsher-mitzvah*. The actual fulfillment of the mitzvah is *yeshiva*, living in the Land of Israel.)

Now, consider again the oath *shelo yaalu bechoma*—they shall not go up and storm the Land of Israel. That the oath refers to the Jews while they are in exile is evident from the *halachic* understanding of the word *yaalu*—they shall go up.[448] For the word *yaalu* (or any of its cognates) relates only to the Land of Israel. That is to say, in every place where the Talmud and Midrash speak of anyone coming to Eretz Yisrael, the sages always use the language of "*aliya*," which means ascending or "going up" to the Land. Conversely, whenever anyone left Eretz Yisrael, the sages always use the language of "*yerida*," which means descending or "going down" from the Land.[449]

In his Responsa (1-3), the Rashbash (Rabbi Shlomo ben Shimon, 1400-1467) elaborates on the concept of *aliya*. Quoting the Ramban and the Tashbatz (the work of Rabbi Shimon ben Tzemach), the Rashbash points out that *aliya* to the Land of Israel is a *hechsher-mitzvah* (a *pre-mitzvah*), whereas living in the land is a *kiyum-ha'mitzvah* (the *mitzvah per se*). Furthermore, Rabbi Abraham of Sochochov, in his *Avnei Nezer* (Ch. 454), affirms the preceding and adds that an oath made by a man not to make *aliya* is not a violation of the Torah because, like *yerusha* it is only a *hechsher-mitzvah* (*pre-mitzvah*).[450]

With the above *halachic* definitions and applications, resolved is the 700-year difficulty in the Ramban, whose understanding of the commandment to conquer the Land of Israel seems to contradict the "Three Oaths," specifically the oath that prohibits such conquest. Since *aliya* means to go up to Eretz Yisrael from the Diaspora, then, clearly, the prohibition *shelo yallu bechoma*—they shall not conquer the land through *aliya*—only applies against Jews in exile who might want to mobilize for an invasion of Israel from the Diaspora itself. On the other hand, the oath does not apply to Jews who, individually, by way of immigration and the permission of the nations, have already settled in the land. Indeed, once they have done so, the mitzvah of conquering the land comes into force. They may then wage war from within Israel to liberate the land from foreign rule. *Halachic*ally, this constitutes a perfectly logical reversal of the liberation and settlement of Eretz Yisrael. Since conquering the land is only a *pre-mitzvah*, it can be undertaken after the *mitzvah per se*, the settling in the land. This is why the commandment to conquer the land can be realized even today in complete consistency with the great Ramban.

It is astonishing that, in his commentary to the *Song of Songs*, the Ramban predicted that the Jews will enter Eretz Yisrael with the approval of the nations! Hence it is in conformity with the Ramban's *halacha* that the Jews, having been allowed by the nations to enter the Land of Israel (and thereby to fulfill the mitzvah of settlement or *yeshiva*), were thereafter able to conquer the land and establish their own sovereign and independent state (thereby fulfilling the mitzvah of conquest or *yerusha*). Nor is this all.

Once the Jews have settled and conquered the Land of Israel, then, according to the Ramban, they are forbidden by the commandment of conquest (*yerusha*) to give up their possession of any part of this land. This commandment, as understood by the Ramban, together with the previous *halachic* analysis of the oath, *shelo yaalu bechoma*, refutes all arguments of those who quote this oath to disqualify the Jewish possession, conquest, and government of the Land of Israel.[451]

Furthermore, this refutation is clearly and explicitly defined in the Midrash, and in a most telling way. As is known to any talmudic student, the *Halacha* uses very concise and even abbreviated (though logically defined) language. In contrast, the Midrash is usually elaborate and explicit. Thus, referring to the *Song of Songs*, the Midrash (in II, 7) quotes the oath under discussion using the following words: "*shelo yaalu bechoma min ha'golah*"—which clearly states that the Jews should not storm *Eretz Yisrael* from the *Galut*—the Diaspora! We see here that, for the sake of those who are not *Halacha* men, and who therefore may not know the definition of the word *yaalu*, the Midrash—which is written for everyone—made the effort to state explicitly that the term *aliya* means *min ha'golah*—from the Diaspora. (See Rashi on *Shabbat* 30b.)

Conclusion

At this point let us summarize the previous analysis. According to the Ramban, it is the duty of Jews who live in the Land of Israel to establish their sovereignty over the land. This *halacha* (specific ruling) of the Ramban is valid for all times and therefore applies to the Jews who live in Israel today.[452] As a result of the exile and dispersion of the Jews, there took place a logical reversal of the commandment to conquer and settle the Land of Israel. Settlement had to occur first, consistent with the oath prohibiting armed invasion, followed by conquest. The order in time is not restrictively determined because "conquest" is only a *pre-mitzvah* and can be accomplished after fulfilling the commandment to settle the land.

It is therefore profoundly interesting to see that the Beginning of the Redemption has in our time taken place in accordance with the *Halacha*. First, there were waves of Jewish immigration to Eretz Yisrael for centuries preceding 1948. Second, in that year, and with the approval of the United Nations (as predicted by the Ramban), the Jews established the State of Israel. Then, by means of two wars—the War of Independence of 1948 and the stunning Six-Day War of 1967—the Jews conquered the heartland of Israel, the land which belongs to them as decreed in the Torah. By this logical reversal in the Torah, first settlement (*yeshiva*) and then conquest (*yerusha*), the divine oath was not violated, as the history of the establishment of the State of Israel bears witness, because this new State of Israel was created exactly through this process. In the Divine Plan for the rebirth of Israel, the order of the Beginning of the Redemption clearly followed the laws of Torah and *Halacha*. The reverse order would have failed, for it would have violated the divine oath.

But what is utterly astonishing and incredible is that in Psalms 69:36, King David predicted the Beginning of the Redemption in the special sequence in which it has actually occurred! This psalm, which is almost a condensation of the *Book of Lamentations*, describes the tribulations the Jews will have in exile. It begins: "*Save me, O God, for the waters are come into my soul. I sink in a deep mire, where there is no standing. I am come into deep waters and the flood overwhelms me. I am weary with my crying; my throat is dried. My eyes fail while I wait for my God.*" Then, after elaborating on the suffering of the Jews in exile, King David assures them that, in the end, "*God will help Zion, and He will rebuild the cities of Judah, and they shall live there (**yeshiva**) and conquer it (**yerusha**)!*"[453] Everywhere else in the Bible of Israel the word *yerusha* is written first, whereas the word *yeshiva* always occurs second. But here, in his prophecy of the future redemption, King David first mentions *yeshiva*—living in the

Land of Israel—and only second does he mention *yerusha*—conquering the land. ***This is the only place in the Bible of Israel where the order is reversed!***

The arguments that the present State of Israel cannot exist *halachically* because of the divine oath have thus been shown by Dr. Zimmerman to be completely invalid, as are all other arguments which deny the instrumental function of the State of Israel in the *Atchalta d'Geula*—Beginning of the Redemption. To the contrary, not only has the oath not been violated, but the Jews now living in Eretz Yisrael should bear in mind their duty to liberate the land as stated in the Torah and as understood by the great Ramban.

*   *   *

Notes

[1] See Paul Eidelberg, *Jewish Statesmanship: Lest Israel Fall*.
[2] See Paul Eidelberg, *Demophrenia: Israel and the Malaise of Democracy*.
[3] See Akiva Tatz, *Worldmask*, pp. 13-15.
[4] This is denied by certain "ultra-orthodox" Jews.
[5] Yisachar Shlomo Teichtal, *Eim Habanim Semeichah*.
[6] In this essay, no distinction will be made between the political Zionism of Theodor Herzl and the cultural Zionism of Ahad Ah'am.
[7] Dr. Chaim Zimmerman has shown, citing numerous biblical and post-biblical sources, that the State of Israel is an integral part of the redemption process. See his *Torah and Existence*, ch. 1, which the present author, with Dr. Zimmerman's permission, edited and published under the title *Israel's Return and Restoration* (1987), a version of which appears in the Appendix of this book.
[8] Rambam is the acronym of Moshe ben Maimon (1135-1204); Ramban is the acronym of Moshe ben Nachman (1194-1270).
[9] Teichtal, pp. 49-50.
[10] The founders needed these Jews to counterbalance the country's Arab population, and they had to secularize them to maintain their control over the new government.
[11] See Yoram Hazoni et al., "The Quiet Revolution in the Teaching of Zionist History: A Comparative Study of Education Ministry Textbooks on the 20th Century."
[12] *Agudat Yisrael* was almost alone in its attempt to save Jews from the Nazi Holocaust.
[13] See Isaac Breuer, *Concepts of Judaism*, pp. 6, 31, 309.
[14] In 1994 the religious parties even supported the surrender of 330 square kilometers of Jewish land to Jordan, a country that posed no threat to Israel!
[15] Michael B. Oren, *Six Days of War*. Page references appear between parentheses in the text.
[16] See Robert Baer, *Sleeping With The Devil*, pp. xxiv, 60, 78, 206-207.
[17] At the behest of Washington, Israel prevented Syria from overrunning Jordan in 1970. Thereafter the United States offered Israel significant loans and became its primary military supplier.
[18] Bernard Lewis, "Did You Say American Imperialism," *The National Review*, December 17, 2001, p. 30. See Eidelberg, *Jewish Statesmanship*, ch. 9, on "Democratic versus Martial Diplomacy."

[19] A thousand years ago the Arab moralist Ibn Hazm said: "He who treats friends and enemies alike will arouse distaste for his friendship and contempt for his enmity."

[20] Prominent rabbis from Israel met with and dignified Muslim clerics in Egypt by joining the latter in a statement which deplored suicide bombings. But the only suicide bombers are Muslims! Muslim clerics have been notoriously silent even about the September 11 terrorist destruction of the World Trade Center, let alone the Arab suicide bombings occurring in Israel.

[21] To abbreviate a passage from the Midrash: "The Holy One Blessed be He said to Israel, 'The Land of Israel is My portion…and you are My portion…[Hence] it is befitting that My portion dwell in My portion.'"

[22] See Roger A. Gerber and Rael Jean Isaac, *What Shimon Says*, cover.

[23] The quoted words were expressed by Israel's former air force chief General Eitan Ben-Eliyahu at a February 2002 international conference at Haifa University on "The City in the 21st Century and War." See *Jerusalem Post*, February 15, 2002, p. B4. Israeli generals are notoriously part of Israel's left-wing establishment, as witness Yitzhak Rabin, Ehud Barak, Ezer Weisman, and, contrary to his reputation, Ariel Sharon.

[24] See Caroline S. Glick, *Jerusalem Post*, September 26, 2003, pp. 1, 15.

[25] The "grandfather clause" permits any person whose grandfather is a Jew to immigrate to the State of Israel even if the person's parents and grandmother are not Jewish, and even if the grandfather is dead or not living in the State.

[26] *Jerusalem Post*, May 16, 2003, p. 2.

[27] Yoram Hazony, *The Jewish State*, p. 72.

[28] Moshe Brody, *Troubleshooting in the Promised Land*, pp. 94-95. See also Eidelberg, *Demophrenia*, p. 41.

[29] Although Israel is not a democracy from an *institutional* perspective, the mentality of its political and intellectual elites is thoroughly democratic. See Eidelberg, *Jewish Statesmanship*, pp. 89, 155.

[30] Cited in Yehoshafat Harkabi, *Arab Attitudes to Israel*, p. 348.

[31] Although Thomas Jefferson, the author of the Declaration, was not a religious man, the document, in his words, "was intended to be an expression of the American mind," which, as is well-known, was very much influenced by the Bible of Israel. See Paul Eidelberg, *On the Silence of the Declaration of Independence*, p. 1, which develops an aristocratic interpretation of this extraordinary document.

[32] John Stuart Mill, *Utilitarianism, Liberty, and Representative Government*, p. 96.

[33] Ibid., pp. 239-240.

[34] *The Wall Street Journal* (*Jerusalem Post* edition, Oct. 10, 2001), p. 15.

[35] *The Collected Works of Abraham Lincoln*, III, 315.

[36] Cited in Mordechai Nisan, *Israel and the Territories*, p. 119, referring to statements made in 1971.

[37] Ibid.

[38] Unfortunately, Israeli politicians engage in such a charade when "negotiating" with Egypt or its client, Yasser Arafat.

[39] *Washington Post*, August 17, 2001, p. A23. Will quotes Al-Shami as boasting that "no border restriction will stop" suicide bombings.

[40] *Jerusalem Post*, August 24, 2001, p. B3. Prime Minister Ariel Sharon's counter-terrorism adviser warned: "If you are an Israeli and you go downtown in Amman you are in danger of being lynched." But in no country does Jew-hatred thrive as in Egypt. See Arieh Stav, *Peace—The Arabian Caricature: A Study of Anti-Semitic Imagery*. See also John Derbyshire, "Kill a Jew for Allah: The Mideast Problem," *National Review*, March 22, 2002, for a devastating critique of Islamic culture.

[41] As reported by Knesset Member Yossi Sarid, in *Ha'aretz*, August 17, 1990.

[42] The sooner this is accomplished the less the bloodshed. Every delay increases the likelihood that Arafat will acquire much deadlier weapons.

[43] In *Preachers of Hate*, Kenneth R. Timmerman (who is not Jewish) writes: "Four weeks before Arafat ordered the beginning of the second *intifada*, Arab Knesset member Abd al-Malek Dahamsha appeared on Palestinian television to comment on the Camp David talks. Responding to a viewer's call that 'our problem with Israel is not a border problem, but one of existence,' Dahamsha agreed. "We exaggerate when we say 'peace'...what we are [really] speaking about is *hudna* [a cease fire]" (p. 194). Timmerman relates how Arafat's representative in Jerusalem, Faisal al-Husseini, compared the Oslo Accord to a "Trojan horse." Israel saved Arafat, who was languishing in Tunis, by bringing him into Gaza ("Gaza First") in 1994. Arafat thereby obtained a foothold in Palestine, the first stage in what the PLO calls its "phased plan" for the conquest of Palestine as a whole. Arafat's deputy Otham Abu Arbish explained in 1999: "The goal of this stage is the establishment of a Palestinian state, with its capital in Jerusalem....The Palestinian state is a stage after which there will be another stage and that is the democratic state in all of Palestine [that is, in place of Israel]" (p.195).

[44] See Machiavelli, *The Prince*, ch. 3.

[45] Having formed no distinct culture or solid infrastructure in Judea and Samaria, the Arab's attachment to the land is superficial—avowals to the contrary notwithstanding. Indeed, while Jordan ruled the area from 1949 to 1967, the 400,000 Arabs mentioned moved from Judea and Samaria to the eastern side of the Jordan River. During and immediately after the 1967 war, 200,000 more Arabs—roughly one of every five inhabitants—moved to the East Bank.

[46] Chaim Zimmerman, "Death of Zionism," pp. 12-13.

[47] For details, see Yoram Hazony, et al., "The Quiet Revolution in the Teaching of Zionism."

[48] Cited in Randolph S. and Winston S. Churchill, *The Six Day War*, pp. 200-201.

[49] Cited in Mordechai Nisan, "A Radical Approach to the Arab-Israeli Conflict: Toward Peace Without Negotiation," Ariel Center for Policy Research, July 2003, p. 31.

[50] See Eidelberg, *Jewish Statesmanship*, ch. 10.

[51] Suffice to mention Basic Law: Freedom and Human Dignity enacted in 1992 by a vote of 32-21, i.e., with less than half the Knesset voting! Strange as it may seem, this law can be amended by a vote of two MKs to one, since there is no quorum or minimum majority required to make changes! Yet this law, *as interpreted by Supreme Court President Aharon Barak*, initiated a "constitutional revolution" by endowing the court with the power of judicial review. See notes 52-54, 63 below. See, also, Ariel Bin-Nun, *The Law of the State of Israel*, p. 38.

[52] See Knesset Speaker Reuben Rivlin's interview in *Ha'aretz*, June 5, 2003, concerning Aharon Barak. Rivlin speaks of a "gang of law" that rules Israel. See also Evelyn Gordon, "Fast Track to Anarchy," *Jerusalem Post*, April 23, 2002, who cites examples of public officials who, in imitation of the Barak court, have substituted their personal preferences for the laws of the State.

[53] Regarding the Supreme Court, it nullified the Knesset Elections Committee decision to disqualify Arab Knesset Member Azmi Bishara, who was indicted by the Attorney General for violating the Prevention of Terrorism Act; ignored the Attorney General's decision, affirmed by the Knesset Elections Committee, to disqualify the Balad Party for violating Basic Law: The Knesset, which prohibits any party that negates the Jewish character of the State; quashed the Attorney General's indictment of Arab MK Talib a-Sana for incitement (of which, more later); ordered the Interior Minister to recognize homosexual adoptions performed overseas, even though Israeli law does not recognize such; declared parental spanking a criminal offense, contrary to a consensus of the Knesset; nullified a law permitting the Film Censorship Board to ban pornographic movies by ruling that nothing can actually be declared pornography, as one man's pornography is another man's art (a manifestation of the court's relativism).

[54] This may also be said of the Supreme Court, which has always been dominated by left-wing secularists. Because the three sitting judges of the judicial selection committee (of nine members) have de facto control of judicial appointments, the Court has been called a self-perpetuating oligarchy by professors and retired judges across the political spectrum. For the method of appointing the Supreme Court judges, see Eidelberg, *Jewish Statesmanship*, p. 155.

[55] David Ben-Gurion, *Israel: A Personal History*, p. 552.

[56] See notes 53 and 54 above.

[57] Montesquieu, Baron de, *Considerations sur les Causes de la Grandeur des Romains et de leur Decadence*, p. 4 (my translation).

[58] For example, Israel has a variety of competing school systems: the state system, the state-religious system, the Tami school system, the "independent" Hareidi system, the Ma'ayan (Shas) system, etc. Each of these systems is linked to a particular political party. This politicization of the schools has pernicious consequences. The allocations of Education Ministry are based not on educational criteria but on political power.

Moreover, when one political group succeeds in obtaining a larger slice of the education budget for its constituents, other groups bitterly complain that this has come at the expense of their children. The politicized nature of the schools thus breeds intercommunal hatred and rivalry.

[59] See *Ma'ariv*, August 1, 1989. Then cabinet minister Ezer Weisman was also implicated in such illegal contacts.

[60] See High Court of Justice No. 2805/94. A more comprehensive petition (HC 3414/96) was submitted to the Supreme Court two years later. See Howard Grief, "A Petition to the Supreme Court of Israel Challenging the Legality of the Oslo Accords," *International Journal of Statesmanship* (Foundation for Constitutional Democracy), Vol. I, No. 2, Summer, 1996, pp. 1-78.

[61] Cited in Mordechai Nisan, *Toward a New Israel*, p. 120.

[62] See *Jerusalem Post*, December 4, 1990, p. 4.

[63] The libertarianism of Israel's Supreme Court encourages Arabs to test the limits of the law by subtle and not so subtle forms of insurrection.

[64] The same thing happened in 1982, when the government allowed hundreds of foreign journalists to cover the "Peace for Galilee" operation in Lebanon. Israel was portrayed as having committed "genocide." See Edward Alexander, "Israel and the News Media," in Robert Loewenberg & Edward Alexander (eds.), pp. 47-58; Stephen Karetzky, *The Cannons of Journalism: The New York Times Propaganda War Against Israel*; Yedidya Atlas, "Israel Bashing and the Media," *Nativ: A Journal of Politics and the Arts*, 1:1 (English edition), 1990, pp. 26-32.

[65] See Yisrael Harel, "People Against the Media," *The Jerusalem Report*, November 29, 1990, p. 56, who writes:

> The roots of the widespread, almost general hatred of the media in Israel seems to be that the press has in recent years divorced itself from the national, Zionist aspirations and consensus.... In the eyes of many Israelis—apparently the majority—the media, and the state-run electronic media in particular, no longer represent the national interest. More and more Israelis...agree that the Israeli media are more sympathetic to some PLO leaders in Jerusalem than to, say, MK Rehavam Ze'evi...

[66] On August 12, 1990, ten days after the Iraqi invasion of Muslim Kuwait, *Al-Fajr* published the following letter of the Mufti of Jerusalem, Sheikh Saad Al-Din Al-Alam, to Saddam Hussein: "From the God-favored Al-Aqsa Mosque...and in the name of the Muslim world and Muslim religious law, we call on you to drive the contamination of the US armed forces and their helpers out of the Arabian Peninsula. May you purge these sanctified Muslim lands of the contamination of the American armed forces...May God help you against your enemies and the enemies of Islam and

268   A Jewish Philosophy of History

Muslims. All the Muslim peoples are behind you..." The editor of *Al-Fajr*, Hanna Siniora, was a top leader of the *intifada*. *Al-Quds* headlined, "America sinks in Gulf war." Its front-page also featured casualty figures according to Iraqi releases: 160 coalition planes down, etc. See *Jerusalem Post*, February 1, 1991, p. 11.

[67] This effectively discriminates against Jews in favor of Arabs.

[68] Richard B. Bentall (ed.), *Reconstructing Schizophrenia*, pp. xiii, xv, 24, 284. (All further page references will appear in the text between parentheses.) See also D. G. Garan, *Our Sciences Ruled by Human Prejudice*, pp. 119-122; Daniel R. Weinberger & Richard Jed Wyatt, "Structural Brain Abnormalities in Chronic Schizophrenia: Computed Tomography Findings," in Claude F. Baxter & Theodore Melnechuk (eds.), *Perspectives in Schizophrenia Research*: "One of the oldest issues in schizophrenia research is whether the brains of schizophrenic patients are morphologically different from the brains of normal individuals. Despite 70 years of research, the question remains unresolved" (pp. 29-30); Joseph Zubin, "Chronic Schizophrenia from the Standpoint of Vulnerability" (ibid.). "Despite the notable advances made with each of these models [genetic, internal environment, neurophysiological, ecological, developmental, learning theory], we have not yet found any necessary or sufficient causes for schizophrenia" (277). Even of those psychiatrists who regard schizophrenia as a neurological disorder or brain deficit, few claim that its causes are known (24, 229).

[69] David Shakow, *Adaptation in Schizophrenia: The Theory of Segmental Set*, p. 67 (partly paraphrased). Shakow cites Freud: "Protection *against* stimuli is an almost more important function of the living organism than *reception* of stimuli" (ibid., pp. 8-9).

[70] In D. Kemali et al. (eds.), *Schizophrenia Today*, pp. 211-232. (All further page references will appear in the text between parentheses.) For a fuller analysis, see Ignacio Matte-Blanco, *The Unconscious as Infinite Sets*, ch. 2, *passim*.

[71] Sigmund Freud, *An Outline of Psycho-Analysis*, pp. 30-31, J. Strachey, trans.

[72] See Ignacio Matte-Blanco, *Thinking, Feeling, and Being*, Introd., Rayner & Tuckett, p. 7.

[73] I have substituted the term "characteristic" for "prepositional function."

[74] *Yediot Achranot*, October 1, 2001, cited in Roger A Gerber and Rael Jean Isaac, *What Shimon Says*, p. 15.

[75] Harkabi, *Arab Attitudes to Israel*. Further reference will appear between parentheses in the text.

[76] See ibid., p. 471, and Harkabi, *Israel's Fateful Hour*, p. 179.

[77] Ibid., p. xii.

[78] Ibid., p. 41.

[79] *Ma'ariv*, May 23, 1996, cited in Roger Gerber and Isaac, *What Shimon Says*, p. 4. This inane statement, which negates memory, reduces the human to the subhuman. Another indication of the pathological character of Israel's ruling elites.

[80] Harkabi, *Arab Attitudes to Israel*, p. 465.

[81] Yair Evron, *The Middle East: Nations, Superpowers and Wars*, p. 9.

[82] Caroline B. Glick, *Jerusalem Post*, December 26, 2003, pp. 1, 18.

[83] Albert Einstein & Leopold Infeld, *The Evolution of Physics*, p. 257.

[84] Ibid., p. 312.

[85] Hans Reichenbach, "The Philosophical Significance of the Theory of Relativity," in P. A. Schlipp (ed.) *Albert Einstein: Philosopher-Scientist*, p. 289.

[86] Bertrand Russell, *The ABC of Relativity*, p. 16.

[87] Max Planck, *Scientific Autobiography and Other Papers*, pp. 46-47.

[88] Albert Einstein, *Out of My Later Years*, p. 8.

[89] Ibid., p. 10.

[90] See Paul Eidelberg & Will Morrisey, *Our Culture 'Left' or 'Right': Litterateurs Confront Nihilism*, p. 182, for evidence that Einstein also succumbed to historicism, which indicates that he even denied the finality of any scientific truths! He says as much in *Out of My Later Years*, p. 98, and thus anticipates Thomas S. Kuhn, *The Structure of Scientific Revolutions*, on which see Steven Weinberg, *Dreams of a Final Theory*, pp. 184-185.

[91] Einstein, *Out of My Later Years*, p. 205. Must we not say that Yasser Arafat's genocidal intentions toward the Jews of Israel were also "clear beyond the possibility of misunderstanding"? Did he not repeatedly declare jihad against Israel since the day after he signed the Israel-PLO Declaration of Principles of September 13, 1993? Did not the Palestinian Arabs repeatedly hear Arafat's declarations of war against Israel, yet nonetheless elected him as their Fuhrer? Must they not therefore be held collectively responsible for the brutal murder of Jews perpetrated by their government, the "Palestinian Authority"? And must they not be punished, as Einstein said of the German people, "if there is justice in the world and if the consciousness of collective responsibility in the nations is not to perish from the earth entirely"? Who does not know that these Palestinian Arabs glorify the suicide bombers that have reduced Jewish men, women, and children to human debris? Poll after poll of the Arab population of Judea, Samaria, and Gaza reveals their desire to exterminate Israel. Hence, must we not conclude that Einstein's message honoring the heroes of the Warsaw ghetto stands as a profound denunciation of Israel's or rather of its government's unheroic policy of self-restraint toward Arab terrorism?

[92] Martin Buber, *Israel and the World*, p. 223.

[93] See Leo Strauss, *Natural Right and History*, ch 1.

[94] Cited more fully and discussed in Eidelberg, *Jerusalem vs. Athens*, p. 195.

[95] Steven Weinberg, *Dreams of a Final Theory*, p. 184.

[96] Moral relativism is inherent in the irrational domain of the unconscious.

[97] Hans Reichenbach, *The Rise of Scientific Philosophy*, p. 280. Having decreed what constitutes a "statement," Reichenbach shifts from the grounds of logical positivism to historicism or historical determinism: "The attempts of philosophers to fashion ethics as a system of knowledge have broken down. The moral systems thus constructed were nothing but reproductions of the ethics of certain sociological groups; of Greek bourgeois

society, of the Catholic church, of the Middle Class of the preindustrial age, of the age of industry and the proletarian. We know why these systems had to fail: because knowledge cannot supply directives…. Science tells us what is, but not what should be." Ibid., p, 287. See Moshe Koppel, *Meta-Halakhah: Logic, Intuition, and the Unfolding of Jewish Law*, p. 126 n. 6, who writes: "I can accept the basic positivist premise that a sentence is meaningful only if there is a criterion for distinguishing its truth from its falsehood. I do not accept the stricter premise that this criterion must be experimentally testable and hence finite."

[98] Hobbes, *Leviathan*, p. 32.

[99] Ibid., p. 46.

[100] The following discussion is adapted from *Jerusalem vs. Athens*, pp. 246-254.

[101] Cited in ibid., p. 62.

[102] Alex Bein (ed.), *Arthur Ruppin: Memoirs, Diaries, Letters*, Afterword by Moshe Dayan, pp. 315-323, K. Gershon, trans. For an extensive analysis, see Eidelberg, *Demophrenia*, pp. 143-146.

[103] Hobbes, *Leviathan*, p. 46.

[104] Ibid., especially chapters 2-6.

[105] Alan E. Kazdin, "The Modification of 'Schizophrenic' Behavior," in Peter A. Magaro (ed.), *The Construction of Madness*, p. 153. One wonders whether Kazdin has ever visited an insane asylum?

[106] Karl Marx & Frederick Engels, *The German Ideology*, p. 14 (italics added).

[107] See William James, *The Principles of Psychology*, II, 449-450. Yet James admits that "One may get angrier in *thinking* over one's insult than at the moment of receiving it" (II, 443, italics added). James' Darwinism (II, 683) leads him to reduce aesthetic and moral principles to matters of taste (II, 672, 677).

[108] Sigmund Freud, *An Outline of Psycho-Analysis*, p. 54.

[109] Ibid., p. 23. See Hobbes, p. 37.

[110] Freud, *An Outline of Psycho-Analysis*, pp. 51-53, 68.

[111] Freud, *The Ego and the Id*, p. 51.

[112] See Carroll E. Izard et al. (eds.), *Emotions, Cognition, and Behavior*, pp. 69, 80. Although the editors admit that cognition is sufficient to activate the emotions (p. 1), their uncritical acceptance of evolution compels them to insist on the primacy of the emotions as opposed to the intellect. On evolution, see the critical works cited in Nathan Aviezer, *In the Beginning: Science and Torah*, pp. 54-59. Alfred North Whitehead, *The Function of Reason*, p. 15, rejected the modern inversion of mentality long before the accumulation of paleontological evidence contradicting interphylum evolution. Whitehead argued that even if one were to accept the evolutionary hypothesis, neither logic nor observation requires us to affirm the primacy of the emotions: what occurs later in phylogeny might well dominate that which came earlier. Nevertheless, instead of the primacy and potential autonomy of reason, modern psychology has posited the primacy of an autonomous unconscious. A contrary position

is presented by Yakov Rofé, *Repression and Fear*, pp. 218, 246, who cites current research indicating that the behavior even of paranoid schizophrenics can be explained as reactions to consciously perceived entities, and that therapy does not require the postulation of any autonomous unconscious agency.

[113] Izard, pp. 17, 24. Albert Ellis, *Reason and Emotion in Psychotherapy*, a cognitive psychologist, seems to affirm the primacy of reason vis-à-vis the emotions. The impression is misleading. Ellis happens to be a moral relativist. This being so, his "reason" is incapable of apprehending objective or suprapersonal standards of good and evil or of how one should live. Reason must then be an instrument of one's personal desires or aversions. We are back to Hobbes. Unlike Hobbes, however, Ellis regards negative emotions such as hate (and anger) as irrational. This follows logically from his moral relativism. Even in this relativistic age people tend to regard the object of their hatred as evil. But to hate anything as evil is irrational, for nothing is truly evil in the world of moral relativism. (But if hatred is irrational, surely the same must be said of love.) Rational-emotive therapy would then seem to be limited to dissolving those (erroneous) moral judgments of a patient which he deems objectively valid, but which judgments arouse in him disturbing or "maladaptive" emotions. Although such therapy may sometimes be salutary, it leaves reason as a mere instrument of one's desires. Contrast D. G. Garan, *The Paradox of Pleasure and Relativity*, who provides a devastating critique of the hedonistic foundation of all schools of modern psychology. And yet, Garan, too, reduces reason to an instrument of the emotions (p. 30) and succumbs to moral relativism (p. 265). Only his good sense saves him from sheer folly. He not only reaffirms the partial autonomy of reason (pp. 132, 136), but repeatedly emphasizes that mental health necessitates moral restrictions.

[114] C. G. Jung, *Modern Man in Search of a Soul*, pp. 116-117; but contrast pp. 41-45. See Bertram P. Karon, "The Psychoanalysis of Schizophrenia," in Magaro, p. 206, who concludes that, contrary to Jung and Freud, "there is no collective unconscious, that symbolism based on word origins are not necessarily valid, that there is no prenatal memory, that there is no death instinct...and that libido is at most a useful metaphor."

[115] D. G. Garan, *Our Sciences Ruled by Human Prejudices*, p. 156.

[116] D. G. Garan, *The Key to the Sciences of Man*, p. 123. See also L. Willerman & D. B. Cohen, *Psychopathology*, p. 20, who offer this criticism of the Freudian and psychoanalytical model: "First, many of the assumptions [of this model] are either scientifically untestable or, when tested, found to be unsupportable. For example, the role of early childhood experience in indelibly shaping adult personality is inconsistent with the research evidence suggesting a less powerful role for these early experiences. Second, scientifically more defensible explanations involving biology, conditioning, and cognition often seem to fit the facts about abnormality better." Stephen Jay Gould, *The Hedgehog, The Fox, and the Magister's Pox*, p. 134 is less kind: "...in our last century, Sigmund Freud

rose to preeminence as a paramount social force through his unparalleled literary gifts, and surely not for his cockamamie and unsupported theory of the human psyche."

[117] Freud, *The Problem of Anxiety*, p. 39.

[118] S. J. Rachman, *Fear and Courage*, pp. 28, 38.

[119] David Pilgrim, "Competing Histories of Madness," in Richard P. Benthall (ed.), *Reconstructing Schizophrenia*, p. 228. See also P. A. Berger & K. L. Davis, "Pharmacological Studies of Tardive Dyskinesia: Implications for Future Research," in Charles F. Baxter & Theodore Melnechuk (eds.), *Perspectives in Schizophrenia Research*, p. 333.

[120] Rofé, p. 283.

[121] Ibid., pp. 255-256.

[122] Ibid. p. 259.

[123] Cited in Garan, *Our Sciences Ruled by Human Prejudice*, p. 142.

[124] See Garan, *The Key to the Sciences of Man*, p. 134.

[125] Garan, *Our Sciences Ruled by Human Prejudices*, p. 139.

[126] See ibid., p. 140.

[127] Jung, p. 29.

[128] Garan, *Our Sciences Ruled by Human Prejudices*, p. 139.

[129] Although Ignazio Matte-Blanco pursued at length the hypothesis that the emotions may be measurable, the idea is not even alluded to in his more recent work on thinking and feeling. See his *The Unconscious as Infinite Sets*; also *Thinking, Feeling, and Being*.

[130] Freud, *The Problem of Anxiety*, p. 17.

[131] Garan, *The Key to the Sciences of Man*, pp. 131-132; 122-129.

[132] Henri Baruk, *Tsedek*, pp. 2-5, 24, 123-127, 133-134. See Lev. 17:11, 14; Deut. 12:23; Isaiah 5:20-24, 44:24-25.

[133] See David V. Edwards, *The American Political Experience*, 1988, pp. 372-373.

[134] Garan, *The Key to the Sciences of Man*, p. 156.

[135] Spinoza, *Ethics*, Part IV, Prop. VII.

[136] But then it is not merely the emotion of fear but the anticipation of those consequences which are necessary to overcome the desire for "X." Fear may be necessary but certainly not sufficient.

[137] See S. J. Rackman, *Fear and Courage*, 2d ed., pp. 28, 38, 43. Rackman's study reveals that "fearful cognitions" or "catastrophic misinterpretations of bodily sensations can" induce panic, indeed, that panic can be induced by "meditational states" as well as by hyperventilation (pp. 131, 135). This is not to suggest that panic can be prevented merely by acts of the intellect. But as Aristotle understood, true courage, like all the moral virtues, requires proper habituation and the use of reason. What Aristotle terms "habituation" is equivalent to the conditioning associated with behavioral psychology. Aristotelian conditioning, however, is intended to maximize the role of reason in human life.

[138] Rackman (p. 55) notes that ideology significantly increased the fighting capacity and resistance to fear among those who volunteered on the side of the Republicans

during the Spanish Civil War. This only confirms the well-attested phenomenon of religious martyrdom, which dramatically illustrates the power of ideas or rather, of the intellect, over the fear of violent death. Thus, referring to the "state of mind of religious men," William James admits that "Fear is not held in abeyance as it is by mere morality; it is positively expunged and washed away." See his *Varieties of Religious Experience*, p. 47 (originally published in 1902). It should also be noted in passing, however, that the primacy of the intellect is manifested even in anxiety, an emotional disorder whose prevalence since the outset of the twentieth century coincides with the ascendancy of skepticism and moral relativism in the democratic world.

[139] James, *Varieties of Religious Experience*, p. 53. Here James rejects reductionism. For a critique of reductionism in biology, see Gould, *The Hedgehog, The Fox, and the Magister's Pox*, pp. 221-260. See also Richard Feynman & Steven Weinberg, *Elementary Particle and the Laws of Physics*, p. 66, where Weinberg says, "It is true, of course, that a naïve reductionism can have terrible effects, no where more so than in the social sciences."

[140] See C. F. Levinthal, *Introduction to Physiological Psychology*.

[141] Gerald L. Schroeder, *The Science of God: The Convergence of Scientific and Biblical Wisdom*, p. 80.

[142] Steven Weinberg, *The First Three Minutes*, p. 32, states that more significant than general relativity for cosmology is the density of the universe as formulated by Alexander Friedman in 1922. Specifically, "If the average density of the matter of the universe is *less* than or equal to a certain critical value, then the universe must be spatially infinite. In this case the present expansion of the universe will go on forever. On the other hand, if the density of the universe is *greater* than this critical value, then the gravitational field produced by the matter curves the universe back on itself...so that it will eventually implode back to infinitely large density" (p. 34). See also Hugh Ross, *The Creator and the Cosmos*, pp. 24-25. Ross points out that the idea of an expanding universe is suggested eleven times in the Bible, which refers to the heavens as being "stretched out": Job 9:8, Psalms 104:2, Isaiah 40:22, 42:5, 44:24, 45:12, 48:13, 51:13, Jeremiah 10:12, 51:15 and Zechariah 12:1. Seven of these verses—Job 9:8, Psalms 104:2, Isaiah 40:22, 42:5, 44:24, 51:13 and Zechariah 12:1—employ the active participle form of the verb *nata*. This form of the verb, conjoined with its object, the heavens, literally means "the stretcher out of the [the heavens]" and implies continual or ongoing stretching.

[143] See Aryeh Carmell & Cyril Domb (eds.), *Challenge: Torah Views on Science*, p. 282, n. 10.

[144] Ramban (Nachmanides), *Commentary on the Torah*. I, 23, C.B. Chavel trans.

[145] Cited in Ross, p. 31. See Weinberg, *The First Three Minutes*, pp. 180-182; Weinberg, *Dreams of a Final Theory*, pp. 267-269; Stephen Hawking, *The Theory of Everything*, pp. 98-101 (cited hereafter as TOE); Hawking, *The Universe in a Nutshell*, pp. 94-95. In March 2004, the Space Telescope Institute announced that the orbiting Hubble space

telescope collected light from the youngest stars, that is, from a point just a few hundred million years from the beginning of the universe.

146 See *Philo*, I, 21, Colson & Whitaker, trans. Commenting on the term "beginning" in Genesis 1:1, Philo points out that it is not to be construed "in a chronological sense, for time there was not before there was a world."

147 Schroeder, pp. 45-47, writes: "In addition to providing a calculated age of the universe, having a time period for each day permits us to compare the sequence of scientific observations of cosmology and paleontology with the events of each day described in Genesis. The match, day by day, between the biblical description of our cosmic genesis and the description provided by science is extraordinary" and is summarized by Schroeder in the following table (p. 67):

The Six Days of Creation

Day Number	Start of day (years B.P.) (B.P.=Before Present)	End of day (years B.P.)	Main events of the day Bible's description	Scientific description
One	15,750,000,000	7,750,000,000	The creation of universe; light separates from dark (Gen.1:1-5)	The Big Bang marks the creation of the universe; light literally breaks free as an electron bond to atomic start to form nuclei; galaxies form
Two	7,500,000,000	3,750,000,000	The heavenly firmament forms (Gen. 1:6-8)	Disk of Milky Way forms; Sun, a main sequence star, forms
Three	3,750,000,000	1,750,000,000	Oceans and dry land appear (Gen. 1:9-13); Kabala states this marked only the start of plant life, which then developed during the following days	The earth has cooled and liquid water appears 3.8 billion years ago followed almost immediately by the first forms of life: bacteria and photosynthetic algae
Four	1,750,000,000	750,000,000	Sun, Moon, and stars become visible in heavens (Talmud *Hagigah* 12a)(Gen. 1:14-19)	Earth's atmosphere becomes transparent; photosynthesis produces oxygen-rich atmosphere
Five	750,000,000	250,000,000	First animal life swarms abundantly in waters; followed by reptiles and winged animals (Gen. 1:20-23)	First multicellular animals; waters swarm with animal life having the basic body plans of all future animals; winged insects appear
Six	250,000,000	approx. 6,000	Land animals; mammals; humankind (Gen. 1:24-31)	Massive extinction destroys over 90 percent of life. Land is repopulated; hominids and then humans

See also Gerald L. Schroeder, *Genesis and the Big Bang: The Discovery of Harmony Between Modern Science and the Bible*. See Stephen Hawking, *A Brief History of Time: From the Big Bang to Black Holes*, updated edition, p. 7 (cited hereafter as *Time*). Lacking knowledge of the Jewish sources, the renowned mathematical physicist does not relate the six days of creation in the Book of Genesis to time dilation. For a concise and lucid analysis of how those six days are consistent with science, see Aviezer, *In the Beginning*.

148 Cited in Lawrence Kelemen, *Permission to Believe: Four Rational Approaches to God's Existence*, p. 40. See Gould, *The Hedgehog...*, p. 87, which rejects the dichotomy of religion and science.

149 Ibid.

150 J. R. Oppenheimer, *Science and the Common Understanding*, pp. 42-43.

[151] Cited in Arthur Koestler, *The Roots of Coincidence*, pp. 51, 53. See Hawking, *Time*, p. 189, who writes: "The unpredictable, random element [of particle-wave duality] comes in only when we try to interpret the wave in terms of the positions and velocities of particles. But maybe that is our mistake: maybe there are no particle positions and velocities, but only waves. It is just that we try to fit waves to our preconceived ideas of positions and velocities. The resulting mismatch is the cause of apparent unpredictability." For a more precise analysis of particle-wave duality, see Weinberg, *Dreams of a Final Theory*, p. 73.

[152] Ibid., p.78.

[153] Eugene P. Wigner, *Symmetries and Reflections*, p. 202.

[154] Schroeder, *The Science of God*, p. 173.

[155] Hawking, *Time*, pp. 126, 138, 152. More recently, *TOE*, p. 94, Hawking suggests that "quantum mechanics allows the universe to have a beginning that is not a singularity. This means that the laws of physics need not break down at the origin of the universe." This, he cautions, is only a "proposal" (p. 121). I ask: Where did the *initial* quantum of energy come from, and would that energy be equivalent to the matter comprising the universe?

[156] Freeman J. Dyson, *Scientific American*, September 1971, p. 59.

[157] Schroeder, *The Science of God*, p. 5.

[158] Extracted from the Internet. According to Hawking, *Theory*, p. 104, "If the rate of expansion one second after the Big Bang had been smaller, by even one part in a hundred thousand million million, the universe would have recollapsed before it ever reached its present size."

[159] The references in this paragraph are cited in Ross, pp. 157, 159. Hawking, *Time*, p. 199, defines the Anthropic Principle as follows: "We see the universe the way it is because if it were different, we would not be here to observe it." See also ibid., pp. 130-134. Weinberg, *The First Three Minutes*, p. 154, rejects the Anthropic Principle.

[160] Carmell & Domb, pp. 132-134.

[161] Stephen Jay Gould, *Wonderful Life*, pp. 319-320. Gould rejects the Darwinian doctrine that evolution is progressive and posits "contingency" (or chance) as its basic principle. See ibid., pp. 24-35, 54-58, 228-233, 304-310. Gould is silent about the Anthropic Principle.

[162] Such a being is capable of speech, of abstract reasoning, including numerical, aesthetic, and moral modes of expression. As for writing, "Archeological finds that predate the invention of writing five to six thousand years ago are referred to by the scientific community as prehistoric, because these finds are artifacts, and not deliberately recorded accounts of events. Cuneiform, the first form of writing, dates to the biblical time of Adam and Eve." Schroeder, *The Science of God*, p. 130.

[163] Ibid., p. 137.

[164] Ibid., pp. 138-139. See *Philo*, I, 167, who speaks of two types of men, one "earthly," the other "heavenly."

165 Cited in Schroeder, *The Science of God*, p. 141.

166 Ibid., p. 145.

167 Ibid., p. 135 (italics added, and spelling adjusted to our own text). The year of Rabbi Lipschitz's lecture, 1842, is most significant. In the previous decade, a basic controversy raged between partisans of two renowned geologists, Georges Cuvier, who posited "catastrophism" in the biological history or fossil record of the earth, and Charles Lyell, who argued for "uniformitarianism" or gradualism. Although Lyell's theory triumphed in the 1830s and dominated geology for the next 150 years, Rabbi Lipschitz sided with catastrophism, now the prevailing view. See Michael J. Benton, *When Life Nearly Died: The Greatest Mass Extinction of All Time*, pp. 58-69.

168 Gould, *Wonderful Life*, p. 54. For references to contemporary biologists, mathematicians, and physicists who reject the neo-Darwinian doctrine of evolution via chance mutation and natural selection, see Kelemen, pp. 54-65.

169 Schroeder, *The Science of God*, p. 85.

170 Cited in *Encyclopedia Judaica*. See Carmell & Domb, pp. 55-96 *passim*; Chaim Zimmerman, *Torah and Reason*, pp. 24-26, 29-49.

171 See Eidelberg, *Jerusalem vs. Athens*, pp. 91-92.

172 Alfred North Whitehead, *Science and Philosophy*, p. 75.

173 Cited in *Pathways to the Torah*, p. A6.2.

174 Friedrich Nietzsche, *The Joyful Wisdom*, p. 289, T. Common, trans.

175 Judah Halevi, *The Kuzari*, p. 182, H. Hirschfeld, trans.

176 Joseph M. Soloveitchik, *Worship of the Heart*, p. 4.

177 Zvi Yaron, *The Philosophy of Rabbi Kook*, A. Tomaschoff, trans., pp. 55, 64.

178 Abraham Isaac Kook, *Orot*, pp. 148-149, B. Naor, trans.

179 Ibid., pp. 15-151, 148, 233, n. 119.

180 Malbim, *Commentary on the Torah*, I, 27-28, Z. Faier, trans. See also Judah Halevi, p. 187.

181 *The Zohar*, I. 68-69, H. Sperling & M. Simon, trans.

182 Schroeder, *The Science of God*, p. 162.

183 Menahem Stern, *Greek and Latin Authors on Jews and Judaism*, I, 10.

184 Ibid., I, 50. See Josephus, *Complete Works, Against Apion*, p. 948.

185 Stern, II, 210. Numenius lived in Apamea, which had a considerable Jewish population.

186 I am indebted to Eliyahu A. Green's unpublished research on the denial of Jewish influence on Greek philosophy.

187 Paul Johnson, *A History of the Jews*, p. 2.

188 Cited in *Pathways to the Torah*, p. A6.2.

189 Quoted by Geoffrey Wheatcroft, *The Controversy of Zion*, p. xi.

190 Matthew Arnold, *Literature and Dogma*, p 58.

191 Quoted by J. H. Hertz, p, 177.

192 Cited in Alan M. Dershowitz, *Chutzpah*, p. 105.

193 Baruk, *Tsedek*. pp. 80, 133-140.

194 Friedrich Nietzsche, *The Dawn of Day*, pp. 203-206, J. Volz, trans.

195 The following discussion of Abraham is drawn from *Jerusalem vs. Athens*, pp. 74-75.

196 Breuer, *Concepts of Judaism*, p. 68.

197 Hugo Grotius, the renowned seventeenth-century legal scholar, often cited the Noahide laws as an early source of international law. But as Aaron Lichtenstein has shown in *The Seven Laws of Noah*, these laws are actually general categories which involve no less than 66 of the 613 basic laws of the Torah codified by Maimonides. Also, to convey the humane and progressive character of this most ancient body of laws, Lichtenstein quotes extensively from that remarkable work, *The Unknown Sanctuary*, in which the French author, Aime Palliere, tells of how his knowledge of Hebrew led him to renounce Catholicism, how he sought to convert to Judaism, to which end he consulted the Italian rabbi, Elijah Benamozegh, who introduced him to Noahism as the "true catholicism."

198 Leo Jung, *Judaism in a Changing World*, pp. 15-16.

199 Schroeder, *The Science of God*, pp. 76-78.

200 Max Jammer, *The Philosophy of Quantum Mechanics*, p. 521.

201 See Aviezer, ch. 1.

202 See Moshe Katz, *CompuTorah: Hidden Codes in the Torah*; Eidelberg, *Judaic Man*, ch. 10.

203 See Abraham H. Rabinowitz, *The Jewish Mind*, pp. 29-33; Tatz, *Worldmask*, pp. 13-14.

204 Hence no discussion here of Hinduism, Buddhism, Bahai, Confucianism, Taoism, Jainism, and Shintoism, which is not to say they are morally inferior to Christianity and Islam. A word, however, about Zoroastrianism, which interacted with Judaism in Babylon. Some commentators contend that the Persian Zoroaster (Zarathustra) was a monotheist. This is not so, strictly speaking. It is true that Zoroaster rejected the pagan view that man's sustenance and success depend on worshipping and sacrifices to nature deities. Indeed, he taught that man's happiness depends on his being truthful and just. (See Herodotus, I, 131-139.) But Zoroastrian dualism regarding the forces of light versus the forces of darkness is not the pure monotheism of the Torah: "*I form light and create darkness; I make peace and create evil...*" (Isaiah 45:7). It should also be noted that Zoroastrianism spread far and wide throughout the Persian Empire and shaped its religious life. Its ethical teachings and religious toleration spread rapidly through Babylon following the latter's conquest by Cyrus the Great, perhaps because that country had already been influenced by a large influx of exiled Jews. The reader should bear this in mind when we discuss Islam.

205 Cited in Rafael Eisenberg, *Survival: Israel and Mankind*, pp. 161-162.

206 Nietzsche, *Beyond Good and Evil*, in *Basic Writings of Nietzsche*, Aph. 52, W. Kaufmann, trans.

207 Josephus, *Against Apion*, p. 970.

[208] Clearly the Greek and Hebrew alphabets have much in common. Interestingly, Jewish law states: "A Sefer Torah may be written in no language but Greek (other than the Holy Tongue)." See Matis Weinberg, *Patterns in Time: Chanukah*, p. 66, citing the Babylonian Talmud, *Megilah* 8b.

[209] Schroeder, *The Science of God*, p. 97.

[210] Diogenes Laertius, *Lives of Eminent Philosophers*, I, 35, R. D. Hicks, trans.

[211] As interpreted by Nietzsche, *Early Greek Philosophy*, p. 93.

[212] Josephus, *Against Apion*, p. 946. See Elliot A. Green, "Did Pythagoras Follow Nazarite Rules?" *The Jewish Bible Quarterly*, Vol. XX, No. 1 (77), pp. 35-42.

[213] Josephus, *Against Apion*, p. 977.

[214] See John Burnet, *Early Greek Philosophy*, 3d ed., p. 176.

[215] Spinoza not only identifies God with nature. He maintained that "the love of God toward man, and the intellectual love of the mind toward God are identical." See his *Ethics*, V, Prop. XXXVI, cor.

[216] Burnet, pp. 132, 134-138.

[217] See P.C.W. Davies, *Space and Time in the Modern Universe*, pp. 188-192 on the "oscillating" universe.

[218] Burnet, p. 199.

[219] Ibid.

[220] Diogenes Laertius, p. 376.

[221] Nietzsche, *Early Greek Philosophy*, pp. 111-113.

[222] Burnet, p. 258.

[223] Ibid.

[224] Ibid., pp. 259-260.

[225] See Diogenes Laertius, pp. 389-395.

[226] By no means is the philosopher to be confused with the academic professor of philosophy. No one has portrayed the difference more powerfully that Nietzsche in *Beyond Good and Evil*, Part Six, "We Scholars."

[227] See Joseph B. Soloveitchik, *Halakhic Man*, p. 6.

[228] Diogenes Laertius, pp. 397-398.

[229] Werner Heisenberg, *Natural Law and the Structure of Matter*, p. 20.

[230] Philo identified the Idea of the Good with Divine Reason: *On the Creation*, I, 17.

[231] Plato calls it the "Receptacle" (49a). Commentators refer to it as "space"; but if space is vacuous, it is hard to see how it can rightly be described as the "mother of all Becoming."

[232] Compare Aristotle's *aether* in *On the Heavens* 270b22.

[233] Philo, *On the Creation*, I, 15.

[234] See Plato, *Statesman* 269-270.

[235] As Professor Will Morrisey puts it—referring to Plato and Aristotle in a letter to the author: "The course of events for them [and which moderns call 'history'] is a series of moments in which human nature either does or does not realize itself, a realization

dependent in part upon theoretical wisdom and in part upon practical wisdom or prudence. Political philosophy and statesmanship bring out the meaning or purpose of human life, a life lived within the course of events."

236 *Philo*, VI, 459, 461, F. H. Colson, trans.

237 Ibid., VI, 457.

238 Ibid., p. 473.

239 Ibid., VI, 475.

240 Soloveitchik, *Halakhic Man*, p. 6.

241 See Harry Austryn Wolfson, *Philo*, I, 17, and contrast Maimonides, *Guide*, II, 14, 17; *Basic Writings of Thomas Aquinas*, II, xliv; *Summa Contra Gentiles*, I, 13.

242 See Maimonides, *Mishneh Torah, Book of Knowledge*, I, 7.

243 See Maimonides, *Guide*, II, 14-15. Dr. Zimmerman pointed out to the present writer that in a Responsa to the Jewish congregation of Marseilles, Maimonides emphatically declares that all those who deny creation *ex nihilo* are atheists and strike at the root of Judaism. That Maimonides does not and would not make such a statement in the *Guide* is readily understandable. (See ibid., II, 1, 4.) Given Aristotle's unique reputation in the Middle Ages as *The* Philosopher, it would have been futile and even harmful to have called him an atheist.

244 Aristotle's theory of nature and its relation to politics is discussed more fully in my *Jerusalem vs. Athens*, pp. 122-129.

245 Alfred North Whitehead, *The Principle of Relativity*, pp. 41-42.

246 Cited in E. A. Burtt, *The Metaphysical Foundations of Modern Science*, p. 76.

247 The Greek atomists (such as Democritus) speculated about the infinity of space, but their speculations, which became well known in modern Europe after the discovery of Lucretius' *De Rerum Natura* in the fifteenth century, had little influence on the main currents of Greek philosophical and scientific thought. See Alexander Koyre, *From the Closed World to the Infinite Universe*, p. 5.

248 Koyre, *Infinite Universe*, pp. 8-23.

249 The falsity of Aristotle's physics, which underlies his politics, does not of itself invalidate his politics. But to retain his politics (including his ethics), another foundation must be found. Aristotelians have yet to do so.

250 Alfred North Whitehead, *Science and the Modern World*, p. 17.

251 Cited in Burtt, p. 88.

252 See Alfred North Whitehead, *Concept of Nature*, p. 37 *et seq.* for a critique of the doctrine in question. See Descartes, *Principles of Philosophy*, LXX; Locke, *Concerning Human Understanding*, Bk. II, Ch. III.

253 Whitehead, *Science and the Modern World*, p. 54. For a most radical reductionism, one that would explain life in terms of particle physics, see Weinberg, *Dreams of a Final Theory*, pp. 61-62.

254 This rendering is adapted from Chaim Zimmerman, *Torah and Reason*, pp. 160-161.

[255] See C. S. Lewis, *The Abolition of Man*, ch. 1. This charming little book, originally published in 1947, reveals the pernicious effects of positivism-cum-relativism on the human soul.

[256] I say this as one who studied with the incomparable Leo Strauss.

[257] It is worth noting that in addition to the Euclid of Alexandria (c. 325-265 BCE), there is a Euclid of Magara (c. 430-360 BCE) who was a pupil of Socrates. His philosophy was that "the good is one, though it is called by many names, sometimes wisdom, sometimes God, and sometimes reason."

[258] Gian Carlo Duranti, *Terzo Numero Binomiale Di Euclide E Terze Civilta Di Ammon-Zeus*, cited hereafter as *Opus*. The preface (p. XL) cites a key passage from my *Beyond the Secular Mind*, which Duranti avows, in a 106-page letter to the author, utterly transformed his view of the Torah.

[259] Citing Max Jammer in *Jerusalem vs. Athens*, p. 3, "Such is the state of quantum mechanics that physicists disagree not only about its conceptual foundations, but even about its empirical dimension—*measurement.*"

[260] The page in the text is unnumbered; it is the first of four such pages.

[261] Duranti, *Opus*, p. VII.

[262] Ibid., p. XVII. This does not contradict Plato's "atoms" as consisting of geometric figures.

[263] Ibid., p. XXXIII.

[264] Ibid., fourth unnumbered page of the preface.

[265] We know that each letter of the Hebrew alphabet represents a number, its "*Gematria*." The *Gematria* of a word is the sum of the numerical values of the letters that compose it. For example: the letter Y (*yod*) represents the number 10; the letter H (*hei*) 5; the letter V (*vav*) 6. Hence the *Gematria* of the Ineffable Name YHVH is 10+5+6+5 = 26. Now, as the renowned Talmudist and Torah philosopher Dr. Chaim Zimmerman indicated to the present writer, to use the *Gematria* in a non-arbitrary way, one must have a mastery of the Kabala, which, far from being reducible to mysticism, contains a qualitative mathematics.

[266] Daniel Michelson, "Codes in the Torah" (Jerusalem: "Shamir," 1976), No. 6, pp. 7-39.

[267] Gian Carlo Duranti, "Codes in the Pentateuch and Egyptian-Platonic Mathematics," *Filosofia Oggi*, N. 66–F. II—April 1994, p. 161 (italics in the original).

[268] Duranti, *Opus*, p. XC.

[269] Ibid., p. 201.

[270] See Eidelberg, *Beyond the Secular Mind*, ch. 4, "Why Judaism is Not a Religion."

[271] James E. Holton, "Marcus Tullius Cicero" in Leo Strauss and Joseph Cropsey, eds., *History of Political Philosophy*, p. 131.

[272] See ibid., for Holton's incisive analysis of the esoteric and exoteric intentions of Cicero's two dialogues.

273 The historical as opposed to the philosophical material mentioned here is drawn from the Internet Encyclopedia of Philosophy.

274 Ibid.

275 Hirsch, *Judaism Eternal*, I. 140-141 (italics added). I have substituted "gentile" for "heathen."

276 Breuer, *Concepts of Judaism*, pp. 69-70. The idea of the human community is implied by the Roman Stoic philosopher Epictetus (c.55–c.135 CE), who said: "…there is but one course open to men, to do as Socrates did: never to reply to one who asks his country, 'I am an Athenian,' or 'I am a Corinthian,' but 'I am a citizen of the universe'"? See Whitney J. Oates, ed., *The Stoic and Epicurean Philosophers*, p. 239.

277 See David T. Runin, *Philo in Early Christian Literature*, pp. 3-22.

278 See Wolfson, I, 234, 240.

279 Ibid., I, 254-255.

280 See Runin, p. 191.

281 In Egypt, Horus, Osiris, and Isis; in India, Siva, Brahma, and Vishnu; in Babylon, Ishtar, Sin, and Shamash.

282 See Harvey Falk, *Jesus the Pharisee*. Compare Rabbi Shmuley Boteach, "The Gospel of Untruth," which reveals the source of Christian anti-Semitism:

> The argument that the Jews, rather than the Romans, killed Jesus, rests on one central, absurd premise, namely that Pontius Pilate tried to save Jesus's life but the Jews demanded that he be executed. "Pilate said to [the Jews], 'Then what shall I do with Jesus who is called Christ?' They all said, 'Let him be crucified.' And he said, 'Why, what evil has he done?' But they shouted all the more, 'Let him be crucified.' So when Pilate saw that he was gaining nothing, but rather that a riot was beginning, he took water and washed his hands before the crowd, saying, 'I am innocent of this man's blood; see to it yourselves.' And all the people answered, 'His blood be upon us and on our children'" (Matthew 27:22).
>
> These verses are cheap forgeries, contradicted by all serious history of the time and by other verses in the New Testament itself. Pilate was known to be one of the cruelest Roman proconsuls ever. He killed thousands of people on an absolute whim….

After citing evidence from Philo and Josephus, Rabbi Boteach continues:

> The idea that he [Pontius Pilate] fought to spare the life of a Jew who allowed himself to be called King of the Jews (Matt. 27:11, Mark 15:2, Luke 23:3) and who was rebelling against Roman authority is not just implausible but laughable. Hyam Maccoby's brilliant book *The Mythmaker* demonstrates how shortly after the death of Jesus a concerted effort was made to curry favor with the Roman

authorities by implicating the Jews and exonerating the Romans in Jesus's and his disciples' deaths....

To be sure, there is a famous Talmudic citation that says that the high Jewish court condemned Jesus to death (*Sanhedrin* 43a). But the Jesus it is referring to cannot be the founder of Christianity. In the Talmud there is more than one Yeshu (Jesus). A case in point is where the Talmud says that Jesus of Nazareth was a student of Yehoshua ben Perahia (*Sotah* 47a), a sage who died at least 100 years before the Jesus of the New Testament was born. More importantly, whoever this "Yeshu" is, it most certainly is not Jesus of the New Testament because the narrative of their deaths is completely different. There is no Roman involvement, no crucifixion, and a number of students are put to death with this Yeshu, something that does not happen in the New Testament.

Rabbi Boteach says in the sequel:

> To my Christian brethren, who will be scandalized at the assertion that the Christian Bible contains forgeries, I remind them that sadly, many parts of the New Testament were doctored to demonstrate Christ's break from his people and their retribution against him for rebuking them. What emerged in the final text was sadly a tragedy for both Jews and Christians, namely, an anti-Semitic and hateful Jesus who is often unrecognizable as the same man who taught such wondrous ethical precepts as the Sermon on the Mount.
>
> In what arguably ranks as the greatest act of character assassination ever, some early Christians took the prince of peace and lover of his people and turned him into the source of Christian anti-Semitism. Dagobert Runes wrote: "The New Testament contains 102 references to the Jews of the most degrading and malevolent kind, thereby creating in the minds and hearts of the Christian children and adults ineradicable hatred toward the Jewish people." The reconstructed Jesus regularly labels his Jewish brethren deceivers and murderers. In John 8:44 he goes so far as to say, "You are of your father the devil, and your will is to, do your father's desires. He was the murderer from the beginning..." In Matthew 23 he tells the Jews they are destined for the damnation of hell.
>
> But could this possibly be the same man who so loved his people that he instructed his original 12 apostles: "Go nowhere among the gentiles, and enter no town of the Samaritans, but go rather to the lost sheep of the house of Israel" (Matt. 10:5-7). Could this be the same Jesus who famously told the Canaanite woman who begged him to exorcize a demon from her daughter, "I was sent only to the lost sheep of the house of Israel.... It is not fair to take the children's bread and throw it to the dogs" (Matt. 15:22-26)?

> Jesus's hatred of his people is an utter fabrication designed to justify later Christian antipathy toward Jews for rejecting Christianity. The great underlying secret of the New Testament, and what its later anti-Semitic falsifiers tried so desperately to bury, was that Jesus hated not the Jews, but the Romans. He tried to overthrow the authority not of the rabbis—among whose number he counted himself—but the Romans, whom he detested and despised for their cruelty and paganism.
>
> And because he preached revolt against the Romans, Pilate had him killed. Hence the High Priest, Rome's corrupt political appointee, says to Pilate of Jesus: 'We found this man…forbidding us to give tribute to Caesar and saying that he is a king (Luke 23:2). Jesus preached revolt against Rome and tried to usher in a Messianic age in which Jewish political dominion would be reestablished. That Jesus believed he was the Messianic king I have no doubt.

But then, in principle, any Jew can believe he is the Messiah, since the Jewish belief is that the Messiah is a human being rather than a deity. Such a person will be judged solely by whether he fulfills the Messianic prophecies.

> In Jesus' case…he was killed without having fulfilled the prophecies and was therefore deemed definitively not to have been the Messiah. But that did not mean that the Jews could not embrace some of his beautiful teachings. In the end, they rejected everything about Jesus not only because his followers made him into a god, but principally because they made him the fountain of anti-Semitism…. (*Jerusalem Post*, November 13, 2003).

[283] Kook, *Orot*, p. 108, B. Naor, trans.
[284] Isaac Breuer, "Judaism and the World of Tomorrow," in Leo Jung (ed.), *Israel of Tomorrow*, pp. 87-91.
[285] Kook, *Orot*, pp.105-106. Rabbi Kook referred to Christianity as "the daughter who bites her mother's [= Judaism's] breasts." Ibid., p. 254n140,
[286] Ibid., p. 150.
[287] Ibid., p. 201.
[288] Soloveitchik, *Halakhic Man*, pp. 55, 102.
[289] Maimonides, *Guide of the Perplexed*, Introduction and III, 51.
[290] Fouad Ajami, *The Dream Palace of the Arabs*, pp. 123; 121, 220-222, 310-311.
[291] Gerald L. Schroeder, *The Science of God*, p. 72. The Zohar, commenting on the Second Commandment, declares: "Thou shalt even avoid conceiving Me in those aspects which form Ishmael's religion" (Exodus 87a). See http://yu.showsit.info/ for worldwide commentary on the character of Islam.

292 The idea of free will can even be found in Epictetus: "He gave us this gift free from all let or hindrance or compulsion—nay, He put it wholly in our hands, not even leaving Himself any power to let or hinder us." Oates, *The Stoic and Epicurean Philosophers*, p. 235. This is Jewish, in fact, rabbinical doctrine.

293 Hirsch, *Judaism Eternal*, II, 498.

294 St. Thomas Aquinas, *Summa Contra Gentiles*, pp. 73-74.

295 Bat Ye'or, *Islam and Dhimmitude: Where Civilizations and Collide*.

296 Bernard Lewis, *What Went Wrong?* The book was in page-proofs when the Twin Towers were destroyed by Muslim terrorists.

297 See below, note 317 *in re* Dore Gold, and note 318 *in re* John L. Esposito.

298 Serge Trifkovic, *The Sword of the Prophet: Islam, History, Theology, Impact on the World*.

299 The Quran is spelt variously as Qur'an, Koran, Kuran, etc. "Quran" will be the preferred spelling in this book.

300 Trifkovic, p. 43.

301 Ibid., pp. 44, 50.

302 Ibid., p. 50. See Ibn Warraq, *Why I am Not a Muslim*; originally published in 1995, p. 97, who rejects this relativism.

303 Trifkovic, p. 132. Muir's statement also appears in Ibn Warraq, p. 88.

304 Abraham Geiger, *Judaism and Islam*, p. 19.

305 Ibn Warraq, pp. 35-48.

306 Ibid., pp. 112-113.

307 See Lewis, *Islam in History*, pp. 148-149.

308 Ibid., pp. 193-198

309 See Muhsin Mahdi, *Alfarabi's Philosophy of Plato and Aristotle*, pp. 3-10. Ajami, pp. 215-216, points out that the ninth-century *Mu'tazilah* philosophers, influenced by Greek philosophy, concluded that the Quran was a human creation.

310 Ibid., pp. 196-199. See Ibn Warraq, pp. 272-274 *re* Ibn Khaldun, Ernest Renan, and G. E. von Grunebaum on Islam's antagonism toward science and Greek philosophy. Compare, Lewis, *What Went Wrong*, p. 156.

311 Quoted in Trifkovic, p. 208.

312 See Paul Eidelberg, "The Clash of Two Decadent Civilization: Toward a Hebraic Alternative" (Ariel Center for Policy Research, December 2002).

313 Daniel Pipes, *Militant Islam Reaches America*, pp. 5-6.

314 See Bernard Lewis, *Islam in History*, 2d ed., p. 5. It should be borne in mind that Syria, like Iraq, is a secular state.

315 Daniel Pipes, *In the Path of God: Islam and Power*, ch. 9.

316 See John J. Donohue & John L. Esposito (eds.), *Islam in Transition*, p. 182.

317 Bat Ye'or, *Islam and Dhimmitude*, p. 371. See Dore Gold, *Hatred's Kingdom*, pp. 11-12, 214-215, who ignores the Armenian genocide in developing the simplistic idea that

Saudi-based Wahhabism is the basic source of international terrorism. This compels him to argue that Wahhabism is an aberration of Islam, which he regards as a basically tolerant religion. He curiously supports this assertion by quoting Bernard Lewis: "The application of jihad wasn't *always* rigorous or violent" (p. 14, italics added). Significantly, Gold makes no reference to Bat Ye'or's *Islam and Dhimmitude*, whose thoroughly documented research refutes his "politically correct" view of Islam.

[318] The leading apologist is John L. Esposito, *Unholy War: Terrorism in the Name of Islam*, pp. x-xi, who claims that fundamentalists have "hijacked Islam for their unholy purposes." See also his *The Islamic Threat: Myth or Reality.*, ch. 6. Esposito, a liberal democrat, concludes that the Islamic threat is a myth. In response, see Daniel Pipes, "Jihad and the Professors," *Commentary*, November 2002.

[319] In contrast to Bat Ye'or, Bernard Lewis treats Islam's persecution of infidels rather politely. See his *The Multiple Identities of the Middle East*, p. 128.

[320] See G. E. Von Grunebaum, *Modern Islam: The Search for Cultural Identity*, p. 47.

[321] Daniel Pipes, "The Long Life of Arab Rejectionism," *Commentary*, December 1997 (italics added).

[322] Pipes, *Militant Islam Reaches America*, pp. xiii-xiv, 29-30, 47; Lewis, *Islam in History*, ch. 25.

[323] Bat Ye'or, "A Culture of Hate," *National Review*, August 2, 2002.

[324] See Lewis, *What Went Wrong*, p. 114, who compares Christian tolerance unfavorably.

[325] Lewis, *Islam in History*, p. 416.

[326] Lewis, *What Went Wrong*, p. 151. See, also, Olivier Roy, *The Failure of Political Islam*, pp. 194-195.

[327] Turkey is a special case. The Ottoman Empire had just dissolved when Kemal Ataturk separated religion and state. This did not change the *sharia*. Also, Turkey is tied to Europe, and if this were not the case, it would probably revert to type, judging from the resurgence of "Islamism."

[328] Lewis, *Islam in History*, pp. 149-150.

[329] According to Malcolm Yapp, fundamentalists "are strictly traditional in their formulations [of the law] and modern in their practice and they care little for the resulting contradictions." Cited in Pipes, *In the Path of God*, p. 130.

[330] *New York Times*, November 24, 2002. For a contrary view of the *sharia*, see Donahue & Esposito (eds.), *Islam in Transition*, pp. 261-271.

[331] See Lewis, *What Went Wrong*, pp. 10-112. See also Roger Scruton, *The West and the Rest: Globalism and the Terrorist Threat*, pp. 98-99.

[332] See Pipes, *Militant Islam Reaches America*, p. 82.

[333] Needless to say, modernity also places in question the divine origin of the Bible, which does not prompt Jews and Christians to engage in holy wars. As for the human-all-too-human origin of the Quran, enough to read Ibn Warraq's *Why I am Not a Muslim*. He weakens his case, however, by his dogmatic secularism.

[334] Roy, *The Failure of Political Islam*, pp. 3-4.
[335] Ibid., p. 4.
[336] Ibid., p. x.
[337] Lewis, *Islam in History*, p. 402.
[338] Roy, p. 8. Compare Lewis, *Islam in History*, pp. 405-406.
[339] Ibid., p. 410.
[340] See Steven Emerson, *American Jihad: The Terrorists Living Among Us*, ch. 3.
[341] Eric Hoffer, *The True Believer*, p. 149.
[342] Cited in Donohue and Esposito, *Islam in Transition*, p. 144.
[343] See Pipes, *In the Path of God*, p. 182.
[344] See Bernard Lewis, *Islam and the West*, p. 136.
[345] Lewis, *Islam in History*, p. 7.
[346] See Daniel Pipes, "Who will stand up for Moderate Muslims," *Jerusalem Post*, September 24, 2003, p. 7 (italics added). Contrast Robert Spencer, *Onward Muslim Soldiers: How Jihad Still Threatens America and the West*, p. 300, who writes: "Ultimately, if moderate Islam is ever to become the dominant form of Islam around the world, the impetus must come from Muslims themselves. They must do it by renouncing some aspects of Islamic tradition and history—most especially jihad and dhimmitude."
[347] Pipes, *Militant Islam Reaches America*, pp. 46-47. Roy, p. 41, defines "moderates" in secular Islamic regimes as those who are "partisans of reIslamization from the bottom up (preaching, establishing sociological movements) while pressuring leaders (in particular through political alliances) to promote Islamization from the top (introducing the *sharia* into legislation)…" But if the government should take an anti-Islamic stance unaffected by peaceful protest, revolution becomes a right and an obligation.
[348] Cited in Bat Ye'or, *Islam and Dhimmitude*, p. 339.
[349] Pipes, *In the Path of God*, p. 167.
[350] See Lewis, *Islam in History*, p. 271.
[351] Roy, pp. 195-196.
[352] Ibid., p. 203.
[353] See Allan Bloom, *The Closing of the American Mind: How Higher Education Has Failed Democracy and Impoverished the Souls of Today's Students*; Dinesh D'Souza, *Illiberal Education*.
[354] See Lewis, *Islam in History*, who writes: "Khomeini was working within the historic and religious traditions of Islam" pp. 399, 403.
[355] Pipes, *In the Path of God*, p. 63. See p. xi of said preface, to which contrast pp. 63, 93, 118 of the book itself.
[356] See above, note 318 *in re* Daniel Pipes.
[357] See Donohue & Esposito (eds.), *Islam in Transition*, p. 79.
[358] Cited in Huntington, *The Clash of Civilizations*, p. 213.
[359] Ibid.

360 Ibid.

361 Cited in von Grunebaum, p. 161 (italics added).

362 Cited in Harkabi, *Arab Attitudes to Israel*, p. 97. See also Lewis, "The Roots of Muslim Rage," *The Atlantic Monthly,* September 1990, pp. 48-60.

363 For a profound analysis of this subject, see James Kurth, "The Real Clash," *The National Interest*, October 1994.

364 Cited in Weinberg, *Dreams of a Final Theory*, p. 189.

365 Scruton, *The West and the Rest,* pp. 78-79.

366 See Samuel P. Huntington, *Who Are We?* chs. 5 and 7. That Huntington does not speak of moral or cultural relativism as one of "The Challenges to America's National Identity"—the subtile of his book—may be indicative of his own philosophical predilection.

367 The following exposition is based largely on Chapter 1 of my book *Beyond the Secular Mind*.

368 All references to *The Prince* are from the annotated and literal translation of Leo Paul de Alvarez, *The Prince*.

369 Ibid., pp. 93-94.

370 Actually, eleven vices are mentioned, since "miserliness" and "rapaciousness" are listed in opposition to "liberality." See Leo Strauss, *Thoughts on Machiavelli*, pp. 311n63, 338n139 (cited hereafter as *Thoughts*). This is by far the most profound work on Machiavelli, a work to which the following analysis is very much indebted.

371 *The Prince*, p. 108 (italics added).

372 See de Alvarez, pp. xi-xiv; Strauss, *Thoughts*, pp. 179, 207-208.

373 A smiling Machiavelli would remind us from the grave that when Mao Tze-tung and Chou En-lai died, Western statesmen and intellectuals praised these tyrants as "great men." The author of *The Prince* writes in Chapter 18: "And with respect to all human actions, and especially those of princes where there is no judge to whom to appeal, one looks to the end. Let a prince then win and maintain the state—the means will always be judged honorable and will be praised by everyone; for the vulgar are always taken in by the appearance and the outcome of a thing, and in this world there is no one but the vulgar." Among the most notable adulators of Mao Tze-tung and Chou En-lai—the two must be held responsible for the slaughter of millions of Chinese—were an American president and his professorial Secretary of State.

374 *The Prince*, ch. 18 (italics added). See de Alvarez, pp. vi-vii.

375 See Machiavelli, *The Discourses*, I, 26.

376 See de Alvarez, pp. ix-x. Founding an entirely new state must be the work of only one man. See note 384 below.

377 See Strauss, *Thoughts*, pp. 26, 29. Although the concept of the common good appears in *The Discourses*, I, 2, Machiavelli asserts that the origin of justice is

force. Incidentally, this chapter reveals what Machiavelli thought of Aristotle's classification of regimes. For a defense of the concept of the common good in opposition to behavioral political science, see my *Discourse on Statesmanship*, pp. 9-14.

[378] See Strauss, *Thoughts*, pp. 26, 29. Note that whereas *The Prince* is dedicated to a ruler, *The Discourses*, which does refer to Hiero as a "tyrant," is dedicated to two subjects. See de Alvarez, pp. xv-xix, and Harvey Mansfield, Jr., *Machiavelli's New Modes and Orders*, pp. 21-23.

[379] See *The Prince*, ch. 18. Contrast *The Ethics of the Fathers*: "Be the tail among lions rather than the head among foxes" (4:20).

[380] See Strauss, *Thoughts*, p. 26.

[381] *The Prince*, ch. 9. Machiavelli explains in the sequel that whereas the great want to oppress, the people only want not to be oppressed. By no means does he regard the people as honest per se. "For one can say this generally of men: that they are ungrateful, fickle, hypocrites and dissemblers, evaders of dangers [and] lovers of gain..." (ibid., ch. 17). Of course, only a "prince" can found a state; but thereafter Machiavelli takes the side of the people—as he must if he himself is to be a "founder," that is, of new modes and orders. Accordingly, his best regime is a commercial and imperialistic republic, reversing classical and medieval political philosophy. See *The Discourses*, I, 6, and Mansfield, pp. 152-155, 243.

[382] See Nosson Scherman and Meir Zlotowitz (eds.), *The Wisdom in the Hebrew Alphabet*.

[383] See Strauss, *Thoughts*, pp. 312n22, 313n24, 326n183; Mansfield, pp. 32n12, 67n8, 73n9.

[384] Machiavelli defends Romulus' fratricide in *The Discourses*, I, 9, entitled "To Found A New Republic...Must Be The Work Of One Man Only."

[385] See Strauss, *Thoughts*, p. 59.

[386] Hobbes, pp. 82, 83.

[387] Ibid., p. 104 (italics added).

[388] Emanuel Kant, *Foundations of the Metaphysics of Morals*, p. 80, L. W. Beck, trans.

[389] Ibid., p. 65.

[390] See *Jerusalem vs. Athens*, p. 349, n. 25.

[391] For a discussion of Bacon, see ibid., pp. pp. 176-177.

[392] Shimon Peres still believes there is an economic solution to conflict between Israel and its Arab neighbors. Which reminds me of Orwell's chilling remark: "A generation of the unteachable is hanging upon us like a necklace of corpses."

[393] See Strauss, *Liberalism Ancient & Modern*, p. 244. As Strauss notes, Spinoza hated Judaism as well as Jews, an attitude Hermann Cohen deemed "unnatural" and even as a "humanly incomprehensible act of treason." I mention this in passing because one may find a similar phenomenon among certain Jews in Israel today.

[394] The *Chief Works of Benedict de Spinoza*, I, 207, 257, 263, 265. As others have noted, Spinoza's *Ethics* implicitly identifies God with "nature."

[395] Eidelberg, *Demophrenia*, p. 30. I refute Marx in ibid., pp. 31-32.
[396] Marx and Engels, *The Communist Manifesto*, pp. 12-14.
[397] Whitehead, *Science and Philosophy*, pp. 165-166.
[398] See Zimmerman, *Torah and Reason*, pp. 147-151, on which this historical view of slavery is based.
[399] See Alexis de Tocqueville, *Democracy in America*, II, 104, who attributes the spread of selfishness to democratic individualism:

> *Individualism* is a novel expression, to which a novel idea has given birth. Our fathers were only acquainted with *egoisme* (selfishness). Selfishness is a passionate and exaggerated love of self, which leads a man to connect everything with himself and to prefer himself to everything in the world. Individualism is a mature and calm feeling, which disposes each member of the community to sever himself from the mass of his fellows and to draw apart with his family, so that after he has thus formed a little circle of his own, he willingly leaves society at large to itself. Selfishness originates in blind instinct; individualism proceeds from erroneous judgment more than from depraved feelings; it originates as much in deficiencies of mind as in perversity of heart.
>
> Selfishness blights the germ of all virtue; individualism, at first, only saps the virtues of public life, but in the long run it attacks and destroys all others and is at length absorbed in downright selfishness. Selfishness is a vice as old as the world, which does not belong to one form of society more than to another; individualism is of democratic origin, and it threatens to spread in the same ratio as the equality of conditions.

[400] Jean-Jacques Rousseau, *First Discourse*, in *The First and Second Discourses*, p. 39, R.D. Masters, ed., J.R. Masters, trans.
[401] Ibid., p. 40.
[402] When Hobbes wrote that "desire and love are the same thing," and when Freud reduced love to the merely physical, they were cultivating ground prepared by Machiavelli, who writes, "men forget more quickly the death of a father than the loss of patrimony." Which means that filial affection is weaker than the desire for property. See Hobbes, p. 32; *The Prince*, p. 101.
[403] Doing good or pleasing others is to be understood simply as a means of gaining reputation and power. No wonder *success* in achieving the object of one's desires is the ultimate criterion of praise and blame—a vulgar teaching.
[404] This applies to Jewish movements that have abandoned the Torah.
[405] Breuer, *Concepts of Judaism*, p. 91.
[406] See Mansfield, pp. 202-203, commenting on *The Discourses*, II, 5.

[407] Kook, *Orot*, pp. 110, 195-196. "Formal Logic fails to accommodate the contraries and insists on their separation. In reality, however, opposites combine to fertilize one another, especially in the intellectual context." Yaron, *The Philosophy of Rabbi Kook*, p. 87.

[408] See Avraham Kook, *War and Peace*, pp. 35-36.

[409] Ibid., p. 50.

[410] The following exposition is drawn from Matis Weinberg, *FrameWorks* (Genesis), pp. 61-66.

[411] See Whitehead, *The Function of Reason*, p. 20.

[412] Ibid., p. 4. For a profound analysis of the problem of permanence and change, see Koppel, *Meta-Halakhah*, chs. 1-8.

[413] See Matis Weinberg, *FrameWorks* (Exodus), pp. 156-159.

[414] See Hirsch, *Judaism Eternal*, I, 187. I have taken the liberty of substituting "highest perfection" for the "greatest."

[415] Breuer, *Concepts of Judaism*, p. 31.

[416] Eidelberg, *Jewish Statesmanship*, p. 106.

[417] See *The Jerusalem Post*, November 10, 2002, p. 3.

[418] Jewish monotheism will then animate mankind.

[419] Originally published in Jerusalem by the present author as a separate booklet under the title *Israel's Return and Restoration: The Secret of Her Conquest*. The text (here slightly abridged) represents my rendering of Chapter 1 of Dr. Chaim Zimmerman's *Torah and Existence*. Unless indicated by (P.E.), endnotes are based on that book.

[420] The *Rishonim* lived between the eleventh and fifteenth centuries. They were followed by the *Achronim* who deferred to the superiority of their predecessors. Rashi is the acronym of Rabbenu Shlomo ben Yitzhak (1040-1105). As previously noted, Rambam is the acronym of Rabbi Moshe ben Maimon known as Maimonides (1135-1204); Ramban is the acronym of Rabbi Moshe ben Nachman (1194-1240) known as Nachmanides (P.E.).

[421] What Dr. Zimmerman refers to as the "Beginning of the Redemption" is referred to in Chapter 1 above as the "Third Redemption," and will also be described as Israel's "return and restoration."

[422] The Rambam included belief in the advent of the Moshiach as one of Thirteen Basic Principle of the Torah. These are printed in the Jewish prayer book.

[423] The Kabala and works like the Zohar are not mystical. Rather, they are couched in allegorical form to conceal what are thoroughly rational teachings about man and the universe, but which teachings would confuse the ignorant and arm the wicked. See Chaim Zimmerman *Torah and Reason*, pp. 136, 269-291 (P.E.).

[424] It should be noted that the partial return of Jews to Eretz Yisrael after the destruction of the First Temple was not from the four corners of the earth, as was the case after 1948 (P.E.).

425 It should be noted that Dr. Zimmerman speaks of seven arguments, to which he addresses seven refutations. To simplify the exposition, I have rearranged the order of these arguments and refutations and have combined what he designates as the Third and Fifth Arguments concerning the (supposed) impossibility of the Redemption given the secular character of those who founded the State of Israel. See *Torah and Existence*, pp. 27, 28, 32, 67.

426 For a profound discussion of the role of the miracles in relation to the Redemption and free will, see ibid., pp. 44-67 (P.E.).

427 "*And your seed shall be as the dust of the earth*" (Genesis 28:14). The Midrash comments: "As the dust of the earth can be blessed only through water, so will your children be blessed only for the sake of the Torah, which is likened to water; and as the dust of the earth is trodden upon, so will your children be downtrodden beneath the powers, as it is written, '*And I will put it unto the hand of them that afflict you…*' (Isaiah 51:23); and as the dust of the earth wears out all utensils even of metal, yet itself remains forever, so will your children outlive all and exist forever" (P.E.).

428 These two periods of *B'Eto* and *Achishena* involve different premises and rules for the process of Israel's Redemption. Their states of affairs are *halachically* differentiated. A comprehensive *halachic* discourse of talmudic and Zoharic sources can be found in *Divrei Taam* p. 241. The *Divrei Taam* explains that many talmudic statements, which appear to be contradictory, are actually related to the two different processes concerning Israel's Redemption.

429 See also the Zohar (117b): "Said Rav Jose: 'We have still a long time to be in exile until the day arrives, but all depends on whether the people will repent of their sins, as appears from the passage, '*I the Lord will hasten it in its time*' (Isaiah 60:22), that is, 'if they will be worthy, I will hasten it, and if not then in its time'" (P.E.).

430 The Gemara in *Megilla 17b* alludes to the natural process of redemption. See Third Refutation.

431 No less remarkable is the fact that more and more Jews are applying the Torah to the sciences (P.E.).

432 It should be noted, however, that the reference of *Eruvin* 43b to the prophet Eliyahu and his prophecy regarding the days of the Moshiach has no relation to the Beginning of the Redemption (*Atchalta d'Geula*) but to the later stage of the redemption process.

433 From a purely political perspective, this will require, *inter alia*, a basic shift of power from political parties to the people. This can only be accomplished by transforming Israel from a *single*, nationwide electoral district to a regional or multi-district system in order to make elected officials individually accountable to the people rather than to party oligarchs. The latter can ignore the people because they rank at the top of fixed party lists.

434 See, for example, *Berachot* 34b; *Pesachim* 68a; *Sanhedrin* 99a; *Shabbat* 63a.

435 Many people who deny the Beginning of the Redemption of our time—in Hebrew, the *Atchalta d'Geula*—and who consider this term to be an expression invented by modern religious Zionists, were not aware that the term is used explicitly in *Megilla*17b.

436 In our books it is the tenth psalm, verse 15 (P.E.).

437 The Maharsha (Morenu HaRav Shmuel Eliezer, 1555-1631) resolves the apparent discrepancy between the seventh and tenth benedictions. He says that these represent two stages in the conquest of Eretz Yisrael, but that it will not be until the second stage that Jerusalem will be liberated—thus anticipating its liberation in the Six-Day War!

438 Rashi states that "When the Land of Israel will yield its produce in super-abundance, this will signal the approach of the end of the exile. There is no clearer 'end' than this." As quoted in *Pathways to the Torah*, p. A29.8 (P.E.).

439 See Chaim Zimmerman, *Torah and Reason*, p. 80 referring to the *Yalkut Shimoni* (*Emor* 23), which states that Klal Yisrael will not return to their land unless the wicked and the righteous are combined (like the four species) in one bundle (P.E.).

440 Notice that, since its establishment in 1948, the State of Israel has emphasized the physical development of the country. (Notice, too, Israel's stunning victories over Arab states on the battlefield, victories attributed, as may be expected, to her superior scientific-technological infrastructure and military training programs.) But the emphasis on physical development, so natural for a secular government, could not but lead to the spread of materialism in society at-large. Repelled by the vulgar and hedonistic way of life (which Israel has largely imported from the West), religious people uncritically reject the State of Israel as an instrument of the Redemption. See Mordechai Alexander (ed.), *Torah L'Israel: Selected Teachings of Reb Chaim Zimmerman*, "The Soldier of Israel," pp. 66-69 (P.E.).

441 It should be noted that various Israeli prime ministers and cabinet ministers have openly pursued the goal of transforming Israel into a "state of its citizens," and have sought, with considerable success in the 1990s, to remove Jewish content from the public school curriculum. See Yoram Hazony et al., "The Quiet Revolution in the Teaching of Zionist History."

442 On the question of free choice, see *Torah and Existence*, pp. 49-54 et seq (P.E.).

443 Nevertheless, and as will be demonstrated in the Sixth Refutation, once Eretz Yisrael is under control of the Jews, it would be a violation of *Halacha* to surrender any part of the land, even if its retention would necessitate war. The contention of certain religious Jews that parts of Eretz Yisrael may be sacrificed on grounds of *pekuach nefesh* has no basis in *Halacha*; indeed, it is palpably absurd and even provocative. For on these grounds, Israel would have to surrender land every time her enemies threatened war—and they would be encouraged to do so by the concept in question. Viewed in this light, *pekuach nefesh* would be a formula for national suicide. Hence, contrary

to those who invoke this concept to justify surrendering parts of Eretz Yisrael for the sake of "peace," *pekuach nefesh* entails the very opposite policy (P.E.).

444 The second oath bound the Jews not to rebel against the nations of the world. The third oath concerned the nations themselves: they are not to oppress the Jews unduly. Regarding the latter, it is an incontrovertible historical fact that any nation that cruelly oppressed the Jews has either been destroyed or lost its reigning power: for example, Babylon, Persia, Greece, Rome, Spain, Tsarist Russia, and Nazi Germany. The "Three Oaths" are also discussed in Chaim Zimmerman, *Torah and Reason*, pp. 140-141 and in *Torah L'Yisrael*, pp. 9-22. Some aspects of the latter work have been incorporated into the Sixth Refutation.

What Judaic man calls God's "oath" the non-Torah man calls a "law of nature." A brief explanation: Like the ancient Greek philosophers, who regarded the universe as eternal, classical physics postulated eternal and self-subsisting laws of nature. The Sages of the Talmud refer to laws of nature as *Shevuot*—"oaths." The reason is this. All laws of nature are creations of God (as are the laws or rules of mathematics and logic). These laws are not self-sustaining or independent. Their continued operation depends, every moment, on the Will of God. Were God to withdraw His power, the universe would revert to nothingness. Strictly speaking, therefore, there are no immanent, eternal, and absolute laws of nature. A law of nature is nothing more than God's "oath" or promise that He will not change some stable form or predictable regularity of existence. God allows the world to function within the limits and constraints of the laws He has created. So, what to man is a law of nature is to God an "oath." But the same may be said of "laws of history," which may also be called "Laws of Divine Guidance." For further elaboration, see Chaim Zimmerman, *Torah and Reason*, pp. 137-141, on which this paragraph is based. See also *Torah L'Yisrael*, pp. 17-19.

445 See *Avnei Nezer* the work of the Gaon Rav Avraham of Sochochov.

446 See *Kidushin* 26a. Although the word *yerusha* is often translated as "inherit," its primary meaning is "to expel, seize, take possession or to occupy," usually by force. For various derivatives of this word (or its cognates), see Lev. 20:24; Deut. 1:8, 2:12, 19, 21, 22; 11:23; 12:2; 18:14; 19:1; 31:3; Jud. 11:23; Isa. 14:21; Jer. 8:10; Ps. 44:4, 83:13. See also Nachmanides, *Commentary on the Torah*, Num. 33:53 (P.E.).

447 Chaim Zimmerman, *Torah and Reason*, ch. 23 (P.E.).

448 Cognates of the word *yaalu* also connote "*to go up against*" (P.E.).

449 The terminology of *aliya* and *yerida*—of "going up" when one comes to the Land of Israel, and of "going down" when one leaves this Land—is made explicit in both Talmuds and is emphasized in the Babylonian Talmud. See *Kidushin* 69a, *Berachot* 63a, *Yevamot* 122a.

450 See Chaim Zimmerman, *Torah L'Yisrael*, p. 12 (P.E.).

451 This also refutes those who, on grounds of *pekuach nefesh* and in the name of "peace," would surrender parts of the Land of Israel to the descendants of Ishmael (P.E.).

452 Needless to say, this statement has profound implications for the Government of Israel (P.E.).
453 *V'yashvu shom viyreishua* (P.E.).

Bibliography

Primary Jewish Sources

Tanach: Torah/Writings/Prophets. New York: Mesorah Publications, Ltd., 1998.
The Holy Scriptures. 2 vols. Philadelphia: Jewish Publication Society of America, 1955.
Babylonian Talmud. 18 vols. London: Soncino Press, 1978.
Midrash Rabbah. 10 vols. London: Soncino Press, 1983.
The Zohar. 5 vols. London: Soncino Press, 1973.

Secondary Jewish Sources

Breuer, Isaac. *Concepts of Judaism*. Jerusalem: Israel Universities Press, 1974.
Hirsch, Samson Raphael. *The Pentateuch*. 6 vols. Gateshead: Judaica Press, 1982.
_____. *Judaism Eternal*. 2 vols. London: Soncino Press, 1956.
Judah Halevi. *The Kuzari*. Jerusalem: Sefer ve Sefer Publishing, 2003.
Kook, Abraham Isaac. *Orot*. Northvale, NJ: Jason Aronson, 1993.
_____. *War and Peace*. Jerusalem: Torat Eretz Yisrael Publications, 1997.
Maimonides, *Guide of the Perplexed*. Chicago: University of Chicago Press, 1963.
Malbim. *Commentary on the Torah*. 3 vols. t.d.; Jerusalem: Hillel Press, 1983.
Nachmanides. *Commentary on the Torah*. 5 vols. New York: Shilo Publishing House, 1971.
Soloveitchik, Joseph M. *Halakhic Man*. Philadelphia: Jewish Publication Society, 1983.
Teichtal, Yisachar Shlomo. *Eim Habanim Semeichah: On Eretz Yisrael, Redemption, and Unity*. Mevaseret, Israel: Kol Mevaser Publication, 2000.
Weinberg, Matis. *FrameWorks* (Genesis). Boston: Foundation for Jewish Publications, 1999.
_____. *FrameWorks* (Exodus). Boston: Foundation for Jewish Publications, 1999.
_____. *Patterns in Time: Chanukah*. Jerusalem: Feldheim, 1988.
Zimmerman, Chaim. *Torah and Existence*. Jerusalem: privately published. 1986.
_____. *Torah and Reason*. Jerusalem: HED Press, 1979.

General

Ajami, Fouad. *The Dream Palace of the Arabs.* New York: Vintage Books, 1999.
Aquinas, Thomas. *Basic Writings.* 2 vols. New York: Random House, 1945.
_____. *Summa Contra Gentiles.* New York: Doubleday, 1958.
Aristotle, *Metaphysics.*
_____. *Physics.*
_____. *On the Heavens.*
_____. *De Anima.*
_____. *Politics*
_____. *Nicomachean Ethics.*
Arnold, Matthew. *Literature and Dogma.* London: Smith, Elder, 1876.
Aviezer, Nathan. *In the Beginning: Science and Torah.* Hoboken, N.J.: KTAV, 1990.

Baer, Robert. *Sleeping With the Devil: How Washington Sold Our Soul For Saudi Crude.* New York: Crown Publishers, 2003.
Baruk, Henri. *Tsedek.* Binghamton, NY: Swan Publishing Co., 1972.
Bat Ye'or. *Islam and Dhimmitude: Where Civilizations and Collide.* Fairleigh Dickenson University Press, 2002.
Baxter, Claude F. & Melnechuk, Theodore, eds. *Perspectives in Schizophrenia Research.* New York: Raven Press, 1980.
Bein, Alex, ed. *Arthur Ruppin: Memoirs, Diaries, Letters.* London: Weidenfeld & Nicolson, 1971.
Ben-Gurion, David. *Israel: A Personal History.* Tel Aviv: Sabra Books, 1972.
Bentall, Richard B., ed. *Reconstructing Schizophrenia.* London: Routledge, 1990.
Benton, Michael J. *When Life Nearly Died: The Greatest Mass Extinction of All Time.* New York: Thomas & Hudson, 2003.
Bin-Nun, Ariel. *The Law of the State of Israel,* 2nd ed. Jerusalem: Rubin Mass Ltd., 1992.
Bloom, Allan. *The Closing of the American Mind: How Higher Education Has Failed Democracy and Impoverished the Souls of Today's Students.* New York: Simon & Schuster, 1987.
Brody, Moshe. *Troubleshooting in the Promised Land.* Kvar Sava: Judean Hills Publishing, 2003.
Burnet, John. *Early Greek Philosophy.* London: A. & C. Black, 1930.
Burtt, E. A. *The Metaphysical Foundations of Modern Science.* New York: Doubleday, 1954.

Carmell, Aryeh & Domb, Cyril., eds. *Challenge: Torah Views on Science.* Jerusalem: Feldheim, 1976.
Churchill, Randolph S. and Winston S. *The Six Day War.* London: Heinemann, 1967.

Davies, P.C.W. *Space and Time in the Modern Universe.* London: Cambridge University Press, 1977.
Dershowitz, Alan M. *Chutzpah.* Boston: Little, Brown & Co., 1991.
Descartes, Rene. *Principles of Philosophy.*
Donohue John J. & Esposito John L., eds. *Islam in Transition.* New York: Oxford University Press, 1982.
D'Souza, Dinesh. *Illiberal Education.* New York: Free Press, 1991.
Duranti, Gian Carlo. *Terzo Numero Binomiale Di Euclide E Terze Civilta Di Ammon-Zeus.* Venice: Franco Cesati Editore, 1991.

Edwards, David V. *The American Political Experience.* Englewood Cliffs, N.J.: Prentice Hall, 1988.
Eidelberg, Paul. *Jewish Statesmanship: Lest Israel Fall.* Ariel Center for Policy Research, Israel 2000; Lanham, MD. University Press of America, 2002.
_____. *Judaic Man: Toward a Reconstruction of Western Civilization.* (Middletown, NJ: Caslon Co., 1996.
_____. *Demophrenia: Israel and the Malaise of Democracy.* Lafayette. LA: Prescott Press, 1994.
_____. *Beyond the Secular Mind: A Judaic Response to the Problems of Modernity,* New York: Greenwood Press, 1989.
_____. *Israel's Return and Restoration.* Jerusalem, 1987.
_____. *Jerusalem versus Athens: Toward a General Theory of Existence.* Lanham, MD: University Press of America, 1983.
_____. *On the Silence of the Declaration of Independence.* Amherst: University of Massachusetts Press, 1976.
Eidelberg, Paul & Morrisey, Will. *Our Culture 'Left' or 'Right': Litterateurs Confront Nihilism.* Lewiston: Edwin Mellen Press, 1992.
Einstein, Albert. *Out of My Later Years.* New York: Wings Books, 1996.
Einstein, Albert & Infeld, Leopold, *The Evolution of Physics.* New York: Simon & Schuster, 1938.
Eisenberg, Rafael. *Survival: Israel and Mankind.* Jerusalem: Feldheim, 1991.
Ellis, Albert. *Reason and Emotion in Psychotherapy.* New York: Lyle Stuart, 1962.
Emerson, Steven. *American Jihad: The Terrorists Living Among Us.* New York: Free Press, 2002.

Esposito, John L. *Unholy War: Terrorism in the Name of Islam.* New York: Oxford University Press, 2002.

_____. *The Islamic Threat: Myth or Reality.* New York: Oxford University Press, 1999.

Euclid, *Elements.*

Evron, Yair. *The Middle East: Nations, Superpowers and War.* New York: Praeger, 1973.

Falk, Harvey. *Jesus the Pharisee.* Costa Mesa, CA: Paulist Press, 1985.

Feynman, Richard & Weinberg, Steven. *Elementary Particles and the Laws of Physics.* New York: Cambridge University Press, 1997.

Freud, Sigmund, *An Outline of Psycho-Analysis.* London: Hogarth Press, 1940.

_____. *The Problem of Anxiety.* New York: W. W. Norton & Co., 1936.

_____. *The Ego and the Id.* London: Hogarth Press, 1923.

Garan, D. G. *Our Sciences Ruled by Human Prejudice.* New York: Philosophical Library, 1987.

_____. *The Key to the Sciences of Man.* New York: Philosophical Library, 1975.

_____. *The Paradox of Pleasure and Relativity.* New York: Philosophical Library, 1963.

Geiger, Abraham. *Judaism and Islam.* New York: KTAV Publishing House, 1970.

Gerber, Roger A, & Isaac, Rael Jean. *What Shimon Says.* New York: Americans for a Safe Israel, 2001.

Gold, Dore. *Hatred's Kingdom.* Washington, D.C.: Regnery, 2003.

Gould, Stephen Jay. *The Hedgehog, The Fox, and the Magister's Pox.* New York: Vintage, 2004

_____. *The Structure of Evolutionary Theory.* Cambridge: Harvard University Press, 2002.

_____. *Wonderful Life.* New York: W. W. Norton, 1989.

Grunebaum, G. E. Von. *Modern Islam: The Search for Cultural Identity.* Berkeley: University of California Press, 1962.

Harkabi, Yehoshafat. *Arab Attitudes to Israel.* Jerusalem: Keter, 1972.

_____. *Israel's Fateful Hour.* New York: Harper & Row, 1989.

Hawking, Stephen. *The Theory of Everything.* Beverly Hills, CA: Millennium Press, 2002.

_____. *The Universe in A Nutshell.* New York: Bantam Books, 2001.

_____. *A Brief History of Time: From the Big Bang to Black Holes.* New York: Bantam Books, 1998.
Hoffer, Eric. *The True Believer.* New York: Perennial Classics, 2002.
Hazony, Yoram. *The Jewish State.* New York: Basic Books, 2000.
Hazony, et al. *The Quiet Revolution in the Teaching of Zionist History: A Comparative Study of Education Ministry Textbooks on the 20th Century.* Jerusalem: The Shalem Center, 2000.
Heisenberg, Werner. *Natural Law and the Structure of Matter.* London: George Allen & Unwin, 1970.
Hertz, J. H. *A Book of Jewish Thought.* London: Oxford University Press, 1966.
Hobbes, Thomas. *Leviathan.* Oxford: Blackwell, 1955.
Huntington, Samuel P. *The Clash of Civilizations.* New York: Simon and Schuster, 1997.
_____. *Who Are We? The Challenges to American Identity.* York: Simon and Schuster, 2004.

Izard, Carroll E. et al., eds. *Emotions, Cognition, and Behavior.* Cambridge: Cambridge University Press, 1984.

James, William. *The Principles of Psychology.* 2 vols. New York: Dover Publications, 1950/1890.
_____. *Varieties of Religious Experience.* New York: Modern Library, n.d.
Jammer, Max. *The Philosophy of Quantum Mechanics.* New York: John Wiley & Sons, 1974.
Johnson, Paul. *A History of the Jews.* London: Weindenfeld & Nicolson, 1987.
Josephus. *Complete Works.* Grand Rapids, MI: Kregel Publications, 1999.
Jung, C. G. *Modern Man in Search of a Soul.* New York: Harcourt, Brace & Co., 1933.
Jung, Leo. *Judaism in a Changing World.* New York: Jonathan David Publishers, 1939.
_____. ed. *Israel of Tomorrow.* New York: Herald Square Press, 1949.

Kant, Emanuel. *Foundations of the Metaphysics of Morals.* Chicago: University of Chicago Press, 1950.
Karetzky, Stephen. *The Cannons of Journalism: The New York Times Propaganda War Against Israel.* Stanford: O'Keefe Press, 1984.
Katz, Moshe. *CompuTorah: Hidden Codes in the Torah.* Jerusalem: privately published, 1996.
Kelemen, Lawrence. *Permission to Believe: Four Rational Approaches to God's Existence.* Jerusalem: Targum/Feldheim, 1990.

Kemali. D. et al., eds. *Schizophrenia Today*. Oxford: Pergamon Press, 1976.
Koestler, Arthur. *The Roots of Coincidence*. London: Picador, 1970.
Koppel, Moshe. *Meta-Halakhah: Logic, Intuition, and the Unfolding of Jewish Law*. Northvale, NJ: Jason Aronson, 1997.
Koran. New York: Penguin Books, 1974.
Koyré, Alexander. *From the Closed World to the Infinite Universe*. New York: Harper, 1958.
Kuhn, Thomas S. *The Structure of Scientific Revolutions*. Chicago: University of Chicago Press, 1962.

Laertius, Diogenes. *Lives of Eminent Philosophers*. 2 vols. Cambridge: Harvard University Press, 1959.
Levinthal, C. F. *Introduction to Physiological Psychology*. New York: Prentice-Hall, 1990.
Lewis, Bernard. *The Crisis of Islam: Holy War and Unholy Terror*. New York: Modern Library, 2003.
_____. *What Went Wrong? Western Impact and Middle Eastern Response*. New York: Oxford University Press, 2002.
_____. *The Multiple Identities of the Middle East*. New York: Schocken, 1998.
_____. *Islam and the West*. New York, Oxford University Press, 1993.
_____. *Islam in History*. Chicago: Open Court, 1993.
Lewis, C. S. *The Abolition of Man*. Toronto: Macmillan, 1965.
Lichtenstein, Aaron. *The Seven Laws of Noah*. New York: Z. Berman Books, 1981.
Lincoln, Abraham. *Collected Works*. 9 vols. New Brunswick: Rutgers University Press, 1953.
Locke, John. *Concerning Human Understanding*.
Loewenberg, Robert & Alexander, Edward, eds. *The Israeli Fate of Jewish Liberalism*. Lanham, Md.: University Press of America, 1988.
Lucretius. *De Rerum Natura*.

Machiavelli, Niccolo. *The Prince*. Irving, TX: University of Dallas Press, 1980.
_____. *Discourses*.
Magaro, Peter A., ed. *The Construction of Madness*. New York: Pergamon Press, 1976.
Mahdi, Muhsin. *Alfarabi's Philosophy of Plato and Aristotle*. Ithaca: Cornell University Press, 1962.
Mansfield, Harvey Jr. *Machiavelli's New Modes and Orders*. London: Cornell University Press, 1979.

Marx, Karl & Engels, Frederick. *The German Ideology.* New York: International Publishers, 1947.
Matte-Blanco, Ignacio. *The Unconscious as Infinite Sets.* London: Duckworth, 1975.
_____. *Thinking, Feeling, and Being.* London: Routledge, 1988.
Mill, John Stuart. *Utilitarianism, Liberty, and Representative Government.* New York: E. P. Dutton, 1951.
Montesquieu, Baron de. *Considerations sur les Causes de la Grandeur des Romains et de leur Decadence.* Paris, 1899.

New Testament. New York: Thomas Nelson & Sons, 1946.
Nietzsche Friedrich. *The Joyful Wisdom.* New York: Frederick Ungar Publishing Co., 1960.
_____, *The Dawn of Day.* London: T. Fisher Unwin, 1903.
_____. *Basic Writings of Nietzsche.* New York: Modern Library, 1968.
_____. *Early Greek Philosophy.* New York: Macmillan, 1924.
Nisan, Mordechai. *Israel and the Territories.* Ramat-Gan, Israel: Turtledove Publishing, 1978.
_____. *Toward a New Israel.* New York: AMS Press, 1992.

Oates, Whitney J., ed. *The Stoic and Epicurean Philosophers.* New York: Modern Library 1957.
Oren, Michael B. *Six Days of War.* New York: Ballantine Books, 2002.

Pathways to the Torah. Jerusalem: Aish HaTorah Publications, 1988.
Philo. Works. 10 vols. London: William Heinemann, 1929.
Pipes, Daniel. *In the Path of God: Islam and Power.* New Brunswick: Transaction Publishers, 2002.
_____. *Militant Islam Reaches America.* New York: W.W. Norton, 2002.
Planck, Max. *Scientific Autobiography and Other Papers.* New York: Philosophical Library, 1949.
Plato. *Republic.*
_____. *Timaeus.*
_____. *Laws.*
_____. *Symposium.*
_____. *Statesman.*

Rabinowitz, Abraham H. *The Jewish Mind.* Jerusalem: Hillel Press, 1978.
Rachman, S. J. *Fear and Courage.* New York: W. H. Freeman & Co., 1990.

Reichenbach, Hans. *The Rise of Scientific Philosophy.* Berkeley: University of California Press, 1959.
Rofé, Yakov. *Repression and Fear.* New York: Hemisphere Publishing Co., 1989.
Ross, Hugh. *The Creator and the Cosmos.* Colorado Springs, CO: NavPress, 2001.
Rousseau. Jean-Jacques, *The First and Second Discourses.* New York: St. Martin's Press, 1964.
Roy, Olivier. *The Failure of Political Islam.* Cambridge: Harvard University, Press, 1994.
Runin, David T. *Philo in Early Christian Literature.* Minneapolis: Fortress Press, 1993.
Russell, Bertrand. *The ABC of Relativity.* Fairlawn, NJ: Essential Books, 1958.

Scherman, Nosson & Zlotowitz, Meir., eds. *The Wisdom in the Hebrew Alphabet.* NY: Mesorah Publications, Ltd., 1983.
Schlipp, P. A., ed. *Albert Einstein: Philosopher-Scientist.* LaSalle, IL: Open Court, 1970.
Schroeder, Gerald L. *The Science of God: The Convergence of Scientific and Biblical Wisdom.* New York: Broadway Books, 1997.
_____. *Genesis and the Big Bang: The Discovery of Harmony Between Modern Science and the Bible.* New York: Bantam Books, 1990.
Shakow, David. *Adaptation in Schizophrenia: The Theory of Segmental Set.* New York: John Wiley & Sons, 1979.
Soloveitchik, Joseph M. *Worship of the Heart.* Jersey City, NJ: KTAV, 2003.
_____. *The Halakhic Mind.* New York: Free Press, 1986.
Spencer, Robert. *Onward Muslim Soldiers: How Jihad Still Threatens America and the West.* Washington, DC: Regnery Publishing, Inc., 2003.
Spinoza, Benedict, *The Chief Works of Benedict de Spinoza.* New York: Dover: 1951.
_____. *Ethics.* New York: Tudor Publishing Co., n.d.
Stav, Arieh. *Peace—The Arabian Caricature: A Study of Anti-Semitic Imagery.* Jerusalem: Gefen Publishers, 1999.
Stern, Menahem. *Greek and Latin Authors on Jews and Judaism.* 3 vols. Jerusalem, The Israel Academy of
Scruton, Roger. *The West and the Rest: Globalism and the Terrorist Threat.* London: Continuum, 2002.
Strauss, Leo. *Liberalism Ancient & Modern.* New York: Basic Books, 1968.
_____. *Thoughts on Machiavelli.* Glencoe, Ill.: Free Press, 1958.
_____. *Natural Right and History.* Chicago: University of Chicago Press, 1953.

Strauss, Leo & Cropsey, Joseph, eds. *History of Political Philosophy*. Chicago: Rand McNally, 1972, 2d ed.

Timmerman, Kenneth R. *Preachers of Hate: Islam and the War On America*. New York: Crown Forum, 2003.

Tatz, Akiva. *Worldmask*. Jerusalem: Feldheim, 1998.

Tocqueville, Alexis de. *Democracy in America*. 2 vols. New York: Vintage Books, 1945.

Trifkovic, Serge. *The Sword of the Prophet: Islam, History, Theology, Impact on the World*. Boston: Regina Orthodox Press, 2002.

Warraq, Ibn. *Why I am Not a Muslim*. Amherst, NY: Prometheus Books, 2003.

Weinberg, Steven. *The First Three Minutes*. New York: Basic Books, 1993.

_____. *Dreams of a Final Theory*. New York: Vintage Books, 1993.

Wheatcroft, Geoffrey. *The Controversy of Zion*. London: Sinclair-Stevensohn, 1996.

Whitehead, Alfred North. *Science and the Modern World*. New York: Free Press, 1967.

_____. *The Function of Reason*. Boston: Beacon Press, 1966.

_____. *Concept of Nature*. London: Cambridge University Press, 1963.

_____. *Science and Philosophy*. New York: Philosophical Library, 1948.

_____. *The Principle of Relativity*. London: Cambridge University Press, 1922.

Wigner, Eugene P. *Symmetries and Reflections*. Bloomington, IN: Indiana University Press, 1967.

Willerman, L. & Cohen, D. B. *Psychopathology*. New York: McGraw-Hill, 1990.

Wolfson, Harry Austryn, *Philo*. 2 vols. Cambridge: Harvard University Press, 1968.

Zvi Yaron, *The Philosophy of Rabbi Kook*. Jerusalem: Eliner Library, 1991.

INDICES

BIBLICAL CITATIONS
(Chapter and verse designations follow those of the Hebrew Bible)

Genesis
1:1, 5, 96-97, 100, 107, 108, 125, 143, 218, 253, 274
1:9-13; 5:1, 99
1:26; 2:7, 107
1-27, 125
2:4, 99
2:7, 107, 117
3:7, 105
4:9, 115, 143
4:25, 99. 108, 115, 143, 290
5:3, 99,108, 124-125
9:11, 115
12:1, 121, 124, 216, 227
12:1-3, 121, 124, 191, 216, 227
14:14-24, 18:3-7, 23-32, 55
14:22-23, 16:17, 124
14:22, 55, 124-125, 291
15:7, 9, 118, 246
15:13-14, 9, 96, 117, 118, 128, 238, 246, 290-291
17:5, 125, 228, 233, 238
17:8, 125, 228, 233, 238
18:1-8, 23, 125
18:17, 27, 55, 124-125, 130, 228, 233
19:56, 21:18, 130
23:6, 124-125
26:5, 124
35:10, 241, 246
37:5-10, 50:20, 110

Exodus
3:14, 114
6:17, 128
14:13, 114, 253
18:19, 48
20:1-3, 20: 3-5, 113-115, 117, 174
20:2, 115
20:8, 117
23:10, 114, 250
29:46, 128
31:17, 107, 108
33:20, 23, 114
34:6, 115
20:22, 113-115, 117, 174
25:2-5, 250

Leviticus
20:22, 26-27, 32, 238
21:10, 236
25:2-5, 2590
26:8, 11

Numbers
23:19, 131, 238
33:53, 258

Deuteronomy
1:13, 45, 48
4:25-31, 131, 132
4:39, 114, 117, 128, 131

6:4, 114
14:2, 113, 237
14:12, 113
17:15, 30:8, 30:35, 239
18:14, 237
30:1-6, 128, 221, 233, 239
30:8, 221, 233, 239
30:15, 221, 233, 239
32:7 127
32:21, 21

I Samuel 10:1, 236
II Samuel 2:4, 236
I Kings 19:11-12, 131-134, 233, 235-236, 250-251

Isaiah
1:25, 250, 273
5:20, 14, 272-273
11:2, 237, 252
25:11, 252
28:15, 14
43:21, 113, 253
55:8, 114, 216
60:2-3, 234, 246, 291
60:22, 234, 246, 291

Jeremiah
23:7-8, 241
26:18-20, 21, 106

Ezekiel 36:8, 250
Haggai 2:8, 253

Hosea 3:5, 251
Micah 3:12, 21
Zephaniah 3:9, 242-243

Zechariah
8:3-4, 21, 234, 273
8:23, 21, 234, 273
12:1, 273
14:9, 234, 254
14:19, 234, 254

Psalms
8:6, 105, 160
32:10, 84:10, 239
33:6, 117, 171
75:11, 251
85:12, 109
104:2, 273
105:8-11, 233
122:6, 251
127:1, 243

Proverbs
3:19, 105, 117, 171
11:17, 228

Job
9:8, 273
27:17, 252

Esther 2:21, 6:11, 30, 8:15, 16, 247

TALMUDIC, MISHNAIC. MIDRASHIC, AND ZOHARIC CITATIONS
Babylonian Talmud

Avoda Zara
2b, 252
3a, 116

36a, 48
53b, 9

Bava Batra 10b, 230
Baba Metzia 61b, 255
Berachot 12b-13a, 242
Eruvin 43b, 248
Hagiga 14a, 106
Hullin 89a, 103, 110
Ketuvot
110b, 9
111a, 245, 257

Megilla
13b, 125
17b., 250, 291

Nedarim 32b, 124

Sanhedrin
97b, 243
98a, 20, 246

Shabbat 88b, 105, 106

Mishna
Eduyot 2:9, 246
Sotah 6:14, 20

Midrash Rabbah
Genesis 3:7, 105, 109, 238
Genesis 12:11, 121, 124, 191, 216, 227
Genesis 39:8, 9

Zohar, 127, 192, 267, 300
Zohar (Exodus 32a), 267
Zohar (Exodus 96a), 192

INDEX OF NAMES

Abraham (or "Avraham"), 9, 29, 55, 117-118, 123-125, 127, 130, 140-141, 227-228, 231-232, 238, 239, 257
Adam, 99, 106-109, 206, 216-217, 225, 275
Adams, John, 114, 121
Ajami, Fouad, 181, 200, 284
Akiva, Rabbi, 21
Allah, 13, 24, 118, 181-185, 196, 199-200, 265
Allon, Yigal, 38
Ambrose, 170
Anaxagoras, 139, 141-142, 146-147, 171
Anaximander, 137-139, 148-149
Anaximines, 137
Aquinas, Thomas, 182, 279, 284
Arafat, Yasser, 14-15, 28, 30-31, 34, 36-37, 45, 50, 69, 265, 269

Aristotle, 5, 120, 134, 136-138, 142-146, 153-156, 158-163, 170, 185, 203, 216, 222, 224, 272, 278-279
Arius, 171, 173
Arnold, Matthew, 121, 143, 276
Ataturk, Kemal, 39, 285
Athanaseus, 171
Aviezer, Nathan, 227, 270

Bacon, Francis, 217
Baruk, Henri, 91, 122, 272
Barak, Ehud, 16, 34, 72, 264
Bat Ye'or, 182, 184, 189, 191, 284-286, 296
Beilin, Yossi, 33, 50
Ben-Gurion, David, 42, 185, 266
Boteach, Rabbi Shmuley, 281
Boulad, Henri, 197
Bourguiba, Habib, 192
Burbidge, Geoffrey, 100

Bishara, Azmi, 266
Breuer, Isaac, 10, 125, 169, 177, 221, 232, 263, 283
Burbidge, Geoffrey, 100
Buber, Martin, 76, 269

Chofetz Chaim, 8, 243, 251
Churchill, Winston, 121
Cicero, 136, 166-169, 203, 280
Clearchus, 120
Clement, 120, 170
Constantine, 173, 206
Corey, Michael A., 104
Crescas, Rabbi Hasdai, 216
Cuvier, Georges, 276

David, King, 105, 134, 160, 216, 219, 236, 238-240, 246, 262
Davies, Paul, 104
Dayan, Moshe, 11, 38, 80, 270
Democritus, 143, 146, 159, 279
Descartes, Rene, 297
Duranti, Gian Carlo, 297

Eban, Abba, 38
Emden, Rabbi Jacob, 174
Empedocles, 141-142, 147
Epictetus, 281, 284
Epicurus, 143, 167-168, 215
Eshkol, Levi, 38, 185
Euclid, 110, 129, 138, 157-158, 161-164, 280, 298
Eusebius, 170
Esposito, John L., 297-298
Evron, Yair, 298

Feynman, Richard, 298
Freud, Sigmund, 62, 77, 78, 80, 85-91, 268

Galileo Galilei, 77, 143, 155, 158, 159, 161, 165, 214-217,
Gamow, George, 98
Garan, D. G., 88, 89, 91, 268, 271
Glick, Caroline S., 73-74
Gold, Dore, 284
Gregory of Nyssa, 173
Grossman, David, 20
Grotius, Hugo, 277
von Grunebaum, G. E., 284

Harkabi, Yehoshafat., 67, 79, 80, 82, 198
Hazony, Yoram, 20
Heraclitus, 140, 142, 231
Herzl, Theodore, 8
Hirschfeld, Yair, 33
Hirsch, Rabbi Samson R., 169, 179, 184, 191
Hobbes, Thomas, 77, 78, 80, 83, 85-87, 92, 95, 143, 167, 168, 206, 214, 215, 217
Honor, 15, 25, 43, 52, 126, 142, 152, 195, 219, 247
Hussein, Saddam, 33, 68, 73, 195, 267

James, William, 86, 270, 273
Jammer, Max, 277, 280
Jefferson, Thomas, 26, 264
Jesus, 170, 173, 176, 184, 281-283, 298
John of Damascus, 173
Jung, Carl, 88
Jung, Leo, 127, 277, 283

Khaldun, Ibn, 284
Kalischer, Tzvi, 8, 19
Kellam, S., 89
Kelly, Jack, 30
Kook, Rabbi Avraham, 116, 177-178, 223, 226, 283

Lang, Robert D., 79
Lapid, Tommy, 18

Laroui, 'Abdallah, 196
Leonardo de Vinci, 146
Lewis, Bernard, 13, 183-184, 189, 192, 196, 201, 202
Lincoln, Abraham, 28, 264
Lipschitz, Rabbi Israel, 105
Locke, John, 225
Lucretius, 143, 167-168, 279
Lyell, Charles, 276

Machiavelli, Niccolo, 6, 35, 81-83, 92, 144, 155-156, 205-213, 216-218, 220-222, 225, 287, 288, 289
Macaulay, Thomas B., 121
Mahdi, Muhsin, 184, 284
Maimonides (Rambam), 8, 115, 174, 179, 229, 230, 235, 237, 239, 240, 242, 243, 245, 246, 248, 249, 252, 254, 255, 273, 277, 279, 290
Malbim, Rabbi Meir, 117
Marx, Karl, 86, 204, 206, 207, 217, 218, 219, 225, 288
Matte-Blanco, Ignacio, 62-64, 272
Meir, Golda, 185
Mill, John Stuart, 26
Montesquieu, Baron de, 266, 301
Morrisey, Will, 269, 278
Mubarak, Hosni, 30
Muhammad, 24, 34, 181-185, 188, 196-197, 200

Nachmanides (Ramban), 8, 97, 98, 100, 107, 235, 257-262
Nasser, Gamal Abdal, 192
Netanyahu, Benjamin, 16, 200
Newton, Isaac, 77, 134, 155, 165, 214
Nietzsche, Friedrich, 83, 114, 122-123, 130, 131, 141, 199, 208, 209, 221, 222, 231
Numenius, 120, 276

Oppenheimer, Robert J., 102
Oren, Michael B., 301
Origen, 120, 170, 172-173

Parmenides, 140-142, 154, 231
Penrose, Roger, 104
Penzias, Arno, 98
Peres, Shimon, 14-15, 36-37, 50, 65, 67-69, 71, 189, 202, 288
Philo, 120, 149, 151-152, 170-172, 274-275, 278
Pipes, Daniel, 188-189, 197, 199, 200
Planck, Max, 75, 269
Plato, 5, 48, 94, 120, 134-135, 138, 143-156, 158, 161-167, 170-172, 184, 203, 216, 219, 222-223, 278
Poraz, Avraham, 18-19
Protagoras, 139, 146
Pundak, Ron, 33
Pythagoras, 120, 136, 138-139, 146, 278

Rabin, Yitzhak, 14-15, 36, 56, 72, 264
Rachman, S. J., 88, 272
Reichenbach, Hans, 74, 77, 161, 269
Renan, Ernest, 184, 284
Rivlin, Reuben, 266
Rousseau, Jean Jacques, 289
Roy, Olivier, 194, 198, 285
Ruppin, Arthur, 80, 270, 296
Russell, Bertrand, 74, 269

Sadat, Anwar, 34
a-Sana, Talib, 59, 266
Sarid, Yossi, 50, 265
Schroeder, Gerald L., vii, 96, 98, 100, 103-104, 107-109, 118, 127-128, 181, 227, 274
Shakow, David, 61, 62, 268
Shamir, Yitzhak, 15, 50, 56
Sharett, Moshe, 15

Sharon, Ariel, 11, 14, 16, 20, 41, 58-60, 71-72, 264-265
Smith, Adam, 217, 225
Smoot, George, 98
Socrates, 29, 139, 144-146, 150, 166-167, 169, 280-281
Solomon, King, 105, 134
Soloveitchik, Rabbi Joseph B., 115, 153, 179
Spencer, Robert, 286
Spinoza, Benedict de, 288, 302
Strauss, Leo, 3, 76, 212, 280, 287, 288
Swift, Jonathan, 222

Teichtal, Rabbi Yisachar Shlomo, 7-10, 19-20
Tennyson, Lord Alfred, 179
Tertullian, 174
Thales, 120, 134-139, 142
Theophrastus, 120, 137, 139, 152

Tocqueville, Alexis de, 185, 289
Toynbee, Arnold, 130
Trifkovic, Serge, 183-185

Uris, Leon, 190-191

Warrak, Ibn, 184
Weinberg, Rabbi Matis, 227
Weinberg, Steven, 76, 98, 103, 269, 273, 279
Weisman, Ezer, 264, 267
Whitehead, Alfred North, 113, 124, 150, 157, 159, 219
Will, George, 30
Wilson, Robert, 98

Ze'evi, Rehavam, 59
Zimmerman, Rav Chaim, vii, 3, 6, 235, 258, 262, 263

Subject Index

Accountability, 38
Anthropic Principle, 103-105, 110, 164, 275
Anti-Semitism, 8, 54-55, 58, 71, 174, 281-283
Arab Knesset Member, 60, 266
Arabs, 12-13, 15-16, 20, 23-25, 27-29, 31-38, 40, 51, 55-58, 65, 67-71, 74, 80, 133, 181, 184-188, 190-191, 195, 238, 257, 265, 267-269, 283

Barbarism, 30, 52-53, 59, 116, 169, 178-179, 183, 196, 224
Basic Laws, 41, 277
Big Bang, 96, 98-99, 104, 107, 119, 143, 164, 231, 274-275

Cabinet, 35, 37-38, 42, 44, 49-51, 53, 57, 59, 65, 267

Cardinal virtues, 156, 207
Checks and balances, 42-43, 45, 51
Chosen People, 5, 8, 13, 76, 113, 115, 119-120, 123-124, 127, 132
Clash of civilizations, 6, 40, 181, 187, 190, 199-202, 205, 286, 299
Codes, Torah, 129
Constitution, 41, 44, 192
Cosmology, 5, 96-97, 103, 122, 136, 143, 146-147, 149-150, 158, 214, 222, 273-274
Creatio ex nihilo, 5, 96, 101, 103, 110, 119, 136, 140, 142, 147, 149-150, 154
Creation, 5, 23-24, 26, 92, 96-100, 103, 105-108, 110, 113-114, 117, 123-124, 126, 129, 135, 137, 140, 142, 147, 149-150, 156, 160, 169, 171, 180-181, 214, 216, 220-221, 227-229, 231, 237, 253-254, 274, 278-279, 284

Cro-Magnon, 107-109
Czechoslovakia, 28

Darwinism, 86, 109, 270
Degradation, 4, 7, 10-11, 14-17, 20, 120, 218-220, 226
Demiurge, 5, 145, 147-149, 151, 154, 156, 171
Democracy, 14, 19-20, 23-25, 27-30, 32-33, 36, 42-45, 48, 54-62, 65-66, 72-73, 82-83, 91, 94, 119, 127, 130, 146, 155, 205, 211-212, 217-221, 225, 263-264, 267, 286
Demographic Problem, 32-33, 35-37, 40
Demophrenia, 4, 54, 59-60, 65-67, 69, 71-72, 158, 217, 263-264, 270, 288, 297
Determinism, 103, 105, 269
Dhimmitude, 182, 284-286

Egalitarianism, 8, 14, 23, 59-60, 62, 64, 70, 87, 186
Egoism, 6, 43-44, 46, 48, 87, 146, 203, 209, 218, 220, 225, 227, 231, 254
Egypt, 7, 11-14, 28, 30, 110, 113, 115-116, 151, 173, 193, 200, 202, 241-242, 246, 264-265, 281
Electoral System, 38, 42, 46, 52
Equality, 23-24, 27, 54, 57, 59, 64, 71, 83, 100, 157-158, 165, 214-215, 218-221, 233, 289
Entropy, 101, 154
Evolution, 68, 86-87, 109, 197, 269-270, 275-276

Feminism, 203
Freedom, 18, 23-24, 27-28, 39, 54, 57-59, 90, 92, 115, 117, 151, 182, 190, 210, 218-221, 223, 232-233, 244, 255-256, 266
Fundamentalism, 204, 222

Gaza, 11-12, 14, 17, 20, 22, 24, 33, 35-36, 38, 55-58, 68, 265, 269
Gematria, 106, 139, 212-214, 280
General Relativity, 5, 97, 100, 103, 110, 113, 129, 150, 158, 273
Germany, 28, 47, 58, 68, 178-179, 293
Government, 3-5, 10-16, 18-20, 26-28, 30, 34-42, 44-50, 52-53, 55-58, 60, 65, 68, 75, 82-83, 85, 117, 122, 126, 150, 167, 176, 187, 193, 204-205, 217-218, 236, 238-239, 242, 245-248, 254-256, 261, 263-264, 267, 269, 286

Halacha (see also Jewish Law), 175, 177, 219, 232, 235, 238, 240, 243, 248, 252, 255-256, 258, 260-262
Human Community, 125, 169-170, 281
Human Nature, 26, 29-30, 43, 85, 90, 92, 94, 146, 207, 210-211, 218, 225, 278
Humility, 119, 208

Idea of Equality, 157-158, 165, 214, 219
Ideas, 5, 65, 87, 93-94, 137, 147-149, 161, 163, 171, 203, 214-215, 273, 275
Idolatry, 3, 5, 114, 116-119, 126, 127, 131, 133, 160, 161, 176, 179, 185, 199, 208, 217, 218, 224, 237, 264
Indeterminism, 102, 105
Individualism, 6, 209, 211, 225, 289
Institutional Reform, 42, 49
Intifada, 15, 18, 31, 56-58, 265, 268
Islam, 5-6, 24-25, 31, 33-34, 67-68, 70, 95, 116, 118, 127, 130, 181-185, 187-202, 204, 227, 229, 231, 233, 267, 277, 283-286
and Democracy, 19-20, 36, 155, 212
Islamism, 196-198, 204, 285
Islamic Law (see also *Sharia*), 25, 188
Israel, 3-24, 27-29, 31-63, 65-76, 80, 82, 85, 95, 105, 113-114, 116, 119, 121-123, 125,

127-128, 130-132, 134, 151, 156-157, 164, 174, 178-179, 182, 185-187, 189-191, 200, 202, 223-224, 226, 233, 235-269, 277, 282-283, 287-288
Israeli Arabs, 33

Jerusalem, 3, 16, 21, 31, 34, 58, 186, 190, 251
Jews, 4-5, 7-20, 22, 28, 30-37, 42-43, 45, 48-49, 51-59, 67-71, 74-77, 80, 82, 109-110, 113-114, 116, 119-128, 130-131, 134, 136, 139, 152-153, 169, 175-176, 178, 182, 186-187, 189-191, 202-203, 235-240, 243-250, 255-263, 268-269, 276-277, 281-283, 285, 288
Jewish law (see also *Halacha*), 8, 18, 48-50, 126, 156, 169-170, 173, 176, 179, 187, 232, 235-236, 238, 240, 270, 278
Jihad, 17, 25, 31, 37, 68, 184, 188, 192, 200, 204, 269, 285-286
Jordan, 12-13, 19, 22, 29, 32, 34, 131, 263, 265
Judea and Samaria, 9, 12, 14, 16, 19-20, 22, 34-35, 37, 56, 265

Kabala, 106, 110, 128, 280
Knesset, 15, 17, 19-20, 32, 36, 38-39, 41-42, 44-46, 48-53, 59, 186, 265-266

Land of Israel, 7-11, 71, 128, 134, 185-187, 238-240, 242, 245-249, 251, 256-262, 264

Mind, 86, 90, 94-95, 98, 103, 105, 118, 119, 129, 136, 140-142, 144, 146, 149-151, 153-154, 171-172, 207, 222, 278
Moderate Islam, 197, 286
Monotheism, 3, 5, 113-114, 116, 118-119, 124-126, 130, 136-137, 145, 170, 173-174, 176, 179, 185, 188, 228, 277

Morality, 6, 70, 76, 78, 81, 86, 94, 126-127, 146, 155, 161, 164, 168, 170, 176-177, 200, 206, 208, 213, 215-216, 218, 220, 222, 224, 227, 233, 254, 273
Moral Relativism, 4, 23-25, 33, 59-62, 69-75, 79, 83, 85-86, 89, 91, 146, 178, 203, 205, 218, 220, 226, 269, 271, 273
Moshiach, 236-246, 248-251, 253-255, 258
Multiculturalism, 203, 205
Muslim, 25, 43, 63, 182, 184-185, 188-189, 191-201, 205, 229, 264, 267-268, 284-287

Neanderthal, 107
Neo-Fundamentalism, 198
Neshama, 107-109
New Testament, 116, 131, 173, 281-283
Noahide Laws, 116, 126-127, 179, 233, 277
Normative Democracy, 23, 48, 54
Normless Democracy, 23, 54

Oslo Agreement, 10, 14-16, 20, 34, 69

Paganism, 31, 113, 133-134, 152, 161, 173, 177-178, 184-185, 224, 283
Palestinian Authority, 16, 31, 34, 52, 55, 269
Palestinian Liberation Organization (PLO), 57, 58, 60, 65, 68, 70, 71, 265, 267, 269
Particularism, 125, 127, 233
Parliamentary, 28, 29, 38, 42, 43, 46-47, 52, 192
Peace, 4, 8-9, 12, 14-15, 17, 19-20, 25, 27, 31-32, 34, 36-38, 45, 49-50, 55, 59, 66-71, 76, 80, 95, 140, 182, 187, 189-191, 200, 215, 221, 226, 233, 236, 251, 265, 267, 277, 282
Philo-Semitism, 120
Polytheism, 5, 113, 124, 136-137, 145, 166, 170, 173, 185
Positivism, 75-78, 80, 161, 209, 269

Presidential System, 38, 49
Prime Mover, 145, 153-154, 156
Psychology, 4, 43, 61, 79, 84-92, 94-95, 270-273
Qualitative mathematics, 161-162, 164-165, 280
Quantitative mathematics, 153, 157-158, 161-162, 164-165

Radiation, 98
Reason & Revelation, 128-129, 176, 194, 231
Reductionism, 158, 273, 279
Relativism, 4, 23-25, 33, 55, 59-62, 67, 69-77, 79-83, 85-87, 89, 91, 146, 178, 183, 187, 199-200, 202-203, 205, 218, 220-221, 226, 266, 269, 271, 273, 284, 287
Religion, 4, 10, 25, 31, 36, 58, 76, 80, 86, 100, 116, 121-122, 128-130, 144-145, 151-152, 161, 165, 167, 170, 172-176, 178-179, 182-184, 187, 190, 195-196, 199-202, 206-208, 212, 217-218, 224, 231, 274, 280, 283, 285
Rome, 121, 152, 166-169, 176, 211, 213, 283
Rule of law, 41-42, 48-49, 52, 126
Schizophrenia, 60-67, 71, 83, 268, 271-272
Secular Man, 206, 208, 210-211, 220, 226
Self-Determination, 22-23, 25-30, 32, 55, 69
Sharia (see also Islamic law)., 25, 188, 191-195, 197-198, 200, 233, 285-286
Six-Day War, 4, 11-12, 14-15, 29, 35, 38, 55, 67, 261
Space-time, 76, 103, 105
Special Theory of Relativity, 74, 76
Statism, 6, 225
Suicide bombers, 17, 30, 34, 56, 264, 269
Supreme Court, 39, 41-42, 45, 49-53, 59-60, 232, 266-267

Talmud, 9, 20-21, 37, 48, 98, 101, 106, 108-110, 116, 156, 191, 232, 236, 241-243, 246-247, 258-260, 278, 282

Teleology, 224
Thought-Experiment, 92-93, 185
Timaeus, 134, 145, 147, 149-150, 152-153
Torah, 3-5, 7-10, 20, 26, 41, 48, 72, 82, 85, 92, 94, 96-98, 100-101, 103, 105-106, 109-110, 113-119, 122, 125-126, 128-133, 136, 139, 141, 145-147, 153, 162, 164-166, 169, 171, 174-176, 179, 185-187, 218, 220, 225, 227-233, 235-251, 253-256, 258-263, 270, 273, 276-280
Trinity, 171-174, 179
Truth, 5, 10, 20-21, 25, 28, 37, 68, 72, 75, 77, 80, 87, 93-94, 109, 116, 125, 139, 159, 172-173, 184, 196, 203, 208-209, 220, 227, 229, 253-254, 270

Ultra-secular, 18, 202
United States, 10-11, 13-14, 28-29, 38, 46-47, 55, 72, 79, 84, 114, 187, 226, 232, 263
Universalism, 125, 127, 169, 233

War, 4, 11-15, 17, 22-23, 25, 27-29, 32, 35, 38, 52, 55, 58, 67-68, 70, 73, 140-141, 144, 168, 178, 182-183, 186, 188, 192-193, 195, 197, 201, 204-205, 214, 217, 225-227, 253-254, 256-258, 260-261, 263-265, 267-269, 273, 285
"West Bank," 14, 20, 22, 28-29, 32-33, 36, 40, 58
Western Civilization, 3, 6, 129, 156, 165, 199, 201, 203-204, 206, 220, 222, 226
Wisdom, 9, 47-48, 74, 76, 105, 110, 113, 117, 124, 130-131, 141, 144, 147, 156, 171-172, 193, 207, 219-220, 228-230, 232-233, 236-237, 242, 248, 252, 254, 273, 276, 279-280
World-Historical Program, 5, 113, 118-119, 133, 145, 165, 187, 225

Zionism, 4, 7-10, 15, 20, 36, 54-55, 57, 59-60, 72, 78, 201, 263, 265

0-595-31695-6

Printed in Great Britain
by Amazon